# Police Organization and Management
## Behavior, Theory, and Processes

**Roy R. Roberg**
San Jose State University

**Jack Kuykendall**
San Jose State University

Brooks/Cole Publishing Company
Pacific Grove, California

To our respective managers, Arlene and Mary,
and to Jack and Mary's littlest manager, Casey.

**Brooks/Cole Publishing Company**
A Division of Wadsworth, Inc.

Printed in the United States of America
10   9   8   7   6   5   4   3   2

**Library of Congress Cataloging-in-Publication Data**
Roberg, Roy R.
    Police organization and management: behavior, theory, and processes /
by Roy R. Roberg and Jack Kuykendall.
    p.   cm.
    Includes index.
    ISBN 0-534-11802-X
    1. Police administration—United States. I. Kuykendall, Jack L. II. Title.
HV7935. R64   1989
351.74′0973—dc20                                    89-1037
                                                    CIP

Sponsoring Editor:   *Cynthia C. Stormer*
Marketing Representative:   *Tina Allen*
Editorial Assistants:   *Mary Ann Zuzow, Catherine Sue Collins*
Production Editors:   *Nancy L. Shammas, Ben Greensfelder*
Manuscript Editor:   *Robin Witkin*
Permissions Editor:   *Carline Haga*
Interior Design:   *Sharon L. Kinghan*
Cover Design:   *David Aguero, Sharon L. Kinghan*
Art Coordinator:   *Sue C. Howard*
Photo Researcher:   *Judy Mason*
Typesetting:   *A-R Editions, Madison, Wisconsin*
Cover Printing:   *Phoenix Color Corporation*
Printing and Binding:   *The Maple–Vail Book Manufacturing Group*
(Credits continue on p. **491**)

# Preface

Organization and management textbooks about the police tend to have one of three frames of reference: police administration, general management, or police management. Police administration texts are explicitly oriented toward police matters and utilize a process approach and a functional approach. The process approach is concerned with administrative activities such as planning, organization, leadership, personnel, and budgeting. The functional aspect emphasizes major police activities such as patrol, investigations, and traffic. This description fit most police management textbooks prior to the early 1970s.

In the mid-1970s, general management-oriented texts, which are at the other end of the continuum, began to appear. They are almost exclusively based on general organization and management knowledge, with only minimal concern for police issues or application to police problems. These books were written in reaction to the belief that police administrative texts were inadequate because they were not based on a conceptually sound, empirically oriented body of knowledge.

Police management books also began to appear in the early to mid-1970s. These books emphasize both generic management and police issues in one of two ways, either by example or through analytical integration. The example approach uses a general management–police example format. The examples are often quite limited, but they may be as extensive as a chapter. When the examples are that long, they usually address such issues as minority group relations, stress, community relations, or police functions such as patrol and investigations. Usually there is no meaningful attempt to integrate the general management concepts and police organization and management problems.

The analytical-integration approach in developing police management textbooks has not been successfully undertaken. Essentially, this approach involves applying contemporary management concepts to the police setting, while attempting to analytically integrate and assess their impact; that is, asking what problems and issues are associated with applying contemporary organization and management techniques to a police agency. The purpose of this textbook is to attempt an analytical-integration approach. To this end, both general and police management research are applied to police organizational behavior, theory, and processes. We hope that this will result in an enhanced understanding of the relationship between management and the police endeavor in a democratic society. In addition, because the text is interdisciplinary in nature and emphasis is placed on general management theory and practice, we believe the text will be useful not only in police-oriented courses, but in courses emphasizing criminal justice related management issues and practices as well.

This book is truly a joint endeavor. Although each author was responsible for separate chapters, we each read and changed all the chapters so often that it is not possible to determine who is completely responsible for any single one. We would like to thank Gary Cordner, Chris Eskridge, and Robert Langworthy, who provided constructive comments that improved the quality of the work. In addition, we would like to thank Arlene Roberg for her valuable comments in several substantive areas, and Arlene Chastant, Oscar Larson, and Gretchen Newby for their conscientious assistance in putting the manuscript together. We would also like to extend our sincere appreciation to our editors Claire Verduin and Cindy Stormer for their valuable support and contributions to the project, and to the rest of the Brooks-Cole team for their outstanding efforts, especially Nancy Shammas and Ben Greensfelder.

Finally, we would like to thank the many police officers, managers, and students with whom we have interacted over the years. Their experiences and insights have given us the basis for many of our ideas. If the reader finds fault with any of these ideas, blame them and not us; the first rule of police management is to learn to avoid responsibility for your mistakes. Or is it? Reading this book should increase your understanding of organization and management concepts, and hence the role of police managers.

*Roy R. Roberg*
*Jack Kuykendall*

# Contents

CHAPTER 2

CHAPTER 3

CHAPTER 7

# Human Resource Management                    **229**

CHAPTER 10

# Critical Issues in Operations                                    **347**

CHAPTER 11

# Planning, Change, and Innovation    373

CHAPTER 12

# Enhancing Organizational Performance     **409**

# Figures

# Tables

# CHAPTER 1

# Police Organization and Management: An Introduction

This book is concerned with the study of police organizations and their management in a democratic society. It is an attempt to understand the organizational behavior of police and how "good" management can make a difference, with respect to employee attitudes and behaviors, and to the accomplishment of organizational goals. Thus, police managers must try to formulate goals and design organizations to meet the expectations and needs of individual employees and the organization as well. The closer management comes to meeting individual expectations and needs, the more likely maximum effort will be expended to accomplish goals, and concomitantly, the more likely goals are to be accomplished.

Individual employees, as well as the organization itself (i.e., its influential members), have certain expectations of one another. For instance, the organization expects employees to adequately perform the tasks and uphold the responsibilities assigned to them and to abide by the rules established to guide work behavior. However, management often expects more from its employees, such as self-supervision, learning new skills, taking the initiative, and so on. On the other hand, employees expect the organization to treat them fairly and in a dignified manner and to provide adequate pay and acceptable working conditions. Like management, employees often expect more, depending on the strengths of individual needs such as security, social interaction, status, power, and self-actualization. Of course, the amount and strength of each party's expectations will vary from organization to organization.

In an attempt to understand and predict the behavior of people in police organizations, recent knowledge gained through behavioral science research (e.g., psychology, sociology, and political science) will be utilized. Much of this knowledge is about general organizational behavior, produced through the study of both public and private institutions. We will use this general knowledge and, when appropriate, apply it to more specific themes with respect to police management practices.

Organizations exist for one reason: to accomplish activities that cannot be accomplished individually. We will define an *organization* as *a social system composed of groups of two or more persons who are interdependent and work in a coordinated manner to achieve common goals*. Because organizations are *goal-oriented*, the purpose of management is to work toward the attainment of these goals by responding to the ever-changing needs of individuals, groups, and the organization itself. Managers should facilitate the *integration* of individual and organizational needs so that each party is fulfilled while both work toward the accomplishment of organizational goals.

We are primarily concerned with the role of *general* police management, rather than with more specialized managerial concerns—such as finance and budgeting—that are not as directly related to the day-to-day decision-making activities that profoundly affect the relationship between the organization and its employees. This is not to suggest that these specialized activities do not affect employee attitudes or behaviors toward the organization. They obviously do, but in a much less direct and forceful manner than general managers. The manner in which general managers interact with their employees on a daily basis, particularly in the expectations they create, the feedback they provide, and the amount of responsibility they delegate, has the most direct influence on the individual-organization relationship. Hence, highly specialized functions pertaining to management practice are discussed only as they relate to the general role of management and police organizational behavior.

## Major Themes

The purpose of this book is to provide the reader with an understanding of how police organizations work and how people behave in police organizations. More specifically, our aim is to help the reader understand how individuals and groups can be effectively managed in these organizations. To this end, we will define the *study of police organization and management* as:

> The scientific study of police organizations, including individual, group, organizational, and external environmental processes, undertaken for the purpose of producing enhanced knowledge that can be used by police managers to improve both organizational effectiveness and individual performance and satisfaction.

Our approach to understanding police organization and management incorporates several major themes that will be used throughout this book. The first theme states that a police organization's most important commodity is its human resources, which include all activities and decisions that affect the relationship between the organization and its employees. Thus, a *humanistic orientation*, where employee expectations, attitudes, capabilities, and goals are taken into account in the managerial process, is deemed essential.

Since understanding and dealing with the expectations of people within the organization (i.e., the internal environment) and outside the organization (i.e., the external environment) is vital to effectively managing the police, an *expectation-integration model* has been developed. This model proposes that general police managers strive to integrate the expectations of the organization's employees, as well as of outside individuals and groups, with the expectations of the organization. This model will be fully described later in the chapter.

We believe that it is also necessary to understand the *interdisciplinary nature* of the study of police organization and management. Relevant organizational and managerial theories, along with important research findings from the field of policing and from well-established disciplines, will be incorporated. Because most of the rigorous empirical research and theory development in organizational behavior and management has taken place in the behavioral sciences (especially psychology and sociology) and in the management field, we have attempted to "blend" these findings with current policing research. Thus, we have developed an extensive knowledge base on which to formulate police managerial practices. The role of research and the *scientific method* is deemed critical; empirical research findings help us to identify and understand important variables and relationships in the study of police organizations and their management.

To further promote an adequate understanding of the complex nature of organizational behavior, *four levels of analysis* will be utilized (see figure 1-1). The basic building block of any organization is the *individual*. The next level of analysis is the *work group* (unit or department) that forms a collection of individuals who work together to accomplish various tasks and objectives. The next level is the *organization*, made up of a collection of groups attempting to accomplish organizational goals. The final level of analysis is the *external environment*, or community, in which the organization interacts. In other words, "outside" individuals, groups, and organizations (e.g., spe-

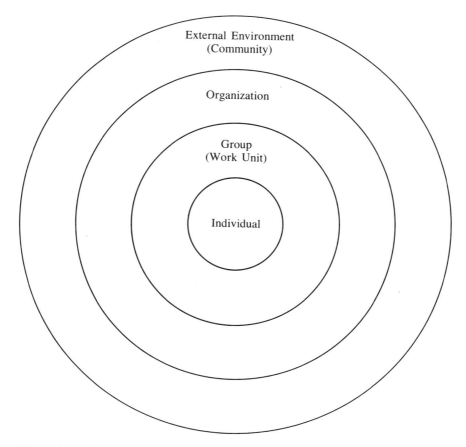

**Figure 1-1**  Organizational Levels of Analysis

cial interest groups, politicians, the courts, and corrections) have a vital impact on police organizational behavior.

By studying police organizations using the four levels described, we are, in effect, utilizing *general systems theory*, which sees a system as a unitary whole composed of interrelated and interdependent parts or subsystems. In other words, the reaction of various groups or units toward events within the system (i.e., organization) will produce a change of greater or lesser magnitude in other parts of the system. For instance, a change in dispatching procedures will have a direct impact on patrol operations, which, in turn, will have an impact on supervisory practices. A change introduced into any part of the system will produce a corresponding change in the other parts as well. While this approach takes into consideration the interrelationships among the parts of the system, it fails to take into account the interactions between the system and its external environment, which, in the case of the police, is the community at large. Consequently, we use an *open systems* approach that allows us to view not only the interrelationships of the parts of the system (police organization), but also the interactions of the system with a dynamic and continually changing environment (community).

By its very nature, general systems theory is broad in scope, relating the parts to the whole. A more pragmatic approach to the study of organizations is *contingency theory*, which stems directly from a general systems approach but is more specific in applying appropriate management concepts and techniques to organizational circumstances. Contingency management is concerned with studying relevant internal and external variables that impact on the organization and attempts to apply appropriate managerial practices and organization designs to particular situations. Each of these theoretical approaches and their importance to police managers will be explored in chapter 3.

Finally, an important focus of this book is on *promoting ethical behavior* throughout the organization. We believe that while employee ethics is important in all organizations, it is especially crucial to police organizations because of their role in a democratic society and because of the degree of trust the public must place in them. These basic issues are described in the following chapter and are interwoven throughout the text as they relate to specific chapter topics. Table 1-1 summarizes the major themes used in the study of police organization and management.

**Table 1-1**   Major Themes of Police Organization and Management

| Themes | Characteristics |
|---|---|
| Humanistic Orientation | The importance of employee expectations, attitudes, and goals is emphasized. |
| Expectation-Integration Model | The importance of integrating individual-organization and community-organization expectations is emphasized. |
| Interdisciplinary Nature | Relevant principles, models, theories, and research findings from the social sciences are utilized. |
| Scientific Method | Scientific methods are used whenever possible to supplement managerial experiences. |
| Four Levels of Analysis | Individuals, groups, the organization, and the external environment are considered in the study of police organizational behavior. |
| General/Open Systems Theory and Contingency Theory Approaches | The interrelated and interdependent nature of the parts of a system to the whole and to the external environment is stressed. Appropriate managerial practices are applied to specific organizational circumstances. |
| Ethical Behavior | An organizational climate that fosters ethical conduct on the part of all employees is established. |

# The Process of Managing

Managers differ from other organizational members in the work that they do. We will define *management* as *the process of working with people in a humane manner to accomplish goals and objectives*. Such work, for example, would consist of supervising the work of a group of patrol officers rather than performing patrol activities.

This definition includes several salient features that should be discussed. First, the idea of working *with* people, rather than through them, connotes a *mutual* participation between managers and employees, thus emphasizing a positive attitude toward employee involvement in the organization. Second, the idea of humaneness, which is infrequently mentioned with respect to management, is an integral part of our definition. Funk and Wagnalls (1953, p. 575), in a timeless fashion, have defined *humane* as "having or showing kindness and tenderness; compassionate." They list several synonyms—benevolent, charitable, gracious, merciful, and sympathetic—and several antonyms—barbarous, cruel, fierce, inhuman, merciless, and selfish. By promoting a humane approach to management, we believe human dignity will be increased in the organization and the quality of the work environment will be improved.

Finally, our definition relates to the accomplishment of goals and objectives. *Goals* are general statements of purpose that tend to be long range. Goals may be, and often are, utilized to identify the role of police; for instance, to prevent and/or deter crime or to help solve community problems. However, goals may also be more specific. For example, a police agency may have as a goal the reduction of property crimes for the next calendar year. Although general in nature, this goal is more specific than "to prevent and/or deter crime," while still supporting that goal.

*Objectives* tend to be more specific than goals, and they are usually time-bounded, quantifiable, and consistent with the organization's broader purposes or goals. For example, an objective might be to reduce residential burglaries by 5 percent in the next six months. Thus, this objective is specific (a single type of crime), time-bound (six months), and quantifiable (5 percent).

Other objectives could also be established relative to reducing burglary rates. These might concern resources to be obtained, programs to be developed, and tactics to be employed, and they might be related to the performance of individual officers.

Both goals and objectives are important because they, in part, identify the expectations held concerning what the police are doing and how productively they perform. Unrealistic and unreasonable expectations, goals, and objectives make the jobs of managers and employees more difficult.

## Management: Art or Science?

The question of whether management is an art, a science, or both is often raised in the literature. This is an interesting and important question regarding the management of complex police organizations.

*Science* can be defined as the systematic study of a subject leading to a general body of knowledge about the subject. In determining whether management is a science, keep in mind that there are different types of science. For instance, if we mean science in the sense of the "exact" sciences, such as chemistry and physics, then management cannot be considered a science. The experimental controls characteristic of the natural and physical sciences, which take place in a laboratory setting, cannot be applied to the study of management and organizational behavior. This does not mean, however, that managers and researchers cannot conduct valuable research on organizational behavior. It does mean that when dealing with the complexity of organizational life, the controls, and therefore the results, are not as exact. In fact, the "inexact" sciences, such as psychology and sociology, have been used to systematically study organizational behavior and to develop general principles and concepts for many years. In this sense, management can be referred to as a developing science.

What about management as an art? *Art* has been defined as "the systematic application of knowledge and skill in order to achieve an objective" (Haiman and Scott 1974, p. 13). The key word in this definition is *application*. Accordingly, managers must apply their knowledge and skills toward the attainment of objectives. This would suggest that "good" management is indeed both an art and a science. To management then, art and science complement each other. Police managers must be able to apply what they have learned through science to the management process in such a manner as to lead others to accomplish goals and objectives. In the final analysis, it is doubtful whether goals and objectives can be attained if managers do not properly balance science with art.

## Expectation-Integration Model

As noted previously, police managers must attempt to integrate two important sets of expectations: those between individual employees and the organization, and those between the community and the organization. A conceptual model has been developed depicting the nature of the relationships between these two sets of expectations and the *degree* to which they are shared or *integrated*. This expectation-integration model (E-I model) is depicted in figure 1-2.[1] The dotted lines denote the degree of integration — substantial, partial, or minimal — and the size of the boxes represented by the broken lines illustrates the growing number of problems that will confront managers as the degree of integration changes. In other words, the model hypothesizes that as the degree of expectation-integration increases, the number of organizational problems decreases.

It is important to note, however, that even with a substantial degree of expectation-integration, numerous organizational problems will still require management's attention. These are recurring types of problems, such as planning, scheduling work, obtaining and allocating resources, evaluating personnel, and so on, that are intrinsic to all organized endeavors. As the degree of integration declines, these problems become more difficult for managers to cope with because dissatisfaction among employees or the community results in reduced cooperation, which leads to a greater expenditure

[1] The expectation-integration model presented here has been adapted from Roberg (1979, p. 5) and has been expanded to include the external environment.

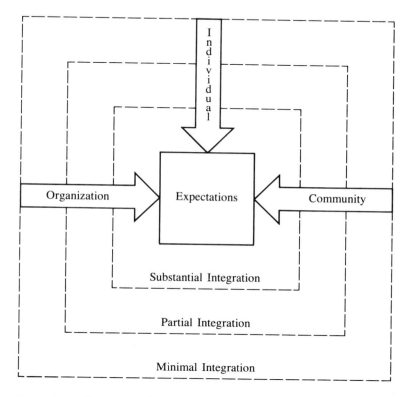

**Figure 1-2**   Expectation-Integration Model

of the manager's time and energy. The resulting problems may be so time-consuming that more basic management endeavors (e.g., long-term planning) may be ignored to the detriment of the long-term vitality and productivity of the organization.

The E-I model is presented as a conceptual frame of reference for police managers to utilize. It is useful for all levels of management, although in different ways. For example, top-level managers should pay more attention to the generalized concerns of employees, while lower-level managers should be more interested in specific individual needs. To utilize the model at all levels, managers need to address themselves to the following questions:

1. What does the organization expect of me and the people I supervise?
2. What do my subordinates and colleagues expect of me and the organization?
3. What does the community expect of the organization and my subordinates and colleagues?
4. When these expectations are compatible, what are the most effective strategies, methods, and ethical considerations involved in attempting to solve the problems?
5. If the expectations are in conflict, what compromises can be agreed on to meet the legal and ethical mandate of law enforcement in a democratic society with a minimum of disruption to productive endeavors?

Each set of expectations indicated by the E-I model will be briefly discussed in the following paragraphs.

## Individual-Organization Expectations

As we suggested earlier, in order to establish a high-quality work environment, the individual employee and the organization must strive to cooperate with and complement one another. An initial sharing of expectations can greatly enhance this process. In other words, what does each party expect from the other? Are their needs and goals similar? Do they feel comfortable with each other? What about the future?

If an honest and trustworthy individual-organization association can be fostered from the beginning, life within the organization will most likely be rewarding and fulfilling. When the individual and the organization both strive toward integration, relationships will improve while sources of discontent will decrease, because each knows what is expected of the other. Each party is then aware of the adjustments (the "give and take") that are necessary for a mutually satisfying association. Simultaneously, many of the dysfunctions that can develop within organizations due to irresponsible or indifferent behavior by either party should be diminished.

Although it may not be feasible to always obtain substantial expectation-integration, each party should strive to reach this goal. Furthermore, it is crucial to understand that *both conformity and deviance* are found within organizations. All too frequently, police organizations view strict conformity to established rules and procedures as acceptable behavior, while viewing deviation from such rules and procedures as a failure by the individual. Some individuals do in fact fail and a certain degree of conformity is desirable; however, a certain degree of conflict is also necessary. In order to achieve expectation-integration, channels of communication must be opened, allowing for constructive input of "deviant" or contrary viewpoints.

In this manner, conflict can lead to positive gains for the individual and organization. While it may appear desirable for organizations to function smoothly and silently, this situation can be deceptive. Lengthy periods of quiet operation could be a sign of organizational stagnation or internal repression of legitimate concerns, which may lead to employee discontent. In any case, stagnation can be a symptom of a lack of organizational change and progress. Those who subvert the rules, speak out against "petty" regulations, or suggest improved methods are often rebelling against stagnation and a lack of timely change. Rather than categorizing such employees as recalcitrant "troublemakers," the organization should observe and listen carefully to those who may represent the "cutting edge" of desirable organizational change.

## Community-Organization Expectations

The community also has expectations for police organizations. Although not all police organizations are an integral part of a specific community, as are municipal and county law enforcement organizations, all have a constituency with whom they interact. For municipal and county law enforcement agencies, expectations are as multifaceted as the economic, cultural, and political diversity of the persons living in the community.

The concept of community has a number of possible meanings. The most obvious and frequently used meaning defines community in terms of the legal, geographical boundary of the city or county jurisdiction. However, within those boundaries exists a number of possible other communities. Any identifiable group of persons who share common values or concerns about crime and law enforcement–related issues is a potential community with expectations. For example, a particular neighborhood may be concerned about vandalism, juvenile gang activity, drug-related problems, or all three. Another neighborhood within the same city may be more concerned about traffic law violations. Both communities will have expectations about the police relative to these problems.

Communities may also be based on ethnic and racial identification, political affiliation, age, and sex. Blacks and hispanics may view the use of force by police differently than whites. Conservatives and liberals may disagree over the rigor with which police enforce "victimless crime" laws. Senior citizens present a decidedly different set of problems for police than teenagers, and as a result both groups may have different expectations. Women may also manifest special concerns, for instance, in the areas of spousal abuse, sexual assault, and equal treatment.

The E-I model recognizes the importance of three major sources of expectations concerning police behavior: the organization, the employee, and the community. Chapter 2 identifies four models of policing in democratic society that have evolved in the United States since the mid-nineteenth century. Each of these models illustrates the types of adjustments police departments have made as a result of conflicting expectations. If one expectation source becomes too influential, other participants in the police process will become disenchanted and eventually will effectuate some type of reform. In fact, it is reasonable to suggest that each of the four models of policing results because an influential group establishes the expectations defining the police role. That is one reason police agencies are characterized by change.

If police organizations, through their managers, ignore or deemphasize the expectations of employees or the community, the resulting frustration will often result in reform. If the conflict between strongly held expectations results in a compromise rather than in an adversarial relationship, it is more likely to create an atmosphere of mutual trust and respect, which will increase the probability of open communication and the likelihood that future accommodations can be realized. Unfortunately, police organizations have been plagued by adversarial relationships between the organization and employees, the organization and the community, and the employees and the community. The E-I model emphasizes the diversity of expectations concerning the police role and the importance of their integration or balance. We hope that this model will underscore, for managers, the importance of recognizing and responding to diverse expectations in order to avoid possible negative consequences.

## Ethical Behavior

A vital aspect of police management, and one that impacts all other organizational processes, is *establishing and promoting ethical behavior*. Promoting ethical behavior is frequently not discussed as an integral aspect of managing. As noted previously, however, we believe that employee ethics is especially important to policing a democratic society. This is particularly relevant given the historic and current problems police have with corruption, violation of procedural safeguards, and excessive or questionable behavior in other areas. Consequently, we will treat promoting of ethical behavior as a separate, and indeed, critical function of police management.

Webster's (1984, p. 210) defines *ethics* as "the study of standards of conduct and moral judgment." Of course, moral judgments, and the standards based on them, change over time. This means that police managers, at all levels, must be cognizant of ethical issues confronting the police and must practice proper ethical conduct as well. Police organizations must firmly establish that unethical behavior on the part of their employees, from brutality or harassment to free meals, will not be tolerated and will be dealt with in an appropriate and swift manner.

A consideration of ethics involves both the discipline of what is good and bad behavior and a set of principles involving moral duties, obligations, and values. For police it includes both the ethics of a profession of policing (i.e., derived from a code of ethics) substantive and procedural criminal laws, and organization policies and procedures. What is morally good and bad in police work? What is right and wrong behavior? How does the socialization theory of police behavior (discussed in chapter 5) influence the ethical frame of reference of police officers?

There are essentially two categories of ethical problems in law enforcement. The first category is concerned with *integrity*—taking payoffs, perjuring oneself, using excessive force, knowingly going outside the law to accomplish an objective, and lying about what happened (e.g., falsifying a report or providing false testimony in court). These are not difficult problems ethically because they are clearly wrong even though they do occur. This type of behavior occurs because the decision to engage in such behavior may be in keeping with being "one of the boys" in the police department. As such, this behavior can most likely be attributed to the socialization process and may be consistent with the values of the police culture and rationalized by the officers. Some police officers, perhaps a substantial number, do not have any difficulty believing they are "special" people who deserve "special" consideration. Accordingly, they come to believe that they are above the law.

The second category of ethical problems is concerned with what might be considered "*hard choices*" (Heffernan and Stroup 1985), which include exercising discretion, using deception in police investigations, selecting targets in undercover investigations, and using force, particularly deadly force. Is there sufficient authority for police officers to exercise discretion? When should officers use deception in investigations? Should investigators allow informants to use drugs or commit crimes in order to secure information? When and how should police agencies decide to target a particular individual or group for an investigation? When should the police use force to accomplish an objective? These are only some of the hard ethical choices police organizations and officers must make.

One of the more interesting aspects of ethics is the arguments that can ensue about police officers' moral obligations and responsibilities. Police officers must take an oath of office to the Constitution and the laws of their jurisdiction. However, they may claim they do not have a moral obligation to honor this oath if their motives are not based on self-interest but, rather, are disinterested. For example, Heffernan (1985, p. 4) says in this regard:

> If the goal of nonenforcement is to conserve police resources to combat more serious crime or to give an offender a break, then, . . . nonenforcement can be morally acceptable [to the officer] despite the existence of the rules of office and the oath to honor them. A similar argument is also advanced in support of violations of the Fourth Amendment that result in no physical harm to the person searched or arrested. . . . Some police claim [that this contributes to the] conservation of law enforcement resources and can also make it possible to punish those who are barely touched by the courts.

In general, students of police ethical behavior would most likely argue that the only time a police officer is justified in knowingly violating the oath of office is for the most serious considerations. Such exceptions would indeed be rare and should be clearly understood by all officers. Managers need to establish strong guidelines and to communicate to officers their ethical responsibilities, as well as have candid discussions with them about the ethical dilemmas of police work. Managers must also be aware of the rationalizations for unethical behavior that officers acquire during the socialization process as they become integrated into the police culture (Heffernan and Stroup 1985).

## Managerial Functions

Managers in every organization perform several essential functions, including planning, organizing, leading, and controlling. How well each of these functions is handled in an organization will ultimately determine whether a manager is successful. Each function is briefly described in the following paragraphs, but the remainder of the book explores these functions and their attendant components (e.g., organizing includes organization structure and job design; leading involves human behavior and motivation, etc.) in detail.

Keep in mind that although managerial personnel perform each function, the effort exerted varies according to the manager's level in the organization. For instance, higher managerial levels, such as assistant chiefs, spend a greater proportion of their time on planning and organizing activities, while lower managerial levels, such as sergeants, spend more time leading and controlling. How management handles each function will determine the nature of the organization's relationship with its employees, and thus the quality of the work environment.

## Planning

*Planning*, the first function of managing, is the process of preparing for the future by setting goals and objectives and developing courses of action for accomplishing them. The courses of action involve activities such as conducting research, developing procedures and policies, identifying strategies, and formulating budgets.

All managers engage in planning, but the scope and nature of the activity differs considerably depending on the managerial level within an organization. For instance, while a patrol supervisor may plan work schedules and operating activities for the upcoming week, a police chief may be planning organizational activities and changes for the upcoming year and beyond. In general, the higher the managerial level, the broader the scope of planning and the longer the time impact for the plans.

## Organizing

*Organizing* is the process of arranging personnel and physical resources to carry out plans and accomplish goals and objectives. Organizational structure, job design, and individual work assignments are part of the organizing process. Although all managers are involved in organizing, once again, the degree and scope differs depending on their level within the organization.

The patrol supervisor is more concerned with job design and work assignments; the chief is more concerned with the structure of the organization and
the overall distribution of personnel and physical resources.

## Leading

*Leading* is the ability to motivate others to perform various tasks that will
lead to the accomplishment of goals and objectives. Since an organization's
success or failure depends on its employee performance, it is important that
managers, as part of their function of working *with* people, create conditions
that will encourage employees to perform well. Motivating others is a difficult and complex process, especially in civil service organizations where
managers have less control over fiscal resources, such as base salaries and pay
increases, than in the private sector. How well a manager motivates employees to perform depends on how extrinsic rewards, such as pay and promotion, and intrinsic rewards, such as praise and feelings of accomplishment,
are utilized. Successful leaders normally motivate their employees by providing a balance between both kinds of rewards.

## Controlling

*Controlling* is the process by which managers determine whether goals and
objectives are being accomplished and whether operations are consistent
with plans. If goals and objectives are not being met or plans, policies, and
procedures are not being followed, managers must take corrective action.
Corrective action may be either informal or formal. For instance, an employee's performance deficiencies may simply be discussed with the individual or
more formalized responses, including a poor performance rating, required
attendance at a training program, or disciplinary actions, may be taken. In
some instances, the manager may determine that the goal/objective or
policy/procedure is flawed, not the performance of the employee.

# Human Resources and the Quality of the Work Environment

While these managerial functions apply to all of the organization's resources (including personnel, material, time, etc.), we are primarily concerned with how they apply to the organization's human resources. The foundation for focusing on human resources was established earlier in this chapter. However, there is another reason for placing increased emphasis on human resources. Police organizations typically spend 80 to 90 percent of their budgets on hiring, training, and paying their employees, which means that economically, they cannot afford to ignore their employees' behavior.

Macy and Mirvis (1976) indicate the importance to the organization of considering the behavior of its employees in terms of economic effectiveness. The conceptual framework underlying their work emphasizes that employees' behavior results from choices they make about (1) being available to work and (2) role performance while on the job. This conclusion assumes that "employees are more likely to come to work and remain in the organization if they obtain satisfaction from their jobs, and that they are likely to put forth more effort and work more effectively if they expect to be rewarded for their efforts and performance" (p. 213). Thus, the employees' satisfaction and reward expectations are influenced by their work environment and the extent to which it provides valued rewards. The work environment includes the employees' jobs, supervisors, work group relationships, and organizational structure.

In the plant studied by Macy and Mirvis, behavioral measures were selected in relation to member participation (e.g., absenteeism, tardiness, turnover, and work stoppages and strikes) and role performance (e.g., productivity, product or service quality, grievances, accidents, and job-related illnesses). During the experimental period, organizational characteristics and employees' reward expectations were altered; therefore changes were expected to occur in the employees' job-related behaviors. Sizable reductions in turnover, accidents, and grievances took place during the experiment. Although absenteeism increased, employees in the experimental groups appeared to select leave days, instead of pay bonuses, as rewards for good performance. Product quality and production levels also improved over the course of the experiment. Thus, by *manipulating* the *quality* of the work environment, management *can* influence employee performance.

Such positive changes in employee job behavior save the organization substantial sums of money and improve both the quality and quantity of the organization's products. Although the "products" of police agencies are usually more difficult to measure than those of most private-sector firms (e.g., administering laws justly or using force appropriately versus the number of welds made or cars assembled), the implication remains the same. Accordingly, this text will adopt the conceptual framework used by Macy and Mirvis in regard to the effective use of human resources: *individual employees who are satisfied with their jobs are more likely to come to work and remain in the organization, and work more effectively, if they expect to be (and, in fact, are) rewarded for their performance.*

The importance of establishing a viable relationship between the individual employee and the organization, and thus achieving a high-quality work environment, cannot be overstated. In order to accomplish this, however, the organization and the individual must be partners—each willing to exercise some "give and take"—in establishing a mutually beneficial relationship.

Neither party can legitimately "fix the blame" or "take the credit" for life inside the organization, because within any organization we find a widely shared interaction process between the organization (i.e., its influential members) and its employees. Most police organizations, for instance, have not thoroughly analyzed job designs to determine which jobs might be redesigned in order to improve the employee's work environment. For example, highly educated and well-qualified patrol officers may be inhibited from utilizing their own decision-making capabilities while on the job. Allowing the officers to maximize their own job skill potential (e.g., by enriching certain aspects of the job) may benefit the employee and the organization. The employee's positive feelings, generated by increased contributions to the organization, strengthen the organization and may be reflected in improved performance. Police organizations may also improve interactions with their employees through a systematic review of promotional and reward systems. It is questionable whether police agencies adequately reward or promote for actions that benefit both the organization and the employee.

Throughout this book, we will emphasize the point that most police organizations can significantly increase the quality of interactions with their employees. However, individual employees must also remember that they need to make sacrifices in order to improve the overall development and operation of the organization. In the final analysis, the organization allows the individual to satisfy many needs and aspirations that could not otherwise be met. Purely self-motivated behavior or substandard work, at the expense of a more common good, can only lead to a decline in the quality of the work environment. Because police work has such a substantial impact on the public, the selfish behavior of an employee or a group of employees may lead to their increased satisfaction but not without causing severe ramifications for the organization, which may lose public trust and support. Accordingly, while the individual employee expects the organization to provide a high-quality work environment, the employee must also expect to contribute substantially to this end.

## The Police Managerial Perspective

The police manager's general roles and functions were identified earlier. It is important to point out, however, that in addition to the responsibilities that all managers have, there are aspects of the managerial role that are unique to policing. Police managers work in public organizations, and they must cope with problems that result from conflict about the role of the police in a democratic society. However, before discussing the unique aspects of police management, we will briefly discuss some of the differences between public and private management.

## Public Versus Private Management

In general, public management differs from private management in terms of *time perspective*, *performance measurement*, *personnel constraints*, *equity*, and *openness and persuasion* (Allison 1983). Due to the political nature of their jobs, public managers tend to have a shorter time perspective; therefore, they may do less long-term planning than managers in the private sector. Performance evaluation is also problematic. There is generally greater diversity in the community's expectations of public organizations. Consequently, performance measures may be vague; that is, they may be more qualitative (or intangible) than quantitative, since there is no clearly identified bottom line such as profits or market share. As we discussed earlier, it is easier to measure the quality of an assembled car than the quality of justly administering laws.

Public managers also tend to operate with more personnel constraints. As a result of merit-based selection processes, civil service rules, and the political interest in the welfare of public employees, public managers have less flexibility in terms of who is employed and how those employees are treated. Accordingly, there is a greater concern for equity in the public sector, even beyond the personnel area. Public managers, for instance, must be sensitive to how their employees treat clients, particularly as this relates to the perception of fairness. Public employees are expected to be not only honest and fair, but also responsive to public demands.

Public organizations tend to be more open than private organizations. In democratic societies, public scrutiny of the behavior of government officials is part of the political process. The public is interested in the police and what they do, as are elected officials, judges, media representatives, and many other diverse interest groups. Finally, because of the lack of comparable concrete work incentives such as pay bonuses and stock options, public managers must rely more on persuasion and informal methods to motivate and lead than private managers. The expectation-integration model indicates that the basic managerial role is to *balance* and *integrate* often-competing expectations. Public managers, because of the openness of the organization, are more likely to rely on persuasion, particularly when they attempt to balance and integrate community and organizational expectations.


## Police Management Versus Public Management

Having discussed how public management can be distinguished from private management, how does police management differ from other publically managed organizations? In general, the difference is in the problems that result from the conflict inherent in the police role in a democratic society. How do the police organize, manage, train, and evaluate personnel to make the concepts of force and authority (characteristics of the police) compatible with the concepts of freedom and participation (characteristics of a democracy)?

Two uniquely characteristic aspects of police work are the use of coercive force and the exercise of discretion. Coercive force involves the use of verbal threats or physical force to accomplish police objectives. This force can be "applied" by either the officer or the organization or both. For example, a police officer may threaten to arrest a suspect and may have to use force to effectuate the arrest. In rare instances, the suspect may even be killed. The degree to which police organizations emphasize the importance of apprehension of suspects rather than the prevention of crime indicates the degree to which that organization is implicitly coercive in the community. The more resources devoted to arrests, the more arrests made, the more intrusive and coercive the police.

Discretion is concerned with the decision-making latitude of officers and the factors that influence those decisions. The types of decisions police officers make include whether or not to intervene with citizens, how to behave when interacting with citizens, when and how to change their behavior if the citizen does not cooperate, and the alternative to use to "solve" the problem. Police officers must decide when to do their job, how to behave when they are doing it, and what to do about the problems that confront them. Organizations must decide how they will allocate their resources, what strategies and tactics they will employ, and how they will guide the behavior of their officers.

The exercise of discretion and the use of coercive force present unique and difficult problems for police managers because police officers often work by themselves or with one other officer. Many officers are widely dispersed throughout a community and may go unsupervised for long periods. As a result, there is considerable potential for abuse in discretion and the unnecessary use of force. Both types of problems have been, and remain, a managerial preoccupation. Other issues that police managers must be concerned with include the following:

1. The model that is most appropriate for police in a democratic society (see chapter 2);
2. the management model that is most likely to balance or integrate diverse expectations, and structure and control the exercise of discretion and the use of force;
3. the qualities that are "desirable" to be a "good" police officer and how best to identify or develop these qualities; and,
4. the changes that police departments should make and how those changes should be made, particularly as they relate to police–democratic society compatibility issues.

These are some of the important differences that police officers must handle in managing law enforcement organizations. Other differences are explored throughout the remainder of the book as we attempt to integrate theory and practice in analyzing the most pressing managerial problems facing contemporary police organizations. As a result, we hope the reader will develop a better understanding of the complex nature of policing and an appreciation for the dynamics of police organization and management.

## Summary

The purpose of this text is to promote an understanding of police organization and management in a democratic society, and the importance of "good" management in making a difference in policing. An organization was defined as a social system composed of two or more persons who are interdependent and work in a coordinated manner to achieve common goals. The study of police organization and management stressed several major themes. Each theme should enhance our understanding of police organizational behavior and how individuals and groups can be effectively managed in these organizations. The major themes include: a humanistic orientation, the expectation-integration model, the interdisciplinary approach, the scientific method, the four levels of analysis, general systems and contingency theories of management, and the promotion of ethical behavior throughout the organization. We believe that promoting ethical behavior in police organizations is especially important because of the nature of policing in a democratic society and the level of trust that the public must place in the police.

We defined management in terms of working with people in a humane manner to accomplish goals and objectives. This definition requires mutual participation between managers and employees to accomplish individual and organizational goals. Four essential functions of management were discussed: planning, organizing, leading, and controlling. Emphasis was also placed on how human resources are utilized and the quality of the work environment. By manipulating the quality of the work environment, police managers can influence the performance of their employees. However, both the organization and the employee must be willing to contribute equally to providing a high-quality working environment. Finally, to properly understand the role of the police manager in a democracy, differences between public and private management and between police and public management were noted.

## Discussion Questions

1. What is an organization, and how would you define the term *management*?
2. Discuss several major themes that can be used in the study of police organization and management.

3. Describe four levels of organizational analysis.
4. In what ways is management an art or a science?
5. Briefly describe the expectation-integration model and how it can be useful in improving organizational performance.
6. Why is it important for police managers to promote ethical behavior?
7. Describe at least three essential functions performed by managers.
8. How can managers influence employee performance by "manipulating" the quality of the work environment?
9. In general, how does public management differ from private management; conversely, how does police management differ from public management?
10. Describe at least four unique problems that confront police managers.

## References

Allison, G. T., "Public and Private Management," in *Readings in Public Administration*, eds. R. T. Golembiewski and F. Gibson (Boston: Houghton Mifflin, 1983), pp. 1–19.

Funk, C. E., ed, *Funk and Wagnalls New College Standard Dictionary* (New York: Funk and Wagnalls, 1953).

Haimann, T. and Scott, W. G., *Management in the Modern Organization*, 2nd ed. (Boston: Houghton Mifflin, 1974).

Heffernan, W. C. and Stroup, T. eds., *Police Ethics: Hard Choices in Law Enforcement* (New York: John Jay Press, 1985).

Heffernan, W. C., "The Police and the Rules of Office," in *Police Ethics: Hard Choices in Law Enforcement*, eds. W. C. Heffernan and T. Stroup (New York: John Jay Press, 1985) pp. 3–24.

Macy, B. A. and Mirvis, P. H., "A Methodology for Assessment of Quality of Work Life and Organizational Effectiveness in Behavioral-Economic Terms," *Administrative Science Quarterly* 21 (1976):212–226.

Roberg, R. R., *Police Management and Organizational Behavior: A Contingency Approach* (St. Paul, MN: West, 1979).

*Webster's New World Dictionary*, (New York: Warner Books, 1984).

# CHAPTER 2

# Police Development
# and Role Debates

Understanding the development of police in the United States is crucial in order to fully appreciate the problems of modern police management. Police agencies live with the legacy of the past and each generation of officers struggles anew with many of the same issues. This chapter will describe police development by presenting four models that have been and still are prevalent in the United States. In addition, the police role in the community and the major role debates will be discussed.

## The Development of Police

Between about 1600 and the 1830s, the basic responsibility for law enforcement gradually shifted from the *volunteer citizen* to the *paid specialist*. This process of role specialization was the result of a growing and increasingly complex society attempting to master the physical environment and cope with human problems. One consequence of these economic, social, and technological changes was an increasing public concern about deviant and disruptive behavior.

Initially, the *constable-nightwatch system* of policing evolved as a response to order-maintenance and law enforcement problems. This system included a limited number of constables who had civil and criminal responsibilities and a patrolling nightwatch staffed with persons who were required to serve as a community obligation. However, this obligation was unpopular and paid substitutes were used until finally the nightwatch became a full-time, paid occupation. Between the 1830s and the 1850s, a growing number of cities decided that this system of law enforcement was inadequate. As a result, paid daytime police forces were created. Eventually the daytime force joined with the nightwatch to create *integrated day-night*, or *modern*, police departments (Bridenbaugh 1964; Johnson 1981; Lane 1967; Miller 1977).

Four theories have been suggested to explain the development of police departments. The *disorder control* theory explains development in terms of the need to control mob violence. For example, Boston had three major riots in the years preceding the establishment of its police department (Lane 1967). Mob violence also occurred in other cities in the 1830s and 1840s (Johnson 1981). The *crime control* theory suggests that increases in criminal activity resulted in a perceived need for a new type of police. Threats to social order such as highway robbers and violent pickpockets (now called muggers) created a climate of fear. Concern about daring thieves and property offenses was widespread in cities (Johnson 1981).

The *class control* theory blames the development of police class-based economic exploitation. Advocates of this theory note that urban and industrial growth coincided with the development of the new police. During this period, many persons of different social and ethnic backgrounds competed for opportunities that would enhance their economic status. The resulting disruption prompted the middle and upper classes, usually white Anglo-Saxon Protestants, to develop a means to control the people involved, usually poor immigrants, sometimes not Anglo, and often not Protestant. This theory holds that modern police forces were merely tools created by the industrial elite to suppress the laborers who were being used as fuel for the engine of capitalism (Cooper 1975; Johnson 1981). The last theoretical view, *urban dispersion*, holds that many municipal police departments were created because other cities had them, and not because there was a real need. Police forces were considered an integral part of the governmental structure needed to provide a stabilizing influence in communities (Mokkonen 1981).

There is some evidence to support all four theories; however, no single theory provides an adequate explanation. While some cities had major urban disturbances before they established new police departments, others did not. Although there was also a public concern about crime, the degree of concern varied among communities. Some cities established after the 1830s and 1840s did not have mob violence or serious crime. Yet, police departments were created because a governmental structure was assumed to include a police component similar to, even if smaller than, the ones that existed in older, larger cities. Police were also used to control class-based, economic unrest; but since many police officers often came from the dissident groups or had friends or family members who were participants, some police officers and organizations resisted brutal or excessive responses.

Once modern police departments were established, they performed a wide variety of tasks and activities. In the nineteenth century, and well into the twentieth century in many cities, the police were an *all-purpose munic-ipal service*. They acted as health officers, tax and garbage collectors, pro-bation officers, social workers, and more. As governments were established and their responsibilities defined, but before specialized roles were created, police were given many governmental tasks to perform because they were available, already being paid, and usually had extra time. In small cities this role diversity is still commonplace; police officers perform tasks that would be the province of nonpolice specialists in larger communities.

The police departments established in the 1830s to 1850s—Boston in 1837, New York in 1844, Philadelphia in 1854—were loosely based on the Peelian model of the London police that emerged in 1829. This model, de-signed by Robert Peel, Charles Rowan, and Richard Mayne, emphasized prevention rather than apprehension. *Prevention* was to be accomplished by dispersing police throughout the community to keep crime from occurring and to intervene when it did. Apprehension was not stressed because it was associated with secrecy, deceit, incitement, and corruption. The London model also included an elaborate organizational structure based on military principles, strict rules of conduct, and well-defined management practices. Great care was taken in the selection and retention of police officers. Since the creation of a new police in England was controversial, the most impor-tant consideration was control of officer behavior. Community expectations and acceptance was the overriding concern in the development and manage-ment of police.

In the United States, however, the establishment of the new police was not as controversial. Departments were generally based on the Peelian's pre-vention concept, but there were minimal similarities beyond that point. Dif-ferences in development were essentially the result of three factors: *social context, political environment,* and *law enforcement policies.* America was more violent, politicians were more meddlesome, and the police were more decentralized and were expected to be locally responsive (Johnson 1981).

By the 1870s most cities had a police department even if it consisted of only one person. However, these departments tended to be dominated by the most influential political groups in the community. Local political concerns were more important to most police leaders than the application of the best available organization and management knowledge. What resulted was the development of the first model of modern policing, followed by subsequent models as existing assumptions about police and police practices were scrutinized, criticized, and gradually changed.

## Models of Policing

Democratic social systems make the job of police more difficult. Democracy is associated with concepts such as freedom, privacy, individual rights, the rule of law, participation, and the value of human life and individual dignity. Policing is often associated with concepts such as restriction, intrusion, responsibility, force, authority, and indifference to the individual. These democratic and police concepts obviously have considerable potential for conflict. How this conflict can be reduced if not eliminated largely depends on how the role of the police is defined and carried out.

The police *role* in any community is determined by changing expectations concerning police activity and behavior. The expectation-integration model (E-I model) described in chapter 1 identified the three major sources of these expectations: the *employee,* the *organization,* and the *community.* The role of the police manager is to integrate, or at least balance, these expectations. Historically, conflicting expectations about what police should do and how they should do it have been commonplace. When conflict exists, police organizations must adjust and this adjustment takes the form of a style of policing. A *style* is the uniquely characteristic manner used by police to practice their craft, both organizationally and individually.

The police have gone through essentially four stages of development. These stages represent different policing models that have evolved since the mid-nineteenth century. Each model describes, in general, the dominant characteristics of policing in a certain time period. This does not mean that as a new model emerges, all police organizations simultaneously change or replace the old model with the new one at the same rate. On the contrary, once a certain approach to policing is established it may change very little. When change does occur in a community it is often a gradual process, unless it is precipitated by a major crisis or scandal (e.g., extensive police corruption). However, police departments do change and they gradually adopt some or all of the characteristics of a policing model that is considered most compatible with democratic concepts, as determined by leading practitioners and researchers. However, since police departments do not adhere to the same timetable for change, more than one model is likely to exist in any particular period of history. In addition, no department exactly "fits" a specific model; usually departments have elements of some or all of the models, but they have distinct tendencies toward one. Before discussing the four police models, it is necessary to first describe the major parts or constructs utilized to build each model.

## Model Constructs

Just as various parts are needed to build a working model plane, conceptual models use parts referred to as constructs. Constructs are the basic, general ideas that are common to all models but that may have different meanings in each model. If a model plane is to fly, it must have an engine, but engines vary in design, power, size, and shape. The same holds true for model constructs; they are necessary if the model is to be adequately understood, but they vary in definition.

Two basic constructs will be used to build the policing models: (1) the major *strategies* that can be utilized in attempting to respond to crime problems and (2) the *behavior* of the officers who implement the strategies, with particular emphasis on the use of coercive force and the exercise of discretion. As noted, strategies are used to conceptualize the various means police departments employ to respond to crime problems. Strategies also provide an organizational level of analysis, whereas behavior is concerned with an analysis at the individual and work-group levels.

## Strategies

Police departments engage in a wide variety of activities that are not related to criminal behavior. For example, police officers provide information, assist the sick and injured, and maintain order in the community. However, one of their most important responsibilities is to respond to crime problems. Consequently, how they decide to do this is an important factor in determining the police role in the community.

Strategies are the police activities that are assumed to have an influence on either the motives of the individuals contemplating a crime or the opportunities available to them. The four basic police strategies are visibility, apprehension, counseling, and education. *Visibility* is a police "presence," frequently mobile, made known in the community by distinctive uniforms and "marked" and painted vehicles and equipment (e.g., cars, motorcycles, boats, helicopters). This strategy is intended to make prospective law violators wary by actually denying them opportunities to commit a crime or by creating the impression that police might be close by. *Apprehension* involves the investigative efforts of police to "catch" suspected criminals. This strategy is intended to deter criminal behavior in one of two ways: by holding accountable those individuals committing the crimes (specific deterrence) or by providing an example to others of what might happen if they violate the law (general deterrence).

*Counseling* is the attempt to resolve or alleviate problems without making an arrest. Counseling, which includes informing, advising, mediating, and referring for expert assistance, occurs most often with juveniles and in cases involving only minor or moderately serious violations of the law. This strategy is directed primarily at the motivation of actual or prospective law violators. *Education* involves police efforts to inform the public on how to avoid being victimized. The intent of this strategy is to make the "target" (person or property) less vulnerable and it is essentially directed at the opportunity to commit a crime.

Strategies have an *organizational* (formal) and an *individual* (informal) character. Patrol officers either formally or informally utilize all four strategies even if they are unaware of doing so. They are often confronted with situations and problems for which they have not been prepared. In such situations, the officer's response tends to be informal, derived primarily from both preemployment and postemployment experiences. In many instances, these informal solutions reflect some form of counseling or education. The counseling may be harsh or supportive, intended to confront or to avoid the problem, and either helpful or harmful. Educational efforts may be informative, useful, and accurate, or none of these. To the degree that responses and solutions are left to the individual officer, the greater the officer's discretion and the less influence the managers have.

An important managerial concern is when to formalize the use of strategies. What should be or has to be left to the experience and wisdom of the officer, and what should the organization attempt to formalize? Formalization requires defining the problem, identifying a body of knowledge that may be useful in responding, developing training in using the necessary methods and skills, and formulating the necessary policies and procedures.

An example of this process of formalization is the changing police response to domestic disturbances or family fights. Until the 1960s the police response was highly informal and incorporated, depending on the officer, use of apprehension (or arrest), separation of the parties involved, and different forms of "counseling." When and how these tactics were used depended on the seriousness of the problem and, perhaps more important, on the personal and police experiences of the officers. At best, it was a haphazard process and the results were not reviewed or analyzed.

Beginning in the 1960s, police organizations began to attempt to formalize a response to this problem. This decision required recognition that domestic disturbances were a serious problem and were amenable to solution by a formalized response that officers could be trained to use routinely and consistently. For example, officers in some agencies received training in violence reduction and background instruction on counseling techniques. Officers were usually provided with a list of community agencies, for long-term assistance, to which the disputants could be referred. While not all agencies developed the same approaches, at least the organization attempted to take the decision away from the officer and make it an organizational endeavor; that is, the response moved from being informal to formal. A more thorough discussion of police responses to this problem and how they have continued to change is found in chapter 10.

It is also important not to confuse strategies with organizational *functions* or *specializations* like patrol and investigations. The officer's presence in a uniform or in a marked vehicle represents visibility; giving a traffic citation or making an arrest represents apprehension; a word of advice to a juvenile about his or her driving behavior or beer consumption involves counseling; a comment to a burglary victim about how to prevent a subsequent crime represents education.

Police strategies also have their functional or programmatic aspects. A police *function* is a basic specialization common to police organizations. The patrol and investigations functions discussed in chapter 8 are good examples. To what degree are police strategies incorporated, informally or formally, into basic functions? Or to what degree do strategies become part of specific *programs* that become more specialized responses to problems? For example, should police educational efforts in crime prevention be integrated into the patrol and investigation functions? Or should crime prevention be a specialized organizational activity, perhaps less basic than primary functions, but nevertheless an important program?

Managers must attempt to deal with the informal–formal, functional–programmatic nature of police strategies. In part, the role of police managers is to constantly try to understand the most effective components of strategies and how to incorporate them into the organization.

## Behavior

An officer's behavior uniquely characterizes his or her interpersonal and occupational *style,* how he or she exercises discretion and employs coercive force. This behavior is strongly influenced by both the formal organization through training, policies, and procedures, and by his or her immediate work group. The organizational culture discussed in chapter 4 is particularly important. How does an officer practice the art or science of policing? Important considerations include what officers consider the most important aspects of their work, and the factors that influence decision making; for instance, police officer discretion, the commitment to the rule of law, officer responses to the ends-means dilemma, how coercive force is utilized, and finally, what typifies the individual officer's style of policing.

Police officers have different opinions about the importance of various aspects of their job. For some, serious felonies receive the most effort, whereas for others, traffic or juvenile problems may be given a higher priority. This is more likely to occur in patrol where there is less task specialization, but even investigators and other personnel, including managers, may invest more effort in the tasks they like or think are important. Other factors also influence the decisions officers make, such as the characteristics (i.e., race, sex, age, appearance, economic and political status) of suspects, victims, or witnesses, the circumstances surrounding police–citizen interaction (i.e., time of day, type of neighborhood, crime problems), and organizational factors (i.e., supervision, incentives to perform specific work like writing traffic tickets).

Police decision making, or *discretion,* involves essentially three important types of decisions: (1) whether to get involved in an event (this is not a choice if the police are requested to become involved), (2) how to behave in that event, and (3) what to do once they are involved. Police officers frequently work by themselves or with a partner. Many of their decisions are known only to one individual or possibly a few other persons (e.g., a suspect, victim, or fellow police officer). If an officer sees a violation of the law and takes no action, it is a discretionary act.

Officers must also choose the type of *initial behavior* they will utilize when they become involved with citizens. Will they be formal or friendly or forceful? Will they be pleasant or harsh? Once involved they may also have to decide how they will change behavior. The third important consideration is the *problem-solving alternative* selected. What should the officer do about the problem? Which alternative is the most effective? Should they issue a citation, make an arrest, give a verbal warning, take the person home, let him or her go, or offer some type of advice? Guidelines for the exercise of police discretion come from the formal organization, the police culture, and the law.

Police officers are formally charged with enforcing the law. A fundamental characteristic of democracy is the principle of the rule of law. Substantive criminal laws make illegal and punishable acts such as rape, robbery, and murder. Procedural criminal laws identify the process to use in pursuing investigations of individuals suspected of violations of substantive laws. Police are supposed to be concerned about the legal justification for arrests, search and seizure, obtaining confessions, and other "suspect rights." As noted, however, officer's opinions about which substantive laws are the most important may vary. Officers may also differ in the degree to which they observe a suspect's legal rights. Some officers take their job "personally" or have a low regard for the effectiveness of the criminal justice system and legal processes. Consequently, these officers may practice "back alley" or "street corner" justice, in which they decide who is "guilty" and what the punishment should be. When police personalize their authority, they tend to "take the law into their own hands."

The *ends-means* dilemmas in police work are analogous to the substantive-procedural law relationship. The ends represent successful apprehension or enforcement of substantive laws and accomplishment of the organization's goals and objectives; the means represent the methods used to obtain a desirable end. Procedural law, along with organizational policies and procedures, techniques taught in training programs and learned from peers, identifies methods of enforcing laws. Do police always follow "acceptable" methods? Does the desire to achieve a successful end, that is, to make the arrest or accomplish the goal, ever outweigh the requirement that acceptable means be employed? How do individual officers balance the ends-means dilemma? The ends-means dilemma and corruption problems represent two major ethical problems for police managers and officers.

Police officers must also make decisions concerning when they will employ *coercive force*. When will they threaten people with whom they interact? When will they use physical means to insure cooperation or make an arrest? When will they use deadly force? The degree to which officers use coercive force is a function of both individual and organizational factors. To a substantial degree, training, policy, and procedures govern the use of coercion, but the organization's culture and how each officer views the police role, the perceived threat in dangerous situations, and what is required to be successful are also important.

Finally, police officers tend to develop a *style* of policing that reflects an orientation based on the above and other considerations. It is not uncommon for styles to change, either situationally or over time. For example, an officer will usually behave differently at a crime in progress than when giving a traffic citation. When giving a traffic ticket, an officer may change styles if the traffic violator is not cooperative. The more stubborn, obstinate, or insulting the violator, the more likely that the officer will change behavior, perhaps more than once. What is the appropriate style for police officers? How should style change when a situation changes? As officers gain more experience, do their styles change? And if they do, what factors influence these changes?

Studies of police behavior, usually of patrol officers, have identified six variables that can be utilized to characterize police officer styles: (1) their work specialization, (2) their response to order-maintenance as compared to law enforcement problems, (3) their selectivity in enforcing the law, (4) their degree of aggressiveness, (5) their degree of compassion, and (6) their degree of comfort in exercising authority.

Banton (1974) found that organizational specialization influenced the development of a policing style, and as a result, officers became either *peacekeepers* or *law enforcers*. Patrol officers became peacekeepers responsible for a wide range of problems that were often resolved without using the alternative of arrest. Investigative or detective specialists and traffic enforcement officers were law enforcers because they were much more likely to issue citations or make arrests than were patrol officers.

Wilson (1968) discussed three organizational styles of policing that are similar to three of the democratic models, but these styles can also be used to identify individual officer styles. Wilson argues that problems confronting patrol officers (and police departments) can be grouped into one of two categories: order maintenance or law enforcement. *Order-maintenance* problems involve no violation or minor to moderately serious violations of the law

**One of the important characteristics of a police officer's style is his or her degree of compassion.**

for which there is no arrest. *Law enforcement* situations involve more serious violations in which an arrest is usually made or a citation is issued.

Wilson found that style differences were based on how police officers handled order-maintenance problems because police usually responded to law enforcement problems in the same way. The *legalistic* style response to order-maintenance problems tends to be in terms of what the law permits. If possible, a legalistic department or officer will make an arrest or issue a citation to "solve a problem." A *watchman* style incorporates an informal, individual approach. The solutions to order-maintenance problems are left to the wisdom and experience of the officer. A *service* style does not leave the solution of order-maintenance problems to the informal response of officers nor does it attempt to view these problems only in terms of the law. Rather, the organization attempts to develop a more formal, but not necessarily an enforcement, response to some of the more typical order-maintenance problems (e.g., juvenile vandalism).

Brown (1981) characterized styles in terms of the selectivity and aggressiveness of police officers. Some officers are *selective,* emphasizing only certain violations of the law, and some officers are not selective, giving all problems about equal consideration. Officers may also differ in degree of *aggressiveness.* Some are highly proactive (e.g., initiate numerous public contacts), whereas others are essentially reactive (e.g., respond only when assistance is requested by a citizen). Muir (1977) used two different variables to characterize police styles: *compassion* and *authority*. Officers can be either compassionate or not compassionate toward people (that is, empathetic about the tragic consequences of life that everyone experiences). Officers may also be either comfortable or uncomfortable with their authority. Some officers are more than willing to confront problems, issue ultimatums, and make arrests, whereas others are more reluctant.

Police managers need to realize that a police officer's behavior can be characterized by these differences and in other ways. To what degree do managers want styles to vary? How selective and aggressive do they want their officers to be? How compassionate? How comfortable are they with their authority? Do organizations want order-maintenance problems left to the experience and wisdom of the officer or do they want more control over responses? And, if so, for which order-maintenance problems? These are some of the questions that police managers need to address.

The two constructs—strategies and behavior or officer styles—are used to identify four models of democratic policing. The models represent four stages on a historical continuum along which police departments have moved. Change does not necessarily mean improvement; rather, it denotes differences in the model constructs. The model, or organizational style of a police department, can most effectively be determined only within the context of the community in which it functions. And one model does not necessarily remain the most effective approach if the character and population of a community change. The adoption of a model is contingent on the role conceptions and performance expectations that result from the interaction of the officer, the organization, and the external environment.

## The Political-Watchman Model: Police Officer as Neighbor

In the 1830s, when integrated day-night, or modern, law enforcement began in the United States, the *political-watchman model* emerged. The political characterization reflects the political context within which community law enforcement evolved. For decades policing was dominated by local politicians and competing political groups. The watchman characterization indicates the continuing lack of professionalism in organization and management practices and in the officers' behavior, the broad range of tasks police officers were expected to perform, and the "watching" role of police, particularly patrol officers. For most of the nineteenth century, many police departments were politically corrupt, and many officers were corrupt, indifferent to their responsibilities, incompetent, or all three.

The strategies emphasized by community police included *visibility* and *apprehension* and, to a lesser degree, counseling and education. The police established patrol and investigation specializations in an attempt to limit opportunities to commit crime and deter criminal behavior. Police officers were also actively involved in providing *social services* to communities (e.g., as probation officers, juvenile counselors, and providers of shelter and food). These wide-ranging services were consistent with the evolving nature of the police role.

Officer behavior was shaped by personal values, political affiliations, the problem to be solved, and the possible negative consequences of behavior. Individual officers tended to be *informal* and *personal*. Knowledge of the citizens, their ethnic and racial identity, socioeconomic standing, and politics influenced police–citizen interaction, particularly when the crime was not serious. Officers tended to be selective in responding to problems, uncomfortable with their authority, and to vary in their degree of compassion and aggressiveness. Coercion was probably used more frequently primarily because citizens were more likely to resist police authority, but also because management had minimal control over officers.

The police officer in this model was like a *neighbor,* available for information, advice, and assistance. Many officers were political lackeys and bullies who periodically discriminated against those persons they did not approve of. The rule of law, and organizational policies and procedures where they existed, often gave way to the rule of personal authority. Officers had a great deal of discretion and were more likely to use coercive force than in any subsequent model. The ends usually justified the means employed. With police functioning essentially as a neighbor, "good men" tended to make good cops while less-than-good men incalculably damaged police credibility and authority.

In the latter part of the nineteenth century, the model came under criticism. Identified problems included excessive political influence, laziness, incompetent and corrupt officers, inadequate selection and training, poor management practices, and ineffective leadership. Reformers from inside and outside police ranks suggested solutions, which gave birth to new democratic policing models. However, the process of replacing the political-watchman model was gradual and piecemeal. As late as the 1950s many community police departments, if not the majority, had a substantial political character and some still do (Fogelson 1977; Johnson 1981; Lane 1967; Richardson 1970).

## The Legalistic-Professional Model: Police Officer as Soldier

In the first three decades of the twentieth century, two competing views emerged about the police role in a democratic society. One view resulted in the emergence of the *legalistic-professional* model and the other resulted in the development of the community-service model, to be discussed later. The former proved to be more acceptable to most police and the public and became the dominant reform orientation until the 1960s, when the community-service model was rediscovered.

The legalistic characterization of this model emphasizes the importance of *rule enforcement*. If police departments were excessively influenced by politics, which meant favoritism and inconsistent behavior, the supposed remedy was to strictly follow the rules. For police the most important rule was the law, followed by the strict, elaborate organizational rules and regulations created to guide and control officer behavior. The professional characterization indicates an emphasis on improving the officers' competence, commitment, and sense of responsibility. If police were to be efficient and effective, organizations had to select the best applicants, pay them well, train them properly, and free them from political influence. However, even though this model emphasizes the importance of well-qualified personnel, it is probably the least humanistic model.

The strategies of *visibility* and *apprehension* are considered the most effective and desirable police responses to deviant and disruptive behavior. Although these strategies were important in the political-watchman approach, they became the primary perspective from which police viewed their role in the legalistic-professional model. This approach emphasized *crime fighting.* Partly, this emphasis resulted from police leaders' trying to obtain support for their reforms, but it was also consistent with their views on how to most effectively "wage war" on crime.

Visibility and apprehension were formalized by emphasizing the importance of patrol and investigations specializations in police departments. Counseling and education tended to be deemphasized by the advocates of the legalistic-professional approach, but they were not abandoned. Rather, they were used informally by individual officers or as part of a limited programmatic effort. In general, however, police organizations, with the exception of the programs created to deal with juveniles, tended to ignore counseling and education.

In this model the behavior of officers, the exercise of discretion, and the use of coercive force are tightly controlled or at least that is the organizational intent. *Standards* of law and organizational policy are to be unswervingly applied in waging the "war on crime." Position descriptions, policies and procedures, and rules and regulations are stressed. Officers were not supposed to be selective (but many were, emphasizing only serious crimes), were comfortable with their authority, were not particularly compassionate, and tended to be aggressive. Ideally, the means or process of enforcement is more important than the ends of deterrence and apprehension, however, the reality proved to be somewhat different because there was a perceived conflict between being organizationally effective in fighting crime and following strict guidelines. Consequently, many officers went outside the law and policy to get results because they believed that "doing the job" was not possible if they "played by the rules."

Organizations contributed to this orientation by rewarding officers for the number of arrests made and tickets issued. For those departments in gradual transition from a political to a legalistic approach, the emphasis on crime fighting, the tendency of officers to exercise personal authority, and the organizational demands that officers be productive legalistically resulted in many dramatic examples of police abuse. While the actual use of coercion by police may have declined, when compared with the political-watchman model, the legalistic-professional model promised more than it delivered.

Officers were supposed to be businesslike, objective, dedicated, and incorruptible with a "no nonsense" approach to problem solving. This was the reformer's vision but as legalistic crime fighters, police became more like soldiers than business persons. The officer became society's soldier—the "thin blue line" between the savages and civilization. They were to be well-trained, incorruptible, disciplined professionals who enforced the law "without fear or favor." Instead, communities in which this model prevailed had many officers who were insensitive, autocratic, and verbally abusive, and who saw police work as "fighting crime." This approach created serious problems for police in some cities, particularly in minority communities where, historically, police have not been well received.

This model was the most prominent approach to reforming the police from the 1920s to the 1960s. It was somewhat influential in many police departments but it was never completely realized in its ideal state. It had to compete with the political-watchman approach that many cities gave up grudgingly, if at all. In the 1960s, the public perception of a "crime wave" plus numerous urban riots led to a general public criticism of police in the United States. Models of policing that existed—political-watchman and legalistic-professional—were criticized as having failed to respond effectively to deviant and disruptive behavior. The political-watchman model was perceived as a failure because of excessive political influence and poor management, and the legalistic-professional model because it emphasized visibility and apprehension too much and had gone so far to eliminate political influence that the police were no longer responsive to the communities they were created to serve (Fogelson 1977; Johnson 1981; Walker 1977). In effect, this model tended to deemphasize the needs of many employees and the expectations of the community.

## The Community-Service Model:
## Police Officer as Teacher

With the so-called police failure of the 1960s, critics began to advocate a model of policing that had existed since the 1920s, but had not played a significant role in changing the political-watchman approach. This model was essentially a reaction to the failure of the legalistic-professional model.

The community characterization reflects a *concern for community problems* and a *social responsibility* that goes beyond rule enforcement. The service dimension suggests police should broaden their approach to responding to crime by providing noncriminal alternatives and programs (e.g., misdemeanor citations, diversion programs, crisis intervention). The police should be more responsive and less formalistic, with a reduced emphasis on legalistic responses. Instead of being a neighbor or a soldier, police officers should be more like a teacher; a person who is a philosopher, a guide, and an educator but who is capable of disciplining the unruly student when appropriate. Instead of a negative, autocratic force in the community, officers should play a more positive, supportive role. However, while this essentially humanistic perspective was advocated in relationships with communities and citizens, management did not always support the approach. Some agencies attempted to adopt this model externally, but internally remained essentially bureaucratic or legalistically oriented in management practices and treatment of personnel.

All four police strategies (i.e., visibility, apprehension, education, counseling) are emphasized in this model. Officers are trained to utilize organizationally prescribed nonenforcement alternatives in dealing with a wide range of problems. Activities related to education and counseling are considered an integral part of the officer's behavior. Often, special programs are

**In the community-service model, the police officer often functions as a teacher.**

developed to implement these strategies. The officer has less latitude than in the political-watchman model because many of the informal alternatives of that model are replaced by organizational policies and procedures. However, there is greater latitude than in the legalistic-professional approach because officers are provided more problem-solving alternatives.

Officer behavior, while more interpersonally oriented, tends to be objective. Situations and individuals are viewed as problems to be solved. Officers are concerned with communication skills, basic interpersonal style, and escalation patterns in utilizing verbal and physical aggression (Caiden 1977; Fogelson 1977; Goldstein 1977; Johnson 1981). Officers tend to be more compassionate, they are neither selective nor particularly aggressive, and they may or may not be comfortable with authority. The organization attempts to control officer discretion by encouraging them to adopt a community-oriented philosophy and by providing nonenforcement alternatives in problem solving. Coercive force is considered a last resort and is actively discouraged. Usually, a strict policy limits its use. The use of verbal persuasion is actively encouraged in order to increase support in the community.

By the early 1980s, the legalistic-professional and community-service models were the two basic reform orientations for community police in the United States. Although the political-watchman model still existed, it was not usually viewed as appropriate within police circles or among critics. However, another emerging trend was beginning to have a significant impact on police organizations. Essentially, this trend resulted from an increasing emphasis on the use of the scientific method. This systematic research emphasis began in the 1960s and by the 1980s resulted in the emergence of a fourth policing model.

## The Rational-Contingency Model: Police Officer as Analyst

The emphasis placed on research about policing by many police organizations has resulted in the development of solutions *contingent* upon problem variables. The organizations using this approach are not wedded to the implicit ideology of one of the other models. They tend to be more pragmatic, with the objective of reducing or eliminating a problem for a reasonable time, utilizing methods that are acceptable to those with expectations about how the problems should be solved. The rational characterization indicates the emphasis on systematic and objective analysis of *problems* confronting the organization. The contingency characterization indicates that solutions are contingent on, or depend on, the results of the analysis (Spelman and Eck 1987).

Strategy selection varies with the problem and the possible remedies. As with the community-service model, all four strategies are utilized by the officer and the organization. A substantial emphasis is given to all strategies in order to balance the police–citizen relationship. Advocates of this model believe that police must be viewed in a supportive, helping role as well as in a rule-enforcing role. Officer behavior varies; in fact, the absence of a well-defined style philosophy associated with the legalistic-professional and community-service models results in a greater variety of police behavior. Ideally, officers are not selective and are capable of adjusting their styles as situational problems change. They can be neighbor, soldier, teacher, and

**Table 2-1**  Police Models

| Constructs | Political-Watchman | Legalistic-Professional | Community-Service | Rational-Contingency |
|---|---|---|---|---|
| **Strategies** | All strategies are utilized but they are haphazardly developed | Visibility and apprehension are emphasized | All strategies are formally developed by the organization | Strategic use is contingent upon analysis of the problem |
| **Behavior** | Neighbor | Soldier | Teacher | Analyst (Plus others) |
| **(Role and Style)** | Selective May be uncomfortable with authority May or may not be compassionate and aggressive | Not selective Aggressive Not compassionate Comfortable with authority | Not selective Aggressive Compassionate May or may not be comfortable with authority | Characteristics vary with the problem Generally comfortable with authority Not selective Aggressiveness and compassion varies |

when necessary, analyst. The four models of policing and their important characteristics are presented in Table 2-1.

## Models in Transition

These models of democratic policing are the result of the *style adjustments* made to accommodate *conflicting expectations* concerning the police role. To resolve this conflict, one of the major expectation sources—the community, the organization, or the employee—tends to dominate the adjustment that is made.

In the political-watchman model, selected communities and the politicians determined the adjustment. In the legalistic-professional model, the reform movement was first instigated by middle-class, civic-minded citizens, but it was taken over and sustained by police leaders, who seized the opportunity for reform that came when the public became disenchanted with the inefficiency and corruption of the political-watchman model. These practitioners believed that the law provided the most effective frame of reference for reform, particularly since rule enforcement would minimize political influence.

The community-service model was, in part, a reaction to the impersonalism of the police activities associated with the legalistic-professional model and the perceived lack of effectiveness in crime control. The public, particularly those groups representing liberal politicians, the media, and academic social scientists, worked to encourage the adoption of this model to reform the police. The impetus for the rational-contingency model began in the 1960s when systematic research into police and related problems became more prevalent. By the 1970s, as a result of substantial financial support from the federal government, the emphasis on research increased dramatically and police departments began to use research findings to develop responses to problems. By the 1980s, this research orientation and flexible response to problems became characteristic of more and more police organizations. This problem-oriented approach to policing is discussed in more detail in subsequent chapters.

In the political-watchman model, the police officer is like a neighbor, either a friend or bully or both. In the legalistic-professional model, the police officer is like a community soldier, who protects society against deviant incursions. In the community-service model, the police officer is the teacher, who educates and counsels but who may have to discipline the unruly citizen. In the rational-contingency model, the police officer is potentially all of the above and an analyst. Some police authorities believe that the rational-contingency model (becoming popularly known as problem-oriented policing) is part of the community-service approach, but the authors believe that it is a separate approach to policing (Goldstein 1987).

Regardless of the time period or the policing model in question, police organizations and managers have had to respond to some of the same basic problems in attempting to make the police more compatible with democratic society. Although the knowledge about, understanding of, and responses to these problems may change, the problems do not. The response to these problems depends, in large part, on how the role of the police is defined and carried out. The next section addresses the police role in democratic society and discusses five role debates.

## The Police Role in Democratic Society

The expectation-integration model helps identify the sources of expectations concerning the *police role*: the officers, the organization, and the community. The community expects the police to respond to certain problems; the organization becomes concerned, along with the community and officers, with the extent, nature, and causes of those problems. The resulting analyses, whether simplistic or complex, general or specific, determine how the police will respond. What strategies will be employed? How will these strategies be organized into functions or specializations like patrol, investigations, traffic, and so on? Which problems will be given the highest priority? To which problems will the organization train its officers to respond? Which problems, in effect, will be ignored and left to the officer to do his or her best?

Expectations concerning police activity and behavior may be diverse. We have already noted the potential diversity of community expectations by identifying the different communities that may exist in one city or county. These expectations are even more diverse when the roles played by citizens when interacting with police are considered. What do citizens expect when they are a suspect? a victim? a witness? a bystander? To what degree do the police organization and the officer take into account these expectations? And, perhaps even more important, to what degree should they take them into consideration? How do the police balance legal requirements and citizen and community expectations? Integrating and balancing expectations requires that managers be aware of the expectations and which ones have the highest priority.

The organization's role is to understand the community's expectations, balance them against the requirements of substantive and procedural criminal law and those civil laws that are applicable, and develop programs, policies, and procedures to productively and effectively respond. However, the third major source of expectations, the officer, also develops opinions about the problems and their causes. What problems should be given priority? Which community expectations are reasonable and which are not? And, which laws, policies, and organizational practices do officers agree with and which do they tend not to support? Officers must work in the "reality of the street," which results in not only an analytical but also an emotional and psychological adjustment to the job. The emotional demands and occasional dangers inherent in police work tend to make many police officers less sympathetic than managers to some community and legal expectations.

The police role, from a managerial perspective, is the part police are expected to play in terms of what they do and how they do it. The most common, and simplistic, method used to identify the police role is the *goals/objectives approach*. The goals or objectives identify the purpose(s) of the police. Another approach to determining the police role is called *task and/or activity analysis*. Police activities have been studied since the turn of the century; however, in the 1960s these studies were more influential because they became the basis for challenging the police view of their role. Task studies examine the time officers spend in various activities. Based on the results of such research, generalizations are made regarding the police role as determined by what police actually do. To conduct this type of study, categories of police activities must be constructed and officer records or activities must be observed to determine how officers spend their time. The design phase of this type of study is crucial since the accuracy of the data, and hence the results, will be determined by how police activities are defined and measured by the researcher.

While task-activity studies are useful to managers, and have been influential in police role discussions, generalizations are often difficult to make. However, such studies do emphasize one aspect of police role discussions that is of vital importance to police managers: the basic debates surrounding the role police are expected to play in a democratic society. There are essentially five important debates: (1) Are police officers *crime fighters* or *social service workers*? (2) Is police work a *profession* or a *craft*? (3) How is the police role most effectively made compatible with democratic society— *politically* or *bureaucratically*? (4) To what degree should police be *proactive* as opposed to *reactive*? and (5) Should the primary orientation in responding to crime be *prevention* or *apprehension*? Table 2-2 relates the debates to dimensions of the police role. The first role debate is concerned with the orientation of individual officers. The second is related to the nature of the police occupation and the last three are concerned with how the police role should be implemented.

**Table 2-2**   Police Role Debates

| Role Dimension | Debate |
|---|---|
| Officer | Crime Fighter or Social Service Worker? |
| Occupation | Profession or Craft? |
| Implementation | Bureaucratic or Political? Proactive or Reactive? Prevention or Apprehension? |

## Role Debate: Crime Fighter or Social Service Worker?

This is an important role debate because it influences strategies that police utilize, the priority given to police tasks, the type of personnel selected, how officers are trained, and it is also influential in interpersonal behavior. *Crime fighters* believe that crime is a function of a rational choice made by criminals and that the most important police tasks are investigating serious crimes and making arrests. Police officers are expected to be aggressive, confident, and tough-minded. Their training tends to emphasize the knowledge and skills required to carry out their job in this way, and physical, mental, and emotional toughness is stressed.

*Social service* officers believe that all aspects of police work are important and that one aspect should not be ignored in favor of others. This approach to policing advocates the use of all strategies. Making an arrest is only one alternative and except in the more serious crimes, it is probably not the best one. The community dictates priorities and police officers are expected to be responsive to citizen concerns and to be empathetic and caring. Training includes the knowledge and skills necessary to meet the requirements for this role.

There are, of course, no pure crime fighters or social service officers; however, the belief that police are or should be one or the other influences how the police role will be constructed in a community. Often the role expectations along this dimension vary by source. Some communities may expect police to be crime fighters, whereas others may want a social service orientation. Often, police officers prefer to think of themselves as crime fighters. In such situations, the organization must balance and integrate these expectations. How do police managers integrate the autocratic toughness of the crime fighter with the supportive community worker requirements of a social service officer?

The ideal officer roles discussed in the previous section provide a good illustration of the conflicts inherent within this role debate. The *cop-as-neighborhood-friend* was an informal social service officer. As *neighborhood bully*, officers were both formally and informally crime fighters, being visible and making arrests, but often with a greater concern for ends than means. The *cop-as-soldier* is a formalization of the crime-fighter dimension of the police role. The police response to serious crime is emphasized and this response is more disciplined and structured, or more formalistic. The *cop-as-teacher* represents a formalization of the social service dimension of the role. The *cop-as-analyst* subordinates all ideal-type models to the requirements of the problem and its solution.

What should the police role be? Should it be determined by assessing what police do (task analysis) or prescribed by those most concerned about and impacted by police activities? What are the implications of emphasizing the crime-fighter dimension of the role? What are the implications of emphasizing the social service dimension? Should role discussions focus on whether police should be neighbor, soldier, teacher, or analyst or when they should be neighbor, soldier, teacher, or analyst? These are some of the questions police managers must address.

## Role Debate: Profession or Craft?

Is the police occupation a professional activity or essentially a craft? Generally speaking, do the tasks to be performed and problems to be solved require systematic and rational analysis and extensive formal preparation, or are common sense, intuitive insights, and experience the most important requirements? Are members of a profession managed differently than those of a craft? Who is to be given the most latitude in decision making? Whose performance is the most predictable and least troublesome? These are some of the questions addressed in this debate.

The *professionalization* of an occupation requires the replacement of trial-and-error learning with a process of rationalization that uses the scientific method. The process of developing knowledge is usually associated with an affiliation with colleges and universities. There are several stages in the movement of an occupation toward professional status: (1) the work is more intellectual than physical (or emotional), (2) selection and training procedures are developed, and (3) organizations are established to facilitate research and discussion of work-related problems. Ideally, a profession has the following features:

1. formal training with an intellectual component
2. certification of quality and competence
3. demonstrated ability in the pragmatic application of skills acquired in training

4. mechanisms to insure that individuals will behave in a social responsible manner
5. a commitment to research to update and improve the body of knowledge and skills required to practice the profession (Cullen 1978; Geison 1983).

An occupation that is a *craft* differs in, or lacks, several of these features. The work is as much physical or emotional as it is intellectual, and often it is more so. While training may exist, it usually emphasizes technical competence rather than intellectual exploration and discussion. Members of an occupation that is craftlike may or may not certify competence and may or may not require demonstrated ability in skill application. These occupations have little or no real commitment to research, but emphasize trial and error and experientially based learning.

The distinction between a profession and a craft is analogous to distinctions between science and art. As a *science*, police work would be viewed as including systems and methods based on a set of principles that convey general truths derived from research using the scientific method. Police work as an *art* involves the use of skill, taste, and creative imagination in problem solving. It differs from science in that it perceives, analyzes, and creates solutions to problems that are not based on identifiable principles.

The view of an occupation as a craft or a profession has obvious implications for police management. Professionalism tends to confer more status and economic benefits but imposes greater responsibility and obligations. Consequently, occupations can move toward professionalism to obtain status and benefits without a meaningful effort to structure and formalize training and problem solving through research. The four police models discussed previously are examples of a gradual movement from essentially a craft status toward more of a professional status (i.e., from political-watchman through rational-contingency).

Some of the questions raised by this debate include: Should police officers be required to go to college? If yes, what subjects should they take? What should be included in a training program for police? How much should be practical and how much intellectual? What obligations do officers and organizations have to participate in research activities and disseminate the results of that research? Do communities and managers really want officers to be professional? Are professional police more difficult to manage and do they cost too much? Should the police profession "police" itself or should this be a community responsibility?

## Role Debate: Bureaucratic or Political?

From a managerial viewpoint, what is the most effective way to integrate the role of police into democratic society? At the extremes there are two alternatives: *rational* and *rule-oriented* or *responsive* and *individualized*. The former is a *bureaucratic* approach, the latter a *political* approach.

The conception of police role implementation as bureaucratic assumes that justice is a product of *consistency*, and that consistency is best defined by precise and strict rules. The rules of law provide the basic requirements while organizational policies, procedures, and well-defined position descriptions provide officers the essentials of their work. Ideally, these rules are rationally developed and free of any biases that would be inconsistent with the fundamental principles of society.

The political view of the police role has two possible explanations. At the worst, laws and the police primarily serve the interests of the most influential persons in a community. Such individuals are considered to be above the law, while others are treated more harshly. This is the politics of *preference*. The second explanation focuses on *responsiveness* and individualization. Advocates of this role conception argue that strict rule enforcement does not take into account the uniqueness of the problems and needs of individuals and neighborhoods in the community. Consistency is not required and preferential treatment is unnecessary. The police need understanding and flexibility to respond to a particular community's needs.

Police managers must ask themselves how to respond to this bureaucratic-political debate. Actually more than a debate, it is tension between two polar views of the police-democratic conflict. When should the interests of the community be given more consideration than law and rules?

How many rules should an organization have? How important is consistency to the perception of justice? How do managers distinguish between interests demanding preference and those that are more representative of the entire community?

### Role Debate: Proactive or Reactive?

*Proactive* police work emphasizes *police-initiated activities* of the individual officer and the organization. *Reactive* police work is more a response to a problem by police when assistance is specifically *requested by citizens*. Giving a traffic ticket or other citation or conducting a field interrogation is a proactive act. Developing a response to a crime or other problem that is designed to prevent or intercept that type of crime is proactive. For example, undercover decoy programs are proactive, as are "stake outs" following suspected career criminals, and picking up truants (who may be committing burglaries when absent from school). Responding to specific problems based on citizen requests and following up on those problems to their conclusion are reactive responses.

The *organizational* dimension of a proactive police response may be difficult to understand. To illustrate, assume that a community is undergoing a series of armed robberies. A reactive response by police would involve conducting an investigation to identify and apprehend a suspect or suspects. A proactive response could include conducting an analysis of all the robberies in an attempt to determine a pattern. If a pattern was identified, the police might develop a series of "stake outs" at locations where future robberies could occur. This is an example of the difference between an organization that is essentially reacting to a problem by conducting an investigation and one that is trying to anticipate problems and respond accordingly.

What is problematic about proactive responses is that they make the police more intrusive in the community; that is, they are more likely to initiate contacts and programs without being asked, and some organizational proactive programs are potentially dangerous (e.g., stake outs and decoy programs). While being proactive can be associated with good management, it may also be excessively intrusive and risky. For example, the issue of entrapment is important here. Can police provide the intent to commit a crime during proactivity? Unless they are careful about how they identify potential "criminal" targets, or what they say when interacting with criminals, this is a definite possibility. In addition, and perhaps more serious, is the issue of incitement. Can police develop programs that may encourage individuals to commit crimes? This is also possible, particularly in so-called sting operations in which undercover police officers purchase stolen property. Does the availability of an outlet to sell stolen property provide encouragement for criminals to steal more?

Which is more compatible with democracy—a police force that is primarily reactive or one that is substantially proactive? Although eliminating all proactive activity (e.g., giving traffic tickets) is probably not possible, it is possible to limit the number of police-initiated contacts and organizational programs designed to prevent crime or to intervene when crimes occur. It is also important to distinguish the degree to which proactive police work is in response to community expectations or the result of managers in the organization. In some instances, professional police work has been associated with being proactive. What is clear, however, is that the more proactive, the more intrusive the police. And the more intrusive, the greater the risk to police officers and the greater the potential threat to democracy. How can the degree of intrusiveness that may be the result of police management be balanced with the expectations of the community? Which is more effective—being essentially reactive or proactive? And is effectiveness relevant to this issue? Even if improved police effectiveness is associated with being highly proactive, is there a point where this proactivity becomes too intrusive? These are some of the important issues in this role debate.

## Role Debate: Prevention or Apprehension

A uniformed patrol officer has just completed investigating a traffic accident and she is writing a report. Her vehicle is parked in a secluded area but she can see a small grocery store about a block away. However, the people coming in and out of the store cannot see her police car. The officer notices a car that fits the description of one used by a robbery suspect drive into the parking lot. The driver gets out of his car and looks at the store. From what she knows about the other robberies, there is insufficient information for an identification of a suspect. What should she do? (If she thought a crime was about to occur, she would undoubtedly call for assistance.) If she waits and the robbery takes place, will the store owner and/or customer be injured or killed? Will she be injured or killed if she tries to apprehend an armed suspect? If she makes an appearance will the person in question, if he is the robbery suspect, simply wait and commit another crime, or perhaps many more, before being apprehended? Are there any other alternatives (e.g., put in an appearance and then have an unmarked police car follow the suspect to obtain additional information, conduct a field interrogation)?

For a police officer to make her or his presence known is a distinctly *preventive* act, while waiting to arrest reflects an *apprehension* orientation. When police act in a manner designed to keep a crime from occurring, they are concerned with prevention; when they act in a manner designed to make arrests, an apprehension emphasis is evident. Ideally, apprehension is related to prevention because an arrest is supposed to prevent (through deterrence) the criminal and others from committing future crimes. Of course, the degree to which this actually occurs is not precisely known but police arrests probably do have some impact in this regard.

The prevention-apprehension debate is reflected not only in the *discretion* of individual officers but also in the manner in which an organization elects to *allocate resources*. For example, if a police department allocates substantial resources to counseling and education strategies then a prevention orientation is evident. On the other hand, if minimal resources are given to such activities then prevention has little support and an apprehension orientation prevails by default. Even in these departments, however, police officers may give informal advice designed to prevent crimes, but the extent and type of advice is not controlled by the organization.

A prevention orientation in police work tends to influence the types of police–citizen interaction in the community. A major emphasis on prevention activities increases the number of contacts in which police interact in a helping, supporting role with citizens. A strong emphasis on apprehension results in more adversarial relationships with citizens. The legalistic-professional model is an example of how this role debate can be resolved in favor of an apprehension orientation. The community-service model reflects more of a balanced concern for both prevention and apprehension.

Police act to prevent crime and to apprehend suspects, and perhaps by apprehension, they prevent future criminal acts. Whether police organizations and officers engage in prevention and apprehension activities is not at issue; rather, the degree of emphasis to be given to one or the other is the issue. Police officers and organizations make prevention-apprehension choices and these choices influence the role of police in society. Do the community, organization, and employee prefer a legalistic-professional model (apprehension-dominated orientation) or a community-service model (strong prevention orientation)? This is perhaps the basic issue in this role debate.

# Summary

This chapter has briefly traced the historical development of police, explained four theories of police development, and discussed four models of democratic policing—political-watchman, professional-legalistic, community-service, and rational-contingency. The role of the individual officer changes in each model, from a neighbor to a soldier to a teacher, and finally, to an analyst. This last role incorporates the other individual officer roles. These models are constructed by using two variables: the four basic police strategies (visibility, apprehension, counseling, and education) and police behavior. Police behavior is discussed relative to task preferences, exercise of discretion, use of coercive force, commitment to the rule of law or personal authority, and responses to ends-means problems. These models represent a continuum of movement from police work as essentially craftlike and politically preferential to more professional and politically responsive.

The police role discussion includes consideration of how the role is determined and five major role debates: Are police officers primarily crime fighters or social service workers? Is police work a profession or a craft? Is the police role most effectively implemented politically or bureaucratically? Should the police be more proactive or reactive? Should the orientation of police in the community be directed primarily toward prevention or apprehension?

The role debates clarify important considerations in the relationship between police and a democratic society. A crime-fighting, proactive, apprehension-oriented police organization or officer creates one type of relationship with democracy. A social service orientation that stresses the importance of prevention creates another type of police-democratic relationship. To help resolve this question, community, organization, and employee expectations must be considered.

## Discussion Questions

1. Identify and explain the four theories of police development.
2. Explain the differences and similarities between the development of police in England and the United States.
3. Identify and discuss the two basic constructs utilized to "build" the four models of policing. Include in your discussion the various aspects of both constructs.
4. Describe the political-watchman model of policing.
5. Describe the legalistic-professional model of policing.
6. Describe the community-service model of policing.
7. Describe the rational-contingency model of policing.
8. Discuss the factors that have influenced the transition from the political-watchman model to the rational-contingency model.
9. Identify and discuss the two role debates related to the officer's role and the nature of the police occupation.

10. Identify and discuss the three role debates related to implementing the police role in the community.

# References

Banton, M. P., *The Policeman in the Community* (New York: Basic Books, 1974).

Bridenbaugh, C., *Cities in the Wilderness: The First Century of Urban Life in America, 1625–1742*, 2 vols. (New York: Knopf, 1964).

Brown, M. K., *Working the Street* (New York: Russell Sage Foundation, 1981).

Caiden, G. E., *Police Revitalization* (Lexington, Mass.: Lexington Books, 1977).

Cooper, L., *The Iron Fist and the Velvet Glove* (Berkeley: Center for Research on Criminal Justice, 1975).

Cullen, J. B., *The Structure of Professionalism* (Princeton, N.J.: Princeton University Press, 1978).

Fogelson, R. M., *Big-City Police* (Cambridge: Harvard University Press, 1977).

Goldstein, H., "Toward Community-Oriented Policing: Potential, Basic Requirements, Threshold Questions." *Crime and Delinquency* 30, no. 1 (1987): 6–30.

———, *Policing A Free Society* (Cambridge: Ballinger Publishing Co., 1977).

Geison, G. L., ed., *Professions and Professional Ideologies in America* (Chapel Hill: University of North Carolina Press, 1983).

Johnson, D. R., *American Law Enforcement: A History* (St. Louis: Forum, 1981).

Lane, R., *Policing the City: Boston 1822–1882* (Cambridge: Harvard University Press, 1967).

Miller, W., *Cops and Robbers: Police Authority in New York and London, 1830–1890* (Chicago: University of Chicago Press, 1977).

Mokkonen, E., *Police in Urban America* (Cambridge: Cambridge University Press, 1981).

Muir, W. K., *Police: Streetcorner Politicians* (Chicago: University of Chicago Press, 1977).

Richardson, J. F., *The New York Police: Colonial Times to 1901* (New York: Oxford University Press, 1970).

Spelman, W. and Eck, J. E., *Newport News Tests Problem-oriented Policing*, NIJ Reports, January–February 1987, pp. 2–8.

Walker, S., *A Critical History of Police Reform* (Lexington, Mass.: Lexington Books, 1977).

Wilson, J. Q., *Varieties of Police Behavior* (Cambridge: Harvard University Press, 1968).

# CHAPTER 3

# Development of Management Theory

Although we are primarily interested in modern management theory and practice, it is important to understand the evolution of traditional views and the manner in which they influence current management concepts. Management practices can be traced back 5,000 years (George 1968); however, systematic study and general theoretical advances in the field have been relatively recent, from the late nineteenth century to the present. This chapter will provide a basic understanding of the major theoretical advances in management thought and their influence on police managerial theory and practice.

In describing the development of management theory, we will focus on two well-established schools of thought: the *classical* school and the *behavioral* school. We will also discuss two contemporary approaches to management that attempt to integrate the other major theories: the general *systems* theory and the *contingency* theory. Each of these schools and approaches differs in its assumptions about individual and organizational behavior, and therefore about how managers should define and attempt to solve problems associated with organizational efficiency and effectiveness.

# Classical School

The first students in this field studied the anatomy of organizations and subsequently devised certain principles of management that were to be followed if an organization was to operate efficiently. Thompson (1967) has suggested three principal stages in the development of classical or traditional management thought: (1) scientific management, (2) bureaucracy, and (3) administrative management.

## Scientific Management

The systematic study of complex organizations and their management can be traced to the work of Frederick W. Taylor (1947) and his associates. Taylor began his work in the latter part of the nineteenth century and continued through the early part of the twentieth. During this period, efficiency in large industrial factories was a major problem. Accordingly, Taylor's work focused on methods of increasing worker productivity. He believed that workers were motivated primarily by *economic* rewards and that organizations should be characterized by a distinct hierarchy of authority comprising highly specialized personnel.

*Scientific management* sought to discover the best method of performing a specific task. For example, in his studies of the Midvale and Bethlehem Steel Companies in Philadelphia, Taylor determined the speed at which workers could carry loads of fifty pounds. Efforts were then made to find less tiring motions that would allow employees to do more work in a given amount of time with the same degree of fatigue. He believed that if workers were taught the best procedures, with pay related to output, they would produce the maximum amount of work physically possible, as calculated by *time and motion studies*. As a result of this approach, Taylor believed that a worker would acquire a "friendly mental attitude toward his employers and his whole working conditions, whereas before a considerable part of his time was spent in criticism, suspiciousness, watchfulness, and sometimes in open warfare" (pp. 143–144).

With respect to this philosophy, the role of management changed abruptly from the earlier use of a "rule of thumb" to a more "scientific" approach. Taylor established the new duties of management as follows:

1. Develop a science for each element of an employee's work.
2. Scientifically select and then train, teach, and develop the worker (in the past, workers had trained themselves).
3. Heartily cooperate with the employees to ensure that all of the work will be done in accordance with scientific principles.
4. Divide the work and the responsibility between management and workers, with management taking over the work for which it is better suited (pp. 36–37).

According to Etzioni (1964, p. 20), out of the scientific management approach came "the characterization of the formal organization as a blueprint

**Frederick W. Taylor (1856–1915) sought to improve worker efficiency through "scientific management."**

according to which organizations are to be constructed and to which they ought to adhere." The primary criticism of Taylor's approach stems from his lack of concern for the individual within the organization and for his over-reliance on economic motives. Nevertheless, his work added greatly to the knowledge of industrial organizations and set the stage for a more comprehensive approach to management theory.

### Bureaucracy

The concept of bureaucracy is generally associated with the work of Max Weber. A contemporary of Taylor and a major contributor to modern sociology, Weber studied the effects of social change in Europe at the turn of the century. He believed that bureaucracy was a rational means of lessening the cruelty, nepotism, and subjective managerial practices common in earlier stages of the Industrial Revolution. Weber's concept of bureaucracy, therefore, cannot be fairly identified with the "red tape" syndrome often associated with the term today.

Weber described an "ideal type" of *bureaucracy*, not intended to mirror reality, but rather to describe how organizations should be structured and managed. His ideal model has the following characteristics:

**Max Weber (1864–1930) identified an ideal type of "bureaucracy" in hopes of improving organizational performance.**

1. A division of labor based on a "specified sphere of competence."
2. A hierarchy of authority where each lower office is under the control and supervision of a higher one.
3. A specified set of rules applied uniformly throughout the organization.
4. Maintenance of impersonal relationships, because rational decisions can only be made objectively and without emotions.
5. Selection and promotion based on competence, not on irrelevant considerations (Gerth and Mills 1946, pp. 196–224).

In short, the bureaucracy was the most rational means of allowing people to attain private and social goals in a capitalistic society. Weber wrote:

It is superior to any other form in precision, in stability, in the stringency of its discipline, and in its reliability. It thus makes possible a particularly high degree of calculability of results for the heads of the organization and for those acting in relation to it. It is finally superior both in intensive efficiency and in the scope of its operations, and is formally capable of application to all kinds of administrative tasks (Henderson and Parsons 1947, p. 337).

The above characteristics reflect a highly formalized, impersonal, and authoritarian approach to the management of organizations. Once again, the primary consideration was given to organizational efficiency with little or no concern for employees. It is not difficult to see the similarities between Taylor's scientific management and bureaucratization as described by Weber. The major criticism of this approach, as of Taylor's, is that employees within the bureaucracy are little more than "cogs in a machine" who have little, if any, control over their work lives. Weber did, however, provide an important theoretical foundation for much of the empirical research on complex organizations.

## Administrative Management

While Taylor was concerned with lower-level organizational production and Weber with the structural characteristics of the organization, a third major area of study developed, known as *administrative management*, during the first half of the twentieth century. This area of study emphasized broad administrative principles applicable to higher levels within the organization. The *classical principles* of management were developed during this era. Henri Fayol, a French industrialist, was the first major contributor to administrative management theory. His most important work, *Industrial and General Administration* (1929), based on his experiences as a manager, was published in 1916 but it was not translated into English until 1929. Fayol realized the need for the development of a theory of administration: "At present, a man who is starting his career has neither theory nor methods of administration to help him, and many people remain in that condition all their lives"

(p. 17). Subsequently, Fayol defined fourteen principles of efficient management that he had applied most frequently during his career. He believed that each of the principles was *universal*, indispensible, and applicable not only to industrial organizations but also to religious, military, and other organizations.

Fayol was careful to note that there was no limit to the number of principles that could be developed or to the manner in which they could be applied. His basic principles, many of which are faithfully followed today, are as follows:

1. *Division of labor*: In order to increase efficiency, labor must be specialized.
2. *Authority and responsibility*: Authority includes both the right to command and the power to require obedience; one cannot have authority without responsibility.
3. *Discipline*: Discipline is necessary for an organization to function effectively.
4. *Unity of command*: An employee must receive orders from only one supervisor.
5. *Unity of management*: There must be only one manager and one plan for all operations that have the same objective.
6. *Subordination of individual interests to the common good*: The interests of an employee or a group of employees must not take precedence over those of the organization.
7. *Remuneration of the staff*: Compensation must be fair, and, as far as possible, satisfactory to both the employer and the employee.
8. *Centralization*: Centralization of authority is always present to some degree; it is not good or bad in itself, but the problem is to find what degree is best for the organization.
9. *The hierarchy*: The hierarchy, or the scalar chain, is the order of rank from the highest to the lowest levels of the organization.
10. *Order*: "A place for everything and everything in its place" applies to material and human resources.

11. *Equity*: The need for fair treatment throughout the organization should be recognized.
12. *Stability of staff*: An employee needs time to adjust to a new function and reach a point of satisfactory performance.
13. *Initiative*: The ability to conceive and execute a plan should be encouraged and developed throughout the organization.
14. *Esprit de corps*: "Unity is strength." Harmony and unity among the staff must be developed.

While some of these principles were undoubtedly practiced before Fayol formally described them, he was the first to state them precisely and thus allow managers to learn them and put them into practice.

A major contribution to administrative management theory in the United States was provided by James D. Mooney and Alan C. Reiley, who wrote *Onward Industry!* (1931). Although they arrived at their findings independently of Fayol's work, several similarities exist. Mooney and Reiley's basic premise is that an organization must be based on certain formalized principles if it is to be efficient. In establishing their principles, they relied not only on their personal business experience but also on historical evaluations of different types of organizations—the army, the church, and industry. In their model, Mooney and Reiley developed the following four principles:

1. The *coordinative principle* provides for a unity of action in the pursuit of a common objective.
2. The *scalar principle* refers to hierarchical responsibility, which should flow in a direct line from the highest executive in the organization to the lowest level employee.
3. The *functional principle* is the same as specialization; specialized jobs are created within the scalar chain.
4. The *staff principle* groups line employees into two categories: employees who have operating authority and staff employees who provide advice and ideas. This distinction should not lead to a divisiveness between line

and staff, but should serve as a unifying principle within the organization.

In judging the contributions of Mooney and Reiley to the field of management, Kast and Rosenzweig (1985, pp. 65–66) have concluded, "their ideas were related to the development of a pyramidal organizational structure with a clear delineation of authority, specialization of tasks, coordination of activities, and utilization of staff specialists. Application of their concepts led to the establishment of formal organization charts, position descriptions, and organizational manuals."

Shortly after Mooney and Reiley published their book, other administrative theorists were developing their own sets of principles or functions. For example, Luther Gulick and Lyndall Urwick edited their classic work, *Papers on the Science of Administration* (1937), in which Gulick contributed a paper describing the major functions of administration by using the acronym *POSDCORB*—planning, organizing, staffing, directing, coordinating, reporting, and budgeting (p. 13). In these papers and other works, most notably Urwick's *The Elements of Administration* (1943), the authors expanded Fayol's work by emphasizing principles such as: unity of command; departmentalization (or specialization) by purpose, process, place, or clientele; authority commensurate with responsibility; and limitations on the span of control. In short, Gulick's and Urwick's primary contributions were their expansion of the principles of administration and their further refinement of the works of earlier administrative theorists.

## Classical Police Theory

The early writers of police management theory were heavily influenced by the classical school. In general, they stressed the need to improve police organizations through reorganization based on classical prescriptions. This is evidenced by the emphasis they placed on Taylor's scientific management approach stressing increased efficiency, Weber's bureaucracy emphasizing hierarchical authority, and the universal principles espoused by the administrative theorists.

In emphasizing classical prescriptions to organizing and managing the police, these early theorists were attempting to create a more professional police organization. This legalistic-professional model was the result of attempts to organize the police along military lines and to insulate police administrators from the influence of partisan politics. As noted, the legalistic-professional model emphasized the crime control function and stressed managerial practices intended to improve law enforcement activities. This improved efficiency was to be achieved by factors such as centralized control, clean-cut lines of organization, improved training, greater police mobility, and an increased use of equipment and reliance on technology (Goldstein, 1977).

Influential writers promoting classical principles as a basis for police management and organizational reform first appeared in the United States in the early 1900s and continued to be influential into the early 1950s. However, some later editions of the textbooks of these classical writers have appeared in the late 1970s and 1980s and still influence police managerial practices and organization designs.

The classical police theorists differed little in their approaches for improving the police. For example, Fuld's *Police Administration* (1909) emphasized the elimination of partisan politics from police management, clearly defined police duties (including the elimination of nonpolice functions), and stressed strong supervision, control, and discipline, clear-cut lines of authority, specialization, and improved selection and training of personnel. Fosdick studied seventy-two American cities and released the results in *American Police Systems* (1915). He discovered that police departments had not defined their function, had no purpose to their organization, and clearly lacked capable leadership. In the early 1920s, Graper's *American Police Administration* (1921) emphasized many of the same prescriptions for improving the police, including hierarchical control, tight supervision, and discipline. He also identified the need for both centralization and decentralization of certain activities and recognized the need for the distribution of police personnel according to a city's geographic layout.

The first edition of Bruce Smith's *Police Systems in the United States* (1940) had a major impact on police reform during the 1940s. While addressing many of the earlier problems of policing, especially partisan politics and the restricted ability of the police to perform their "primary" function of crime control, he felt that not enough attention had been paid to the administrative structure of police organizations. In later editions, Smith (1960) continued to believe that police organizations could be significantly improved if they were properly designed and supervised according to the "principles of organization."

> The broad principles of organization that have won such wide acceptance in military and industrial circles find ready application to the structure of police forces. In general, it is their purpose to simplify as much as possible the complex interrelations of any large-scale human venture; to reduce them to some clear and systematic basis; and thereby to contribute toward making the official leadership effective (p. 208).

Smith focused on the broad principles of organization as they applied to the proper administrative structure of police agencies, and he paid particular attention to a limited span of control, unity of command, and task specialization.

A work that has had an enormous impact on police organizations and their management is O. W. Wilson's *Police Administration*, first published in 1950 and followed by later editions with McLaren as coauthor (Wilson and McLaren 1977). The prescriptions put forth in these texts are still frequently adhered to by police organizations. Like Smith, Wilson and McLaren suggested that an effective crime control organization should be designed and managed according to "fundamental" organizational principles similar to those of commercial, military, and industrial organizations. These major principles included: (1) grouping of similar tasks according to function, time, and place, (2) hierarchy (level) or authority, (3) specialization based on need, (4) chain of command, (5) unity of command, (6) span of control, (7) delegation of authority, and (8) common sense in using the principles (Wilson and McLaren 1977, pp. 73–86).

A year after Wilson's work, V. A Leonard published the first edition of another highly influential text, *Police Organization and Management* (1951), now in its seventh edition. Again, much attention was devoted to the importance of police leadership, certain organizational principles, and organiza-

**O. W. Wilson (1900–1972), author of** *Police Administration,* **which had a major impact on policing in the United States.**

tional structure. Included in the consideration of structure was the impact of relevant internal factors, such as administrative and civil service controls, and relevant external factors, such as public and pressure group demands, on the police department.

Leonard was also a strong proponent of the line/staff principle utilized by military organizations. He subsequently developed a distinction between line and staff functions in police organizations. Activities such as patrol, investigation, and traffic were classified as line functions; while activities designed to promote these primary functions, including planning, personnel, and records and communications, were classified as staff functions (p. 27).

The *legalistic-professional* model of democratic policing described in chapter 2 relies heavily on the classical school for the development of organization and management practices. The "principles" of this school were compatible with the aims of police reformers who wanted to reduce, if not eliminate, the politics associated with police work by making police behavior more "objective" or bureaucratic and less "personal" in the political sense. The classical school was the conventional wisdom of the experts of the period when the legalistic-professional model, with its emphasis on impersonalization, first became popular. Consequently, this model became the foundation for the administrative reforms suggested by Graper, Fosdick, Smith, Wilson, and Leonard.

# Behavioral School

As the earlier discussion indicates, the classical writers emphasized the formal aspects of organizations and principles of management, while basically ignoring the human aspects of organizational life. Managers discovered that workers did not always act rationally or follow predicted patterns of behavior. It was becoming evident that the "people part" of management also needed attention. Out of this void grew the *human relations* movement, which emphasized the *informal* aspects of the organization. The early human relations researchers introduced the use of the scientific method in their studies, which led to a more sophisticated approach to the study of organizational behavior. Later organization researchers were more rigorously trained in the behavioral sciences (i.e., anthropology, psychology, and sociology) and used improved research methods in their studies. This movement toward increased scientific rigor in studying the work environment became known as the *behavioral science* approach.

## Human Relations

The *human relations* movement began with the work of Elton Mayo and his colleagues at Harvard University. A series of studies were conducted at the Western Electric Company's Hawthorne Plant from 1927 to 1932 (Roethlisberger and Dickson 1939). This series of experiments, known as the Hawthorne studies, produced results that contradicted traditions emphasized by classical management theorists. The Hawthorne experiments were sparked by an earlier Hawthorne study on illumination. The experimental group worked under differing intensities of illumination, while the control group worked under a constant intensity. The researchers believed that the different lighting intensities would significantly affect production; that is, better lighting would lead to increased output. However, the actual results were unexpected. As illumination was increased for the test group, *both* groups increased production. Furthermore, when illumination was decreased, productivity continued to increase. Productivity slowed only after the lighting was dimmed to the extent that the workers could not see properly. This finding suggested that variables other than physical ones may have had an influence on the increased output.

At that point, Mayo and his colleagues were called in to continue the investigations. Through improved experimental designs in several sets of studies, they hoped to determine what variables were influencing the workers. In the first set, a *relay assembly experiment*, two groups of six women each were placed in separate rooms and observed over a prolonged period. In the experimental room, the researchers attempted to determine the effects on productivity of various working conditions, such as increased salaries, shortened workdays, and rest periods of varying lengths. The researchers, who were now acting as supervisors, found that regardless of how they altered the working conditions in the experimental group, productivity increased in both groups. They were further surprised to discover that the experimental group's productivity continued to increase even after rest breaks were abolished and the original, longer workday was reinstituted.

The researchers concluded that increases in productivity were influenced by the complex emotional reaction of the groups and were not related to working conditions. Because both experimental and control groups were singled out for special attention, they developed a sense of group pride and increased levels of motivation, which led to improved work performance. Undoubtedly, the sympathetic supervision received by the workers also helped to improve their motivation and work performance.

The results of this experiment led to an important discovery: When special attention is given to employees by management, productivity levels are likely to increase regardless of changes in working conditions. This phenomenon is referred to as the *Hawthorne effect*. Further research indicated that while the Hawthorne effect did have some initial effect, social factors played a more significant role in worker productivity and satisfaction (Roethlisberger and Dickson 1939, pp. 185–186). Suddenly it appeared that, with respect to productivity and satisfaction, human factors and informal group arrangements were more important than physical factors and formal group arrangements.

**The relay assembly experiment led to the discovery of the Hawthorne effect.**

In order to further their knowledge concerning these "social factors" in industrial organizations, the Hawthorne researchers conducted a series of studies consisting of extensive interviews of more than 20,000 workers over a three-year period. The researchers discovered that peers have an important effect on behavior in the workplace. These interviews led to a final set of studies, one of which is known as the *bank-wiring room experiment*. Fourteen employees were set up as a work unit in a separate room and observed for a period of six months. The employees were paid using a piecework incentive system, in which their pay depended on the amount of work they produced. Given this situation, Taylor and other classical theorists would predict that the experimental group would seek to produce the maximum amount possible in order to maximize their earnings. In actuality, the group established an output norm for a "proper day's work." In order to be socially accepted by the group, each worker had to stay within the accepted standards set by that group. Workers who overproduced were labeled "rate busters" and those who underproduced were called "chiselers." Throughout the test period, the production averages were surprisingly close to those dictated by the group. The researchers determined that with respect to productivity levels, social acceptance was more important than monetary rewards.

The Hawthorne studies provided significant breakthroughs in understanding the importance of social and psychological factors in the workplace. Human relationships and informal organization were now considered to be critical factors in organizational behavior and managerial practice. It became apparent to Mayo and his colleagues that in order to maximize production, management had to recognize employee needs for satisfaction and work in harmony with informal groups. The major contributions of these studies can be summarized as:

1. The level of production is set by social norms not by physiological capacities.
2. Noneconomic rewards and sanctions significantly affect the behavior of the workers and largely limit the effect of economic incentive plans.
3. Often workers do not act or react as individuals but as members of a group.
4. Leadership is important for setting and enforcing group norms, and there is a difference between informal and formal leadership (Etzioni 1964, 34–38).

## Behavioral Science Approach

In order to be classified as a *behavioral science*, a field must (1) deal with human behavior and (2) study its subject matter in a "scientific" manner (Berelson 1963, pp. 2–3). The scientific aim is to develop generalizations about human behavior that are supported by data collected in an objective fashion.

As discussed, some of the earliest behavioral science research began with Mayo and his colleagues in the late 1920s. The behavioral science approach did not come into use, however, nor was it applied with any degree of sophistication, until the early 1950s. Behavioral research provided a means for empirically testing earlier theories as well as increasing scientific knowledge. This research led to the decline of the human relations movement when it was discovered that "(1) the satisfied worker was not always the most productive worker; and (2) it was not necessarily the relationships between worker and manager nor the cohesiveness of the work group that led to higher productivity, but that it was the nature of work itself which was important" (Wren 1979, p. 475).

Consequently, the behavioral sciences were regarded as a more thorough and rigorous approach to the study of human problems in the workplace. According to Wren, the philosophy that replaced human relations "sought to offset the authoritarian tendencies of organizations, to provide for democracy and self-determination at work, to integrate individual and organizational goals, and to restore man's dignity at work" (p. 476).

This philosophy is readily apparent in the works of the behavioral scientists of this era. For example, Maslow developed his hierarchy of human needs in the early 1940s and further extended the theory in his work, *Motivation and Personality* (1954). According to this theory, the needs that motivate people fall into a hierarchy, with the need for "self-actualization" at the top of the hierarchy. Recognizing the workers' drive for personal growth and self-enhancement was a major conceptual breakthrough in the study and understanding of individual motivation, group behavior, and the importance of work in people's lives.

A few years later, Argyris wrote *Personality and Organization* (1957), in which he suggested that the human personality and the organization are in conflict. In his immaturity–maturity theory of behavior, he argued that the authoritarian nature of organizations did not allow people to mature or to become self-actualized. Thus, people behave immaturely in the workplace and are not as productive as they might be. Through this and other writings, most notably *Integrating the Individual and the Organization* (1964), Argyris proposed ways of designing and managing organizations to achieve harmony between the worker's personality and the organization. He believed that participatory leadership and job enlargement would lead to greater challenges and more self-control by employees. The result would be increased growth and maturity and greater fulfillment of individual and organizational needs and goals.

Closely associated with Argyris's concept of integrating the individual and the organization is McGregor's theory $X$ and theory $Y$ assumptions regarding human behavior, published in *The Human Side of Enterprise* in

1960. Basically, theory $X$ assumes that man has little ambition, dislikes work, and must be coerced and threatened with punishment in order to perform satisfactorily. Theory $Y$, on the other hand, assumes that man does not inherently dislike work and if properly rewarded, especially by satisfying ego and self-actualization needs, will perform well on the job. McGregor felt that if employees are treated in a mature way by the organization, utilizing theory $Y$ assumptions, they would become committed to organizational goals and perceive them as the most effective way to achieve their own goals. Although he realized that perfect integration is not possible, McGregor believed that a switch to theory $Y$ assumptions by industrial managers would improve existing work environments. Once again, this approach stresses the importance of self-motivation and personal growth on the job and the capacity of employees to integrate their own goals with those of the organization. These behavioral researchers and others will be further discussed in subsequent chapters.

## Behavioral Police Theory

Beginning in the early 1970s, police behavioral theorists began attacking the classic police bureaucracy with its emphasis on hierarchical structure, authoritarian managerial practices, and narrow view of the police role. In line with the behavioral research findings of the 1950s and 1960s that placed a greater emphasis on worker participation and job satisfaction, these writers stressed a more democratic approach to police management, a more flexible and collegial organization model, and recognition of the complex nature of the police role.

By the 1960s, considerable research indicated that the majority of police work was not directly related to law enforcement activities, but rather to order-maintenance activities and the provision of social services. Although this research had methodological problems relative to defining what was and was not a law enforcement activity, it nevertheless provided a "new" perspective on police work by suggesting that adherence to a legalistic and technical approach to the job would not be effective. In short, effective policing required qualified personnel who could use discretion wisely to deal with a broad range of complex problems and situations.

These findings had serious implications for the quasi-military, legalistic-professional model that had become well entrenched in policing. As Bittner noted in *The Function of the Police in Modern Society* (1970), "the core of the police mandate is profoundly incompatible with the military posture. On balance, the military bureaucratic organization of the police is a serious handicap" (p. 51). Bittner viewed the proper use of discretion as central to the professional development of the police role, and he believed that over-reliance on regulations and bureaucratic routine seriously inhibited such development. Furthermore, he suggested that while the military model associated with the legalistic-professional model helped to secure internal discipline, it continued to hinder the development of the police role since "recognition is given for doing well *in* the department, not *outside* where all the real duties are located" (pp. 54–55). In other words, attention to a neat appearance and conformance to bureaucratic routine is more highly rewarded than work methods performed in the community (i.e., dealing with the public).

Shortly after Bittner's work was released, a series of writers produced works calling for a more collegial model of policing based on the recognition of the complexity of the police role and the need to recruit and retain competent employees. This research corresponds with the emergence of the *community-service* model described in chapter 2.

Angell (1971) proposed a "democratic model" of policing to replace the traditional bureaucratic arrangements. He listed criticisms of classical bureaucracies in general and police organizations in particular.

1. Classical theory and concepts are culture-bound.
2. Classical theory and concepts mandate that attitudes toward employees and clients be inconsistent with the humanistic democratic values of the United States.
3. Classically structured organizations demand and support employees who demonstrate immature personality traits.

4. Classical organizations are unable to cope with environmental changes; therefore they eventually become obsolete and dysfunctional (pp. 187–188).

Angell further described three additional problems associated with classical theory as utilized by police managers: (1) the state of police and community relations where well-developed police bureaucracies exist, (2) the state of morale among police employees, and (3) the lack of communication and control in law enforcement agencies (pp. 188–189). Angell believed his democratic model would help alleviate these problems. His model is an attempt to "develop a flexible, participatory, science-based structure that will accommodate change . . . it is democratic in that it requires and facilitates the involvement of citizens and employees in its process" (p. 194). The basic structure of the model is not hierarchical and has no formal ranks or supervisors. Police officers are generalists who work in teams and have considerable flexibility in work assignments; the teams are expected to work closely with the communities they serve in solving problems. Such an organizational model emphasizes a broad service role for the police and is concerned about employee job satisfaction—a much different perspective from the traditional legalistic-professional model.

Other behavioral writers of this era pointed out the importance of recognizing a broad-based police role and the need to change to a more collegial model. For instance, in *The Police and the Public* (1971), Reiss notes that all bureaucracies pose problems for the exercise of professional discretion. And these problems are exacerbated for the police, who operate in what he refers to as a *command bureaucracy*, because they are expected to obey all the bureaucratic rules while exercising professional discretion. Or, as Reiss notes, ". . . a typical line policeman is expected both to adhere to commands and be held responsible for all discretion exercised in the line of duty" (p. 124). Similarly, in its publication, *Standards Relating to the Urban Police Function* (1973), the American Bar Association (ABA) comments that the semimilitary model, "while appropriate for a few of the activities in which the police are engaged, is in fact a serious impediment to effective fulfillment of the overall police function" (p. 227). The ABA further listed several problems associated with overreliance on the use of the quasi-military model:

1. An attachment is developed within the organization to social uniformity and routine and to a somewhat rigid concept of order that makes it difficult for police officers to view community order as being a much more flexible and amorphous condition.
2. An officer is denied, in his work setting, the basic freedoms and values that it is his job to protect and defend in the larger community.
3. An officer is indoctrinated to follow directions from his superior officers rather than make decisions on his own, resulting in a condition that encourages police officers to exercise their discretion in a sub-rosa (secretive) manner and makes appropriate recognition of the officer's discretionary function extremely difficult to achieve.
4. The fact that a police officer does not have the freedom of a professional to exercise judgment and to use discretion detracts from efforts to characterize the police as a profession.
5. Competent persons are dissuaded from joining a police agency because of their dislike for the regimentation of a semimilitary organization.
6. Self-criticism is discouraged, resulting in a serious restraint on the generation of innovative concepts and ideas from within the agency.
7. A high degree of centralization is necessary, resulting in a failure of police officers and police agencies to be sufficiently responsive to the needs of individual neighborhoods.
8. Police officers, once appointed, are all viewed as having the same qualifications and as being interchangeable for police assignments, ignoring the distinctive skills that are required for different aspects of the police function and the desirability of utilizing personnel possessing these skills to perform the tasks requiring them (p. 229).

Finally, in *Policing A Free Society* (1977) Goldstein recognizes the complex nature of the police role: "Those joining a police force must be capable of making complex decisions on their own that have a major impact upon the lives of others" (p. 263). He suggests that in order to retain highly qualified officers, they must be given a new role in the organization.

Goldstein suggests that the *organizational climate* must change if it is to operate properly in a democratic society. Police officers should be more involved in policy making and methods of operation. They should have greater opportunities to realize their "full potential" in ways other than promotion. While Goldstein agrees that a movement toward a more collegial organizational model is in order, he does not believe that a police agency should be run as a democracy. He emphasizes that some situations, such as mobilizing a large number of officers to deal with an emergency, will always require authoritarian management. Furthermore, he does not think that police administrators should commit to a participatory style of management under all conditions. What is called for, according to Goldstein, "is not a substitution of some radical new style of management but, instead, a gradual movement away from the extremely authoritarian climate that currently pervades police agencies toward a more democratic form of organization" (p. 264).

The "extremely authoritarian climate" noted by Goldstein had become a common characteristic of many legalistic-professional-type departments by the 1960s. While police were criticized for ineffectiveness in responding to crime and discriminatory behavior, they were also considered to be using inappropriate management practices. It was suggested that there was even a connection between authoritarian management practices and authoritarian police behavior. Consequently, the human relations and behavioral science bodies of knowledge gradually influenced police circles; however, this new knowledge and the required managerial skills were not always readily accepted by police and, in some instances, still are not.

## Contemporary Approaches

Following the development and increased sophistication of behavioral science research, subsequent theorists have attempted to integrate the knowledge gained from the earlier schools. Such an integrated framework is provided by the relatively recent developments of the systems and the contingency approaches to the study of organizations. Systems theory provides a broad conceptual base from which to study organizations, whereas contingency theory provides a more specific framework for analyzing organizational behavior. Each approach is described in the following paragraphs.

### Systems Approach

Conceptually, the *systems approach* means that all parts of a system (organization) are interrelated and interdependent. Thus, the parts or subsystems of an organization (i.e., the whole) are related and dependent on one another. Keep in mind that although we are using systems theory to study organizations, it was actually developed to study biological and physical systems.

The importance of applying systems theory to organizations is that it allows managers to view organizations as a unitary whole and to understand that the activities of one part affect the activities of other parts of the organization. Thus, a change in any one subsystem will have a direct effect on other subsystems. This understanding is crucial to proper management, in that a manager must be aware that any changes made in his or her unit will have a corresponding impact on other units. Thus, managers throughout an organization must continually be in contact with one another to ensure that the activities of their units are in congruence with the overall needs and goals of the organization.

Figure 3-1 illustrates the interrelated and interdependent nature of a police department's subsystems (depicted by the two-way directional arrows), indicating that the activities of any part of a subsystem are affected by and, in turn, affect the other parts of the system. In this example, the impacts of the personnel, training, and patrol divisions on one another are depicted. For instance, the quality of the police officer selected by personnel has a direct influence on the type of training that can be conducted, which in turn affects how well officers perform their jobs.

Systems can be viewed as either open or closed; a system is *open* if it interacts with its environment and *closed* if it does not. The concept of open/closed, however, is not an absolute, but a relative matter. All organizations interact with their environment, but the degree of interaction varies. For example, police organizations tend to be more open systems than prison organizations. Essentially, those systems that are more open function more effectively due to their environmental adaptability. An open systems model of organizations is shown in figure 3-2.

This illustration indicates that an open system interacts with its environment by importing energy in the form of information and resources, transforming it into usable products or services, and then exporting them back into the environment. The broken lines indicate that the system's boundaries

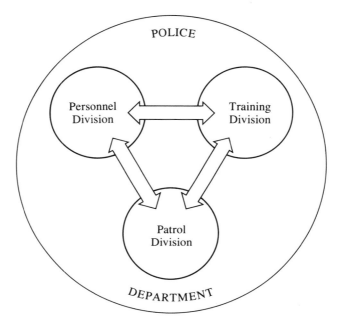

**Figure 3-1**   Police System

are permeable and interact with the environment. Conversely, figure 3-1 represents a closed systems approach; its boundaries are not permeable and are closed to the environment. The open systems approach is applied to a police organization in figure 3-3.

## Characteristics of Open Systems

The following paragraphs present the basic characteristics of open systems theory based on Katz and Kahn's (1966, pp. 19–29) earlier work in which

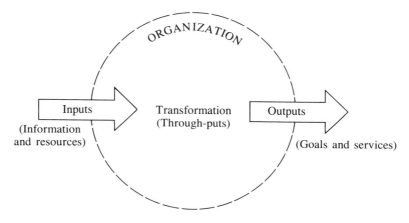

**Figure 3-2**  Open Systems Model

they used open systems theory to analyze complex organizations. These characteristics are applied to the study of police organizations.

1. Importation of energy from the external environment.
2. Throughput or transformation of the energy available into product (or service) form.
3. Output or exportation of the product (or service) back into the environment.

This application indicates that a police organization receives energy inputs from the environment in the form of money, personnel, material, information, and so on. This environmental input is subsequently transformed and used within the system in the form of hiring and training of officers, purchasing materials such as patrol cars and computers, and processing information such as complaints and calls-for-service. These "products" are then exported back into the environment in the form of police services to the community, such as maintaining order, making arrests, or conducting crime prevention programs.

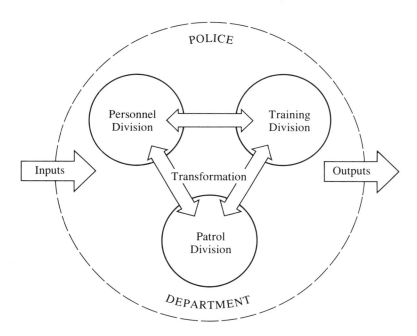

**Figure 3-3**   Open Police System

4. Systems as cycles of events. The pattern of activities of the energy exchange is cyclic; the product exported into the environment provides sources of energy for the repetition of the cycle of activities.
5. Attainment of negative entropy. The entropic process is a universal process of nature in which all forms of organization move toward disorganization or death. To survive, open systems must acquire negative entropy in order not to run down. By importing more energy than it exports, the open system can store energy and therefore acquire negative entropy. All closed physical systems, on the other hand, are subject to entropy and, over time, will cease to exist.

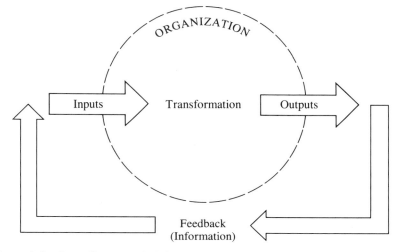

**Figure 3-4** Open Systems Model and Information Feedback

6. Processing of information inputs and negative feedback. Open systems maintain a steady state, known as *homeostasis*, by processing information from the environment and adapting their behavior accordingly. The feedback of information in the open systems model is shown in figure 3-4.

Information feedback from the environment may be either positive or negative. If negative, the system will adapt in order to remain in harmony with its environment and maintain a steady state. Examples of environmental feedback for the police include public opinion, political demands, complaints, and criminal and other statistics. How negative feedback is handled by police organizations, through efforts such as policy changes or patrol practices, greatly determines their success (homeostasis) in the community.

7. Differentiation. As open systems mature, functions are specialized in order to accommodate system growth.

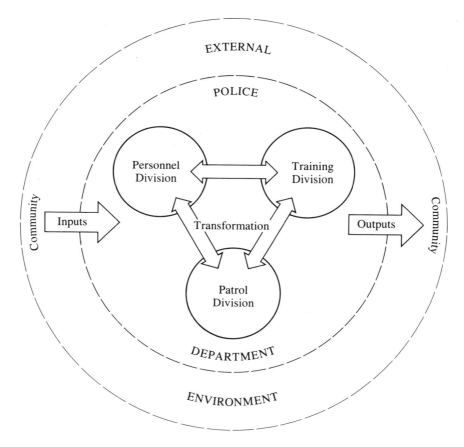

**Figure 3-5**   Police System with Environmental Boundaries

   8. Equifinality. Open systems can reach the same final state from differing initial conditions (inputs) and by a variety of methods.

Further, open systems must export enough transformed resources to the external environment to continue the cycling process—steps 1 through 8. Or, as Berrien (1976, p. 45) notes, "every surviving system must provide some output acceptable usually to a collateral or supra-system."

Another dimension is thus added to open systems theory: The external environment has constraining and identifiable boundaries. With respect to the police, this "supra-system" consists of the community served by the police organization (see figure 3-5). Although we have used the term *community* to represent the external environment of the police, there is no such thing as a single community or constituency to be served. It is crucial that police organizations recognize and respond to the concept of "communities within the community" when determining the police role definition for a given jurisdiction. This concept means that although the police may be responsible for serving a particular set of boundaries, such as a city or county, there is usually no single sense of community within these boundaries. Instead, there are probably many different "communities" comprised of persons of varying minority, ethnic, religious, class, or sexual preference backgrounds. Each of these communities will undoubtedly have different and sometimes conflicting expectations concerning the police. A system's environmental boundaries, however, are limiting and provide for selective input. Thus, police departments in different parts of the country will operate differently, according to the expectations of their external environment.

It is also important to point out that police organizations are a subsystem of the criminal justice system. Actions taken by the police have an impact on both the court and correctional subsystems and vice versa. For instance, if the police increase their number of arrests, an obvious impact will be felt by the courts and eventually by corrections facilities. Conversely, policy changes by the court (e.g., rules of evidence, Miranda warnings) and correctional subsystems (e.g., early release programs) ultimately impact the police as well. Thus, criminal justice system managers need to be aware of the impacts their organizations may have on the other parts of the system.

Clearly, from this description, open systems theory provides a major conceptual scheme that is significant to management; that is, an analytical approach to the interactive nature of a system and its environment. If police organizations are not studied and managed from an open systems perspective, they cannot adapt to changing environmental influences and forces (such as public opinion, community conditions, or court interpretations), and inefficient and ineffective levels of operation will most likely result. When this happens, ultimately, the organization will be forced to change as external critics make demands that cannot be ignored. The change from a political-watchman to a legalistic-professional model is an example of such a process.

## Contingency Approach

The systems approach emphasized the importance of the interrelationships between the parts of the organization and between the organization and its environment. However, because systems theory incorporates natural and biological systems, as well as organizational systems, its concepts are abstract and, in general, cannot be applied to specific situations. Contingency theory utilizes this same perspective and attempts to define important relationships, both internal and external to the organization, that affect organization design and managerial practices.

The *contingency approach* was developed by managers and researchers who found that certain methods and practices are effective in one situation but not in others. For example, why does a certain leadership style or job design work in one type of organization but not in other types or in one part of an organization but not in other parts? The answer appears to be because situations differ, and a managerial method or technique that is effective in one situation may not be effective in other situations. In other words, there are no universal principles that can be applied in all circumstances.

The contingency approach recognizes that many internal and external environmental variables affect organizational behavior. Since these variables differ according to particular situations, there is no one "best" way for structuring and managing diverse types of organizations. The task of contingency managers is to determine in which situations and at what times certain methods or techniques are the most effective. Consequently, the underlying theme of the contingency approach is that *it all depends* on the particular situation.

Contingency management attempts to determine relationships between internal and external variables that are relevant to the organization and, based on the findings regarding the nature of the relationships, recommend appropriate managerial practices and organization designs. In this way, the contingency approach is more pragmatic than the systems approach, while still incorporating concepts of systems theory. Because the contingency approach allows for the most appropriate managerial practices or methods to be applied according to the situation, it can encompass relevant concepts of classical and behavioral theories as well.

An apt description of contingency management has been provided by Kast and Rosenzweig (1985, p. 116):

> The contingency view suggests that there are appropriate patterns of relationships for different types of organizations and that we can improve our understanding of how these relevant variables interact. For example, certain principles of organization and/or management might be appropriate for uniform operations in a relatively stable environment. A mass production operation such as a refrigerator assembly line might operate most efficiently under a rigid hierarchy with precise planning and control as well as routinization of activities. In contrast, other organizations, operating in an uncertain environment and with dynamic technologies, may operate more efficiently under a very different set of principles. An advertising agency, for example, might be characterized by a flexible structure, nonroutine activities, and adaptive planning and control. Contingency analysis thus may lead us to general conclusions about these patterns of relationships.

When patterns of relationships among organizational variables are discussed using the contingency approach, they are generally applied to two distinct forms of organizations: mechanistic and organic (Burns and Stalker 1961, pp. 13–14). *Mechanistic* organizations are characterized by rigid hierarchical structures and authoritarian controls, whereas *organic* organizations are characterized by relatively flexible structures and democratic controls. Consequently, mechanistic systems are much less adaptable to environmental changes than organic systems. With these two organizational forms in mind, Kast and Rosenzweig (1985, pp. 116–117) have suggested that the following patterns of relations generally hold true:

The mechanistic organization form is more appropriate under the following conditions:

1. The environment is relatively stable and certain.
2. The goals are well defined and enduring.
3. The technology is relatively uniform and stable.
4. There are routine activities and productivity is the major objective.
5. Decision making is programmable and coordination and control processes tend to make a highly structured hierarchical system possible.

The organic organization form is more appropriate under the following conditions:

1. The environment is relatively uncertain and turbulent.
2. The goals are diverse and changing.
3. The technology is complex and dynamic.
4. There are many nonroutine activities in which creativity and innovation are important.
5. Heuristic decision-making processes are utilized and coordination and control occur through reciprocal adjustments. The system is less hierarchical and more flexible.

These patterns of relations stemming from contingency analysis, and their importance to police management and organizational behavior, will be explored further in subsequent chapters.

## Contemporary Police Theory

Police theorists began applying the concepts of the systems approach to the study of police organizations in the early 1970s. Among the first writers to incorporate systems theory were Whisenand and Ferguson. In their text, *The Managing of Police Organizations* (1973), they suggested the following reasons for viewing organizations as open social systems:

> (1) the increased complexity and frequency of change in our society, and (2) the limitations of the previously discussed organizational theories, namely, that both the classical and neoclassical [human relations] theories viewed an organization as a *closed* structure. Such nearsightedness produces an inability to rec-

ognize that the organization is continually dependent upon its environment for the inflow of materials and human energy. Thinking of an organization as a closed structure, moreover, results in a failure to develop a feedback capability for obtaining adequate information about changes in environmental forces and goal accomplishment (p. 166).

Whisenand and Ferguson further stated some "specific and compelling" reasons a police organization should consider itself an open system:

1. A police department can be thought of as either a system (a single agency) or a subsystem. If viewed as a subsystem, it is involved in a complex set of interfaces with other subsystems external to its boundary, such as the district attorney, parole agencies, and the courts. The systems approach effectively helps us to cross boundaries and to identify, establish, and make use of significant interrelationships of various organizations.

2. Police organizations are becoming aware of the limitations of simplistic research. The systems approach allows us to synthesize and utilize research of other relevant fields (operations research, educational psychology, etc.).

3. A systems approach provides a new perspective on the internal operations and environmental relationships of police organizations.

4. The systems approach relies greatly on empirical data or hard facts. The data includes facts not only on a particular police department but also on the processes, interactions, goals, and other characteristics of all organizations (public and private) that exert an influence on it.

5. An important benefit of the systems approach is that it is intended to be action-oriented. That is, data are gathered because they are instrumental in fulfilling a set of objectives or in solving a problem (p. 167).

Shortly after Whisenand and Ferguson, Munro wrote a systems-oriented text, *Administrative Behavior and Police Organization* (1974). He noted that ever since the mid-1960s, the role of the police in American society has been vigorously debated and examined but actual changes in policy have been negligible. In spite of a substantial amount of money invested by federal, state, and local governments, few tangible results could be noticed, except in terms of an "escalated police armaments race and an explosion in (largely nonessential) police technology" (p. 9). Munro suggests that this lack of change is due in large part to two major factors: (1) refusal by politicians and police to see the law enforcement function in systems terms and (2) the continued employment of an authoritarian and antidemocratic philosophy of management by police agencies.

Munro recognized the necessity of viewing the police as a part of the criminal justice system and the importance of studying the police from a systems perspective. "The social scientist or managerial analyst," he suggests, "is faced with rather specific consequences resulting from the systematic nature of criminal justice" (p. 12). Munro further asserts:

> Among the more important consequences is the necessity of viewing the behavior of individuals within the organization in terms of their effect on other system elements. If the police chief orders a crackdown on drunk drivers, what are the likely consequences for prosecution, the courts and corrections? Very possibly it may result in flooding with work those other components of the criminal justice system so badly that the ends of good administration, let alone justice, cannot be served. It is the responsibility of the analyst to predict such results of policy or management change. The predictions have little chance of accuracy if the implications of system have been ignored (p. 12).

The importance of applying an open systems approach to policing was introduced by Cordner (1978), who suggested that open and closed models of policing can be viewed as polar extremes on a continuum. The closed (bureaucratic) model is best suited to the performance of routine tasks while operating in stable conditions (stable environment). The open (democratic) model, on the other hand, is best suited to the performance of nonroutine tasks while operating in unstable conditions (unstable environment). Cordner concludes that an open model of police organization is more appropriate than a closed model because, in reality, most police tasks are nonroutine in nature and are performed in unstable environments. Thus, the open model of police organization is in interaction with its environment (community) and, in turn, can more readily adapt to unstable, changing conditions.

In the late 1970s, Roberg was the first to apply contingency theory to policing in his text, *Police Management and Organizational Behavior: A Con-*

*tingency Approach* (1979). He emphasized applying contingency concepts and the necessity of identifying internal and external variables that impact on police organizational behavior. Accordingly, recognition of the complex nature of the police role, the increasing levels of education of those entering policing, and the relatively unstable nature of the police environment (i.e., constantly changing laws, heterogeneous populations, political influences, and so on) must be considered in attempting to determine the most effective management practices and organization designs.

When the above types of variables are taken into account, Roberg asserts that "many of the simplistic classical [bureaucratic] prescriptions which have been applied to police organization design are clearly inadequate" (p. 190) and furthermore, that "organic designs offer more potential for effectiveness . . . than do mechanistic designs" (p. 211). Implicit in these statements is the notion that less authoritarian and more participatory or democratic managerial practices are in order. However, keeping in mind that police organizations vary considerably and that there is no single best way in contingency management, he notes that a particular "mix" of mechanistic-organic conditions is most likely necessary to properly manage and design today's police organizations. As Roberg suggests:

> Because neither the organic nor the mechanistic system is superior under all circumstances, practicing managers must carefully study the pattern of relationships among relevant external and internal variables and decide which system and/or mix of systems would be most effective under existing conditions (p. 211).

The significance in applying the contingency approach to police management lies in the recognition that a variety of managerial practices and organizational designs may be appropriate, depending on the particular situation at hand. Contingency management takes into consideration the dynamics of systems theory, is research-oriented, and yet is pragmatic in its application. Police managers must attempt to recognize relevant internal and external variables affecting their agencies and, based on the pattern of relationships discovered, apply the most appropriate management concepts.

The *rational-contingency* model described in chapter 2 is an example of attempts to apply systems thinking and a contingency perspective to police organizations. In its ideal state it is responsive, flexible, and not wedded to any particular approach to problem solving, yet it recognizes and adapts to legal, political, and resource constraints. The model is consistent with contemporary management perspectives of what is most effective in achieving organizational results.

## Summary

This chapter has emphasized the importance of understanding the development of management thought and its impact on current managerial practices and techniques. To this end, the classical and behavioral schools of theory were described along with two contemporary approaches; namely, systems and contingency theory. The impact of influential writers on theory development from the social and managerial sciences was discussed, as were contributions from significant police theorists regarding each of the schools and approaches.

The classical theorists concentrated on the formal organization and the development of universal principles that could be applied in all organizations, regardless of the situation. Early police theorists were strongly influenced by the classical school, emphasizing strong hierarchical control, a professional orientation, and an emphasis on the law enforcement aspects of the police role. Significant classical police contributors were Fuld, Fosdick, Graper, Smith, Wilson, and Leonard.

The behavioral school emphasized use of the scientific method and increased scientific rigor in studying organizational behavior. The results of early behavioral studies, although relatively unsophisticated in their design, led to the development of the human relations movement. The results of those studies suggested that informal aspects and social factors greatly influenced organizational behavior. Thus, behavioral theorists began emphasizing the importance of worker needs, the conflict between the individual and the organization, and the importance of self-actualization through participation and democratic ideals. Following these developments, police behavioral theorists began to stress the need for a more collegial and participatory approach to police management, along with a recognition of the complexity of the police role. Important behavioral police theorists include Bittner, Angell, Reiss, the American Bar Association, and Goldstein.

Contemporary approaches to management theory have attempted to integrate and utilize the knowledge gained from the earlier schools of thought. The systems and contingency approaches were developed from this prior knowledge. Systems theory relates the parts of any system to the whole, and emphasizes the interaction of a system with its surrounding environment (open system). Because systems theory applies to all types of systems—biological and physical—it is abstract and difficult to apply to organizational behavior. Contingency theory, on the other hand, is more pragmatic in its approach, attempting to define relationships between relevant organizational variables and subsequent organizational designs and managerial practices. Major police contributors to contemporary management approaches include Whisenand and Ferguson, Munro, and Cordner in applying systems theory to policing and Roberg in applying contingency theory to police organizational behavior.

## Discussion Questions

1. Describe the contributions of the following approaches to the development of classical management thought: scientific management, bureaucracy, and administrative management.
2. Who are Frederick W. Taylor, Max Weber, Henry Fayol, Bruce Smith, O. W. Wilson, and V. A. Leonard?
3. Discuss the impact of classical police theory on organization and management practices.
4. Describe the Hawthorne experiments and their contribution to the human relations movement.
5. What effect did behavioral police theory have on traditional police organization and management practice?

6. Compare and contrast the classical and behavioral schools of management theory.
7. Discuss the characteristics of open systems theory and apply them to the study of police organizations.
8. Compare and contrast general systems theory and contingency theory approaches to police organization and management.
9. What are the possible advantages and disadvantages of utilizing a contingency approach to police organization and management?
10. How do you think current police practices have been affected by contemporary police theory?

## References

American Bar Association, *Standards Relating to the Urban Police Function* (New York: American Bar Association, 1973).

Angell, J. E., "Toward an Alternative to the Classic Police Organizational Arrangements: A Democratic Model," *Criminology* 9 (1971):185–206.

Argyris, C., *Personality and Organization: The Conflict Between the System and the Individual and the Organization* (New York: Wiley, 1957).

———, *Integrating the Individual and the Organization* (New York: Wiley, 1964).

Berelson, B., ed., *The Behavioral Sciences Today* (New York: Basic Books, 1963).

Berrien, F. K., "A General Systems Approach to Organizations," in *Handbook of Industrial and Organizational Psychology*, ed. M. D. Dunnette (Chicago: Rand McNally, 1976).

Bittner, E., *The Function of the Police in Modern Society* (Washington, D.C.: Government Printing Office, 1970).

Burns, T. and Stalker, G. M., *The Management of Innovation* (London: Tavistock, 1961).

Cordner, G. W., "Open and Closed Models of Police Organizations: Traditions, Dilemmas, and Practical Considerations," *Journal of Police Science and Administration* 6 (1978):22–34.

Etzioni, A., *Modern Organizations* (New Jersey: Prentice-Hall, 1964).

Fayol, H., *Industrial and General Administration*, trans. J. A. Coubrough (Geneva: International Management Institute, 1929).

Fosdick, R., *American Police Systems* (Montclair, New Jersey: Patterson Smith, 1915).

Fuld, L., *Police Administration* (New York: G. P. Putnam's, 1909).

George, C. S., *The History of Management Thought* (Englewood Cliffs, New Jersey: Prentice Hall, 1968).

Gerth, H. H. and Mills, C. W., *From Max Weber: Essays in Sociology* (New York: Oxford University Press, 1946).

Goldstein, H., *Policing a Free Society* (Cambridge, Massachusetts: Ballinger, 1977).

Graper, E., *American Police Administration* (New York: Macmillan, 1921).

Gulick, L. and Urwick, L., eds., *Papers on the Science of Administration* (New York: Institute of Public Administration, 1937).

Gulick, L., "Notes on the Theory of Organization," in *Papers on the Science of Administration*, eds. L. Gulick and L. Urwick (New York: Institute of Public Administration, 1937), pp. 3–45.

Henderson, A. M. and Parsons, T., trans. and eds., *Max Weber: The Theory of Social and Economic Organizations* (New York: Macmillan, 1947).

Kast, F. E. and Rosenzweig, J. E., *Organization and Management: A Systems and Contingency Approach*, 4th ed. (New York: McGraw-Hill, 1985).

Katz, D. and Kahn, R. L., *The Social Psychology of Organizations* (New York: Wiley, 1966).

Leonard, V. A., *Police Organization and Management* (Brooklyn: Foundation Press, 1951).

—— and More, H., *Police Organization and Management*, 7th ed. (Mineola, New York: Foundation Press, 1987).

Maslow, A. H., *Motivation and Personality* (New York: Harper & Row, 1954).

McGregor, D., *The Human Side of Enterprise* (New York: McGraw-Hill, 1960).

Mooney, J. D. and Reiley, A. C., *Onward Industry!* (New York: Harper & Row, 1931).

Munro, J. L., *Administrative Behavior and Police Organization* (Cincinnati, Ohio: Anderson, 1974).

Reiss, A. J., *The Police and the Public* (New Haven, Connecticut: Yale University Press, 1971).

Roberg, R. R., *Police Management and Organizational Behavior: A Contingency Approach* (St. Paul: West, 1979).

Roethlisberger, F. J. and Dickson, W. J., *Management and the Worker* (Cambridge: Harvard University Press, 1939).

Smith, B., *Police Systems in the United States*, 2nd ed. (New York: Harper, 1960).

Taylor, F. W., "The Principles of Scientific Management," *Scientific Management* (New York: Harper & Row, 1947).

Thompson, J. D., *Organizations in Action: Social Science Bases of Administrative Theory* (New York: McGraw-Hill, 1967).

Urwick, L., *The Elements of Administration* (New York: Harper & Row, 1943).

Whisenand, P. M. and Ferguson, R. F., *The Managing of Police Organizations* (Englewood Cliffs, New Jersey: Prentice-Hall. 1973).

Wilson, O. W., *Police Administration* (New York: McGraw-Hill, 1950).

—— and McLaren, R., *Police Administration*, 4th ed. (New York: McGraw-Hill, 1977).

Wren, D. A., *The Evolution of Management Thought*, 2nd ed. (New York: Wiley, 1979).

# Organization and Structure

In the first chapter we stated that organizations exist for one reason: to accomplish activities that cannot be accomplished individually. Based on this reasoning, a working definition of an *organization* was developed as *a social system composed of groups of two or more persons who are interdependent and work in a coordinated manner to achieve common goals*. The importance of understanding this definition and its relationship to improving work environments in police organizations will be explored in this chapter.

In order to improve work environments, and thus achieve common goals more readily, managers must have an adequate understanding of both the fundamental characteristics of, and the factors that influence, the structure of organizations.

## Characteristics of Organizations

Three characteristics, fundamental to all organizations, are important in understanding organizational behavior. These characteristics include *composition* (individuals and groups), *orientation* (toward goals), and the *methods* used to obtain organizational goals (differentiated functions and intended rational coordination) (Porter, Lawler, and Hackman 1975, p. 69). Each characteristic will be briefly described in the following paragraphs.

### Composition

Organizations are comprised of individuals and groups. Whether or not an individual is a member of any particular group, the influences of others working around that individual, either directly (physically present) or indirectly (psychologically present), are strongly felt. In fact, the organization's social nature is perhaps its primary characteristic.

*Individuals* bring many qualities to the organization. Some qualities are highly beneficial and others are not. For instance, every member brings certain physical attributes and abilities, as well as specific attitudes, prejudices, and emotions. However, the organization never receives the "whole" person. That is, the organization must realize that individual lives are segmented; people play many different roles (e.g., husband or wife, mother or father, homeowner, athlete) and belong to many different organizations and groups (e.g., religious, political, fraternal, social). Accordingly, an individual's total personality or psychological being is not found in any one particular organization. Allport (1933) developed the concept of *partial inclusion* to refer to this fragmented involvement of individuals in social groupings. In other words, the organization must recognize that it will be affected, both in positive and negative ways, by an employee's activities outside of the organization's boundaries, and it must be willing to respond to and to deal with these external influences in a constructive manner.

A *group* can be defined as *any number of people who interact with one another and share, to some degree, norms and values regarding appropriate behavior*. Within organizations there are two primary types of groups: *formal*, those designated by the organization, and *informal*, those with membership left to individual discretion. Informal groups occur naturally, often with little regard to the formal organization. Each type of group membership is largely responsible for the types of attitudes members form toward the organization.

**Formal and informal groups.**    The organization specifically creates *formal groups* in an attempt to realize its goals in the most effective manner. An organization's formal structure can be depicted by an *organization chart*, which defines formal functions and relationships and the flow of communication among designated groups within the structure.

Figure 4-1 presents an organization chart for a medium-to-large municipal police department, consisting of 500 to 1,000 members. The hierarchical nature of this hypothetical organization (i.e., the lines of authority and division of responsibilities) are readily apparent. For instance, the chief of police has a span of control of five (that is, the heads of Internal Affairs, Administrative Services, Field Operations, Criminal Investigation, and Technical Services report directly to the chief). The head (assistant chief) of the Administrative Services Bureau also has a span of control of five (that is, the division heads of Personnel, Budget and Finance, Training, Community Relations, and Planning and Research report directly to the assistant chief).

The division of labor by functional responsibilities, or by specialization, is also readily apparent in figure 4-1. For example, the operations of the departments governing personnel, budgeting, training, public relations, and research and planning activities are perceived to have similar responsibilities and therefore are organized under the same bureau (Administrative Services). Similarly, all general (patrol) and specialized (tactical, juvenile, and traffic) field activities are organized under the Bureau of Field Operations, and all investigative activities (including a crime lab) are organized under the Bureau of Criminal Investigation.

From this description, we can see that a formal organization chart tells us about expected status (authority), communication (chain of command), and functional relationships (job activities) throughout an organization. Formal charts can also tell us something about organizational concerns and priorities. For instance, the location of the Internal Affairs Division in figure 4-1 indicates its importance, since its head reports directly to the chief. Such an arrangement means that the chief wants direct communication with, and control of, this division, which is responsible for investigating alleged improprieties within the organization.

Since organization charts provide information about how an agency is supposed to operate, organizational consultants frequently begin their quest to improve organizational performance by reviewing the formal chart. The consultant gains an understanding of how management perceives organizational priorities, roles, and operations. Although the organization chart can tell us a great deal about formal, or expected, relationships throughout the organization, it tells us virtually nothing about the informal aspects of organizational behavior. The informal relationships and arrangements that inevitably develop will most likely tell us more about organizational "life" than the formally prescribed arrangements depicted on charts.

*Informal groups* are formed naturally, as a result of nonspecified individual interactions. Because these groups are nonspecified, it is difficult, though not impossible, to establish useful charts depicting informal relationships.

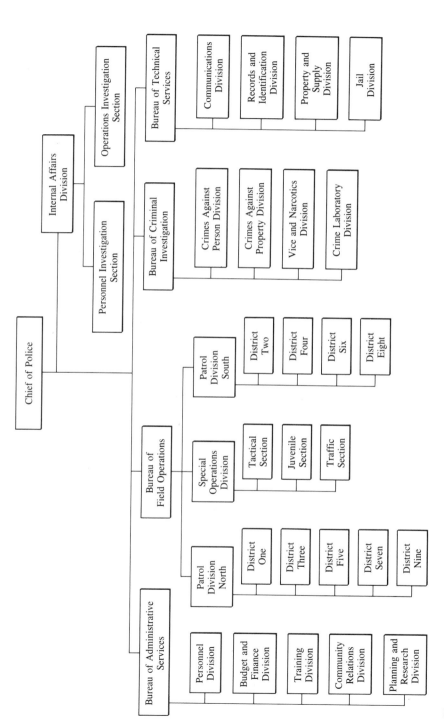

**Figure 4-1**  Medium to Large Municipal Police Department

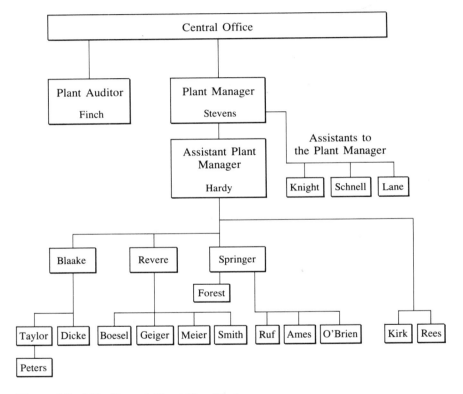

**Figure 4-2**  Milo Formal Chart Simplified

Source: *Men Who Manage,* by M. Dalton. Copyright © 1959 by John Wiley & Sons, Inc. Reprinted by permission.

In his study of the Milo Company, Dalton (1959) was one of the first researchers to empirically verify that differences exist between an organization's formal chart and informal relationships. By comparing figure 4-2 with figure 4-3, the disparity between the formal and informal power and influence of Milo's major executives can be readily observed.

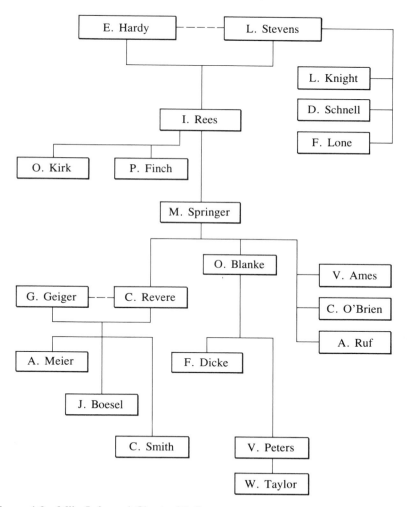

**Figure 4-3**   Milo Informal Chart of Influence

Source: *Men Who Manage,* by M. Dalton. Copyright © 1959 by John Wiley & Sons, Inc.
Reprinted by permission.

In figure 4-3, the managers (except for Forest) on the formal chart in figure 4-2 are reranked according to their informal power within the organization. Dalton used fifteen "reliable" Milo participants or "judges" who evaluated the managers in figure 4-3 based on their perceptions of the managers' actual influence in the organization. All of the judges were, or had been, close associates of the managers they were rating. To enhance validity, Dalton then challenged the rankings; he based his criticisms on his experiences and conversations with executives and their subordinates of all ranks from the level of Taylor down. Dalton discusses his findings as follows:

> In [figure 4-3] the central vertical, dropping from Hardy and Stevens through Rees, Springer, and Blanke, ranks these officers in that order. Rectangles on the same level and horizontal [Hardy-Stevens, Geiger-Revere, Kirk-Finch] indicate that the officers therein were considered to have equal influence. At the same time each division is ranked according to the estimated power of its leader in plant affairs. That is, Springer is above Blanke, and Revere below, as least influential of the division chiefs. The department heads inside a given division are ranked in the same way but are not compared with those of other divisions.
>
> As shown in [figure 4-2] Peters was not a department head. But all the judges agreed that he should be put on the informal chart, and thirteen ranked him above Taylor. There were minor disagreements on the placement of a few officers. For example . . . (t)wo of the judges placed Peters below Taylor. These dissenters were generally foremen who apparently disliked Peters because he had been brought over from a staff organization by his powerful sponsor, Blanke. The informal chart does not of course measurably show that the executives exercised more or less than their given authority, but it does indicate that formal and actual authority differed. Scales and numbers were not used in the rankings because the judges opposed a formal device and believed it was a misleading overrefinement (1959, pp. 20–23).

Although the Dalton study only focused on a single organization, it demonstrates that differences between formal and informal arrangements do exist. Of course, such differences also occur in police organizations and much of a manager's success depends on his or her understanding of, and ability to deal with, informal relationships. In this sense, the informal organization can greatly enhance or impede progress toward the organization's goals.

As Davis (1981, pp. 332–334) has noted, the informal organization brings problems and benefits to the formal management system in organizations. Some of the problems that may arise in dealing with the informal organization include resistance to change, role conflict (i.e., what is good for the employee is not always good for the organization), rumors, and conformity (through group pressure). Conversely, benefits that may accrue from the informal organization if it is dealt with constructively include (1) blending with the formal organization to make a more effective total system (i.e., some requirements in organizations can be better handled through informal relations, which can be more flexible and spontaneous than formal plans and policies); (2) lightening the workload on management (not every detail needs to be checked); (3) lending satisfaction and stability to work groups; (4) providing a useful channel of communication; and (5) acting as a safety valve for employee frustrations and other emotional problems.

**Group influences and police culture.**   As first indicated by the Hawthorne studies, groups greatly affect the attitudes and behavior of individuals in organizations. Groups control many of the stimuli that individuals receive during their organizational activities. These stimuli are transmitted selectively to individual group members at the discretion of their peers (known as "discretionary stimuli") and usually have a significant impact on the *beliefs and attitudes* as well as *job-relevant knowledge and skills* of group members (Porter, Lawler, and Hackman 1975, pp. 370–371, 388–391).

Individuals in organizations do not have a complete or accurate view of their environment unless they obtain information from their work groups. Members usually discover the "social reality" of organizational life through direct communication and observation of others. Frequently, groups pressure members toward uniformity of *beliefs and attitudes* about the work environment because most groups are not usually capable of handling overt disagreements among members. Such pressure is most obvious when new members, whose beliefs and attitudes may be different, join the group. This pressure often occurs in police departments when recruits report for their first tour of duty and hear the veteran officer's advice to rookies: "Forget what you were told in the academy, we'll show you how things really are."

*example*
*of Informal*
*Learning)*
↓
*Coach Officer*

The more experienced officers may also inform recruits that "divergent" points of view are not appreciated.

The pressure toward uniformity of beliefs and attitudes can be functional for the group, as in a task group where uniformity of views is essential for completing the work. However, such pressure is dysfunctional when contrasting views of group members are suppressed. Contrary beliefs and attitudes, if explored, can contribute substantially to the problem-solving abilities of a group.

Another type of group-supplied discretionary stimuli helps group member gain the relevant knowledge and skills needed to perform their jobs or fulfill their organizational roles. Individuals learning how to *behave* in organizations need the group for several reasons. For instance, trial-and-error learning of a new skill or behavior pattern is usually inefficient. The help of group members provides shortcuts to the learning process and lessens the risks involved in the learning process. Furthermore, many skills and role behaviors in police work, such as learning to handle interpersonal conflicts in crisis situations, cannot be effectively learned without the involvement of other people. Field training officers (FTOs) are frequently utilized today to help police recruits learn relevant on-the-job skills and knowledge to adequately perform in the field. Such training may include (1) direct instruction; (2) feedback on appropriate/inappropriate behavior; (3) modeling, whereby the recruit attempts to "match" the behavior of the FTO; or (4) simply observing the activities of the training officer. While FTO programs are one way in which police departments attempt to instill certain beliefs and attitudes and thus influence the behavior of their recruits, the vast amount of what any officer learns on the job is related to the peer group in which he or she works or interacts. Field training officer programs are discussed in greater detail in chapter 7.

In the field of policing, beliefs, attitudes, and behaviors are also strongly influenced by an *organization* or *police culture*. Those persons having common backgrounds, experiences, and interests tend to develop similar beliefs and attitudes, which, in turn, will most likely have an impact on behavior. In policing there also tends to be both a *manager's* and a *worker's* or *street cop's* culture (Reuss-Ianni 1983), as well as a private and public world.

Police managers and employees often have a decidedly different view of their respective jobs. The views of managers are shaped by experiences that tend to remove them from the "street reality" of the officers. One example of this is the ends-means dilemma. Managers tend to be concerned with both ends and means, while officers may be overly concerned with ends. Managers are concerned with organizational priorities, policies, and procedures, while officers are concerned with doing the job according to the "wisdom of the street," often acquired not from the organization's view of reality but from the officer's perspective, determined by "doing the work" and "trying to survive."

The cultures of managers and street cops are a major force of *socialization* and influence in the organization. According to Reuss-Ianni, the "code" of the street cops includes the following maxims:

1. Take care of your partner first, then the other officers.
2. Don't "give up" (inform about) another cop; be secretive about the behavior of other officers.
3. "Show balls"; take control of a situation and don't back down.
4. Be aggressive when necessary, but don't go looking for trouble.
5. Don't interfere in another officer's sector or work area.
6. Do your fair share of work and don't leave work for the next "shift"; however, don't do too much work.
7. If you get caught making a mistake, don't implicate anybody else.
8. Other cops, but not necessarily managers, should be told if another officer is dangerous or "crazy."
9. Don't trust new officers until they have been "checked out."
10. Don't volunteer information; tell others only what they need to know.
11. Avoid talking too much or too little; both are suspicious.
12. Protect your "ass"; don't give managers or the "system" an opportunity to "get you."
13. Don't "make waves"; don't make problems for the system or managers.
14. Don't "suck up" to supervisors.
15. Know what your supervisor and other managers expect.
16. Don't trust managers, they may not look out for your interests (pp. 13–16).

Both the manager's and street cop's cultures, however, must relate to the expectations of the communities they serve; therefore, there is also a private and a public world of policing. The *public world* is presented to the pub-

**Informal communication in which officers share beliefs and attitudes leads to the development of a police culture and contributes to the socialization process.**

lic as the essence of police work. While managers' and officers' presentation of police work and police behavior may differ, neither group is completely candid. Both have a vested interest in manufacturing an image that avoids controversy. If police officers use excessive force to make an arrest, they will probably not admit it because one of the police culture's norms of behavior is to be secretive about illegal or inappropriate behavior. While managers may attempt to uncover the inappropriate behavior, they may not disclose it for one of two reasons: adverse consequences to the organization and/or managers may not be too upset with illegal tactics if a desirable result is obtained.

In general, the *private world* has been characterized as being politically conservative and closed or secretive, having a high degree of cynicism, and emphasizing loyalty, solidarity, and respect for authority (Doyle 1980). This private world of the worker's culture undoubtedly has the strongest influence on the socialization process throughout the organization and thus possibly the greatest impact on police behavior. At times, the behavior dictated by the worker's culture is in conflict with both organizational and community interests. How do managers resolve this conflict? How do managers respond to this apparent deviant behavior by officers? How much deviancy is to be tolerated? How do managers deal with an organizational culture that is frequently at odds with community or organizational expectations?

These are some of the important questions that police managers must be willing to deal with from an ethical perspective. Groups have a significant impact on the beliefs, attitudes, and behavior of organizational members. Accordingly, police managers need to be aware of group pressures, especially with respect to the street cop culture, and how they influence, either positively or negatively, individual group members.

## Orientation

Organizations are oriented toward the attainment of goals. Many organization theorists feel that this particular characteristic is the most essential to "organized life." Etzioni (1964, p. 5), for instance, states that, "Organizations are social units which pursue specific goals; their very raison d'etre is the service of these goals." Parsons (1960) suggests that the orientation of organizations toward specific goal attainment is precisely what differentiates them from other social systems, such as audiences and crowds.

**Establishing goals.**  Because police organizations have multiple goals (e.g., law enforcement, order maintenance, and social services) that may conflict with one another, it is important to understand how departments determine goals and how they attempt to attain those goals. For instance, the models of policing discussed in chapter 2 represent different approaches to goal emphases and identify significantly different strategies in accomplishing these goals. As has been noted, three major influences impact the establishment of police goals: environmental, organizational, and individual. *Environmental influences* consist of the community and its input into organizational priorities. As has been continually stressed, however, there is no such thing as a "single" community or constituency to be served by the police. It is crucial, therefore, that police managers be aware of the various communities they serve and possibly the differing goal expectations of these communities. Thus, departments within a similar geographic area, or even precincts and units within the same department, may need to establish different goals or use different methods to attain goals.

Second, we must be aware of *organizational influences.* The organizational system itself (i.e., influential members, especially top management) seeks certain goals, primarily for efficiency and self-perpetuation, but also to satisfy its members. Finally, we must be aware of *individual influences*, which are generally self-enhancing (e.g., job security, pay, fringe benefits, etc.). Organizational members often have separate and even conflicting goals with those of the organization. As Barnard noted:

> Individual motive is necessarily an internal, personal, subjective thing; common purpose is necessarily an external, impersonal, objective thing even though the individual interpretation of it is subjective. The one exception to this general rule, an important one, is that the accomplishment of an organization purpose becomes itself a source of personal satisfaction and a motive for many individuals in many organizations (1938, p. 85).

It is clear, as the expectation-integration model suggests, that the closer management comes to integrating community and individual member goals with those of the organization, the more likely goal accomplishment is to occur. This can be accomplished by continually monitoring community and individual needs and expectations, and by using practices and procedures that integrate community and employee goals with those of the organization.

Identifying and developing goals is one of the most important tasks of managers attempting to balance and integrate expectations. Goals provide the frame of reference for more specific performance objectives, and the degree to which objectives are accomplished provides the basis for assessing effectiveness and efficiency (when compared to resources utilized). The resulting analyses may also provide an opportunity for learning more about police strategies, methods, and activities. Organization improvement is not usually possible without the knowledge acquired through systematic evaluation.

**Types of goals.** There are essentially three forms of organizational goals: official, operative, and operational. *Official* goals are listed in annual reports, public statements, and other authoritative pronouncements by key officials as the general purposes of the organization (Perrow 1969, p. 66). These goals typically *identify and justify* the activities of the organization. *Operative* goals, on the other hand, designate what the organization is *really* trying to do, regardless of the stated purpose of the official goals (p. 66). An example of each type of goal is illustrated by the police agency that states its goal (official goal) as "protecting and serving" the community in a just manner, while actually promoting a goal (operative goal) of "aggressive" enforcement; that is, rewarding the notion that individual officers must keep their "stats" up (e.g., a high level of traffic citations, "street stops," arrests, etc.), possibly at the expense of justly applying the law.

Goals are said to be *operational* when there is agreement on how to measure their attainment. In other words, for goals to become operational, it is necessary to determine their means of achievement, usually by determining a *set of objectives* that will lead to goal accomplishment. One way of clarifying objectives is to make them specific, time-bounded, and quantifiable. These objectives need to be spelled out so that organizational units and employees understand what is expected of them. Furthermore, objectives must be carefully integrated throughout the organization. For example, most police organizations include investigative units whose primary concern is obtaining information to solve crimes, and community relations units whose primary concern is increasing community rapport and support. If the objectives of such diverse units are not integrated, conflicts between the units may develop to the detriment of organizational goal attainment.

**Measuring goals.**   As we have noted previously, the "products" of police agencies are more difficult to measure than those of most organizations. For instance, how can departments measure diverse activities such as administering laws justly, producing quality arrests, maintaining order, or providing services to the community? Police departments have multiple goals that are difficult to evaluate and, because most departments operate in relatively unstable (changing) environments, goal priorities often change over time.

To properly evaluate a police organization's overall effectiveness, external and internal goals should be assessed. From an external perspective, the organization needs to know the extent to which it is satisfying the community it serves. For instance, are there conflicts between organizational and community goals? Or, if the goals are similar, are the methods used to accomplish the goals acceptable? From an internal perspective, the organization needs to know whether its goals are compatible with those of its employees. Is there conflict between what organizational members feel the goals should be and what the organization actually stresses? Do goal conflicts exist between operating units within the organization and/or between individual members of the units?

To answer these questions, overall organizational goals as well as unit and individual goals must be established and set forth in measurable terms. Accordingly, police managers need to formulate goal statements that are honest enough to be achievable and specific enough to be measurable. In order to be specific, clear and precise objectives that will lead to goal accomplishment need to be set forth. As noted in chapter 1, overall organizational goals such as "preventing and deterring crime" are more difficult to measure than unit goals such as "decreasing residential burglaries by 5 percent." However, measurement of any properly defined goal is usually possible. While it is beyond the scope of this chapter to explore various techniques that can be used by police organizations to assess their performance, several attainable and generally satisfactory methods include community surveys and interviews regarding police performance, representative community boards that participate in departmental goal setting and evaluation, crime statistics, organizational membership input (including surveys and interviews) concerning goal emphases and operating practices and policies, and individual and group performance evaluation measures.

## Methods

Because organizations are oriented toward the attainment of goals, they must maintain systematic means through which goals can be reached. The methods of differentiated functions and intended rational coordination provide such means.

Emil Durkheim Labour
Division of Labour

**Differentiated functions.**   The concept of *differentiated functions* simply means that not everyone in the organization does the same thing. Also known as *division of labor* or *task specialization*, it is needed throughout many organizations because tasks are too varied and too complex for a single individual to be able to perform satisfactorily. Also, it is simply not possible for a single individual (or group of individuals, for that matter) to be in the right place at the right time to perform all organizational functions. Thus, the overall organization task is differentiated so that different units are responsible for the performance of particular activities at particular places and times. Generally, even small organizations with only a few employees involve some degree of differentiation.

Two major types of differentiated functions generally occur in organizations: vertical differentiation, representing the organization's hierarchy or differing levels of authority, and horizontal differentiation, representing different functions or activities performed at approximately equal levels of authority.

*Vertical differentiation* refers to the number of separate hierarchical levels in an organization and the degree of authority and responsibility within each level. In the formal organization, this hierarchy is known as the "chain of command"; the higher the position in the hierarchy, the greater the authority, responsibility, and sphere of influence concerning organizational actions. For example, in the hypothetical police agency described in figure 4-1, the top hierarchical level, the chief of police position, carries the greatest degree of authority and responsibility. Vertical differentiation also facilitates the coordination and direction of specialized activities.

Porter, Lawler, and Hackman recognize four major types of vertical groupings of activities with respect to relatively large organizations:

1. *Top management positions* conduct overall goal formulation and make policy decisions regarding allocation of resources.
2. *Middle management positions* formulate objectives and plans for implementing decisions from above and coordinating activities from below.
3. *Lower management positions* implement decisions made at higher levels and coordinate and direct the work of employees at the lowest level of the organization.

4. *Rank-and-file positions* carry out specific task activities (1975, pp. 90–91).

Examples of each type of vertical grouping can be described using the police agency depicted in figure 4-1. Top management would include the chief of police and assistant chiefs serving at the bureau level; middle management would include the captains and lieutenants serving at the division and section levels; lower management would include sergeants serving at the district level; and rank-and-file positions would include patrol officers and other sworn and civilian personnel under the supervision of lower management personnel. Smaller organizations may have only two or perhaps three vertical groupings.

*Horizontal differentiation* occurs when there is a need to divide activities among groups and individuals who occupy essentially the same level of authority and responsibility. In large organizations, this horizontal specialization of activities is quite apparent and necessary to the effective operation of the organization. Once again using the hypothetical department depicted in figure 4-1, horizontal differentiation is indicated by the various bureaus (i.e., Administrative Services, Field Operations, etc.) at one administrative level and the various divisions (Personnel, Patrol, Communications, etc.) at the next administrative level. Although particular bureaus or divisions are responsible for different functions, they share approximately equal degrees of authority and responsibility.

Even in small agencies, horizontal specialization of functions often occurs. For instance, in a police department with only ten sworn personnel, the primary function of each officer could be that of patrol, although one officer may be in charge of investigating major cases and collecting evidence (thus assuming the specialist role of detective). This kind of differentiation frequently is a result of the individual's natural interests and skills and may even be informal in nature. If these interests and skills are recognized formally by the organization, the individual may be encouraged to attend special training classes and seminars in an attempt to increase skills that further contribute to the organization's goals. While the employee is contributing specialized skills to the organization, he or she may also benefit through increased job satisfaction.

Through differentiated functions, organizational members can accomplish more than they could working alone; therefore, the benefits of this characteristic are obvious. However, there are also consequences that limit the actions of the organization's members, and this may not be beneficial. Depending on the nature of differentiation, it limits the interactions of employees to those they are relatively close to physically. This may or may not contribute to organizational goal attainment or to individual needs and satisfaction. These dimensions may further contribute to a positive or negative impact on the individual's perceptions and attitudes toward the organization. The type of activities performed, and the attitude toward those activities, strongly affects the individual's relationship with other organizational members as well as his or her degree of motivation.

**Intended rational coordination.** *Intended rational coordination* is the rational coordination and integration of activities by management to help organizations run efficiently and accomplish goals. While this coordination of an individual's activities is clearly intended, it may not be completely achieved because of poor planning or other breakdowns that typically occur. Keep in mind, too, that such coordination affects only certain activities; according to the concept of partial inclusion, not all of an individual's behavior can, or should, be coordinated.

Such coordination is necessary because vertical and horizontal differentiation splits the activities and functions required for the organizational goal attainment. In other words, these two dimensions must be *integrated* if the organization is to make substantial progress toward attaining its goals. There is a strong relationship between the need to differentiate functions and the requirements for integration. In general, the greater the differentiation of functions, the greater the difficulty of integration; that is, the more task specialization, the greater the coordination and communication problems for managers.

Organizations must provide mechanisms for achieving coordination.

Three such mechanisms include: the hierarchy, the administrative system, and voluntary activities (Litterer 1965, pp. 223–232). In *hierarchical coordination*, the individual at the top of the organizational pyramid is responsible for coordinating activities. In simple organizations this may be sufficient, but in larger organizations hierarchical coordination is virtually impossible. A top-level manager simply could not handle all of the coordination problems that would come up through the hierarchy. Furthermore, if there are many levels in the organization's structure, the individual at the top does not have enough information to properly coordinate activities at the lower levels.

A second major mechanism for coordinating activities exists in the *administrative system* itself. Memoranda and bulletins are two obvious methods designed to help coordinate work efforts among separate operating units. To the extent that such procedures are routine, specific structural means for coordination are probably not necessary. In the case of nonroutine activities, however, specific units and committees for providing integration may need to be established. For example, police agencies may use ad hoc committees, which are put together to help coordinate or carry out specific activities such as developing or implementing a new policy and are then disbanded.

The third mechanism involves *voluntary coordination*. To a large degree, organizations depend on the willingness and the ability of individual members and groups to voluntarily combine their activities with those of other organizational members and groups. Precisely for this reason, many organizations attempt to tie individual member's identification with, and commitment to, the organization. If identification is achieved, it is believed that individuals will more readily coordinate their activities, which, in turn, will help the organization realize its goals.

Through rational coordination of activities, the organization keeps some measure of control over its operations. For the individual, rational coordination allows the achievement of more than could be accomplished alone. While rational coordination can benefit both the employee and the organization, as with differentiation of functions, it limits the freedom of the individual. If an individual is to coordinate his or her activities with others, his or her actions must be restricted to some degree, which can cause individual–organization conflict. Accordingly, managers must pay attention to the methods used to handle rational coordination and make every effort not to stifle or unfairly restrict individual freedom and initiative.

In the previous sections, we have defined the meaning of organization and described the characteristics of police organizations. We have further discussed several methods that can be used by police managers to help them attain organizational goals. Our attention now turns to a discussion of the structural factors that are important in the proper design of police agencies to meet community, organizational, and employee expectations.

## Organization Structure

In terms of *organization structure*, we are concerned with the arrangements and relationships of the formal structural factors that make up the "design" of the organization. Until recently (Langworthy 1986; Slovak 1986), empirical research on police organizational structure had been largely ignored. Furthermore, an assumption has persisted, based on the classical school of management thought, that a bureaucratic, hierarchical structure was the most appropriate design for virtually all police agencies. Even some departments that have characteristics of community-service and rational-contingency models substantially adhere to this type of organization design. This classical, pyramidal design, is shown in figure 4-4. The relationships among organization members are presumed to follow this structure, as Sayles and Strauss have indicated:

1. Nearly all contacts take the form of orders going *down* and reports of results going *up* the pyramid.
2. Each subordinate must receive instructions and orders from only one boss.
3. Important decisions are made at the top of the pyramid.
4. Superiors have a limited "span of control"; that is, they supervise only a limited number of individuals.

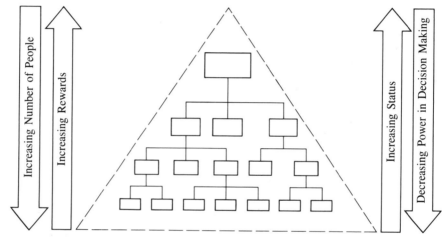

**Figure 4-4**   Organization Pyramid

Source: Adapted from L. R. Sayles and G. Strauss, *Human Behavior in Organizations,* (Englewood Cliffs, N.J.: Prentice-Hall, 1966) p. 349.

5. Individuals at any level (except at the top and bottom) have contact only with their boss above them and their subordinates below them (1966, p. 349).

As the following discussion indicates, total adherence to the classical bureaucratic model, espoused by many of the early police theorists, is no longer appropriate under all conditions. Severe criticism has been leveled against the effectiveness of this paramilitary model (see, for example, Auten 1981 and Sandler and Mintz 1974, among others). Auten, for instance, suggests that the paramilitary model treats the patrol officer like a soldier and thus is based on inappropriate assumptions about patrol work. Auten notes that soldiers are expected to obey orders and to show little, if any, initiative or discretion; they work as part of a larger unit; they perform tasks in a precisely prescribed manner; and they must be uniform in appearance, conduct, and behavior. Problems exist in applying such expectations to the job of policing. First, strict rules cannot be applied to policing because of the nature of the police role. Second, orders are rarely required since most of the work by patrol personnel takes place on the street and out of the purview of supervisors. In addition, if the job is to be performed properly, a great amount of initiative and discretion is required.

Auten further explains that patrol officers seldom work in groups; rather, they perform most of their work alone or in pairs (and thus using the rules or following the "book" cannot be enforced). Auten also criticizes the uniformity of appearance of patrol officers (patterned after soldiers), suggesting that it creates a mind-set and rigidity on the officer's part. Further, such uniformity is depersonalizing, which may be appropriate for soldiers but is antithetical to the police service objective. The decreased flexibility perpetuated by this system is also a problem; that is, there is a prescribed way for an officer (like a soldier) to act. Finally, the managerial philosophy reflected by the paramilitary organization is Theory X–oriented. Theory X is characterized by a philosophy of distrust and control and is punishment-oriented (Theory X and Theory Y philosophies are discussed in chapter 5).

While such criticisms, and their charges of ineffectiveness, are not new, there has been surprisingly little empirical research conducted supporting or refuting the criticisms. A recent study, however, by Franz and Jones (1987) provides empirical evidence that there is some substance to the critics' charges. In this study, police officers were compared with employees in other city organizations (none of which had been exposed to the paramilitary type of organization structure). The researchers found that police employees perceived greater problems with: (1) communications, (2) greater amounts of distrust, particularly with upper management, (3) lower levels of morale, and (4) lower levels of organizational performance. Franz and Jones (p. 161) concluded that "the data presented . . . seriously question the capability of the quasi-military police organizational model to meet today's needs." However, Franz and Jones also caution that additional research is needed on alternative organizational forms before the traditional model can be completely discarded:

Certainly, the "popular inclination" to overgeneralize and overapply the "business organization model and method" to city, county, state, and federal governmental agencies is equally suspect theoretically, administratively, and empirically. If governmental managerial effectiveness in general (and police effectiveness in particular) is to improve, all alternative administrative models demand careful empirical verification (p. 161).

Their statement reiterates that there is no single best way to manage or design police agencies and that managers need to consider relevant external and internal variables or influences if they are to properly design their organizations. A statement made approximately two decades ago by two organization design theorists, Lorsch and Lawrence, still rings true today:

During the past few years there has been evident a new trend in the study of organizational phenomena. Underlying its new approach is the idea that the internal functioning of organizations must be consistent with the demands of the organization task, technology, or external environment, and the needs of its members if the organization is to be effective. Rather than searching for the panacea of the one best way to organize under all conditions, investigators have more and more tended to examine the functioning of organizations in relation to the needs of their particular members and the external pressures facing them (1970, p. 1).

## Mechanistic and Organic Systems

As noted in chapter 3, in the early 1960s Burns and Stalker (1961) distinguished between two types of organizational systems: mechanistic and organic. The *mechanistic* system is characterized by a rigidly defined organization structure, with hierarchical control, authority, and communication. Methods, duties, and powers attached to each functional role are precisely determined. Interactions within the system tend to be vertical, that is, between superior and subordinate. "Management," according to Burns and Stalker, "often visualized as the complex hierarchy familiar to organizational charts, operates a simple control system, with information flowing up through a succession of filters, and decisions and instructions flowing downward through a succession of amplifiers" (p. 5).

By contrast, the *organic* system is characterized by a relatively flexible organization structure, with much less emphasis on functional roles and duties. "Jobs lose much of their formal definition in terms of methods, duties and powers, which have to be redefined continually by interaction with others participating in a task. Interaction runs laterally as much as vertically. Communication between people of different tasks tends to resemble lateral consultation rather than vertical command" (p. 5–6).

Table 4-1 depicts the major characteristics of each system. As can be seen, the mechanistic structure tends to be more rigid with permanent, structured positions, rules, and communication patterns, whereas the organic structure is more flexible with regard to positions, rules, and communications. It is important to point out, however, that a strict duality between the two systems does not exist in reality; organizations have characteristics that fit somewhere between the two extremes. As Kast and Rosenzweig, two contingency theorists, have aptly warned:

> Concepts about these relationships have not been "proven" via substantial empirical research. In fact, it is doubtful whether or not they can ever be proven conclusively. Organizations and their environments are much too dynamic to allow us to set forth "laws" about relationships. Rather, we can only expect to identify tentative patterns of relationships among organizational variables (1974, p. 509).

Kuykendall and Roberg (1982), in attempting to apply mechanistic and organic systems to policing, defined five core characteristics that are applicable to each type of organization. As table 4-2 indicates, the mechanistic system tends to be more bureaucratic and specialized, whereas the organic system tends to reflect a more democratic, generalist approach. The authors are also careful to point out that although such "pure" systems do not exist in the real world, they do provide an accurate description of two differing theoretical orientations, representing polar extremes along a continuum.

In applying mechanistic and organic characteristics to police agencies operating in a democracy, some mention should be made regarding the attention given to means (rule-oriented behavior) as opposed to ends (situation-oriented behavior); see table 4-2 (characteristic number 4). For instance, due process procedures such as probable cause for arrest and re-

**Table 4-1**   Organizational Characteristics of Organic and Mechanistic Structures

| Organizational Characteristics Index | Types of Organizational Structure | |
|---|---|---|
| | **Organic** | **Mechanistic** |
| Span of control | Wide | Narrow |
| Number of levels of authority | Few | Many |
| Degree of centralization in decision making | Low | High |
| Proportion of persons in one unit having opportunity to interact with persons in other units | High | Low |
| Quantity of formal rules | Low | High |
| Specificity of job goals | Low | High |
| Specificity of required activities | Low | High |
| Content of communications | Advice and information | Instructions and decisions |
| Range of compensation | Narrow | Wide |
| Range of skill levels | Narrow | Wide |
| Knowledge-based authority | High | Low |
| Position-based authority | Low | High |

*Source:* R. M. Hower and J. W. Lorsch. "Organizational Inputs." In *Systems Analysis in Organizational Behavior*, ed. J. A. Seiler (Homewood, Ill.: Richard D. Irwin, Inc. and The Dorsey Press 1967), p. 168. Reprinted by permission.

strictions against unreasonable search and seizure have an important impact on how the job is to be performed. Because the organic model emphasizes ends rather than means, there appears to be a conflict, since rule-oriented

**Table 4-2**  Core Characteristics of Organizational Systems

| Mechanistic | Organic |
|---|---|
| *Specialization*: Organizational tasks and activities are specialized into clearly defined positions; members are concerned primarily with their own work and not that of the organization as a whole. | *Generalization*: There is a deemphasis on specialized jobs and tasks; concern is oriented toward a contributive nature of special knowledge and experience to organizationwide objectives rather than those of a subspecialty. |
| *Hierarchical*: Interactions between members tend to be vertical (i.e., between superior and subordinate) in nature, and relationships are governed by the instructions and decisions issued by superiors; status and rank differences are emphasized. | *Collegial*: Interactions between members tend to be horizontal (i.e., between different ranks and units) as well as vertical and are governed by information and advice (i.e., by consultation); status and rank differences are deemphasized. |
| *Authority*: The location of knowledge is inclusive only at the apex of the hierarchy where the final reconciliation of distinct tasks and assessment of relevance is made; prestige is internalized (i.e., personal status in the organization is determined largely by one's office and rank). Influence derived from organizational position. | *Power*: The location of knowledge may be anywhere in the organization with this location becoming the ad hoc center of control, authority, and communication; prestige is externalized (i.e., personal status and influence are determined largely by one's ability and reputation). |
| *Rule-oriented*: The precise definition of rights, obligations, and methods of performance is attached to each functional role to guide member behavior; means (or the proper way to do a job) are emphasized rather than the end product or service. | *Situation-oriented*: There is a "shedding of responsibility" regarding rights, obligations, and methods of performance (i.e., functional roles are deemphasized in favor of all members contributing to the solution of organizational problems); ends (or getting the job done) are emphasized. |
| *Position-oriented*: Accountability is based on job description and rewards are chiefly obtained by precisely following instructions. | *Goal-oriented*: Accountability is based on task achievement and rewards are chiefly obtained through excellence of performance in accomplishing a task; commitment to organizationwide goals and objectives and progress is emphasized. |

*Source:* Adapted from J. Kuykendall and R. R. Roberg, "Mapping Police Organizational Change: From a Mechanistic Toward an Organic Model," *Criminology* 20 (1982): 243–244.

behavior (e.g., due process procedures) is not stressed. An emphasis on situation-oriented behavior, however, simply means that rules applying to due process should be accepted as the parameters within which attempts to adapt to the environment must be considered. This suggests that while procedural safeguards will always be an integral part of job performance, greater attention should be focused on a more precise definition and measurement of ends. According to Kuykendall and Roberg:

> One of the advantages of the organic model is the increased interaction with the community providing for a neutral exchange of viewpoints. For example, the community may wish to provide for input into the degree that substantive laws should be enforced, while the police can communicate the legal parameters as this relates to means, or vice versa (1982, p. 253).

After studying a number of companies, Burns and Stalker concluded that the mechanistic system was most appropriate to a stable environment, and the organic system was most appropriate to an unstable, changing environment. The researchers were careful to point out that neither design is superior to the other under all circumstances. Burns and Stalker (1961, p. 125) suggest that although the organic system appears superior in a changing environment, "nothing in our experience justifies the assumption that mechanistic systems should be superseded by organic in conditions of stability."

Based on the research findings of Burns and Stalker and other organizational theorists, most notably Woodward (1958, 1965), Lawrence and Lorsch (1967), and Perrow (1970), it became apparent that organizations operating in different types of environments require different designs if they are to be effective. Consequently, as the contingency approach suggests, the most appropriate structural characteristics should be applied to an organization according to the current conditions in which it operates.

Designing police organizations is a continual process. Police agencies must continually monitor, and be willing to adapt to, changing environmental influences, such as public opinion, new laws and ordinances (or changing interpretations of the old ones), political pressures, and special and minority group interests. One must keep in mind, however, that the environments of police agencies operating in large metropolitan communities are likely to be more unstable or turbulent than those of agencies operating in small rural communities. Nevertheless, as Kuykendall and Roberg argue, the distinction of police environmental uncertainty is basically one of degree. The authors state that police work can be characterized as "having a changing and complex work technology in which a variety of nonroutine tasks are performed in unstable environmental conditions" (1982, p. 243). In order for police agencies to be able to adapt to their changing environmental conditions, the authors conclude that attempts must be made to move away from mechanistic, toward relatively more organic, designs. In attempting not to overgeneralize, Kuykendall and Roberg do note that not all police environments have the same degree of turbulence, and that other factors such as size of community, population composition, and degree of crime problem all have an impact. Thus, while the trend for police structures should be toward organic, the degree to which they should be organic or, for that matter, mechanistic, depends on a department's particular environmental circumstances.

While the researchers described focused primarily on the effects of *external* influences on an organization's structure, an agency's *internal* influences, or human resources, are also important. For example, the level of employee skills and abilities as well as their need strengths will have a significant impact on the structure of an organization; these internal organizational influences will be discussed in the following section.

We have thus far discovered that both external and internal influences affect organization design and that different designs are appropriate depending on the situation. Keeping these factors in mind, Porter, Lawler, and Hackman, after reviewing several national studies, suggest that the organic and mechanistic models are more appropriate under the following conditions (1975, p. 272):

> Organic, low-structured, nonbureaucratic-type designs are most effective when:
>
> 1. Individuals have relatively high skills that are widely distributed.
> 2. Individuals have high self-esteem and strong needs for achievement, autonomy, and self-actualization.
> 3. The technology is rapidly changing, nonroutine, and involves many nonprogrammable tasks.
> 4. The environment is relatively dynamic and complex.
>
> Mechanistic, high-structured, more bureaucratic-like designs are most effective when:
>
> 1. Individuals are relatively inexperienced and unskilled.
> 2. Individuals have strong needs for security and stability.
> 3. The technology is relatively stable and involves standardized materials and programmable tasks.
> 4. The environment is fairly calm and relatively simple.

Porter, Lawler, and Hackman defend these basic generalizations by taking a practical view:

> Lest anyone be tempted to conclude that these involve invidious comparisons, let him be reminded that not all employees are highly skilled and experienced, not all individuals want high degrees of freedom and autonomy in work situations, not all technology involves highly intricate tasks, etc. The trend over time may well be in this direction, but at present there is still so much variation across organizational situations on all these dimensions that sophisticated analysis continues to be required for achieving appropriate designs (pp. 272–273).

## Factors Affecting Design

We now turn our discussion to several relevant external and internal influences that should be considered in determining the structure of police organizations.

## External Influences

In one of the few empirical investigations on police organization design, Langworthy (1986) analyzed data collected on 175 municipal police agencies to study the effects of agency size, technology, and environment on organization structure. Agency size was measured as the number of police officers, as well as the total number of employees, including civilians. Technology, or the degree that organizations use routine or nonroutine policing methods, was measured by the amount of resources devoted to patrol. The environment included measures of the size of the population served by the agency, the complexity of the population (i.e., stable/homogeneous or mobile/heterogeneous), and the type of local government (e.g., council-manager, nonpartisan mayor-council, partisan mayor-council).

The major findings and implications of the study revolved around strong relationships found between agency *size* and *spatial differentiation* (as measured by number of beats and number of precinct stations) and between *technology* and *functional differentiation* (as measured by task specialization).

The findings of a strong association between agency size and spatial differentiation (i.e., the larger the agency, the greater the number of beats and precinct stations), while predictable and even obvious, has serious implications for police organization design. This finding means, in general, that large police agencies serve large populations and are widely dispersed geographically. This geographic dispersion mitigates against centralized, bureaucratic organization models. Put another way, the tendency of large police agencies is toward a hierarchically flat, decentralized model (i.e., authority and decision making are widely dispersed throughout the organization). These characteristics are associated with a democratic model of policing.

These findings tend to refute the classical emphasis that has often influenced police organization design. As noted in the last chapter, many of the early police theorists, such as Smith (1940), Wilson (1950), and Leonard (1951), suggested that large police organizations should be based on the bureaucratic (i.e., mechanistic) model of organization, with strong reliance on centralization, specialization, unity of command, and hierarchy of control.

Such a model, it appears, may only be an appropriate option for smaller departments that do not service wide geographic areas. This does not mean that all large police agencies that are based on the bureaucratic model will be ineffective or that the bureaucratic model is never appropriate for large organizations. What it does mean is that managers who choose the bureaucratic model, as Langworthy (1986, p. 132) notes, "must recognize that the tendency of the organization is toward decentralization, and the designer must purposely build in measures to overcome this tendency." For example, such measures may include tying officers to a central control by radio, making it impossible for them to be out of contact with headquarters. Changing shifts, beats, and partners on a regular basis can promote centralization and the bureaucratic model by encouraging allegiance to the organization (centralization) rather than to the geographic area (decentralization). While such methods are often used in the design of police organizations, the implications and consequences are not always clearly understood.

The second major finding is a strong association between a routine or nonroutine technology and functional differentiation (task specialization). Routine and nonroutine technologies are defined by Langworthy as the number of employees assigned to patrol. Thus, police agencies that devote a larger proportion of their resources to patrol are characterized as using a nonroutine production technology. Conversely, police agencies that devote fewer resources to patrol are characterized as having a routine technology.

The results of the study revealed that police organizations utilizing a *routine technology* (i.e., low degree of resources devoted to patrol) have a high degree of functional differentiation (task specialization). In contrast, those organizations utilizing a *nonroutine technology* (i.e., a high degree of resources devoted to patrol) tend to be less specialized and therefore are more generalized, or organic, in their structural characteristics. In other words, the manner in which a community is policed, in terms of specialist or generalist operations, has implications for the structure of the entire organization. If emphasis is placed on generalist operations, there is a tendency for the whole organization to generalize, or to be less specialized, in nature.

The practical implications of these findings suggest that if a manager is contemplating a generalist approach to police operations in a community, such as a team policing model, he or she would need to consider the potential costs (loss) of specialized activities or functions. This does not mean that managers cannot manipulate or combine a generalist operation with specialization; for instance, Angell's (1971) democratic model integrates the generalist approach with functionally specialized support units. However, it is important for police managers to recognize that technology (i.e., the way a community is policed) has a strong impact on structural considerations of organization design. Specialization in both the patrol and investigative functions is discussed in chapter 8.

There is an important distinction that needs to be made between organization design and models of democratic policing. Police reformers can attempt to move from a legalistic-professional model to a community-service and/or a rational-contingency model while maintaining a classical, bureaucratic, and directive approach in design and management practices. However, the diversity and flexibility required of the community-service and rational-contingency models are inconsistent with classical, bureaucratic features. Consequently, the success of one depends to a substantial degree on changing not only the police model but also the design features and managerial style within the organization. In addition, attempts to utilize a bureaucratic approach in large, urban departments may be ineffective given the tendency of such organizations toward decentralization.

## Internal Influences

The Langworthy study described the effects of external factors on police organization structure. As mentioned earlier, internal influences, or the organization's human resources, also have an impact on design. Several important employee characteristics that should be taken into consideration when determining organizational structure include skill and ability levels and need strengths (Porter, Lawler, and Hackman 1975). .

With respect to the *skills and abilities* of the human resources in an organization, two dimensions are critical to design: mean level and degree of dispersion. Regarding the *mean or average level* of employee skills and abilities in an organization, Porter, Lawler, and Hackman suggest:

> If any organization is composed of employees who have a very high mean level of skill—as evidenced, say, by experience in jobs requiring a high degree of skill and by considerable amounts of appropriate formal education—then it is presumed that the nature of the structural-operational features of the organization should take cognizance of this. To be more specific, if employees tend to be especially skilled and well educated, it is likely that a high degree of formal specification and standardization of activities, and the imposition of close and severe controls, would result in an inefficient use of human resources, both from the organization's standpoint and from the individual's standpoint. Resulting behavior could be presumed to be characterized by performance much lower than potentially possible, frustration, and perhaps overt expressions of resentment against the organization (1975, p. 243).

They add, "many organizations that . . . employ individuals with high skill levels fail to take this factor into account and are designed as if their employees constitute a low level of human resources when actually their potential is much greater" (p. 243). This statement appears to have important implications for today's police agencies, especially for those agencies that are attempting to attract more highly educated personnel into their ranks. It would appear that the traditional organizational climate and reward structure greatly discourage the presumed attributes acquired through higher education. For instance, there is some evidence that more highly educated and/or intelligent recruits are more likely to terminate their careers in policing (Cohen and Chaiken 1972; Levy 1967, 1973; Marsh 1962; Stoddard 1973; Weirman 1978).

An organization can also be inappropriately designed if the opposite mistake is made and the skills of the employees are judged to be high, when in fact they are low. However, due to the relatively mechanistic designs of many police agencies, this mistake is unlikely. Also, some theorists (Miles 1965) argue that it is better for organizations to expect too much rather than too little from their employees because "self-fulfilling" prophesies will occur, and individuals will strive to meet the levels of performance expected of them.

The *degree of dispersion* (distribution) of the mean or average level of skills and abilities among employees throughout an organization is a second important dimension to be considered in organization design. For example, two police agencies might have employees with the same amount of experience, skills, and levels of education, but one might assign them throughout the organization (i.e., generalist approach) and the other might concentrate them in a few specialized units. In such a situation, it would be inappropriate for both agencies to adopt the same structures. The agency with the greater dispersal of experience, skills, and education would be more likely to utilize its employees appropriately in an organic rather than mechanistic structure. Conversely, the agency with the narrow dispersion would most likely be better off adopting an organic form for those units containing employees with high skill and ability levels, while utilizing a more mechanistic structure throughout the rest of the organization.

Employee *need strengths* may also significantly influence the effectiveness of the organization's design. Not all individuals need or desire a highly flexible, organic organization where they have a great amount of individual responsibility and decision-making powers. The reverse is also true; many individuals do not want to be part of a highly structured, mechanistic style of operation. According to Porter, Lawler, and Hackman:

> It is not just a matter of how individuals differ in their needs, say, for achievement or affiliation. It is also a matter of how they differ in their characteristic modes of behaving and in their own views of themselves. These kinds of regularities, commonly referred to as personality traits, also have an impact on the effectiveness of different types of organization design for the person and for the organization. We can hypothesize that if individuals have strong needs for independence and self-actualization and have relatively high self-confidence, they will prefer organic-type organizations and will do better in them. Individuals who have less of these traits can be presumed to fare better in a relatively more highly structured organization (1975, p. 244).

Because individuals with higher levels of education tend to possess many of the traits described above (for example, see Feldman and Newcomb 1969, p. 326), as mean levels of education increase in police organizations, managers will need to continually examine the structural characteristics of their

agencies. Indeed, if the level of higher education increases in police departments, existing organization designs and managerial styles may become increasingly dysfunctional to the effective utilization of an agency's human resources.

Taking into consideration the external and internal influences affecting
design, it would appear that there is a need to change from highly mechanistic police structures toward more organic designs. We agree that such a
generalization is accurate, but keep in mind that "it all depends." Thus,
while a majority of police departments would most likely benefit from a shift
toward more organic structural characteristics, such determinations can only
be made after careful examination of appropriate environmental variables.

Finally, it should be noted that many of the nation's police organizations
are relatively complex (especially those serving large urban populations) and
it is unlikely that any one type of design is going to be appropriate for all parts
of the agency. Managers in such organizations will need to determine which
combination of mechanistic/organic characteristics best fits their organization's needs according to existing conditions and circumstances.

## Summary

In this chapter the importance of understanding the fundamental characteristics that make up organizations, the impact of these characteristics, and the
relevant external and internal factors that influence the structure of police
agencies have been discussed. A working definition of an organization was
developed as a social system composed of groups of two or more persons who
are interdependent and work in a coordinated manner to achieve common
goals.

The three fundamental characteristics of all organizations include the
composition of the organization, the orientation of the organization, and the
methods of the organization. An example of a formal organization chart was

presented to depict the formal arrangements and relationships of the department's employees. An example of an informal chart (indicating actual power relationships) was also presented, which suggests that while formal charts may tell us a great deal about how management perceives the organization, informal relationships that develop naturally may have a greater influence on how the organization actually operates. Several effects of group influences and police culture on individual group members were also noted.

All organizations are oriented toward the attainment of goals. Three major influences on police goal formulation (i.e., environmental, organizational, and individual) were described as were different types of goals (i.e., official, operative, and operational) and the process of measuring goals. The final organizational characteristic, methods used to accomplish goals, was divided into two parts: differentiated functions (including vertical and horizontal differentiation) and intended rational coordination.

Organization structure is concerned with those structural arrangements that make up the design of the organization. In other words, how the fundamental characteristics are organized by the agency determines its structure. Further, how police organizations are structured is critical if they are to utilize their resources properly and fulfill community expectations. Two types of organizational models were set forth: mechanistic, which is relatively bureaucratic in nature, and organic, which is relatively democratic.

The external factors that affect police structure included environmental or community influences, agency size, and technology (how a community is policed). Relevant internal factors included the primary characteristics of the agency's human resources, namely, employee skills and abilities and employee need strengths. How these employee characteristics are dispersed throughout a police agency will ultimately have an impact on how the organization should be designed. In general, some movement toward more organic structural characteristics would seem to benefit many of the nation's police agencies. Contingency theory suggests, however, that the particular circumstances of each agency must first be considered before an appropriate design can be determined.

# Discussion Questions

1. Discuss three fundamental characteristics of organizations that are important to understanding organizational behavior.
2. Discuss the nature of formal and informal groups in organizations.
3. What is the "police culture," and how are beliefs, attitudes, and behaviors affected by such a culture?
4. What influences must be considered when establishing police organizational goals?
5. Describe the three forms of organizational goals. Why are police agency goals difficult to measure?
6. How do the concepts of differentiated functions and intended rational coordination help police organizations reach their goals?
7. Describe the classical organization design. Discuss several criticisms that have been leveled against the effectiveness of this model when applied to the police.
8. Describe the five core characteristics of mechanistic and organic systems.
9. Discuss the contingency approach to organization design and under what conditions organic and mechanistic structures tend to be most effective.
10. What external and internal factors should be taken into consideration when determining the structure of police organizations?

# References

Allport, F. H., *Institutional Behavior* (Chapel Hill: University of North Carolina Press, 1933).

Angell, J. E., "Toward an Alternative to the Classic Police Organizational Arrangements: A Democratic Model," *Criminology* 9(1971):185–206.

Auten, J. H., "The Paramilitary Model of Police and Police Professionalism," *Police Studies* 4(1981):67–78.

Barnard, C. I., *The Functions of the Executive* (Cambridge: Harvard University Press, 1938).

Burns., T. and Stalker, G. M., *The Management of Innovation* (London: Tavistock, 1961).

Cohen, B. and Chaiken, J., *Police Characteristics and Performance* (New York: Rand Institute, 1972).

Dalton, M., *Men Who Manage* (New York: Wiley, 1959).

Davis, K., *Human Behavior at Work: Organizational Behavior*, 6th ed. (New York: McGraw-Hill, 1981).

Doyle, M. A., "The Police Culture: Open or Closed," in *Fundamentals of Law Enforcement: Problems and Issues*, ed. V. A. Leonard (St. Paul, Minn.: West, 1980), pp. 61–83.

Etzioni, A., *Modern Organizations* (Englewood Cliffs, N.J.: Prentice-Hall, 1964).

Feldman, K. A. and Newcomb, T. M., *The Impact of College on Students* (San Francisco: Jossey-Bass, 1969).

Franz, V. and Jones, D. M., "Perceptions of Organizational Performance in Suburban Police Departments: A Critique of the Military Model," *Journal of Police Science and Administration* 15(1987):153–161.

Hower, R. M. and Lorsch, J. W., "Organizational Inputs," in *Systems Analysis in Organizational Behavior*, ed. J. M. Seiler (Homewood, Ill.: Richard D. Irwin, 1967).

Kast, F. E. and Rosenzweig, J. E., *Organization and Management: A Systems Approach* (New York: McGraw-Hill, 1974).

Kuykendall, J. and Roberg, R. R., "Mapping Police Organizational Change: From a Mechanistic Toward an Organic Model," *Criminology* 20(1982):241–256.

Langworthy, R. H., *The Structure of Police Organizations* (New York: Praeger, 1986).

Lawrence, P. R. and Lorsch, J. W., *Organization and Environment: Managing Differentiation and Integration* (Homewood, Ill.: Richard D. Irwin, 1967).

Leonard, V. A., *Police Organization and Management* (Brooklyn: Foundation Press, 1951).

Levy, R. J., "Predicting Police Failures." *Journal of Criminal Law, Criminology and Police Science* 58(1967):265–275.

——, "A Method for the Identification of the Higher Risk Police Applicant." *The Urban Policeman in Transition*, eds. J. R. Snibbe and H. M. Snibbe (Springfield, Ill.: Charles C. Thomas, 1973), pp. 25–52.

Litterer, J. A., *The Analysis of Organizations* (New York: Wiley, 1965).

Lorsch, J. W. and Lawrence, P. R. *Studies in Organization Design* (Homewood, Ill.: Richard D. Irwin and Dorsey Press, 1970).

Marsh, S. H., "Validating the Selection of Deputy Sheriffs," *Public Personnel Review* 23(1962):41–44.

Miles, R. E., "Human Relations or Human Resources?" *Harvard Business Review* 43(1965):148–163.

Parsons, T., *Structure and Process in Modern Societies* (Glencoe, Ill.: Free Press, 1960).

Perrow, C., "The Analysis of Goals in Complex Organizations," in *Readings on Modern Organizations*, ed. A. Etzioni (Englewood Cliffs, N.J.: Prentice-Hall, 1969).

——, *Organizational Analysis: A Sociological View* (Belmont, Calif.: Wadsworth, 1970).

Porter, L. W., Lawler, E. E., and Hackman, J. R., *Behavior in Organizations* (New York: McGraw-Hill, 1975).

Reuss-Ianni, E., *Two Cultures of Policing: Street Cops and Management Cops* (New Brunswick, Conn.: Transaction Books, 1983).

Sandler, G. B. and Mintz, E., "Police Organizations: Their Changing Internal and External Relationships," *Journal of Police Science and Administration* 2(1974):458–463.

Sayles, L. R. and Strauss, G., *Human Behavior in Organizations* (Englewood Cliffs, N.J.: Prentice-Hall, 1966).

Slovak, J. S., *Styles of Urban Policing: Organization, Environment, and Police Styles in Selected American Cities* (New York: New York University Press, 1986).

Smith, B., *Police Systems in the United States* (New York: Harper, 1940).

Stoddard, K. B., "Characteristics of Policemen of a County Sheriff's Office," in *The Urban Policeman in Transition*, eds. J. R. Snibbe and H. M. Snibbe (Springfield, Ill.: Charles C. Thomas, 1973), pp. 281–297.

Weirman, C. L., "Variances of Ability Measurement Scores Obtained by College and Non-College Educated Troopers," *Police Chief* (August 1978), pp. 34–36.

Wilson, O. W., *Police Administration* (New York: McGraw-Hill, 1950).

Woodward, J., *Management and Technology* (London: H. M. Stationery Office, 1958).

——, *Industrial Organization: Theory and Practice* (London: Oxford University Press, 1965).

# CHAPTER 5

# Behavior, Motivation, and Job Design

In the previous chapter, we described the fundamental characteristics of police organizations and the factors that influence their structure or design. Our attention now turns to the individuals working in police organizations. If policies and practices that lead to the attainment of both organizational and individual goals and objectives are to be implemented, practicing managers need to have a basic understanding of human behavior, of how people are motivated, and finally, of how job design impacts individual behavior and levels of motivation.

## Human Behavior

*Behavior* refers to an individual's conduct or the manner in which an individual acts or reacts to environmental stimuli. Although individual behavioral patterns may vary substantially, the process by which behavior occurs is the same for everyone. Leavitt (1978, p. 10) suggests three related assumptions regarding human behavior:

1. Behavior is caused.
2. Behavior is motivated.
3. Behavior is goal-directed.

This basic behavioral model, shown in figure 5-1, is applicable to all human behavior.

If these three assumptions are valid, then behavior must be purposeful in nature. First, there must be a goal to be achieved, whether implicit or explicit. Second, the behavior related to goal accomplishment must be caused by reacting to a stimulus. The stimulus is generated through a system of needs and wants, which, if not satisfied, may cause tension or discomfort. A "feedback loop" from goal to stimulus, as shown in figure 5-1, indicates that this process is sequential. For example, if an individual is thirsty, the resulting behavior may involve drinking a glass of water. If the goal of quenching thirst is achieved, then the individual moves on to some other behavior. If,

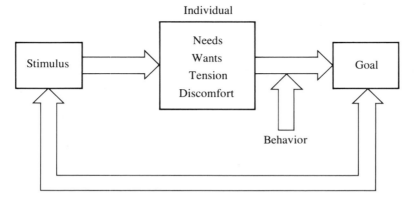

**Figure 5-1**   Human Behavior Model

*Source*: Adapted from H. J. Leavitt, *Managerial Psychology,* 4th ed. (Chicago: University of Chicago Press, 1978), p. 8.

however, the goal is not achieved, the individual may drink a second or third glass of water until the need (thirst) is satisfied.

While this human behavior process is the same for all individuals, actual behaviors can vary substantially. Individuals with different perceptions or motivations may behave differently, even though they are receiving the same or similar stimuli. In other words, because people have different backgrounds (e.g., cultural and educational) and value systems, they may react differently to the same environmental stimuli. Additionally, because needs and wants within the individual vary, individual responses to the same stimuli may also deviate from time to time. A police officer, for instance, may issue a traffic citation for a certain violation one day (depending on the officer's needs, wants, expectations, etc.), whereas on another day he or she may simply give a verbal warning. The point is that because of individual differences with respect to needs and wants, and tension and discomfort, human behavior, even under similar circumstances, is difficult to predict.

## Police Behavior

There are two major theoretical orientations regarding the behavior of in-dividuals in police organizations: the predispositional theory and the social-ization theory. The predispositional theory was more prevalent until the 1960s when the socialization theory began to gain support. The *predisposi-tional theory* suggests that the behavior of a police officer is primarily ex-plained by the characteristics, values, and attitudes that the individual had before he or she was hired. If an officer is dishonest or brutal, he or she prob-ably had those character flaws or psychological problems before being hired as a police officer. This explanation of police behavior resulted in police de-partments' becoming more careful about screening candidates during the se-lection process.

Beginning in the 1960s, largely as a result of research by Skolnick (1966) and Neiderhoffer (1969), social scientists began to suggest that police officers are influenced more by their work experiences than by preemployment val-ues and attitudes. For example, police officers who become corrupt learn the behavior from the *socialization process* in which the corrupt values of the po-lice culture are acquired. Or, if officers become more concerned with ends than means or use excessive force, their behavior is reflecting the values of the organizational culture. The socialization process actually begins before employment because the candidates may begin to adopt the values and at-titudes they think are appropriate for police work, and it continues during the selection process, the training program, and when officers begin to "work the street."

Both theories are useful in understanding police behavior. While both what and who an individual is shapes behavior, work experiences are also important. It is difficult to determine which is most influential, but it is most likely the socialization process. As a general rule, individuals accepted into law enforcement are usually emotionally stable, reasonably intelligent, po-litically conservative or moderate, and basically honest. If officers become emotionally unstable or corrupt, or they change politically, it is probably the socialization process at work. Problem police behavior is more likely to be caused by the socialization process, rather than result from preemployment attitudes and values (Bennett and Greenstein 1975; Harris 1973; Lundman 1980; Neiderhoffer 1969; Muir 1977; Van Maanen 1972; and Skolnick 1966).

## Individual Differences

It is important to recognize that if police managers are to effectively manage or lead, they must keep in mind that individual differences exist and that people behave according to these differences. Thus, employees may need to be managed differently, *even under similar conditions*. Although numerous factors can account for individual differences in behavior, differences in motivation are probably the most important consideration in predicting human behavior. We should keep in mind, however, that while motivation leads to the degree of *effort* exerted, it has no relationship to *ability* level. Therefore, if an individual has low ability levels, he or she may be highly motivated and put forth a great deal of effort but still not perform well. Conversely, if ability levels are high, even relatively low levels of motivation and effort may produce satisfactory performance. Without a high degree of motivation and effort, however, even employees with considerable ability will perform at a level below their capability.

Because employees will not perform to their ability levels unless they are sufficiently motivated, managers must have at least a rudimentary understanding of what motivates people to perform or behave in certain ways on the job. The more a manager understands about individual behavior, the easier it will be to predict how an individual will react to certain organizational stimuli, and consequently, which stimuli in the work environment can be used most effectively to motivate individual employees. This will also help the manager understand more about why different styles of policing develop and how the socialization process of police behavior works.

# Motivation

A *motive* "is what prompts a person to act in a certain way or at least develop a propensity for specific behavior. This urge to action can be touched off by an external stimulus, or it can be internally generated in individual physiological and thought processes" (Kast and Rosenzweig 1985, p. 286). Motivation is a complex concept that involves the factors described in the human behavior model in figure 5-1, including needs, wants, tensions, discomforts, and individual expectations. Each factor varies from individual to individual and within any individual over time. As people grow and mature, their needs, values, expectations, and goals also change. What may have been rewarding, challenging, and motivating at one time may later cause tension and discomfort. Thus, understanding individual motivation is a challenging process that must be continually monitored. Since good management entails knowing how to motivate individuals to perform well, our discussion turns next to several relevant theories of motivation.

# Theories of Motivation

Basically there are two ways to view motivation and what causes people to behave in certain ways. The first way is to focus on the individual's internal states, which include needs, wants, values, and expectations. This is a *cognitive* approach; that is, it takes into consideration how people feel and think in relationship to how they behave. The cognitive approach emphasizes two views of motivation: *content theories*, which identify *what* motivates behavior (e.g., money, status, satisfaction, etc.), and *process theories*, which describe *how* motivation is translated or "energized" into behavior. Although content and process theories are not mutually exclusive, most research has focused on one approach or the other.

In addition, there is a *noncognitive* approach to motivation. Pioneered by B. F. Skinner (1971), this approach does not recognize an individual's internal states or the motivation process. Instead, Skinner believes that behavior is shaped through a conditioning process of reinforcement. In other words, individuals behave in a certain way because they have learned that certain behaviors are associated with pleasurable outcomes (i.e., rewards) and other behaviors are associated with outcomes that are not pleasurable (i.e., punishments). Since people generally prefer pleasurable outcomes, they are likely to avoid behaviors with negative consequences.

If this approach to motivation is emphasized, managers will not pay attention to the internal processes of individuals but will concentrate instead on shaping behavior through positive or negative reinforcements. Managers attempt to find ways to reward employees for desired behavior and punish them for unwanted behavior. These rewards and punishments may be either formal (e.g., pay increases/decreases, promotions/demotions) or informal (e.g., praise, lectures, warnings). Most researchers believe that rewarding desired behavior is more effective than punishing unwanted behavior.

## Content Theories

Traditionally, the management approach to the study of motivation has focused on separate human drives that motivate people to work. For instance, Taylor and other classical theorists viewed economic rewards as the primary motivating factors, while human relations theorists emphasized the importance of "social factors" and informal relationships (see chapter 3). These approaches, however, tended to be simplistic and did not provide managers with an adequate understanding of the complexity of the motivational process in working environments. Three major contributions that have led to a better understanding of the *content* of work motivation are discussed in the following paragraphs.

**Need hierarchy.** In 1943, Abraham Maslow postulated a "hierarchy" of human needs that incorporated several levels (figure 5-2). Basic to his theory is the concept that the satisfaction or satiation of "lower" physiological needs activates "higher" social and psychological needs (Maslow 1943). This does not mean that two levels could not operate concurrently, but lower-level needs take precedence. The foundation of the theory is that once a given level of need is satisfied, it is no longer a motivating factor, and the next level of need must be activated in order to motivate the individual. Maslow identified the needs as follows:

1. Physiological needs, such as hunger, thirst, sleep, and sex.
2. Safety needs for security, such as protection against danger and deprivation.
3. Social needs for friendship, affection, affiliation, and love; the need to belong.
4. Esteem needs for self-respect and the respect of others; ego or status needs.
5. Self-actualization needs, which are at the top of the hierarchy and represent a culmination of all other needs; the need for self-fulfillment or the realization of one's potential.

**Figure 5-2**   Maslow's Hierarchy of Needs

**Abraham Maslow (1908–1970) developed a need hierarchy which differentiated between lower-level physiological needs and higher-level social and psychological needs.**

Maslow's need hierarchy is not specifically directed at work motivation, but it has become popular with managers over the years, probably because of its simplicity and its appeal to common sense: managers only need to learn five needs and their sequence. Although the theory is virtually untestable because of measurement problems, it is not generally supported by available research. However, research has been able to differentiate between two basic levels of needs: higher order and lower order.

While lower-level needs generally must be fulfilled before higher-level needs become influential, people can have overlapping needs and may have a fixation on a particular need after a long period of deprivation. Also, needs tend to change during an individual's psychological development. For instance, physiological and safety needs are relatively more important early in life and social, esteem, and self-actualization needs become more important as the individual matures. Although some generalizations can be made about higher-level needs becoming more important with maturity, significant individual differences in motivation exist in the work environment.

Individual differences in need levels must be taken into consideration by police managers who need to use a number of methods for motivating employees. For example, Lefkowitz (1973, 1974) found that police officers' lower-level needs (i.e., security and social) appear to be reasonably fulfilled in their jobs, but higher-level needs (i.e., esteem, autonomy, and self-actualization) are not. On the other hand, Van Maanen (1975) observed that police obtain the greatest satisfaction of their self-actualization and social needs and the least satisfaction of their esteem, autonomy, and security needs. The low degree of fulfillment of security needs in the Van Maanen study represents an exception to Maslow's theory, which suggested that lower-level needs must be met prior to the fulfillment of upper-level needs. Although Van Maanen's findings contradict Maslow's, especially with respect to lower-level needs, it is possible that such differences exist across many police organizations. Not only do the types of individuals recruited into policing vary, but the managerial practices, organization structures, and job designs of police agencies also differ significantly.

Again, the styles of police officers can be used to illustrate this point. One of the most important variables in determining an officer's style is the selection of tasks or problems he or she considers to be the most important. For example, if an officer decides to emphasize serious crimes (a crime-fighter approach), the associated work probably meets certain of the officer's needs. Perhaps it is that officer's way of self-actualizing or perhaps it is a way of fulfilling social expectations from the work group (informal organization or culture).

**Theory X and Theory Y.**   In *The Human Side of Enterprise* (1960), Douglas McGregor described general assumptions concerning human nature. Although his assumptions cannot be considered a theory of motivation per se, police managers should be aware of his contrasting views of worker behavior. A manager's basic philosophy or set of assumptions about employee behavior determines to a great extent how he or she will treat people in the workplace. In essence, McGregor distributed his assumptions along a continuum, with extremes labeled Theory X and Theory Y.

The assumptions of Theory X are

1. The average human being inherently dislikes work and will avoid it if he [or she] can.

2. Because of their inherent dislike of work, most people must be coerced, controlled, directed, and threatened with punishment if they are to work adequately toward the achievement of organizational objectives.
3. The average human being prefers to be directed, wishes to avoid responsibility, has relatively little ambition, and wants security above all (pp. 33–34).

The assumptions of Theory Y are:

1. Work, whether physical or mental, is as natural as play or rest.
2. External control and the threat of punishment are not the only means of bringing about effort toward organizational objectives. People will exercise self-direction and self-control when they are committed to objectives.
3. Commitment to objectives is a function of the rewards associated with their achievement.
4. The average human being learns, under proper conditions, not only to accept but to seek responsibility.
5. The ability to exercise a relatively high degree of imagination, ingenuity, and creativity in the solution of organizational problems is widely not narrowly distributed (pp. 47–48).

It is easy to see why organizational practices and job designs can be radically different, depending on which view of human nature is accepted by management. Each of these theories can be related to the need hierarchy in the sense that classical management concepts and principles are based on the assumption that lower-level needs are dominant in motivating people to work. Theory X assumes that people work to satisfy physiological and safety needs, primarily through financial gain; the average employee must be coerced and controlled by the threat of punishment. Theory Y, on the other hand, assumes that higher-level needs are dominant. Employees are motivated by esteem and self-actualization needs and will exercise self-direction and self-control if they are committed to their objectives. McGregor further differentiates Theory X and Theory Y:

The central principle of organization which derives from Theory X is that of direction and control through the exercise of authority—what has been called "the scalar principle." The central principle which derives from Theory Y is that of integration: the creation of conditions such that the members of the organization can achieve their own goals best by directing their efforts toward the success of the enterprise. These two principles have profoundly different implications with respect to the task of managing human resources, but the scalar principle is so firmly built into managerial attitudes that the implications of the principle of integration are not easy to perceive (p. 491).

As contingency theory suggests, neither Theory X or Theory Y assumptions are appropriate under all conditions. Depending on the situation, each approach is likely to have some validity. Each human being is a complex individual, who generally cannot be placed at either end of the continuum but lies somewhere in between. However, police managers have clearly subscribed more heavily to Theory X than to Theory Y assumptions; and it is not clear that even as models of democratic policing change, managerial assumptions will change. The failure of some team policing projects, discussed later in the chapter, illustrates this point.

Further, as we pointed out in the last chapter, even police departments with characteristics of a community-service or rational-contingency model may still adhere substantially to the classical prescriptions. Rensis Likert (1967), who has completed extensive research on diverse organizations, has concluded that a managerial system stressing Theory Y assumptions tends to make better use of human resources and enhances both the effectiveness and efficiency of the organization. Additionally, as research presented by Franz and Jones (1987) in the previous chapter indicated, the quasi-military model of organization contributes substantially to problems with communications, distrust, morale, and organizational performance. Although these conclusions cannot be generalized to all police departments, they do apply to many. Thus, while police managers must not only be aware of individual differences, they may also need to reassess their basic assumptions regarding employees.

**Motivation-hygiene.**   In the late 1950s, Frederick Herzberg (1959) and his associates conducted an extensive interview of engineers and accountants, focusing on events that made them feel good about their jobs and events that made them feel bad. The results indicated that job satisfaction and job dissatisfaction come from two separate sets of factors, which Herzberg termed *satisfiers* or "motivating" factors and *dissatisfiers* or "hygiene" factors.

The satisfiers related to the nature of the work or the *job content* and to the rewards that result directly from performing job-related tasks. The major satisfiers included achievement, recognition, the work itself, responsibility, and advancement. Dissatisfiers arose from the individual's relationship to the organization's environment or to the *job context* in which the work was being performed. The major dissatisfiers included company policy and administration, supervision, salary, interpersonal relations, and working conditions.

Some of the factors police officers consider most stress-producing are related to supervision, departmental policy, and working conditions. These job context factors were called dissatisfiers because they did not lead to job satisfaction but merely prevented dissatisfaction; that is, they did not motivate employees to put forth extra effort on the job.

This two-factor theory of motivation can be related to Maslow's need hierarchy in that *hygiene factors* correspond to *lower-level needs*, while *motivators* correspond to *higher-level needs*. According to Herzberg, lower-level needs such as working conditions and salary are not effective motivators, as such, their fulfillment should not be expected to improve job performance. On the other hand, the two-factor theory suggests that, assuming the organization's environmental conditions are acceptable (e.g., working conditions and salary), higher-level needs (e.g., recognition and responsibility) should be emphasized in order to improve motivation and work performance. If higher-level needs are to be satisfied, Herzberg suggests that the employee must be given a sense of psychological growth:

> The hygiene factors are not a valid contributor to psychological growth. The substance of a task is required to achieve growth goals. Similarly, you cannot love an engineer into creativity, although by this approach you can avoid his dissatisfaction with the way you treat him. Creativity will require a potentially creative task to do (1966, p. 75).

Research stimulated by the two-factor theory suggests that it is an oversimplification. For example, several studies have indicated that the same factors may result in job satisfaction for one person and job dissatisfaction for another (House and Wigdor 1967; Schwab, DeVitt, and Cummings 1971). The contention, however, that job satisfaction can be separated into "extrinsic'' (job context) and ''intrinsic'' (job content) factors received support in a study of work satisfaction and municipal police officers (Slovak 1978). Herzberg's work has also been criticized for his method of data collection, his assumptions that people will report their satisfying and dissatisfying experiences accurately, and that employees are more likely to give credit for satisfaction to their own achievements and blame company policies for dissatisfaction (Vroom 1964).

Although the literature reveals contradictory findings in regard to Herzberg's theory, he did apply and extend Maslow's need hierarchy specifically to work motivation. And, as we will discuss later in this chapter, the work of Herzberg and his colleagues has had a significant impact on job expansion programs.

Even though some problems exist in the interpretation of the content theories presented, they have allowed managers to reevaluate the classical prescription that only lower-level needs (i.e., hygiene factors) are important to work motivation. Plainly, employees are motivated by more than these needs. Furthermore, by dealing with the motivational effects of the nature of the job, content theories have extended the simplistic human relations approach (which focused on extrinsic factors) through the study of the motivational effects of intrinsic factors. We now turn our attention to a discussion of two widely respected process theories of motivation.

## Process Theories

Whereas content theories are concerned with attempting to identify specifically what motivates behavior, process theories attempt to explain *how* behavior is energized, *how* it is directed and sustained, and *how* it is stopped. Process theories attempt to define the major variables that lead to motivation and explain how these variables interact to produce certain behavior patterns. The two most influential process theories with respect to organizational behavior are expectancy theory and equity theory. A motivational model developed by Porter and Lawler (1968), which incorporates both expectancy and equity theories, will follow the discussion of the two theories.

**Expectancy theory.** The most widely acknowledged expectancy model of work motivation was developed by Victor Vroom (1964) and views individual motivation as a rational choice people make about the rewards they expect to receive before they perform their jobs. In general, the model rests on two basic assumptions regarding motivation:

1. Individuals have cognitive expectations about what outcomes are likely to result from their behavior.
2. Individuals have preferences among these outcomes.

According to Vroom,

$$\text{Motivation} = \Sigma \text{ Valence} \times \text{Expectancy}$$

This means that motivation equals the summation of valence times expectancy.

*Expectancy*, in this model, incorporates the belief that a particular act will be followed by a particular outcome (if I work hard, I will receive a pay increase). The degree of belief ranges from a certainty that it will follow ($+1$) to a certainty that it will not ($0$). The individual's perception of what is likely to occur is important, not the objective reality of the situation.

*Valence* involves the strength of an individual's preference for a particular outcome. Depending on their desire for the outcome, individuals have either a *positive* ($+1$), *neutral* ($0$), or *negative* ($-1$) preference. Again, the perceived value of an outcome, not its objective value, is important.

*Instrumentality* involves the relationship as perceived by the individual between a *first-level outcome* and a *second-level outcome*, each with its own valence. First-level outcomes are associated with the work itself and include productivity (quality and/or quantity), turnover, and absenteeism. Second-level outcomes are those consequences (rewards or punishments) that first-level outcomes are likely to produce, including pay increases, promotion, transfer, and group acceptance or rejection. Thus, individual preferences for first-level outcomes are dictated by the extent to which individuals believe that attainment of second-level outcomes will occur. For example, an employee expects that his or her performance (first-level outcome) will lead to a desired result (second-level outcome). However, if there is a perception

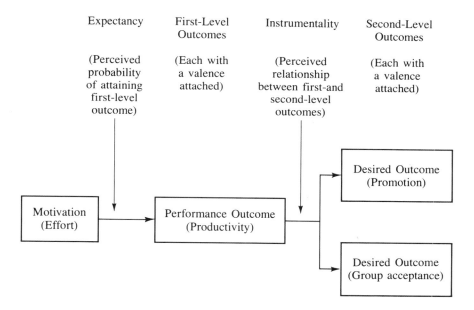

**Figure 5-3**    Expectancy Model of Motivation

that one's effort is not instrumental in producing a desired outcome, there will be little motivation to perform well. For instance, if a patrol officer perceives that the organization does not reward or places little value on social and community service activities, he or she will probably not put much effort into this part of the job. The role police play in the community is significantly influenced by the manner in which police agencies attempt to motivate employees. Figure 5-3 presents an example of the general expectancy model of motivation.

Although expectancy theory does not provide specific solutions to motivational problems, it does help to explain the process of motivation. Furthermore, several clear implications for police managers can be derived from this theory. The first implication is to *clarify expectancies that employee effort will lead to task accomplishment.* If employees are to be motivated to perform well, they must understand what is expected of them and that it is possible for them to attain a desired level of performance. Thus, if a department expects its officers to perform community service activities equally as well as law enforcement activities, this expectation must be communicated throughout the department, and specific methods must be developed (i.e., the way officers are trained and rewarded by managers) that will lead to the accomplishment of such activities.

A second implication is to *relate valued second-level outcomes to performance.* Police managers should attempt to enhance instrumentality or strengthen the beliefs that certain behaviors will lead to valued rewards. Once again, one way to ensure that community service activities will be taken seriously is for managers to base rewards on such performance.

A third implication is to *remember that individual differences must be taken into consideration.* If employees are to be motivated, they must be able to attain rewards that are desirable, or positively valent, to them personally. Some police officers, for example, may be more highly motivated by job satisfaction, others by peer group influences or attention from supervisors, and still others by departmental recognition through improved pay or promotion, and so on. If police managers can take individual differences into account and make highly valent rewards available to their officers, motivational levels should also increase.

In applying expectancy theory to police performance, Van Maanen (1975) measured whether perceptions of "working especially hard" on a particular activity would lead to one of five outcomes: (1) receiving favorable responses from the community, (2) receiving favorable responses from the department, (3) receiving favorable responses from the supervisor, (4) receiving favorable responses from peers, and (5) receiving greater personal satisfaction. The specific activities designed to represent the major areas of a patrol officer's job included field investigation, routine patrol, inspection, administration, service, community relations, and self-development activities. The study was designed to measure the motivation level of recruits during their first thirty months of employment. The results were compared with the motivational levels of a control group of veteran officers. The results were clear: over time, the recruits' motivational levels decreased significantly. Interestingly, the lowest level was recorded at the thirty-month interval, which was similar to, but not as low as, the veterans' level of motivation.

The overall decrease in motivation was basically due to decreased expectancies. This was apparent because the valences or attractiveness of all five outcomes remained relatively constant for the time period examined. This finding suggested a growing perception on the part of the recruits that "working especially hard" was linked to few, if any, of the organization's rewards. With respect to specific reward categories, four of the five declined sharply, including beliefs regarding favorable responses from the community, the department, the supervisor, and fellow officers. Motivation associated with greater personal satisfaction was the only belief that did not decline significantly.

Expectancy theory has been widely tested and applied successfully to many different types of organizations. In general, however, research supporting the theory has been mixed. For example, research tends to support the impact of expectancy and instrumentality on motivation, but not the relationship between valance and motivation (Garland 1984; Behling, Dillard, and Gifford 1979; Campbell and Pritchard 1976). Regardless of the mixed empirical support, expectancy theory is the dominant approach to the study of work motivation, largely because of its clear implications for managerial practice.

**Equity theory.**    The early development of equity theory (Adams 1963) predicted the effects of perceived inequity of pay on job performance. However, the theory has been expanded to include a variety of job inputs (e.g., effort, skills and abilities, knowledge, etc.) found in work environments. According to this theory, individuals compare their own job inputs and job outcomes with others in similar situations. When an inequitable comparison is perceived to exist, tension or dissonance results. The greater the perceived inequity, the greater the motivation to reduce the tension or dissonance. Festinger (1957) first described this concept as part of a general theory of "cognitive dissonance." Individuals may pursue a number of alternatives in order to reduce this dissonance. For example, they may (1) *increase* or (2) *decrease* their *efforts* in order to make their inputs or contributions more equitable with outcomes or rewards. They may also (3) *rationalize* their perceptions by deciding that inputs or outcomes are really greater (or smaller) than originally perceived or that the outcomes being received are really of more (or less) value than previously thought. Finally, individuals may solve the problem by (4) *not associating* with the *comparison other*, by (5) *changing comparison others*, or by (6) *changing the situation*, such as quitting the job or transferring to a new unit or location. Equity theory suggests that each of these methods reduces the dissonance created by the perception of inequity.

Equity theory implies that managers need to "open up" the reward process in order to reduce employee misperceptions. By communicating truthfully with each employee and clarifying expectations, managers should be able to reduce feelings of tension and dissonance. Accordingly, practicing managers should base their rewards as much as possible on objective and tangible (as opposed to subjective) criteria. It follows that employees should be allowed to participate in, but not dictate, the setting of their own goals and objectives and to assist in evaluating their own performance. As a result, individuals who fail to meet expectations will be more likely to understand why their rewards are less than the rewards of more productive employees.

Because individuals have different job inputs (skills, abilities, and knowledge), managers may need to use different performance standards and levels of rewards. Ultimately, however, the best performers must receive the greatest rewards or they will eventually lose their motivation to perform well. The practical application of this concept is critical to police organizations. Frequently, salary increases and promotions are based more on seniority (time spent with the organization) than on actual job performance. Employees often receive yearly across-the-board salary raises regardless of their performance or are promoted on the basis of their seniority or loyalty to the organization, not because of their knowledge or leadership abilities. Such practices reduce motivation to be an outstanding performer. Although police managers are generally required to follow civil service salary structures, they might consider withholding yearly step increases from those employees who did not perform as expected, while granting salary increases to those individuals who exceeded standards of expected performance.

Much of the research on equity theory has focused on pay as the primary outcome (Goodman and Friedman 1971). The failure to include other relevant outcomes in the workplace limits the usefulness of the theory. Nevertheless, it is significant for managers who must deal with civil service salary structures that can decrease motivation for lower-level employees. In many police agencies, for example, patrol officers reach their maximum level of pay within five or six years of initial employment. When this happens, pay increases, other than cost-of-living adjustments, usually come only as a result of promotions. This can create problems because there are a limited number of managerial positions within an organization and many individuals do not want a supervisory role. Such a pay system can force outstanding performers to leave the organization or to seek opportunities in the organization that are of no interest to them. There is no valid reason, for example, why a senior-level patrol officer who is an excellent performer should not be paid a salary equal to, or in excess of, certain managerial positions. Such changes are discussed in more detail in chapter 9.

While equity theory has been most useful with respect to employee motivation and pay, it has also emphasized the importance of comparisons in the work environment. Since inequitable situations can lead to morale, absenteeism, and turnover problems, managers need to develop methods for resolving inequities and for restructuring reward systems.

**Porter-Lawler model.**   In their study of the relationship between motivation and performance, Porter and Lawler (1968) tied expectancy and equity theories together. In so doing, they expanded theory development in this area and further emphasized the complex nature of attempting to determine human behavior. As figure 5-4 illustrates, many different variables need to be considered in predicting what motivates behavior: (1) the value of a reward and (2) perceived effort-reward probability lead to (3) effort, which is affected by (4) abilities and traits and (5) role perceptions, which, in turn, lead to (6) performance (or accomplishment). Performance is mediated by

(7A) intrinsic rewards (e.g., feelings of accomplishment, recognition, and responsibility) and (7B) extrinsic rewards (e.g., working conditions and salary), which are affected by (8) perceived equitability of rewards (i.e., comparing one's own intrinsic and extrinsic rewards with those of others). Each of these variables, in turn, leads to employee satisfaction.

It is important to point out the relationship between work performance and job satisfaction in this model. Figure 5-4 treats performance as the causal variable and satisfaction as the assumed outcome; in other words, *performance leads to satisfaction.* Stated another way, an individual must perform well in order to be satisfied on the job. This proposed relationship is contrary to the human relations view that satisfaction causes performance or that a "satisfied" worker will automatically perform well. Most of the research to date supports the Porter-Lawler view that performance causes satisfaction. Many researchers suggest, however, that these findings are not conclusive and that additional research is necessary. At any rate, enough evidence has been gathered to indicate that satisfaction does not necessarily lead to performance. With these findings in mind, police managers should take a second look at managerial practices based on this particular assumption.

The Porter-Lawler model is comprehensive in that it attempts to explain the relationships among numerous variables, all of which affect the motivational process. Consequently, this model offers a more satisfactory explanation of work motivation and can be valuable to the practicing manager. The model takes expectancy and equity theories into account and proposes that in addition to effort, abilities, traits, and role perceptions affect performance. In other words, there may be a difference between effort and performance due to abilities and traits (i.e., job skills and/or knowledge), as well as to how an individual perceives his or her role in the organization. This analysis explains how employees with low abilities or inaccurate role perceptions may perform poorly even though they exert a great amount of effort, and ultimately, why they may be dissatisfied with their jobs. Based on this information, it again becomes apparent why it is important for managers to take individual differences into account when attempting to motivate employees to their highest levels of performance.

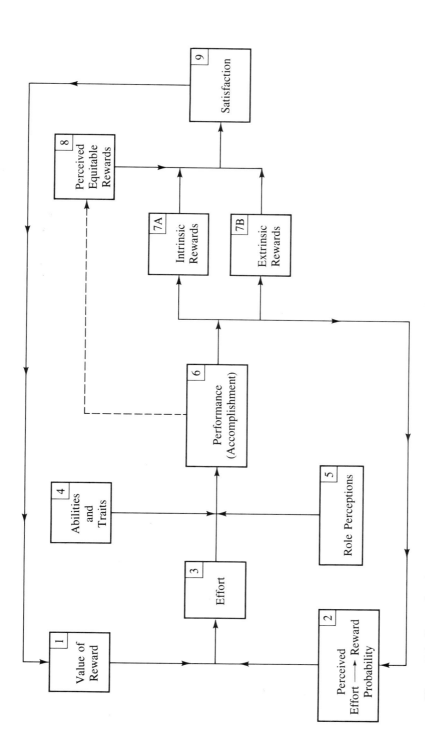

**Figure 5-4** Porter-Lawler Model of Motivation

*Source:* L. W. Porter and E. E. Lawler, III, *Managerial Attitudes and Performance* (Homewood, Ill.: Richard D. Irwin, 1968), p. 165. Reprinted by permission.

The discussion of content and process theories of motivation indicates that managers *can* influence employee motivational levels. To do so, however, requires some knowledge of individual needs, expectations, preferences, and comparisons. By understanding and applying such concepts, astute police managers should be able to improve motivational levels and work performance throughout their organizations. We next turn our discussion to one of the best vehicles managers have to improve motivation, namely, job design.

## Job Design: Work as Motivator

The design, or redesign, of jobs in order to make them more rewarding for employees can have a vital impact on improving employee motivation and performance. This approach can be traced to Frederick W. Taylor (1947) and his attempt to improve worker productivity by "scientifically" designing jobs. As the reader may recall, Taylor designed jobs to be highly efficient by simplifying them and tying productivity to pay. This approach, however, ignored the impact of the individual worker. Subsequently, the Hawthorne studies indicated the importance of considering the human aspects of organizational behavior and management. By ignoring the human element in work design, scientific managers failed to consider that some employees are dissatisfied in jobs that are repetitive and boring, provide little challenge, and over which they have little or no control. Job dissatisfaction can lead to behavior that hurts the organization's effectiveness because it contributes to low morale, absenteeism, and high turnover. Consequently, an attempt should be made to design jobs that are efficient and pleasing to the employees who must perform them.

While scientific management concentrated on *extrinsic* rewards of the job (e.g., pay and fringe benefits), newer approaches focus on *intrinsic* rewards that can be obtained from the work itself, such as feelings of achievement, esteem, and self-actualization. We now turn our attention to a discussion of the major approaches used to improve intrinsic rewards by expanding job content. This form of redesign includes efforts to enlarge and enrich jobs and the use of a job characteristics model developed in the mid-1970s.

## Expanding Jobs

Attempts to fit jobs to individual employee needs in order to improve satisfaction and motivation have emphasized the expansion of jobs. Expansion can take one of two forms: job enlargement or job enrichment. *Job enlargement* refers to expanding the content of a job by increasing the number or variety of tasks of similar difficulty. This is known as *horizontal job loading*, since employees perform a greater number of tasks at approximately the same level of difficulty. The second approach to expansion, known as *job enrichment*, increases both the variety and the importance of tasks. Employees assume responsibility for and control of some tasks normally assigned to those holding a higher (vertical) position in the organization. This is known as *vertical job loading*, since employees perform work that has a greater degree of difficulty. Efforts to expand or load jobs horizontally and vertically are also referred to as job enrichment.

The impetus for loading jobs vertically was provided by Herzberg's (1974) motivation-hygiene theory. As noted previously, this theory states that only factors labeled as "motivators" that are intrinsic to the work itself (higher-level needs such as achievement, recognition, and responsibility) can increase employee motivation to perform. On the other hand, dissatisfiers or "hygiene factors" (such as company policies, supervision, and salary) are extrinsic to the work and, therefore, are not capable of improving employee motivation.

In the 1970s, it was suggested that the performance of patrol officers would improve more by using job redesign based on "motivators" (Baker 1976) than by attempting to change the individual selected for the job (e.g., increasing educational levels). This suggestion became part of a concept known as *team policing*. In general, team policing differs from conventional patrol in at least five aspects, which can be considered forms of job enrichment: (1) geographic stability of the team patrol, (2) a combination of patrol and investigative functions; (3) lower-level flexibility in policy making; (4) maximum interaction among team members, and (5) maximum communication among team members and the community (Sherman, Milton, and Kelly 1973). Through such methods, patrol officers would have greater job responsibilities and recognition and greater chance for achievement and personal growth. (Team policing is also discussed in chapter 8.)

Although job enlargement and job enrichment programs can be beneficial, managers should be aware of several potential problems. Job expansion programs may not *account for individual differences* and, consequently, may not be acceptable to all employees. In other words, the same motivating factors included in a job's redesign may not motivate *all* employees in that job. This, of course, also applies to the team policing concept. Some officers (e.g., those who have been used to working "by the book" for most of their careers) may not feel comfortable with increased levels of responsibility and decision-making authority. Further, as contingency theory suggests, job expansion programs may not be appropriate for all employees.

Another problem that often has an impact on the success of job expansion programs concerns *implementation*. Whenever a major change is introduced into an organization, resistance to the change is likely to result (chapter 11 discusses how resistance to organizational change can be reduced). The team policing concept represents an interesting example of implementation problems. While team policing has received support from many police scholars and some police chiefs, it has not always met with success. In their study of team policing in seven cities, Sherman, Milton, and Kelly (1973) found that team policing either failed or reached only partial success in all seven cities because of (1) a lack of support from mid-level management (who viewed the teams as a threat to their power and, in some cases, actively sabotaged the plans), (2) a lack of dispatching technology that did not allow patrols to remain in their neighborhoods, and (3) a lack of a clear definition of how the role of a team officer differs from that of a regular officer (team officers also were considered an elite group by their peers, who resented not having been chosen for the project). These results clearly show that job expansion programs must be carefully planned and monitored for possible implementation problems.

## Job Characteristics Model

A promising approach to job redesign that attempts to integrate aspects of both job enlargement and job enrichment is the *job characteristics model*. This model, developed by Hackman and Oldham (1976), specifies the conditions under which individuals become psychologically motivated to perform more effectively on the job. The model, shown in figure 5-5, identifies five *core job dimensions* that help to stimulate three *critical psychological states*, which lead to several beneficial *personal and work outcomes*.

The model indicates three job dimensions—skill variety, task identity, and task significance—that result in an individual experiencing *meaningfulness of the work*. *Skill variety* refers to the different activities (skills and tasks) involved in carrying out the work. *Task identity* refers to the degree to which the job requires completion of a whole piece of work from beginning to end. Finally, *task significance* refers to the degree to which the job affects the lives or work of other people.

A fourth job dimension, *autonomy*, refers to the degree to which a job allows the individual freedom, independence, and discretion in scheduling the work and in determining the procedures to be used to carry it out. Autonomous jobs help an individual experience *responsibility for work outcomes*.

The final job dimension, *feedback*, refers to the degree to which an individual obtains direct and clear information about the effectiveness of his or her job performance. Jobs that are designed to provide a high level of feedback to the worker lead to increased *knowledge of the actual results of the work*.

The job characteristics model specifies that by redesigning jobs to increase variety, identity, significance, autonomy, and feedback, the worker's psychological states toward the work will change and should result in improved work outcomes. These work outcomes include greater internal motivation, higher quality of work performance, greater satisfaction with the work, and lower absenteeism and turnover.

It should be pointed out, however, that the model theorizes that only employees who have high *growth-need strength* (i.e., the need for personal

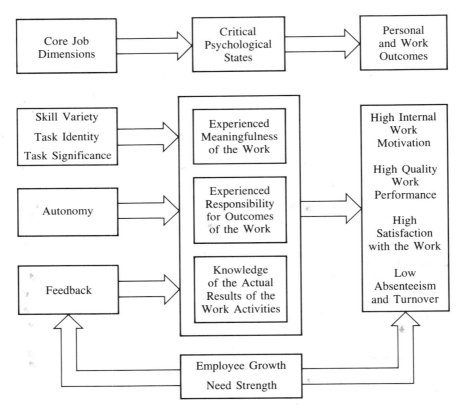

**Figure 5-5** The Job Characteristics Model

*Source*: Adapted from J. R. Hackman and G. R. Oldham, "Motivation Through the Design of Work: Test of a Theory," *Organizational Behavior and Human Performance* 16 (1976):256.

growth and accomplishment) are likely to be affected by the redesign of work advocated by the model. Of course, this recognizes the importance of individual differences.

A number of methods or steps can be taken to enrich jobs (Hackman, Oldham, Janson, and Purdy, 1975). Five steps that can be used to enrich different core job dimensions are identified in table 5-1. As we will discover, each of these steps may have some use in enriching police jobs.

**Table 5-1**    Steps to Enrich Core Job Dimensions

| Job Enrichment Method | Description of Method | Core Job Dimension |
|---|---|---|
| 1. Forming work units | Distributing work in a logical way so that workers have "owner-ship" and a sense of responsibility | Task identity<br>Task significance |
| 2. Combining tasks | Combining tasks that have been functional-ized or specialized into new, larger modules of work | Skill variety<br>Task variety |
| 3. Establishing client relationships | Providing the worker contact with the user of his or her product or service | Skill variety<br>Autonomy<br>Feedback |
| 4. Vertical loading | Increasing worker re-sponsibility for plan-ning, doing, and con-trolling the work | Autonomy |
| 5. Opening feedback channels | Providing the worker with as much direct in-formation as possible about his or her perfor-mance | Feedback |

*Source:* Adapted from J. R. Hackman, G. R. Oldham, R. Janson, and K. Purdy, "A New Strategy for Job Enrichment, *California Management Review* 27(1975):63–65.

Research on the job characteristics model has produced mixed results (Loher et al. 1985); however, given the relatively complex nature of the model, such results are not surprising. Consequently, it is important to point out that several studies have clearly demonstrated the model's ability to effectively enrich jobs (Orpen 1979). The job characteristics model has not yet been tested specifically on police jobs, although one study on a group of correctional officers tested several dimensions of the model (Brief, Munro, and Aldag 1976). The results indicated that those officers with strong higher-order need strength (i.e., recognition, achievement, advancement) responded more favorably to the degree to which jobs were enriched than did officers with weak higher-order need strength. In fact, the researchers concluded that in an institution where a preponderance of the staff sought higher-order needs, low levels of morale could be expected *unless* the employees were offered enriched jobs. We believe that this would be the case in police organizations.

These results support the theoretical orientation of the job characteristics model; that is, employees with high growth-need strength are more likely to be influenced by changing core job dimensions. How this might apply to police jobs is discussed in the next section.

## Traditional Police Job Design: Implications for Policing

Just as police organizations have been criticized for overreliance on the paramilitary model, so too has the traditional design of police jobs. Many police organizations, particularly those emphasizing a legalistic-professional model, have tended to emphasize a narrow perspective concerning the police role. However, with the increasing recognition and acceptance of the complex nature and diversity of that role (Roberg 1976; National Advisory Commission: Police 1973; President's Commission: The Police 1967), new approaches to police work and job design are being debated and implemented throughout the nation (Brown and Wycoff 1987; Eck and Spelman 1987; Goldstein 1987; Williams and Pate 1987; and Skolnick and Bayley 1986).

Police job designs in many agencies are not meeting the requirements of the contemporary police role or the needs of the individual officers performing the job. Since many aspects of police work involve providing needed services, maintaining order, making referrals, and providing temporary solutions to community problems, it is apparent that the job "requires a whole set of human relations and problem-solving skills that can be applied to the wide range of complex situations which police confront daily" (Sandler and Mintz 1974, p. 460). Along with a recognition of the need to change role conceptions and thus job designs has come an emphasis on the recruitment of more highly educated officers. As Goldstein has observed, however:

> without changes in the function and working environment of the police, the potential contribution that these officers could make to policing has not been fully realized. Furthermore, the very qualities we have sought in more educated officers have been smothered in the atmosphere of traditional policing (1987, p. 28).

With these points in mind, we focus on a discussion of the potential for enriching traditional police jobs.

As previously noted, employees who have high growth needs are more likely to be affected by job enrichment practices. Although parts of the job characteristics model have been tested and confirmed on correctional officers, there has been no direct attempt to apply the model to policing. Numerous studies have been done, however, on the work attitudes and personal growth needs of police, individual officer characteristics, and job satisfaction. A closer inspection of several of these studies points to the need, under appropriate conditions, for enriching traditional police jobs.

Lefkowitz (1973, 1974) found that police appear to attach a great deal of importance to the potential gratification of personal needs through their jobs. He discovered that upper-level needs (self-actualization, esteem, and autonomy) are not satisfied through the job, while lower-level needs (security and social) are relatively well satisfied. Van Maanen (1975), on the other hand, found mixed results with respect to growth needs. In his sample of police officers, he found that they are most satisfied with self-actualization and social needs and most dissatisfied with esteem, autonomy, and security. With respect to higher-level needs, these findings are not that dissimilar from

Lefkowitz's; that is, esteem and autonomy needs are not being met. The Van Maanen study further suggested that recruits' motivational levels decrease the longer they are on the job. A more recent study, directly testing the self-actualization needs of Australian police officers (Cacioppe and Mock 1985) supports Lefkowitz's findings. This study notes that self-actualization needs are not often met in traditional police work. Cacioppe and Mock suggest the development of "personal and organizational programs in police departments to enhance the opportunities for self-actualization" (p. 181).

As was noted in the last chapter, some research indicates that more highly educated or intelligent police recruits are more likely to terminate their careers in policing. This may be attributable, at least in part, to the unfulfilled growth needs of officers who are "smothered in the atmosphere of traditional policing." For example, there is some evidence that college-educated officers are less authoritarian (Dalley 1975; Smith, Locke, and Fenster 1970) and more open-minded (Roberg 1978) than their noncollege-educated colleagues. Officers possessing such attitudes are likely to respond unfavorably to highly structured jobs and to bureaucratic, inflexible managerial practices.

Research has further indicated that more highly educated officers may hold differing views on job satisfaction. For instance, one study (Griffin, Dunbar, and McGill 1978) found that as officers' educational levels increase, their feelings of job satisfaction relate to whether or not they feel in control of their own environment—either "externally" (relationship with the public) or "internally" (relationship with the organization). The more highly educated officers believed they were not in control of either their external or internal environment. Unless steps are taken to change these feelings, there is a likelihood of increasing job dissatisfaction, frustration, and ultimately resignation" (p. 181). Another study (Mottaz 1983) on work alienation and the police found that more educated officers tend to place greater importance on self-fulfillment in work and therefore are more sensitive to alienating conditions such as powerlessness and meaninglessness. To reduce alienation on the job, the author suggests that it will be necessary to focus on the officer's tasks and provide greater opportunities for autonomy and accomplishment. In conclusion, "job enlargement and job rotation have, in some cases, reduced alienation in industrial settings, and may also be successful in police organizations" (p. 29).

Traditional police job designs are not meeting the needs of many of those in police work, especially those with higher levels of education. In the final section, we will examine some steps that can be taken to redesign and enrich police jobs.

## Police Job Redesign: Enriching Police Work

As greater emphasis is placed on a broader police role, the focus is not only on responses to crime (and recognition that traditional policing methods have little impact on controlling crime), but also on non-law-enforcement functions that have a vital effect on the quality of life in the community (Goldstein 1987, p. 6). Accordingly, new approaches emphasizing this expanded role concept are being developed that may have a significant impact on police job satisfaction. The most noteworthy are known as community policing and problem-oriented policing (see chapters 8 and 13).

In problem-oriented policing (Goldstein 1979), officers are encouraged to view their role primarily in terms of identifying and dealing with community problems. In attempting to solve these problems, they frequently use alternatives other than those available primarily through the criminal justice system, including counseling, mediation, referral to social agencies, and obtaining services from other public and private agencies.

Although originally designed to reduce the fear of crime in the community, problem-oriented policing can also be regarded as a major job enrichment program. In this approach, patrol is redesigned to broaden officer discretion in an effort to help them determine community problems in their assigned area. Then, in combination with others, they attempt to find solutions to the problems. While "working with others" frequently means other departmental members, it may also include members of public and private agencies outside the department (e.g., health, welfare, fire, transportation, animal control, housing, counseling, etc.). Officers and other "team" members may be quite creative in developing solutions, "perhaps pressuring municipal agencies to carry out existing responsibilities or to invest new resources in an area. They may push for changes in the policies of other government agencies or advocate legislation that would enable police to deal more effectively with a problem that clearly warrants arrest and prosecution" (Goldstein 1987, p. 17).

This approach to job redesign uses many, if not all, of the enrichment methods specified in the job characteristics model (table 5-1). In identifying and solving community problems, for instance, responsibility for planning, implementation, and control is paramount (i.e., vertical job loading). Furthermore, various tasks are combined, new work groups are formed (depending on the defined problem), client or community relationships are enhanced (through increased contact), and feedback channels (especially from the community) are opened. This typifies the use of the expectation-integration (E-I) model, as attempts are made to balance and integrate the expectations of the individual, organization, and community.

Because of the types of enrichment methods "built into" a problem-oriented police job design, motivational levels, especially for those officers with high growth-need strength, would be expected to increase over traditional job designs and even remain relatively high. This would be in sharp contrast to the Van Maanen (1975) findings regarding traditional police job designs, where motivational levels were initially high but declined substantially over time with respect to favorable responses from the community, the department, supervisors, and fellow officers.

The preliminary evidence on the effects of problem-oriented policing on police officer attitudes lends support to the notion that such a job design has a positive impact on job satisfaction. In Baltimore County, Maryland, a policing strategy known as COPE (Citizen Oriented Police Enforcement) was implemented in 1982 and progressed through three stages of development. The third stage emulated Goldstein's (1979) problem-oriented approach, where COPE units analyzed neighborhood problems and then searched for appropriate tactics to solve those problems. In an analysis of police officer

**Police job enrichment may include seeking out citizens to solicit their help in defining and solving neighborhood problems.**

attitudes over the first three years of operation, Hayeslip and Cordner (1987) compared a group of officers participating in COPE with a control group of officers performing traditional policing. The findings indicated that the

COPE officers had higher levels of job satisfaction, more cooperative and service-oriented attitudes about the police role, and more positive attitudes toward the community. Additionally, although COPE officer job satisfaction had been higher than that of control officers at the outset of the project, the difference slightly increased over the three years. According to Hayeslip and Cordner:

> Citizen oriented patrol appears to be a structural change which can contribute to lasting changes in work-related attitudes of police officers. [P]olice officers who are placed into an organizational structure which emphasizes routine motorized patrol may develop potentially problematic work-related attitudes such as cynicism, alienation and rigidity. A citizen-oriented strategy, on the other hand, appears to be a structure which minimizes these potentially problematic attitudes and indeed fosters favorable work-related attitudes, regardless of officers' background (pp. 116–117).

It is important to note the researchers controlled for several important background characteristics (e.g., age, education, and length of service) and found that within each category, COPE officers reported more satisfaction with their assignment than did the control officers with traditional policing. In other words, the attitude changes were caused by the job itself and not by the officers' age, experience, or level of education.

While we have continually emphasized the need to take individual differences into account, this study suggests that the COPE job design had a positive influence on the majority of officers in the program. If similar results can be produced in other police organizations, it may mean that a majority of today's police officers could benefit from a similar redesign of police jobs.

Future research is most likely to reflect that not all police officers will benefit from enriched jobs and others will benefit in different ways. This means that police managers will need to use job expansion methods that offer the most general benefit to their officers and then make individual and work group adjustments as necessary. From this perspective, the importance of applying contingency theory in attempting to match police officers with appropriate job designs becomes clear. Further, the E-I model suggests that community expectations regarding role emphasis must be considered in addition to officer expectations about their jobs. Problem-oriented policing ap-

pears to offer substantial potential in each of these areas. Finally, if enrichment strategies applied to problem-oriented policing turn out to be beneficial to the more highly educated officers being recruited into policing, police
managers and executives will need to place increased emphasis on recruiting
and retaining individuals whose background characteristics are compatible
with the duties required by an expanded police role concept.

## Summary

If organizational and individual goals are to be accomplished, police managers will need to have a basic knowledge of human behavior, motivation,
and job design. Without an adequate understanding of these concepts, it is
not possible to understand what motivates individuals to perform and how
to design jobs to improve performance.
   The concept of individual behavior was discussed and a human behavior
model was presented. Regarding police behavior, two major theories were
presented: predispositional and socialization. The importance of recognizing individual differences was stressed, and the point was made that employees may need to be managed differently, even under similar conditions. The
two major approaches to the study of motivation included: content theories,
which attempt to identify what motivates behavior, and process theories,
which attempt to describe how motivation is energized into behavior. Influential content theories discussed were Maslow's need hierarchy, McGregor's Theory X and Theory Y, and Herzberg's motivation-hygiene theory of
satisfiers and dissatisfiers. The process theories of motivation are known as
expectancy and equity theory. Expectancy theory views individual motivation as a rational choice people make about the rewards they expect to receive before they perform their jobs; several clear implications for police
managers were suggested from this theory. Equity theory states that individuals compare their own inputs and outcomes on the job with others in similar
situations and, when an inequitable comparison between inputs and outcomes is perceived, tension or dissonance occurs. A number of ways individ-

uals attempt to reduce dissonance were described, as well as steps police managers could pursue in order to avoid potential problems resulting from inequitable situations in the workplace.

By tying together both expectancy and equity theories, the Porter-Lawler motivational model greatly expands theory development in this area. It emphasizes the complex nature of human behavior by taking into account a number of variables in attempting to explain the motivational process. Contrary to the human relations approach, the model predicts that performance leads to job satisfaction. Furthermore, the model suggests that in addition to effort, abilities, traits, and role perceptions affect performance. The comprehensive nature of the Porter-Lawler model helps the manager understand why human behavior is difficult to predict and the importance of taking individual differences into account when attempting to increase motivational levels of employees.

The final chapter topic, job design, was described as a potentially significant method of enhancing motivation, satisfaction, and job performance. Expanding jobs to better fit employee needs has taken two general approaches: job enlargement, which expands the content of a job by increasing the number or variety of tasks at the same organizational level, and job enrichment, which expands not only the variety of tasks but also the level at which they are performed. Thus, job enlargement is known as horizontal job loading and job enrichment is known as vertical job loading. One promising approach to job redesign that attempts to integrate aspects of both job enlargement and job enrichment is the job characteristics model. The model specifies that by redesigning jobs to increase variety, identity, significance, autonomy, and feedback, the worker's psychological states toward work will change, which should lead to improved satisfaction and performance.

Although the job characteristics model has not been directly tested on the police, one new approach to police job design, known as problem-oriented policing, appears to include many of the enrichment practices specified in the model. Consequently, motivational levels from officers with high growth-need strength could be expected to increase. Some initial research suggests that police officers who perform problem-oriented policing have higher levels of job satisfaction, a more service-oriented attitude toward the police role, and more positive attitudes toward the community. The future of such an approach toward enriching traditional police work appears promising.

## Discussion Questions

1. Why is the human behavior model important for police managers to understand?
2. Differentiate between the predispositional and socialization theories of police behavior. Which do you think is the most valid?
3. How important do you think Maslow's hierarchy of needs and McGregor's Theory X and Theory Y assumptions are to the practicing manager?
4. Discuss Herzberg's motivation-hygiene theory of motivation and compare this theory with Maslow's need hierarchy.
5. What are the general managerial implications of Vroom's expectancy model of motivation? What does the research on expectancy theory and police performance suggest?
6. In what ways can equity theory be useful to practicing managers?
7. Discuss the significance of the Porter-Lawler model of motivation with respect to the relationship between work performance and job satisfaction.
8. Differentiate between job expansion and job enrichment. Provide an example of how each could be applied to policing.
9. Discuss how the job characteristics model attempts to improve personal and work outcomes. How can this model be applied to traditional police job designs?
10. In general, what does the research indicate with respect to traditional police job designs and officer satisfaction? How would you design police work to meet future needs?

# References

Adams, J. S., "Toward an Understanding of Equity," *Journal of Abnormal and Social Psychology* 67(1963):422–436.

Baker, T. J., "Designing the Job to Motivate," *FBI Law Enforcement Bulletin* 45(1976):3–7.

Behling, O., Dillard, J. H., and Gifford, W. E., "A Test of Expectancy Theory Predictions of Effort: A Simulation Study of Comparing Simple and Complex Models," *Journal of Business Research* 7(1979):331–347.

Bennett, R. R. and Greenstein, T., "The Police Personality," *Journal of Police Science and Administration* 3(1975):439–445.

Brief, A. P., Munro, J., and Aldag, R. J., "Correctional Employees' Reactions to Job Characteristics: A Data Based Argument for Job Enlargement," *Journal of Criminal Justice* 4(1976):225–229.

Brown, L. P. and Wycoff, M. A., "Policing Houston: Reducing Fear and Improving Service," *Crime and Delinquency* 33(1987):71–89.

Cacioppe, R. L. and Mock, P., "The Relationship of Self-Actualization, Stress and Quality of Work Experience in Senior Level Australian Police Officers," *Police Studies* 8(1985):173–186.

Campbell, J. P. and Pritchard, R. D., "Motivation Theory in Industrial Organizational Psychology," in *Handbook of Industrial and Organizational Psychology*, ed. M. D. Dunnette (Skokie, Ill.: Rand McNally, 1976), pp. 84–95.

Dalley, A. F., "University vs. Non-University Graduated Policemen: A Study of Police Attitudes," *Journal of Police Science and Administration* 3(1975):458–468.

Eck, J. E. and Spelman, W., "Who Ya Gonna Call? The Police as Problem-Busters," *Crime and Delinquency* 33(1987):31–52.

Festinger, L., *A Theory of Cognitive Dissonance* (New York: Harper & Row, 1957).

Franz, V. and Jones, D. M., "Perceptions of Organizational Performance in Suburban Police Departments: A Critique of the Military Model," *Journal of Police Science and Administration* 15(1987):153–161.

Garland, H., "Relation of Effort-Performance Expectancy to Performance in Goal-Setting Experiments," *Journal of Applied Psychology* 69(1984):79–84.

Goldstein, H., "Improving Policing: A Problem-Oriented Approach," *Crime and Delinquency* 25(1979):236–258.

———, "Toward Community-Oriented Policing: Potential, Basic Requirements, and Threshold Questions," *Crime and Delinquency* 33(1987):6–30.

Goodman, P. S. and Friedman, A., "An Examination of Adam's Theory of Inequity," *Administrative Science Quarterly* 16(1971):271–288.

Griffin, G. R., Dunbar, R. L. M., and McGill, M. E., "Factors Associated with Job Satisfaction Among Police Personnel," *Journal of Police Science and Administration* 6(1978):77–85.

Hackman, J. R. and Oldham, G. R., "Motivation Through the Design of Work: Test of a Theory." *Organizational Behavior and Human Performance* 16(1976):250–279.

Hackman, J. R., Oldham, G. R., Janson, R., and Purdy, K., "A New Strategy for Job Enrichment," *California Management Review* 27(1975):57–71.

Harris, R., *The Police Academy: An Inside View* (New York: Wiley, 1973).

Hayeslip, P. W., Jr. and Cordner, G. W., "The Effects of Community-Oriented Patrol on Police Officer Attitudes," *American Journal of Police* 6(1987):95–119.

Herzberg, F., *Work and the Nature of Man* (Cleveland, Ohio: World, 1966).

———, "The Wise Old Turk," *Harvard Business Review* 52(1974):70–80.

Herzberg, F., Mausner, B., and Snyderman, B., *The Motivation to Work* (New York: Wiley, 1959).

House, R. J. and Wigdor, L. A., "Herzberg's Dual-Factor Theory of Job Satisfaction and Motivation," *Personnel Psychology* 20(1967):369–389.

Kast, F. E., and Rosenzweig, J. E., *Organization and Management: A Systems and Contingency Approach*, 4th ed. (New York: McGraw-Hill, 1985).

Leavitt, H. J., *Managerial Psychology*, 4th ed. (Chicago: University of Chicago Press, 1978).

Lefkowitz, J., "Attitudes of Police Toward Their Job," in *The Urban Policeman in Transition*, eds. J. R. Snibbe and H. M. Snibbe (Springfield, Ill.: Charles C Thomas, 1973), pp. 203–232.

———, "Job Attitudes of Police: Overall Description and Demographic Correlates," *Journal of Vocational Behavior* 5(1974):221–230.

Likert, R., *The Human Organization* (New York: McGraw-Hill, 1967).

Loher, B. T., Noe, R. A., Moeller, N. L., and Fitzgerald, M. P., "A Meta-Analysis of the Relation of Job Characteristics to Job Satisfaction," *Journal of Applied Psychology* 70(1985):280–289.

Lundman, R. J., *Police and Policing: An Introduction* (New York: Holt, Rinehart & Winston, 1980).

Maslow, A. H., "A Theory of Human Motivation," *Psychological Review* 50(1943):370–396.

McGregor, D., *The Human Side of Enterprise* (New York: McGraw-Hill, 1960).

Mottaz, C., "Alienation Among Police Officers," *Journal of Police Science and Administration* 11(1983):23–30.

Muir, W. K., *Police: Streetcorner Politicians* (Chicago: University of Chicago Press, 1977).

National Advisory Commission on Criminal Justice Standards and Goals, *Police* (Washington, D.C.: Government Printing Office, 1973).

Neiderhoffer, A. E., *Behind the Shield* (Garden City, N.Y.: Doubleday, 1969).

Orpen, C., "The Effects of Job Enrichment on Employee Satisfaction, Motivation, Involvement and Performance: A Field Experiment," *Human Relations* 32(1979):189-217.

Porter, L. W. and Lawler, E. E., III, *Managerial Attitudes and Performance* (Homewood, Ill.: Richard D. Irwin, 1968).

President's Commission on Law Enforcement and Administration of Justice, *Task Force Report: The Police* (Washington, D.C.: Government Printing Office, 1967).

Roberg, R. R., *The Changing Police Role: New Dimensions and New Issues* (San Jose, Calif.: Justice Systems Development, 1976).

———, "An Analysis of the Relationship Among Higher Education, Belief Systems, and Job Performance of Patrol Officers," *Journal of Police Science and Administration* 6(1978):336–344.

Sandler, G. B. and Mintz, E., "Police Organizations: Their Changing Internal and External Relationships," *Journal of Police Science and Administration* 2(1974):458–463.

Schwab, D. P., DeVitt, H. W., and Cummings, L. L., "A Test of the Adequacy of the Two-Factor Theory as a Predictor of Self-Report Performance Effects," *Personnel Psychology* 24(1971):293–303.

Sherman, L. A., Milton, C. H., and Kelly, T. V., *Team Policing: Seven Case Studies* (Washington, D.C.: Police Foundation, 1973).

Skinner, B. F., *Beyond Freedom and Dignity* (New York: Knopf, 1971).

Skolnick, J. H., *Justice Without Trial* (New York: Wiley, 1966).

Skolnick, J. H. and Bayley, D. H., *The New Blue Line* (New York: Free Press, 1986).

Slovak, J. S., "Work Satisfaction and Municipal Police Officers," *Journal of Police Science and Administration* 6(1978):462–470.

Smith, A. B., Locke, B., and Fenster, A., "Authoritarianism in Policemen Who Are College Graduates and Non-College Police," *Journal of Criminal Law, Criminology and Police Science* 6(1970):313–315.

Taylor, F. W., "The Principles of Scientific Management," *Scientific Management* (New York: Harper & Row, 1947).

Van Maanen, J., *Pledging the Police*, (Ph.D. diss., University of California at Irvine, 1972).

———, "Police Socialization: A Longitudinal Examination of Job Attitudes in an Urban Police Department," *Administrative Science Quarterly* 20(1975):208–228.

Vroom, V., *Work and Motivation* (New York: Wiley, 1964).

Williams, H. and Pate A. M., "Returning to First Principles: Reducing the Fear of Crime in Newark," *Crime and Delinquency* 33(1987):53–70.

# CHAPTER 6

# Leadership Theory and Practice

Leadership is a crucial managerial activity. All police officers function as leaders when they attempt to obtain compliance, if not cooperation, from other persons in performing a task, solving a problem, or accomplishing a goal or objective. Patrol officers, investigators, and other operational personnel act as leaders when dealing with victims, suspects, informers, and witnesses. All police managers and executives—sergeants, lieutenants, captains, deputy chiefs, assistant chiefs, chiefs of police, sheriffs, and undersheriffs—also have leadership responsibilities.

## Defining Leadership

*Leadership* is a difficult concept to define. Stodgill (1974) identifies eleven possible perspectives or definitions, including leadership as a function of group processes, the art of inducing compliance, a form of persuasion, the exercise of influence, a power relationship, and an instrument of goal achievement. Davis (1972, p. 100) suggests that leadership is "the ability to persuade others to seek defined objectives enthusiastically." Hunsaker and Cook (1986, p. 303) define leadership as "a process that involves actions taken by one person to influence the behavior of one or more others toward goals desired by the leader." The most important concepts in these definitions are "ability and actions," "process and persuasion," "enthusiastic others," and "goals and objectives." Leaders act to convince other persons to support, if not work hard to accomplish, a purpose.

Sometimes a distinction is made between leadership and management. *Leadership* may be considered more esoteric and abstract and primarily concerned with the future. *Management* may be identified with the more immediate and pragmatic concerns related to administering an organization, program, or work unit. Although the degree to which managers are concerned with the abstract or the pragmatic, or the present or the future, may vary with orientation or organizational level, effective management and leadership include a consideration of all these factors. While management includes more than functioning as a leader, the terms managing and leadership are used interchangeably in this chapter.

As we will discuss, police leadership consists of two major components or roles: style and community. An important part of each of these roles is the knowledge—technical, managerial, historical, and political—necessary to function effectively. Unlike the managers in many organizations, police managers at all levels must be aware of and understand problems and issues that transcend the immediate concerns of their jobs. Police personnel must have technical knowledge and understand the significance of its application within a historical, political, and organizational context. Of particular importance is the political context in which police work. As what Muir (1977) calls "streetcorner politicians," police officers have enormous power and a great deal of discretion.

Leaders must also understand the managerial concepts and skills associated with their position. The belief that police managers should have in-depth technical knowledge concerning how operational personnel perform their jobs is controversial. Students of organization and management are often taught that as they move up in the organizational hierarchy they should become less involved with the specifics of work and more concerned with general and strategic concerns. While this also applies to police managers, they cannot abandon an interest in, or knowledge about, the specific requirements of the tasks of police work.

In many police departments, there are so few personnel that even the chief executive is invariably involved in operational matters. But more important, a significant product—perhaps the most significant—of police departments is the behavior of officers and other personnel. If what police officers do and why they do it is not understood by leaders at all levels, there is little reason to believe that police departments can be managed effectively. In addition, the ability to persuade others to pursue goals and objectives in police organizations is often directly related to the officers' perceptions of the leader's technical competence and managerial ability.

## Leadership: Style and Community Role

The style aspect of leadership focuses on the body of knowledge that has been developed to explain what is characteristic about how managers or leaders function. These unique characteristics are associated with a *leadership style*. Just as there are different styles of policing, there are also different styles of leadership. What is the individual's managerial or leadership style? What is the most effective leadership style? Attempts to answer these two questions have resulted in the development of three schools of thought or theories concerning leadership effectiveness: *trait*, *behavioral*, and *situational* or *contingency*. This chapter will attempt to explain these three theories and to describe selected research concerning police managerial styles. In addition, there is a discussion about how different styles can be used to manage employees. Although these style theories are applicable to leadership inside and outside the organization, they primarily apply to the internal management or administration of police organizations.

The *community leadership role* of the police manager, primarily at the executive level, is partially that of philosopher because the major issues of policing must often be addressed. The philosophical role bridges the gap between the style of the manager and his or her community activities. The manager's position on integrity or ethics, the rule of law, the rights and responsibilities of dissenters, the appropriate policing model for the community, whether police should be crime fighters or social service workers, and so on is part of this philosophical dimension of leadership. In this role, the manager helps to define the values of the organization for both the employee and the community and also helps to identify the issues for debate and discussion that will shape the future of policing.

The manager's involvement in the community's decision-making processes governing the allocation of resources and expectations about police activity is also of concern. Should a police executive be an active or passive voice in this process? To what degree should the police manager attempt to influence this process by forcefully identifying the police position on issues? To what degree should the manager allow elected officials and others to dictate the direction of the organization? Invariably, when a police leader becomes directly involved in the decision-making process of the community, he or she assumes a political role. When engaged in this role, the manager must be alert to the distinction between the politics of *preference* and *responsiveness*. The former is motivated by self-interest, whereas the latter is more consistent with the mutuality of interests shared by many citizens.

# Understanding Leadership:
# Influence, Authority, Power, Politics, and Conflict

In addition to the leadership components identified in the previous section, five important concepts require explanation: influence, authority, power, politics, and conflict. Leadership and the organizational behavior of employees are associated with these components, but they are not directly considered part of the leader's style and community role. Each of these concepts is briefly addressed to provide a foundation for understanding leadership.

## Influence and Authority

*Influence* is more general than either power and authority but it is closely related to them. Influence is the process of altering, impacting, or changing attitudes, behaviors, values, or beliefs. The process involves the person (or persons) who attempts to change the behavior and the person, group, or target of the influence process. Leadership, in a general sense, is a process by which the manager attempts to influence others individually, in a work group, in the organization, and in the community.

*Authority* is the right to lead. In police organizations, the right to lead is granted by the police agency that provides rank and status. The designation of sergeant, lieutenant, or captain indicates that the person is a manager in an official leadership position. The formal methods of granting authority suggest that the organization has the right to designate leaders and implicitly assume that members of the organization will accept that authority. However, acceptance does not always occur because authority also comes from the "bottom up"; that is, authority is granted by employees. Leaders only have the authority that the employees are willing to give them. If employees do not perform as expected most of the time, leaders, for all practical purposes, have no authority.

Employees accept and reject authority and influence. Rejection in-cludes failing to perform productively, violating policies and procedures, disobeying laws, or being absent. Usually these behaviors occur when em-ployees are not being "watched" or supervised. This is a significant problem because police officers often are unsupervised for long periods. During this time, they can avoid their responsibilities or hide their activities by visiting friends, sleeping, or failing to take action when problems are observed.

## Power

Authority is related to the right to command; *power* is related to the ability to lead or command, or more precisely, to influence others. When one per-son is influenced by another person, he or she is subject to the power of the influential person. Any personal characteristic or ability or practice that al-lows one person to influence another is related to power. While authority gives some power, there are a number of ways to influence others even when an individual is not in a position of authority (Kuykendall and Unsinger 1979). There are sources of power and distinct means of utilizing that power. French and Raven (1959) have identified five sources or types of power: re-ward, coercive, legitimate, referent, and expert.

*Reward power* requires giving something of value to others. By virtue of their formal authority, managers have reward power, however, this power varies considerably by rank and type of organization. Public managers, in-cluding police, usually have less reward power than managers in the private sector because they have only minimal influence on employees' salaries and fringe benefits. But even police managers can reward officers through per-formance evaluations and positive feedback. *Coercive power* is the "other side of the coin" and involves taking away (or threatening to take away) something valued. Coercion uses fear by threatening to or actually denying such things as money, job, promotion, status, acceptance, or love. Belief in the primacy of coercive power as a tool to control employees is based on the same logic that resulted in the development of the legalistic-professional model of policing.

*Legitimate power* is similar to the concept of authority because persons grant to others the right to influence them. Managers have legitimate power because employees give them the right to direct their behavior. Primarily, this happens because the manager is in a position to reward and punish the employee, but it may also be related to the personality, ability, or knowledge of that manager. Police officers are excellent examples of individuals with legitimate power because they represent the legitimate force of government in the use of coercive power.

*Referent power* is given to others by the desire to associate with or identify with another person. This desire is usually based on that person's personality, attractiveness, resources, or accomplishments. Officers who are admired, for whatever reason, may have considerable influence. *Expert power* is granted to those people who have knowledge or expertise. To the degree that an individual is influenced by the ideas, advice, or guidance of another, expert power is at work. The managers who combine legitimate with referent or expert power are often the most influential persons in a police organization. However, managers and subordinates may disagree on who has the real "expertise." One of the most frequent complaints voiced by patrol officers about managers is that managers lose their understanding of "street reality" and become more concerned with their own political and organizational survival (e.g., see the list of the norms of the "street cop" culture in chapter 4). Supposedly, the higher in the organization a manager goes, the less expertise and understanding he or she has about the "street."

## Consequences of Using Power

Numerous studies have attempted to analyze the impact of using French and Raven's sources of power. Selected results of this research follow:

1. A decrease in reward power may result in an increase in the use of coercive power.
2. The use of coercive power results in greater resistance than does reward power, and individuals using coercive power are not as well liked as those emphasizing the use of reward power.

3. The more legitimate the use of coercion, the greater the conformity; the greater the strength of the threatened coercive act, the greater the conformity.

4. Coercive power is effective in the short run in securing compliance but it may also produce fear, frustration, alienation, and a desire for revenge among employees. The resulting negative impact on performance may result in greater reliance on coercion.

5. The more expert a person is perceived to be in one area, the more likely he or she is to be capable of exerting influence in other areas.

6. The use of expert power has the strongest correlation with employee performance because it is closely related to a climate of organizational trust.

7. Referent power has an impact similar to expert power if it is essentially emotional in nature, but the influence may be short-lived and is easily manipulated for selfish gain.

8. Legitimate power, or the authority of position, is often depended on initially by the manager but continued and sole utilization of this type of power creates dissatisfaction, resistance, and frustration among employees.

9. Reward power can be most influential in determining employee behavior; however, tangible rewards like pay and promotion may be limited by factors outside the manager's control. The rewards available to the manager may not be valued by the employee or employees may come to feel manipulated (Luthans 1985, pp. 445–460).

Based on these research findings, police managers may be able to initially obtain effective performance by virtue of their position (legitimate power), but eventually expert and even referent power become important if higher levels of effectiveness are to be realized and sustained. While reward and coercive power are important, both can be overused and dependence on coercive methods can be, and often is, counterproductive. To be successful, police officers need to become capable and respected, even admired, task performers before they can become effective managers.

## Politics

At times the concept of power has negative connotations; however, it is not power itself that is negative but how it is used. How power is acquired and used is related to *politics*. Organizational politics involves the use of power and authority to enhance or protect a person, a career, a work unit, or a department. The political activity of leaders may be motivated by the concerns of the organization but often self-interest is the driving force. Organizational politics can involve *maneuvering*, *infighting*, and *"game playing."* Often such activities take place outside the legitimate system of influence (i.e., the organization hierarchy or chain of command). The informal organization and the police culture discussed in previous chapters are the result, at least in part, of the political activity that takes place in police organizations.

"Playing politics" in an organization is facilitated by "knowing the right people," forming coalitions, and co-opting those whose support is needed to accomplish an objective or goal. Knowing the right people involves *networking*. Individuals, regardless of their rank or position, who know influential persons often have an advantage. An individual can also advance his or her interest by obtaining the support of others and forming a coalition. Unions and associations are examples of this approach. Finally, power can be exercised politically by attempting to co-opt those persons or groups who disagree with, or may impede progress toward, a goal. Getting these persons involved with others who may neutralize their opposition is one approach to co-optation (White and Bednar 1986, pp. 449–545). Another approach involves obtaining support by agreeing to what the individual or group wants in areas not related to the immediate goal or objective.

Leadership and playing politics are interrelated concepts. Managers must continually decide how they will use their power and for what purpose. They cannot always depend on the rational processes of the organization to obtain a successful outcome. "Being political" may be the reality of organizational life in some police departments. However, when authority or power are utilized illegally, unethically, or to advance personal or work group interests to the detriment of the organization, playing politics becomes more destructive than constructive.

## Conflict

*Conflict* is intrinsic to organization life. The strategies and tactics for identifying and resolving conflict require more discussion than can be provided in this chapter. However, a general understanding is necessary because leaders must often attempt to resolve conflict between individuals, work groups, and organizations. Conflict involves the perception of incompatible goals and the resistance or interference of one or both parties in attempting to achieve goals. Conflict can have both positive and negative results. It may lead to new ideas, creative solutions, and more effective ways to perform a task or service. However, when conflict is negative it can produce distrust, resentment, and anger, which may impede the effective resolution of problems and impair productivity.

Managers can attempt to address the negative consequences of conflict by engaging in *bargaining*, by providing a *broader goal* toward which the parties in conflict can aspire, or by involving a *third party* to assist in working out the disagreement (White and Bednar 1986, pp. 458–461). At times, however, conflict about certain issues may remain an integral part of organization life. For police organizations, the role debates discussed in chapter 2 are examples of such conflict. For some issues there may not be a permanent solution; rather, there is an ongoing debate that may either result in creative problem solving or damage morale and affect organizational productivity.

# Leadership Styles

The concepts of influence, authority, power, politics, and conflict provide an important foundation for understanding leadership. Historically, leaders' or managers' styles have been discussed from three major theoretical perspectives: trait, behavioral, and situational or contingency. Each of these theories will be discussed along with several leadership perspectives that do not fit into one of the major theories. This discussion is followed by a presentation of selected research concerning the leadership styles of police managers.

In addition, an example will be given as to how general "types" of police employees can be managed using a contingency model.

### Trait Theories

This approach studies effective leaders to determine their *traits*. Often these leaders are considered to be *"great men or women"* who were born with traits or abilities that led them to greatness. However, research in this area produced little agreement on qualities of outstanding leaders or how they could be identified (White and Bednar 1986, pp. 491–492). There are two other components of this theory: *intuitive* and *research*. The intuitive component is based on general observation and judgment. The problem with this approach is that the traits identified are too general and difficult to define (e.g., honesty, industriousness, sincerity, intelligence, dependability, friendliness). The research perspective is more systematic in that careful consideration is given to definitions and the measurement of traits.

Stodgill (1974) analyzed a number of studies and identified twenty-six leadership traits that were listed three or more times. The most frequently listed traits were technical skills, friendliness, task motivation, supportiveness, interpersonal skills, emotional control, intellectual ability, willingness to assume responsibility, decisiveness, and personal integrity. Interviews with heads of some of the nation's largest companies, universities, and governmental agencies found that these "superleaders" are happiest when working and have five distinct characteristics:

1. Vision—the creation of a desirable state of affairs that is inspirational.
2. Communication skill—the ability to present the vision clearly, effectively, and in a manner that enlists support.
3. Persistence—"staying the course" regardless of the obstacles encountered.
4. Empowerment—the ability to design a system that utilizes the energy of others to accomplish the vision.
5. Organizational ability—the capacity to oversee activities, learn from mistakes, and make use of what is learned to improve organizational performance (French, Kast, and Rosenzweig 1985, p. 201).

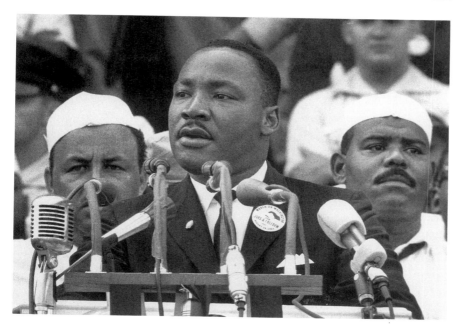

**Martin Luther King, Jr. (1929–1968) possessed all the characteristics of a "super leader."**

The police also approach leadership from the trait perspective. In a survey of 1,665 police chiefs, the most important characteristics identified for executives were integrity, common sense, intelligence, open-mindedness, self-control, and self-confidence. The management skills considered to be the most important were to maintain morale, develop subordinates into effective teams, relate to the community, organize personnel, maintain internal review and control, communicate effectively, and establish priorities and objectives (National Advisory Commission 1977, pp. 22–26). Table 6-1 presents a list of traits commonly associated with leadership effectiveness.

The major criticisms of trait theory include inconsistent research findings and the inability to distinguish between successful and unsuccessful leaders or even nonleaders. Also, as noted earlier, the definition and measurement of traits is problematic. Leaders may be effective because of what they have learned rather than because of some inner trait. In addition, situational demands may be more important than traits in determining desirable leadership qualities (White and Bednar 1986, pp. 491–493).

Despite these criticisms, this approach remains important in leadership discussions. Kenny and Zacarro (1983) found that, to some degree, leadership effectiveness can be attributed to stable characteristics. For example, the ability to identify group members' needs and goals is an important trait in determining who will emerge as a leader. Those persons who have the in-

**Table 6-1**  Trait Theories of Leadership

| Intuitive Component | Research Component | Police Component |
|---|---|---|
| Honesty<br>Intelligence<br>Friendliness<br>Responsibleness<br>Sincerity<br>Industriousness | Integrity<br>Intellectual skills<br>Supportiveness<br>Responsibleness<br>Emotional control<br>Motivation<br>Task competency<br>Decisiveness<br>Persistence<br>Interpersonal skills<br>Communication skills<br>Vision | Integrity<br>Intelligence<br>Common sense<br>Open-mindedness<br>Self-control<br>Self-confidence |

sight to determine needs and to adjust their behavior accordingly have the type of flexibility that appears to be important in leadership effectiveness. However, criticisms of the trait theory resulted in a focus on leaders' behaviors rather than their qualities. These major behavioral theories are presented and briefly discussed in the following paragraphs.

## Behavioral Theories

This approach to the study of leadership concentrates on the *activities* or *behavioral styles* of leaders. Rather than measuring traits, this perspective focuses on patterns of behavior that can be observed and measured. The emphasis is on what leaders do rather than on their individual traits (Roberg 1979, pp. 160–161). Initial research established the groundwork for future inquiries by describing three basic leadership patterns of behavior or styles: authoritarian, democratic, and laissez-faire (Luthans 1985, p. 476). These patterns are important because they identify a major recurring theme in behavioral theories; namely, the degree to which leaders allow subordinates to participate in deciding what will be done and how it will be done in the work environment.

The *authoritarian* manager directs employees, allowing minimal participation. The *democratic* manager encourages the employees to participate, and the *laissez-faire* style essentially allows complete freedom, providing little or no direction (Luthans 1985, p. 476). Subsequent research has built on these important insights and added to the understanding of leadership behavior. In examining the summaries of the following studies, remember that although the terms used to describe leadership characteristics are different, they are essentially based on two factors: the individual employee or work group and the task to be performed or goal to be achieved. Managerial behavior can vary in the degree of interest and concern shown to the employee and work group, and the tasks and goals of the organization. Behavioral theories attempt to determine which managerial styles are most effective.

**Ohio State and University of Michigan studies.**   In the 1940s and 1950s, researchers at Ohio State University analyzed over 1,700 descriptors of behavior that could be related to leadership. They found two primary dimensions or characteristics related to effectiveness: initiating structure and consideration. *Initiating structure* refers to the degree to which a leader attempts to define and organize tasks for subordinates or followers. Leaders who tend to emphasize a high degree of structure are *task-oriented*. *Consideration* refers to the degree to which the manager is aware of and sensitive to *employee needs*. A high degree of concern for consideration is reflected in an emphasis on friendship, mutual trust, and respect, interest in an employee's ideas, and sensitivity to the feelings of others. At about the same time, University of Michigan researchers also conducted studies utilizing similar variables. The two major variables they focused on were the degree to which leaders were either *employee-centered* or *production-centered*.

Based on the two important variables discovered in these studies, it is possible to identify four leadership styles:

1. High concern for both structure (or production or task or goal) and consideration (or employees).

2. Low concern for both structure and consideration.
3. High concern for structure, low concern for consideration.
4. Low concern for structure, high concern for consideration.

The research that has attempted to assess these four styles has been mixed. Some effective leaders tend to emphasize either a high degree of structure or a high degree of consideration. Often subordinates tend to prefer a leader who is primarily concerned with consideration, while the leader's superiors tend to prefer one who is more concerned with initiating structure. Although the Ohio State research did not identify one style as being consistently most effective, other researchers found that a high concern for both structure and consideration is often related to greater employee satisfaction and productivity (White and Bednar 1986, pp. 494–496; Hunsaker and Cook 1986, pp. 308–310; Roberg 1979, pp. 160–165).

**The managerial grid.**   One of the best-known leadership models based on the Ohio State and Michigan research is Blake and Mouton's *managerial grid* (1964, 1968, 1978, 1986). They utilized the variables of *production* (similar to initiating structure and emphasizing tasks and organization needs and goals) and *people* (similar to consideration and emphasizing relationships and individual needs and goals) to construct a grid that identifies five managerial styles. The grid axes, horizontal for production and vertical for people, measured the degree of concern for both variables on a 1–9 scale. This results in five styles of management, numerically characterized as 9/9, 5/5, 9/1, 1/9, and 1/1. While Blake and Mouton state that all five styles are utilized by managers, they believe that the 9/9 style is the most effective.

The *9/9 or team style* (high concern for both production and people) emphasizes the integration of task and human requirements in realizing goals. The *5/5 or middle-of-the-road style* (moderate concern for both production and people) tends to stress production but with an awareness that morale cannot be ignored. The *9/1 or task style* (high concern for production, low concern for people) tends to concentrate on production or the tasks to be performed with little regard for employee needs. The *1/9 or country club style* (low concern for production, high concern for people) tries to avoid conflict and maintain good fellowship by being nice to people even when they have performance problems. Finally, *the 1/1 or impoverished manager* (low concern for both production and people) is generally indifferent to both organizational and employee needs, emphasizing instead organizational rules and regulations.

In their most recent analysis of leadership, Blake and Mouton (1986) also incorporated the trait approach, or what they call *elements*, in identifying effectiveness. They believe executives should take the initiative, inquire into the background and substance of problems, and express their opinions while encouraging others to do likewise. Executives must also be adept at resolving conflict, making decisions, and critiquing or evaluating organizational activities.

Figure 6-1 identifies the relevant variables in these two behavioral theories. *Organizational goals* are related to initiating structure and production, whereas *employee needs* are essentially the same as consideration and people. Managers can have a high concern for both organizational goals and employee needs (HH), neither one (LL), or a mixed concern (HL or LH). Each combination identifies distinctly different managerial behavior.

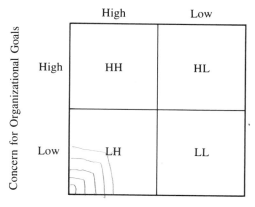

**Figure 6-1**   Behavioral Theory Factors

Behavioral theories of leadership have been criticized on several grounds. The Ohio State and Michigan studies, for example, could not identify a most effective style. Increasingly, researchers found that effectiveness could not be separated from the specific circumstances in which the leader functioned. By the 1960s, situational or contingency theories began to emerge in an attempt to explain the complex interaction of traits, behavior, and situational variables.

## Situational or Contingency Theories

By the 1960s and 1970s, the limitations of both the trait and behavioral theories were becoming increasingly evident. A third major set of variables began to be influential—those concerned with the *managerial problem or situation*. Research to determine which leadership styles were most effective in different types of situations resulted in contingency theory.

**Continuum model.** Tannenbaum and Schmidt (1973) developed one of the better-known approaches to contingency leadership. They base their styles on the degree of managerial authority and the amount of freedom exercised by subordinates. At one extreme is a *boss-centered* or autocratic leadership style; at the other extreme is the *subordinate-centered* or democratic style. The three factors that determine the manager's style are forces in the manager, forces in the subordinates, and forces in the situation.

*Forces in the manager* include his or her value system, confidence and trust in subordinates, managerial inclinations, and feelings of security. What are the basic assumptions that managers make about employees (e.g., Theory X or Theory Y)? How much participation should they be allowed? How much does the manager trust his or her subordinates? How knowledgeable and competent are those subordinates?

Managerial inclinations also influence both values and the degree of confidence in subordinates. Is one style more comfortable than another? Finally, the manager's feelings of security or lack thereof also influence style choice. The more the manager relinquishes control over decision making, the greater the risk, or unpredictability, of the outcome. Insecure managers are more likely to emphasize structure and control and deemphasize employee participation.

*Forces in the subordinate* that leaders should consider in selecting a leadership style are the degree of their:

1. Need for independence
2. Readiness to assume responsibility for participation in decision making
3. Tolerance for ambiguity
4. Perceived importance of the decision or problem
5. Understanding of and commitment to organizational goals
6. Possession of the required knowledge, skills, and experience
7. Expectation of being asked to participate in decisions

Subordinates who are independent, responsible, and tolerant of uncertainty; who value the problem being addressed; who understand organization goals; who are knowledgeable; and who expect to participate in decision making respond more to democratic approaches. On the other hand, subordinates who do not possess one or more of these characteristics should be treated less democratically; that is, the manager should become more autocratic.

*Forces in the situation* are the final set of factors that determine a manager's style. These include type of organization, group effectiveness, type of problem, and time constraints. Some organizations by virtue of their tasks, community expectations, or superiors may prefer one style over another. Managers must also decide how effectively groups work together. Excessive conflict detracts from participatory problem solving. Also, if the problem is outside the knowledge, skills, and experience of subordinates, their participation in solving the problem may not be meaningful. Lastly, the manager may not have time to allow subordinates to participate.

**Fiedler's contingency theory.** Another major contributor to the situational approach is Fiedler (1967). This approach is unique because it suggests that a leader's effectiveness can be improved by *structuring the job to fit his or her style*. Fiedler argues that it is easier to change a leader's work environment than to change his or her style or personality. Not only does leadership performance depend on the manager, it also depends, perhaps to a greater degree, on the organization. Although an attempt can be made to develop leaders, an organization can also be designed to accommodate the leadership styles of current or future managers (Roberg 1979, pp. 170–171).

The basis for Fiedler's ideas is a twofold leadership style that emphasizes *tasks* (production, organization) and *human relations* (individual goals, relationships among people). Fiedler characterizes the situations facing managers by the strength of the *leader-employee relationship*, the degree to which the work or *task is structured* or spelled out, and the degree to which the leader has the *authority* and *power* formally attributed to the leader's position.

When the leader-employee relationship is strong, when the work is structured, and when the leader has authority, the style should be *task-directed*. In this type of situation the leader is accepted and liked, and employees need and want direction. The leader should also use the task-directed style when situational conditions are unfavorable because employees do not want to work and need firm direction. When the tasks or activities are not highly structured or the leader's relationship with the employees is not well established and accepted, he or she should use a *human relations approach*. Showing more concern for relationships and the people involved, and emphasizing cooperation in determining tasks and activities, is most effective in this type of situation.

**Path-goal theory.** House and Mitchell's (1975) *path-goal approach* is another important contingency or situational theory of leadership. They believe that a leader's effectiveness is determined by *subordinate motivation*, *ability to perform*, and *job satisfaction*. Leaders motivate subordinates by clarifying the paths utilized to accomplish goals. The most important factors are the expectations of subordinates and the belief that performance will lead to desired results or rewards. This approach is related to the expectancy theory discussed in chapter 5.

Four types of leadership are identified: directed, supportive, participative, and achievement-oriented. *Directed leadership* lets subordinates know what is expected of them, maintains standards of performance, and expects compliance with these standards. This style is most effective when subordinates work on ambiguous (as opposed to clear and easily understood) tasks. When expectations are unclear, the manager's role is to ensure that subordinates understand how they are to perform.

*Supportive leadership* is characterized by friendliness, approachability, and concern for the needs of subordinates. This style is most effective when tasks are stressful, frustrating, or unsatisfying. When engaged in such endeavors, employees need psychological and emotional support more than expectation clarification, although that continues to be important.

*Participative leadership* involves consulting with employees, asking for suggestions, and using employee input in decision making. This approach to leadership results in helping employees understand what is expected of them. It also tends to create a greater commitment to goals, a greater feeling of control, and more ego involvement. Usually, employees who participate in decisions that influence their work life develop a sense of ownership about the process and results of those decisions.

*Achievement-oriented leadership* involves setting challenging goals for subordinates and expecting them to strive hard to realize those goals. This style tends to assume that subordinates are responsible, will work hard, and can be successful. This leadership style usually results in subordinates' striving for higher standards and having more confidence in their ability to perform effectively. This is particularly true when employees are performing ambiguous, nonroutine tasks.

**Employee maturity theory.**   The last contingency theory to be discussed was developed by Hershey and Blanchard (1977). While this theory has little empirical support, it has added to the conceptual development of leadership styles. Hershey and Blanchard argue that effective leadership is the result of the emphasis given to *task* and *relationship* behavior as they relate to different types of *situations*. Task behavior is defined as the degree to which leaders engage in one-way communication by explaining when, where, and how tasks are to be accomplished. Relationship behavior is defined as the extent to which a leader engages in two-way communication by providing emotional and facilitating support. This results in four possible leadership styles: telling, selling, participating, and delegating. The types of situations can be analyzed by the degree of maturity of the employee, or the degree to which employees are competent and willing to work.

The *telling style* (high task, low relationship) is characterized by one-way communication in which the manager defines the subordinates' roles and tells them what, how, when, and where to perform. The *selling style* (high task, high relationship) uses two-way communication and emotional support to get subordinates to psychologically "buy into" decisions. The *participating style* (low task, high relationship) involves two-way communication and facilitating behavior to encourage shared decision making. The *delegating style* (low task, low relationship) lets followers "run their own show." Delegating is considered to be the most effective style with employees of high maturity, whereas participating should be used with somewhat less-mature workers. For employees with low to moderate maturity, the selling style is considered most effective. When employees are organizationally immature, a telling orientation is appropriate. This model has been utilized to assess police managers and as a basis for suggesting how to manage different police employee "types." This research will be presented later in the chapter.

Figure 6-2 depicts a general integration of the contingency theories discussed in this section. Managers can have different levels of concern relative to the extent of employee participation in work-related decisions and to the emphasis given to integrating and balancing organizational goals and employee needs. These emphases are a function of such factors as managerial inclinations, situational forces, and employee maturity.

Contingency leadership theories have received mixed empirical support. The research on which each theory (except Hershey and Blanchard) is based provides some support; however, studies conducted separately have not always provided verification. This does not mean that the theories do not have value. On the contrary, each one identifies variables that leaders need to be aware of when deciding what style to employ and how to make decisions. In addition, there is considerably more empirical support for the contingency approach to leadership than for either trait or behavioral theories. Leaders will often have to alter or modify their styles to maximize their ef-

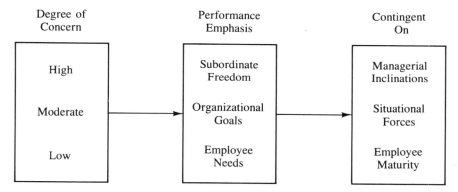

| Degree of<br>Concern | Performance<br>Emphasis | Contingent<br>On |
|---|---|---|
| High | Subordinate<br>Freedom | Managerial<br>Inclinations |
| Moderate | Organizational<br>Goals | Situational<br>Forces |
| Low | Employee<br>Needs | Employee<br>Maturity |

**Figure 6-2**   Contingency Theories of Leadership

fectiveness. Understanding the factors that may make this necessary will enhance the probability of being successful.

## Recent Trends in Leadership Research

Several new perspectives on leadership have emerged in recent decades that do not fit into one of the three theoretical categories. We will briefly discuss the reciprocal approach, the postheroic leader, attributional theory, and implicit theories (Siegel and Lane 1987, pp. 507–517) and Peters and Waterman's (1982) views on organizational excellence.

The *reciprocal approach* is based on the concept of mutual influence; leaders influence followers and vice versa. Instead of considering subordinates or followers as homogeneous groups, each leader-follower or manager-subordinate relationship needs to be examined separately. Contingency theories tend to identify an "average" or "typical" leadership style to be used in a "typical" situation, which results in a failure to understand what is unique about the dynamics of the interaction between a leader and each follower.

Bradford and Cohen (1984) take a somewhat different approach to analyzing leadership. They believe that behavioral and contingency theories include assumptions about managers that prevent the realization of excellence. Managers are placed at the center of the action and are expected to know everything that is going on in their units, to be task-competent, and to solve any problem. Effective leadership has come to be associated with a *heroic role* conception. The unreasonable expectations associated with this role identify a standard of performance that is unrealistic. Instead, managers do not depend enough on subordinates and may come to feel inadequate.

Social psychologists have long studied leadership within the context of *attribution theory*. While not new for behavioral scientists, attribution theory has only recently been applied to management. This theory attempts to explain the causes of leader and follower behavior. To what do leaders and followers attribute the successes and failures of their endeavors? Beliefs held by leaders and subordinates about why things happen shape their behavior in subsequent activities. The leader is an information processor, who observes subordinate behavior, collects information about it, and attributes that behavior to certain causes. Subsequent leader behavior is the result of the analysis of those causes.

*Implicit theories* of leadership suggest that the degree of effectiveness is primarily the result of the subordinates' perceptions of the leader and not leader behavior. If this is accurate, then most of the leadership research to date is flawed because follower perceptions have not been adequately taken into account. It is possible that this will be the next frontier in leadership research, eclipsing the contingency approach. Understanding follower perceptions of leadership may replace traits, leader behavior, and situational factors as the primary basis for research and leadership training.

It is difficult to determine the impact of these theories. It seems likely that one or more will be incorporated into contingency theory because most of the theories identify factors that leaders may wish to consider when adopting a management style. As a result, contingency theory will become more complex and more predictive of obtaining successful results.

Another important perspective related to leadership is concerned with the "principles" that managers should emphasize in order to ensure organizational excellence (Peters and Waterman 1982). These eight principles are listed, in an abbreviated form, as follows:

1. There should be a preference for action rather than undergoing endless analysis and committee meetings.
2. An organization should stay close to clients or customers.
3. The organization should decentralize into small groups or units and encourage them to be independent and innovative.
4. The importance of productivity should be emphasized by working through people. Managers must make employees aware that their best efforts are necessary if the organization is to be effective.
5. Managers should be actively involved in the essential activities of the organization and they should promote the values that are important to success.
6. The organization should do the things it knows best.
7. There should be as few people as possible in upper-level management and a limited number of organizational levels.
8. Organizations should be decentralized to encourage innovation but centralized for the most important organizational values (e.g., serving the client, active involvement of managers, employee participation, ethical behavior).

While this approach to *organization excellence* has received widespread attention, it is not without its critics. Some of the companies that Peters and Waterman (1982) identified as excellent have had financial and managerial difficulties. Some critics have suggested that this approach is simplistic and fails to consider the environment in which organizations operate, government regulations, and other factors (*Businessweek*, 1984).

Perhaps more important, will these eight principles, if applied to police organizations, ensure organizational excellence? Of course, the answer to this question is unknown but they might be somewhat useful as a leadership framework. Stressing the importance of employees, maintaining close ties with the community, and getting managers involved in the nature of the work are advocated in this book. Having a specific set of values, and communicating them, is also an important consideration. However, having a preference for action, doing what the organization knows best, maintaining a lean staff and few managerial layers, and decentralizing to encourage innovation may prove less useful as guides for excellence in police organizations.

For example, a preference for action suggests that police should be highly proactive and this may not always be appropriate in a democratic society. Many decisions in police work (e.g., whether or not to have foot patrol) should probably be discussed extensively before being implemented. Also, what police do best is largely a function of their role in a particular community, and this role may be so diverse that no specific service can be emphasized. The nature of a police bureaucracy, often with numerous layers and a large staff, may be the result of factors outside managerial control (e.g., civil service systems, the police union). Finally, while decentralization to enhance independence and innovation is at times useful in police organizations, historically it has also contributed to problems of abuses in police authority.

## Research on Police Leadership Styles

A limited amount of research has been done on the stylistic tendencies of police managers and it has been based on all three theories. One trait study has already been identified. Other trait research includes Price (1974), who studied the emergence of women in police leadership roles. She found that women tended to have more of the traits associated with leadership effectiveness. Her subjects—women supervisors and managers—tended to be more emotionally independent, intellectually aggressive, flexible, and self-confident than their male counterparts. She also found women leaders were more "liberal" and creative than men.

Pursley (1974) studied what he called traditional and nontraditional chiefs of police. He found that the nontraditionalist's style was characterized by a willingness to delegate and involve subordinates in decision making. In contrast, the more traditional chief executive tended to emphasize structure (or organization goals) and wanted to control the work of subordinates.

Kuykendall (1977) used Blake and Mouton's managerial grid to assess the leadership styles of twenty-five executives in the San Francisco Police Department. Overall, the executives were found to often use what Blake and Mouton consider the most effective grid style (i.e., the 9/9 or team manager). However, these executives tended to change styles as activity changed. When they thought about how to manage and when they set goals and objectives, they were team-oriented; but when they implemented plans and evaluated performance, they changed styles and became less effective, at least as determined by the grid model. Swanson and Territo (1983) also used the grid to identify the styles of 104 police supervisors and managers in four states. They found that 40 percent preferred the 9/9 style, while about 29 percent preferred the 9/1 (or task) approach. The remaining supervisors (31 percent) were about evenly divided among the other three styles.

Perhaps the most extensive study of police managerial styles was conducted by Kuykendall (1985). Using the managerial grid, he analyzed the styles of 225 police managers, representing over one-hundred police agencies in four states. The research instrument identified managerial styles in four areas of performance: philosophy of management, planning and goal-setting orientation, implementation of plans, and evaluation of personnel (Hall, Harvey, and Williams 1973).

The findings indicate that as activity changes, so does the manager's style. As Blake and Mouton define effectiveness, the majority of police managers tended to use the more effective styles (team and middle of the road) in the philosophical and planning and goal-setting activities and the less effective styles (task, country club, and impoverished) during implementation and evaluation activities.

The last study to be discussed is based on contingency theory. Kuykendall and Unsinger (1982) used the employee maturity model developed by Hershey and Blanchard to assess the styles of 155 police managers, representing over one-hundred police agencies in four states. As previously discussed, these styles are based on the degree of emphasis managers give to task (similar to production) and relationship behavior (similar to people) and how they assess employee maturity. The four possible styles, as noted, are telling, selling, participating, and delegating. It was found that police managers tend to be most effective in using styles with a high task emphasis (telling and selling) and least effective in the styles requiring a low task orientation (participating and delegating). Finally, and perhaps most significantly, it was discovered that police managers rarely employ the delegating style, suggesting that they have a difficult time allowing employee participation in decision making.

The available research concerning police managerial styles has been limited in its usefulness. Assessments using Blake and Mouton's managerial grid and Hershey and Blanchard's employee maturity contingency model provide some interesting insights into police manager's styles. However, both of these leadership models are suspect because it is not clear whether or not police managerial, and as a result organizational, effectiveness is enhanced by their use. In the absence of more reliable and valid research, the only reasonable conclusion is that very little is known about what makes an effective police manager. One limited attempt to address this problem is presented and discussed in the following section. The Hershey and Blanchard (1977) leadership model, as adapted by Kuykendall and Roberg (1988), is used to describe how different types of police employees can, in general, be effectively managed.

## Managing Police Employees

The police employee "types" discussed in this section are the result of discussions with over 400 participants in lower- and mid-level police management training programs (Kuykendall and Roberg 1988). During these discussions, the police managers tended to classify employees in terms of their perceptions of *general productivity*, emphasizing the quality and quantity of work performed without consideration of unique or specific police problems. Three important variables were identified: degree of motivation and competence (either high, moderate, or low) and work-related attitudes (either positive or negative). *Motivation* is essentially the manager's perception of how hard the employee works. *Competency* refers to job knowledge and the skills and techniques needed to perform effectively. A positive or negative *work-related attitude* is the degree to which the employee actively expresses support of, and commitment to, organizational goals and objectives. Table 6-2 identifies the characteristics of each of the six employee types identified by the managers.

Table 6-3 identifies, in general, the most effective styles to use in managing each employee type. The styles suggested for each type of employee are the ones perceived by police managers as needed to maintain a performance level, possibly realize some improvement in performance, or simply respond to the problems associated with the type described. It is also important to remember that more than one style may be necessary for each type of officer.

**Rookies.**   As neophytes, rookies are primarily concerned with proving themselves as police officers. Consequently, their primary frame of reference is the expectations of the organization. Rookies tend to have positive work-related attitudes and are highly motivated; however, they are not very competent initially. While usually interested in the work, they have not mastered the knowledge and skills necessary to perform effectively. Assuming that they have the ability (which is not always the case), rookies have the potential to become highly competent.

The maturity level of the rookie is considered to be low; therefore, the *telling* style with considerable structuring of task requirements is required. As the rookie demonstrates his or her competency, the selling style should be employed more frequently. When the manger stresses relationship behavior, it is appropriate to provide feedback on both the employee's attitude and his or her performance.

**Table 6-2** Police Employee Typology

| Employee Type | Employee Characteristics | | |
|---|---|---|---|
| | Motivation | Positive Work-Related Attitudes | Competency |
| Rookie | High | High | Low |
| Worker | Moderate-High | High | Moderate-High |
| Star | High | Moderate-High | High |
| Cynic | Low-High | Low-High | Moderate-High |
| Retiree | Low | Low-Moderate | Moderate-High |
| Depleted | Low | Low | Low |

*Source:* J. Kuykendall and R. R. Roberg, "Police Manager's Perceptions of Employee Types: A Conceptual Model," *Journal of Criminal Justice* 16, no. 2 (1988):134. Reprinted by permission.

**Workers.** This type of employee tends to be moderately motivated, has generally positive work-related attitudes, and is either moderately or highly competent. Often, workers' increasing familiarization with the job or lack of advancement results in somewhat of a decline in motivation without a decline in attitude. This change may be accompanied by the development of important interests outside the organization. Basically, workers are responsible, dependable employees who perform an "average to good day's work" and cause few problems.

In responding to this type of employee, the basic managerial style should be *participating*, although selling may occasionally be required. Workers are basically competent and responsible, therefore a task emphasis is not often necessary. The manager needs to encourage an open and candid dialogue about tasks and be supportive of the employee's endeavors. Positive feedback for significant performance accomplishments should be provided.

**Table 6-3**  Matching Managerial Styles with Employee Types

| Employee Type | Maturity | Managerial Style |
|---|---|---|
| Rookie | Low | Basic: Telling<br>Secondary: Selling |
| Worker | Moderate | Basic: Participating<br>Secondary: Selling |
| Star | High | Basic: Delegating<br>Secondary: None |
| Cynic | Low-High | Basic: Selling<br>Secondary: Telling<br>          Participating |
| Retiree | Low | Basic: Telling<br>Secondary: Selling |
| Depleted | Low | Referral: Professional<br>       Assistance |

*Source:* J. Kuykendall and R. R. Roberg, "Police Manager's Perceptions of Employee Types: A Conceptual Model," *Journal of Criminal Justice* 16, no. 2 (1988):136. Reprinted by permission.

**Stars.**  Stars are highly motivated and highly competent but may have only moderately positive work-related attitudes. From a managerial perspective, some stars tend to be too openly critical of traditional practices. The aggressive pursuit of excellence often places a strain on organizational protocol. However, they tend to be talented, they work hard, and they are ambitious.

This type of employee is highly mature in an organizational sense; consequently, the *delegating* style is most effective. Within the limits of making a constructive organizational contribution, stars should be given as much latitude as possible. The manager-star relationship is more one of two peers than superior-subordinate. Unfortunately, some stars may become workaholics who develop stress-related problems that may have a negative impact on both the employee and the organization. Managers may have to encourage this type of employee to moderate his or her organizational commitment.

**Cynics.**   While cynics tend to be competent, their motivation and attitudes are a function of specific tasks rather than the work in general. They tend to be pessimistic and suspicious, even distrustful. Their cynicism may be general in scope or directed toward specific aspects of the job. When the cynicism is directed toward a particular task, the motivation level is low and the attitude is negative. Cynics are either stars or workers in performing those tasks they consider to be important but they become indifferent if not destructive in other areas, particularly those they view as being incompatible with their definition of the police role.

   This is probably the most difficult type of employee to manage because while competent, the cynic's motivation and attitude is a function of the task to be performed. The maturity level of this type of employee ranges from low to high based on task interest and perception of importance. Managers must utilize several styles to respond effectively. The basic style should be *selling* but with a readiness to change to *telling* or *participating*. The telling style should be utilized in dealing with inadequate task performance while the participating style is most effective when this employee performs as a worker or a star.

**Retirees.**   This type of employee also tends to be competent but has a low level of motivation and a moderate or negative work-related attitude. Performance is at the minimum acceptable level or lower. Retirees are disenchanted with their job as a result of personal problems, a loss of interest in the intrinsic nature of the work, proximity to retirement, or a combination of these factors. Whatever the specific cause, this employee is unwilling to perform even though he or she is competent. This type of employee is of low maturity organizationally. The most appropriate style is *telling* with a willingness to use a selling style if performance improves. However, until the retiree performs at a minimally acceptable level, the manager should specify task requirements.

**Depleted.**   This type of employee has low organizational maturity. The depleted employee has no energy, is disinterested and mistake-prone, and tends to function below an acceptable level of performance. These employees fit the classic "burned out" syndrome and cannot be managed in any conventional sense, nor can they be ignored. Employees who are depleted should be removed from the police operational environment and referred to appropriate professionals (e.g., medical doctor, psychologist, or other counselor) for assistance because managers do not usually have the resources or skills needed to help depleted employees.

# Leadership: Community Role

As noted in the first part of this chapter, leadership includes both stylistic and community concerns. The community role involves attempting to balance and integrate community and organization expectations, including interaction with other law enforcement and criminal justice agencies. This role is particularly important for police managers who have the burdensome responsibility of attempting to make the role of police compatible with democratic society.

## Community Leadership

Wasserman (1982) suggests that a police manager, particularly the chief executive, should become a *community leader*. He believes managers should be proactive, open and honest about police operations, and available to all segments of the community. Farmer (1984) argues that openness about police matters will actually improve police effectiveness rather than make it more difficult for the police to do their job. He thinks police need an intimate relationship with the community to ensure maximum effectiveness. Obtaining citizen input into major policy decisions is one approach to establishing this intimacy.

**A police executive, functioning as a community leader, addresses a town meeting.**

The community leadership role of police managers, particularly executives, also involves responding to and influencing *social change*. According to Reiss (1985), this includes developing and participating in community research projects that facilitate problem solving. Such activities may result in the police having a broader concern for both the causes of problems and the quality of life in the community. However, when doing this, managers may have a tendency to look too much to the past and emphasize traditional, often reactive, strategies and tactics. This tendency can be overcome if police are willing to rely more on research findings in policy and program development. The more informed managers are, the more likely their participation in social change will be meaningful and effective.

## Leaders and the Political Process

The active involvement of police leaders in the community will result in a number of dilemmas. The more community participation, the more effort managers must expend to balance and integrate organizational and community expectations. Issues concerning how responsive police should be to community groups will have to be resolved again and again, as interests of one group are balanced with those of another and with legal requirements and employee concerns.

Potts (1983) believes that this is part of the police responsibility because they have both a *social* and *governmental* role. The police–democratic conflict is that the police must control yet be controlled. For police leaders, the key to understanding and living with this conflict is awareness that responsible administrative behavior is essentially a *political* issue. As such, the community, and therefore political, role of police leaders requires them to provide guidance and direction while working with citizens, elected officials, and other criminal justice personnel in the development of important policies. According to Potts:

> The emphasis must be on institutional relationships. [Those individuals] directing the police agency must remain attentive to their gatekeeper function. They must recognize that they need to work in concert [while] . . . representing diverse [community and employee] interests. Through representations of . . . differing societal needs [police leaders] assure that policy making will be democratic (1983, p. 168).

The community involvement of police leaders requires that they make a distinction between "good" and "bad" politics. Good politics is the *politics of responsiveness*, in which the police are open, share information, and are sensitive to community inputs in the planning and policy formulation process. Bad politics is the *politics of preference*, in which community representatives and elected officials intrude (often based on self-interest) in a non-public, often secretive, manner in an attempt to influence the decision-making processes in the police department (Farmer 1984).

In the political-watchman model, police leaders are either victims of or active participants in bad politics. The legalistic-professional model is so sensitive to the problems of political corruption that leaders attempt to divorce themselves from the political decision-making process. They want to remain either politically uninvolved or neutral. The community-service and rational-contingency models are more sensitive to the political realities of police work. But both models distinguish between the "bad" politics of preference and the "good" politics of responsiveness. At times the distinction between "good" and "bad" politics is vague; consequently, it is not always clear how police can be responsive but not discriminatory.

## Police as Ministers of the Law

The importance of community and political roles of police and police managers is underscored by the manner in which the police enforce the law. Police do not literally enforce the law, rather they function as *ministers of the law* in deciding who will be stopped, who will be arrested, and, at times, who will be punished. This exercise of discretion is critically important in democratic society because police officers and organizations often decide who will and who will not be brought into the criminal justice system. This means, as noted in chapters 1 and 2, that many of those decisions may have low visibility.

Police officers often decide "cases" (e.g., a drunk in public, a loud party, a domestic dispute) based on their own values and judgments. Organizations, by establishing priorities about how resources should be utilized and how policies and procedures should be developed, determine who will and who will not be arrested or issued a citation. For example, an organization may instruct its officers not to issue a traffic citation for speeding unless the violator is exceeding the speed limit by five or ten miles per hour.

The ministerial role of the police emphasizes the importance of community input in terms of reviewing police decisions and having a voice in what police do and how they allocate their resources. However, this voice must be representative of all "communities," lest the politics of preference, rather than responsiveness, prevail.

## Police Leaders as Statesman

Sherman believes that police leaders should be *statesmen*. The professionalism that has emphasized the development of managerial skills needs to be tempered by values and politics. Police leaders need to strive to improve by examining past "failures" and testing new strategies. These new strategies should emphasize prevention based on learning more about the community's social life and human relations. The strategies should also reflect an interest in the needs of the entire community and use research to guide police behavior in developing programs and in police–citizen encounters.

Sherman further believes that instead of undertaking *new* approaches to policing, leaders have tended to be more concerned with *survival* than in accomplishing organizational goals. Accordingly, trying new approaches that might result in a more productive police response is too risky for the professional manager whose vision is limited to current strategies and technical competence. It is important to change this perspective because the police leader's values about strategies and behavior are influential in the development of the work culture of an organization.

Sherman notes that as statesmen, police leaders should infuse their organization with the "right" values by becoming "a leader of a democracy, . . . who can transcend the current values of the day and lead both police and the public into accepting a better set of values and strategies for policing" (1985, p. 462). Statesmanship requires a "constant dialectic between expertise and accountability, [and] between . . . research and public demands" (p. 465).

Although this view of police leadership is intriguing, it has the potential of creating an *elitist* attitude among those who see themselves as statesmen. Such a conception of leadership may result in the belief that only the "leader," and not the employees and community, has the "right" values and strategies that will lead to success. While police leaders can be statesmenlike in moderating a dialogue about police values and strategies, their views may be no more valuable or useful than those of a community or group of employees.

## Summary

The role of police managers is to balance and integrate the expectations of the community, organization, and employees. Awareness of the different types of power, the varying styles of managing subordinates and the broader responsibility of police leaders should help managers become more effective.

The stylistic tendencies of leaders were discussed from three theoretical perspectives: trait, behavioral, and contingency. Each theory has made an important contribution to the understanding of leadership effectiveness; however, the contingency approach has probably been the most influential.

Trait theory emphasizes the characteristics of individuals in leadership positions. Behavioral theory is concerned with the pattern of activity of managers. Contingency theory takes into consideration the leader, employee, work group, and organizational problem. Contingency theory further recognizes that effectiveness is a function of how the leader is able to consider all these factors and adjust accordingly. Other leadership and related theories were also noted but these theories, except for the one concerned with organizational excellence, are not as prominent as the trait, behavioral, and contingency theories.

Leadership research on police managers has been limited. Recent studies suggest that managers may be more effective when engaged in planning and goal setting than when implementing plans and evaluating personnel. Police managers also appear to be flexible in selecting styles, using two and often more styles as situations change. Police leadership research has also included an attempt to use the employee maturity model as a basis for managing different types of police employees. Using this model, six types of employees were identified: the rookie, the worker, the star, the cynic, the retiree, and the depleted.

Police leaders need to understand that police work is often political work. The legalistic-professional model with its emphasis on separating police from the political process failed to acknowledge the differences between the "good" and "bad" political reality of the police role. Both the community-service and rational-contingency models tend to stress the importance of police involvement in "good" politics. The police leader as statesman who avoids an elitist perspective provides an example of how managers can be politically responsive without being politically corrupt.

## Discussion Questions

1. Define leadership and distinguish between leadership and managing.
2. Define influence, authority, and power as they relate to leadership.
3. Identify and define the five types of power. What are the consequences of using the different types of power?
4. Explain the trait theory of leadership and give examples of this leadership approach. What are the criticisms of trait theory?
5. Explain the behavioral theory of leadership and give examples of this leadership approach. What are the criticisms of behavioral theory?
6. Explain the situational or contingency theory of leadership and give examples of this leadership approach. What are the criticisms of the situational or contingency theory.
7. Identify and explain at least three of the more recent trends in leadership research?
8. Summarize the major findings of the research that has been conducted on police leadership styles.
9. Describe the six types of police employees and explain how each one should be managed based on the Hershey and Blanchard leadership model.
10. Discuss the community role of police managers. To what degree do you think police should take a leadership role in the community? How can research findings be used by police leaders?

## References

Blake, R. R. and Mouton, J. S., *The Managerial Grid* (Houston: Gulf Publishing, 1964).

———, *Grid Organization Development* (Houston: Gulf Publishing, 1968).

———, *The New Managerial Grid* (Houston: Gulf Publishing, 1978).

————, *Executive Achievement* (New York: McGraw-Hill, 1986).

Bradford, D. L. and Cohen, A. E., *Managing for Excellence* (New York: Wiley, 1984).

*Businessweek*, "Who's Excellent Now?" November 5, 1984, pp. 76–78.

Davis, K. *Human Behavior at Work*, 4th ed. (New York: McGraw-Hill, 1972).

Farmer, D. J., *Crime Control: The Use and Misuse of Police Resources* (New York: Plenum Press, 1984).

Fiedler, F. E., *A Theory of Leadership Effectiveness* (New York: McGraw-Hill, 1967).

French, J. R. P., Jr. and Raven, B., "The Bases of Social Power" in *Studies in Social Power*, ed. D. Cartwright, (Ann Arbor, Mich.: Institute for Social Research, 1959). Cited in Luthans, F., *Organization Behavior*, 4th ed. (New York: McGraw-Hill, 1985), pp. 449–457.

French, W. L., Kast, F. E., and Rosenzweig, J. E., *Understanding Human Behavior in Organizations* (New York: Harper & Row, 1985).

Hall, J., Harvey, J. B., and Williams, M., *Styles of Management Instrument* (Conroe, Texas: Teleometrics International, 1973).

Hershey, P. and Blanchard, K., *Management of Organization Behavior*. (Englewood Cliffs, N.J.: Prentice-Hall, 1977).

House, R. J. and Mitchell, T. R., "Path-Goal Theory of Leadership," *Organizational Behavior and Industrial Psychology*, eds. K. N. Wexley and G. A. Yurkl (New York: Oxford University Press, 1975), pp. 177–186.

Hunsaker, P. and Cook, C. W., *Managing Organizational Behavior* (Menlo Park, Calif.: Addison-Wesley, 1986).

Kenny, D. A. and Zacarro, S. J., "An Estimate of Variance Due to Traits in Leadership," *Journal of Applied Psychology* 68(1983):678–685.

Kuykendall, J., "Police Leadership: An Analysis of Executive Styles," *Criminal Justice Review* 2, no. 1(1977):89–102.

————, "The Grid Styles of Police Managers," *American Journal of Police* 4, no. 1(1985):38–70.

Kuykendall, J. and Roberg, R. R., "Types of Police Employees: A Managerial Analysis," *Journal of Criminal Justice* 16, no. 2(1988):131–138.

Kuykendall, J. and Unsinger, P. C., *Community Police Administration* (Chicago: Nelson-Hall, 1979).

———., "The Leadership Styles of Police Managers," *Journal of Criminal Justice* 10, no. 4(1982):311–322.

Luthans, F., *Organizational Behavior Modification and Beyond* (Glenview, Ill.: Scott Foresman, 1985).

Muir, W. K., *Police: Streetcorner Politicians* (Chicago: University of Chicago Press, 1977).

National Advisory Commission on Criminal Justice Standards and Goals, *Police Chief Executive* (Washington, D.C.: Government Printing Office, 1977).

Peters, T. J. and Waterman, R. H. Jr., *In Search of Excellence* (New York: Warner, 1982).

Potts, L. W., *Responsible Police Administration: Issues and Approaches* (Tuscaloosa, Alabama: University of Alabama Press, 1983).

Price, B. R., "A Study of Leadership Strength of Female Police Executives," *Journal of Police Science and Administration* 2, no. 2(1974):219–226.

Pursley, R. D., "Leadership and Community Identification: Attitudes Among Two Categories of Police Chiefs," *Journal of Police Science and Administration* 2, no. 4(1974):414–422.

Reiss, A. J., Jr., "Shaping and Serving the Community: The Role of the Police Chief Executive," in *Police Leadership in America*, ed. W. A. Geller (New York: Praeger, 1985), pp. 61–69.

Roberg, R. R., *Police Management and Organizational Behavior: A Contingency Approach* (New York: West, 1979).

Sherman, L. W., "The Police Executive as Statesman," in *Police Leadership in America*, ed. W. A. Geller (New York: Praeger, 1985), pp. 446–459.

Siegel, L. and Lane, I. M., *Personnel and Organizational Psychology*, 2nd ed. (New York: Richard D. Irwin, 1987).

Stodgill, R. M., *Handbook of Leadership: A Survey of Theory and Research* (New York: Free Press, 1974).

Swanson, C. R. and Territo, L., *Police Administration* (New York: Macmillan, 1983).

Tannenbaum, R. and Schmidt, W. H., "How to Choose a Leadership Pattern," *Harvard Business Review* (May–June, 1973), pp. 162–180.

Wasserman, R., "The Governmental Setting," in *Local Government Police Management*, ed. B. L. Garmire (Washington, D.C.: International City Manager's Association, 1982), pp. 30–51.

White, D. B. and Bednar, D. A., *Organizational Behavior* (Boston: Allyn and Bacon, 1986).

# Human Resource Management

As we have stressed throughout the book, human resources are an organization's most precious commodity. In police organizations, personnel are particularly important because their skills, attitudes, values, and enthusiasm determine to a substantial degree the nature of the police role in a community. While the development of these employee attributes is influenced by other factors, such as group processes, leadership styles, motivation techniques, and organization and job design, the personnel system, or management of human resources, is also critical.

Gordon (1986, p. 5) uses the term *human resource management* to describe what are usually discussed as personnel issues in police management. She defines human resource management as "the use, development, assessment, reward and management of individual organizational members or worker groups." Human resource management includes areas of concern such as selection, employee development, management of career growth, evaluation of performance, determination of compensation, and labor relations.

A discussion of police personnel matters, or human resource development, can be addressed both generally and in terms of specific police issues. This chapter will present a general overview of human resource management in police organizations. Chapter 9 identifies specific contemporary police management issues, including some that are often considered to be part of human resource management (e.g., affirmative action, women and minorities, stress, and labor relations). The general discussion in this chapter will include an identification of the major problems and processes associated with the selection, training, performance and evaluation, and development of police officers.

Any discussion of police personnel and their development requires an understanding of the community's *social, political, administrative,* and *economic* environment. To what degree is the population homogeneous or heterogeneous? To what degree do elected, appointed, or influential citizens attempt to involve themselves in personnel matters? Who is responsible for the selection and development process? Is it the police agency (a centralized personnel unit responsible for selection and promotion of all government employees), or an areawide organization that may serve more than one police department? How much money is available to support the personnel system?

What salaries and benefits are to be given to employees? What is the available labor pool? What are the general economic conditions? The answers to these questions determine the approach and limitations in the design and implementation of police career development systems.

Although many states have attempted to standardize part of the personnel process (e.g., selection, training, promotion, and some aspects of evaluation) through the creation of statewide standards, commissions, or organizations (e.g., the California Commission on Peace Officers Standards and Training), there is still considerable variation. In addition, in states with standards commissions, some communities do not participate in the personnel process and therefore are not obligated to adhere to specified requirements. Further, not all aspects of career development are covered in the standards established (e.g., evaluation systems, most promotional processes, and salary and benefits).

## Career Development: Scope and Purpose

*Career development* is the identification and work-life enhancement of the human resources of an organization. The appropriate persons must be identified, selected, prepared, and provided the experiences that will allow them to realize their full potential. The purpose of career development is to utilize human resources in the most productive manner possible. Achieving this goal requires more than just a personnel management system, although such a system is essential.

A management commitment to career development reflects an awareness that the potential capability of an organization can only be realized if the employee is allowed to fully develop his or her job-related interests and abilities. Four steps must be taken to provide an appropriate foundation for achieving effective career development in police organizations:

1. Identification of the tasks performed and the requirements necessary to perform those tasks.
2. Identification of individual attributes and interests, including an ongoing assessment of those attributes and interests.

3. Comparison of task requirements with the attributes and interests of available human resources.
4. Development of programs to integrate task requirements with individual attributes and interests (Los Angeles County Sheriff 1973).

The identification of task requirements is essential in designing jobs or positions and in determining the knowledge, skills, and values required to perform in the existing jobs or positions. The attributes and interests of both prospective and current employees must be compared with position requirements to determine those skills that can be prerequisites for employment or assignment and those that must be taught through informal or formal training. As knowledge and skill requirements for a position change over time (as may the interests of the individuals in that position), developmental and growth experiences are also essential (Dunnette and Motowidlo 1976).

To illustrate some of the important issues in this regard, we will discuss an example of decisions that must be made for entrance (and possibly promotion) in police departments. These decisions are listed as questions relating to one specific task—driving an automobile:

1. Should applicants be required to have a license or should they be trained to drive by the organization?
2. Assuming that applicants should be required to have a driver's license, at what degree of proficiency should they be able to drive?
3. Is the driving of a car by a private citizen the same as the type of driving done by a police officer? If not, what are the differences and how important are those differences?
4. Is there a body of knowledge and skills available to use in the development of a program to enhance driving ability? If there are different ideas about how to enhance driving ability, which ones should the agency use? How much will the program cost? Is it worth the costs, given the benefits that might be derived? Does the agency consider the potential legal liability resulting from inappropriate driving as part of the cost?
5. Once officers are trained, do they have to be retrained periodically to ensure a minimal level of proficiency? How will this proficiency be evaluated? How often? By whom? How often will this training have to take

place? How much will this training cost? Will the benefits of the training justify the costs? Should individuals be promoted who have not demonstrated a given level of proficiency in driving?

6. Do all officers have to be trained and retrained or do some already have the required skills upon entrance? Do employees lose proficiency at the same rate? If not, how does the organization distinguish between those employees who have the skills and those who do not? And between those who retain proficiency and those who do not? Is it worth the effort and cost to even attempt to distinguish between employee skills or should all employees receive the same initial and subsequent training?

7. Are there benefits to be derived from the training, other than the knowledge and skills acquired? Is retraining of officers one mechanism to help officers improve their motivation? Are there any stress-reduction benefits from requiring officers to attend training programs?

These questions indicate many of the issues and problems that must be addressed in career development, and they apply to all tasks performed by all employees in all positions in a police organization. Of course, not all these questions are ever completely answered for every task in every position. That is why career development is a continuous process. Police agencies recruit, transfer, or promote employees periodically. Many police agencies have employees who do not have the interests, knowledge, or skills necessary to perform productively. Most, if not all, employees in a police department are evaluated every year and often more than once. The managerial response to these activities requires a systematic and thorough career development system.

## The Career Development Process

This chapter divides career development into four phases: the selection of candidates, their preparation, their performance and evaluation, and finally, their development as police officers. In each section a general overview is

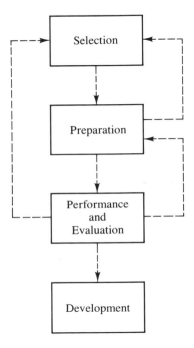

**Figure 7-1** Employee Development Process

provided, followed by a discussion of related issues. Figure 7-1 depicts this process and the relationship between the four phases. As noted earlier, chapter 9 discusses other issues in the police personnel area.

## Selection

There are essentially three selection decisions made in an organization: *entry*, *reassignment*, and *promotion*. Entrance selection decisions are usually for the lowest level or position, but in law enforcement, middle- and upper-level entry is also possible. While rare, some police departments recruit for lower- and middle-level managers (e.g., sergeants, lieutenants, captains) from inside and outside the organization. More common, but still atypical, is the selection of the chief of police from outside the organization. Also, since most sheriffs are elected, potential candidates may include persons outside the sheriff's department, or even outside the law enforcement field.

The selection decision models used historically in law enforcement are the *subjective-political*, *subjective-merit*, and *objective-merit*. The subjective dimension refers to criteria developed based on personal values and experiences. The objective dimension refers to criteria developed through systematic research and analysis. The political dimension refers to criteria based on personal contacts and influences, political ideology, and political party affiliation. Merit refers to the concept of the "best-qualified" person.

In the political-watchman model, selection decisions for entry, reassignment, and promotion were based primarily on subjective-political criteria. While there were other minimal considerations in many departments, like age, education, and health, the primary requirement was who the candidate knew in the dominant political party. Beginning in the later part of the nineteenth century, the concept of merit began to be influential. However, its influence was slow to have an impact, much like the legalistic-professional and subsequent police models. Initially, the concept of merit in policing was highly subjective. The standards picked by law enforcement organizations as a basis for selecting police officers were experientially determined and strongly influenced by the organization's perception of the police role.

Until the 1960s, selection criteria were essentially subjective in nature. Primarily, those criteria required officers to be male, between twenty-one and thirty-five, and at least five feet eight inches tall; to have a high school education or the equivalent; to be in good health and physical condition; to have a certain intelligence level; and to be of good character. These merit criteria define police work as requiring a strong, healthy, young, honest man of average to above-average intelligence. Obviously, this subjective view sees the job as more physically than intellectually demanding. Such criteria are subjective because they are based on the experience and biases of their creators, usually men who had a certain vision of the police role and who advocated, at least implicitly, a certain model of policing. These criteria did not evolve from a systematic analysis of job-related tasks and corresponding requirements, but from a selective and rather limited perception of police activities.

Beginning in the 1960s, as a result of affirmative action, police selection processes gradually began to move more toward an objective merit-based approach. Police departments, pressured by external critics for the most part, began to attempt to make selection criteria valid and reliable. In this context, *validity* refers to the accuracy of a measure; that is, does it measure what it is intended to measure? For example, is the requirement for physical strength, typically a criterion for police officer selection, related to the ability to satisfactorily perform the job? If not, it is not a valid criterion for selection. In contrast, *reliability* refers to a measure's ability to yield consistent results over time. In the physical strength example, the measure would be reliable if a candidate taking the test on more than one occasion received the same or similar strength score on each testing.

To further understand possible differences between valid and nonvalid approaches, two police selection processes will be described. In a subjective merit-based approach, the applicant initially takes a written test designed to measure intelligence, followed by a general physical exam and a physical ability test in which the candidate must run two miles and do a minimum number of push-ups, sit-ups, and chin-ups. The next step is an oral interview, involving a variety of questions that may be different for each candidate. A background investigation is next; the department looks for evidence of a criminal record, the number of traffic tickets, credit problems, and stability in the family and in employment.

In an objective merit-based, or valid, approach, the initial test is related to the tasks of the job; it is not a general intelligence test. The medical exam looks for specific medical problems (i.e., back, knee, circulation) that might result in adverse long-term health consequences for the organization and that might make candidates more vulnerable to performance failures. Instead of testing general physical conditioning, the physical fitness exam includes a process that simulates what a police officer might have to do—pick up or drag a dummy that would weigh as much as an average person, climb over a fence, run an obstacle course, or put on handcuffs simulating the resistance of a suspect to arrest. The oral interview is also more structured. The same questions, primarily related to task and decision requirements, apply to all candidates and all candidates are evaluated in the same way. The background investigation looks for indicators that could be related to performance problems in the organization (e.g., drug use).

The two selection processes described above are substantially different. While it is not possible to identify the exact number of agencies that have moved from a subjective to more objective-based approach in selecting the best-qualified candidates, there is a distinct trend. However, this trend is less well established for reassignment and promotion decision making. While some departments have developed objective-based processes in these areas, many still utilize a subjective approach.

## Police Role and Cultural Matching

A determination of who should be selected is directly related to conceptions of the *police role*. If police work is viewed as a profession, educational preparation becomes important; if it is thought of as a craft, life experience and common sense are more valued. If role implementation is considered more political than bureaucratic, then personalized knowledge of the community is more important than rational detachment, an ideal characteristic of bureaucracies. If police are considered to be proactive crime fighters, then size, strength, and physical and mental toughness are emphasized. If the social service dimension of the role is stressed, more empathetic and humanistic qualities are thought to be important.

An integral part of the selection process is *cultural matching* (discussed in more detail in chapter 9). Depending on the areas and time period, many communities have attempted to match cultural backgrounds of police with the individuals being policed. For example, this process might include suggestions that the Irish ought to be employed to police Irish citizens or black police for black citizens.

## Occupational Status and Applicant Pool

The status of police work is important in the selection process because it influences who applies for employment. The *status* of an occupation is determined by its perceived value to society, the public's (and family's and friends') view of the career, economic rewards, job security, difficulty in obtaining employment, educational requirements, and the activity and behavior of those individuals in the occupation. To a substantial degree, status perception is also influenced by the media's dramatic and comedic presentation of police work. However, the media often distorts the reality of police work and conveys an image that either detracts from or embellishes occupational status. Police organizations can attempt to cope with status concerns by realistically portraying the nature of the work when recruiting. In fact, if candidates are not to become unnecessarily disillusioned, police reality must be depicted accurately to both the police and the public.

The *pool of applicants* available also influences who will be employed. Typically, police agencies establish age, education, health, and background requirements for admission to the pool. Each criterion eliminates applicants who do not qualify. If too many interested applicants are eliminated, the pool shrinks and the choices become increasingly limited. Who the police select is governed not only by interest but also by the number of applicants who possess the designated qualifications.

## Mid-Level and Upper-Level Selection

Although atypical, mid-level and upper-level selection does occur in law enforcement agencies. Mid-level entry (i.e., coming in from another police agency) often involves an objective-based selection process. At the executive level (chiefs of police and sheriffs), both subjective-political and subjective-merit processes are utilized. While chiefs of police and even sheriffs may be "tested" formally or informally on their knowledge, skills, and experience, selections are still based to a substantial degree on the candidate's values and role conception. Prospective chiefs or sheriffs who advocate a legalistic-professional model will not "fit" in a city or county whose expectations are oriented more toward a community-service approach. In this regard, selection decisions are both subjective and political.

The process used to select an individual for the highest position in a police department varies considerably. In some communities, the mayor or city manager simply promotes from within the organization, based on political or professional qualifications. In other cases, one or more chiefs of police may be contacted and asked if they would be interested in the position. Usually, the person contacted is known by reputation and the community is seeking a type of leader who has a particular philosophy of policing. In other communities, a formal selection process may be developed, including an advertisement for the position, a written test, an oral examination, and a background check. In a few instances, a community may employ a consulting firm to assist in the selection process. This selection may be based on the process described or on identifying specific individuals thought capable of performing the job, given the requirements for the position and the organization.

In recent years one approach used by some police organizations for internal promotions, and lateral entry at the management and executive levels, is an *assessment center*. In general, assessment centers are an attempt to determine an individual's capabilities to perform in a specific position. A series of exercises simulate tasks that would be performed in the position in question. In addition, more traditional methods may also be utilized, including written tests or oral interviews. To be successful, this form of evaluation process should be developed and implemented by trained assessors. Ideally, the selection of the most appropriate person for the position will be made by several assessors who combine opinions at the conclusion of the process.

While assessment centers are often more costly than a more traditional process (e.g., a written test and oral interview), they are more objective in determining the most qualified candidates, if properly developed and utilized. Further, if fewer managerial mistakes are made as a result of using this process, there may be long-term savings that will offset the initial expense (Swanson, Territo, and Taylor 1988, pp. 233–236).

*The Entry-Level Selection Process*

The selection of candidates includes measuring abilities and skills in order to predict who will be successful. Within these measurement parameters supposedly exist the only persons qualified to be good police officers. However, the measurement and prediction process also excludes a large number of persons. Therefore, the establishment of criteria is not only important for the candidates it identifies as eligible but also for those it eliminates. Police organizations that establish criteria intended to select crime fighters may exclude candidates who would make good social service officers and vice versa. Some important considerations in the selection process of police officers are discussed in the following paragraphs.

**Attracting candidates.** The first step in selecting police personnel is to attract well-qualified candidates. The relationship of number of applicants to those who qualify for positions is often a major factor in the quality of the personnel employed. Usually, the more applicants, the better qualified will be those employed (Werther and Davis 1985). Five of the most common recruitment methods in police work are advertisement (e.g., television, brochures, radio), requests to special interest groups (e.g., neighborhood, social, political, and minority groups), public announcements (e.g., a public service announcement on television), requests to university and college career planning and placement offices, and referrals from current employees (International City Management Association 1986; Chapman 1982). In some police organizations, officers are offered incentives to recruit (e.g., extra days off or a pay bonus). In some cases, agencies may send recruiters to other cities and states to attract personnel.

One of the major problems with advertising is the *police image* portrayed. Police agencies have always had difficulty in portraying the reality of police work in recruiting. Often they present only the most favorable self-image, usually describing police work as an adventurous and vital public service. This may be done in a brochure with pictures of women and minorities, depicting an exciting and rewarding experience in an ethnically diverse organization. While this image, from an advertising point of view, may be effective, it may also be implicitly deceitful. The recruit's perception of reality after employment rarely matches the advertised image. Such discrepancies may enhance employee disenchantment and frustration.

**Selection criteria.**    Once recruits have been attracted, they are measured against the agency's notion of what is required to be a potentially effective police officer. Before beginning the actual selection process, there are usually minimal criteria that eliminate a substantial number of applicants — age, weight, minimum and maximum height, vision, education, residency, criminal record, and driver's license. Although not all agencies have these requirements, most are common to many agencies. One of the more interesting sidelights is why so many individuals who do not even meet qualifying requirements apply for positions. It is not uncommon for police agencies to claim that only about 5 to 10 percent of the applicants are accepted for positions; however, what is not disclosed is that many who are eliminated do not even meet qualifying criteria.

In general, to be a police officer, an individual cannot be too young or too old, too fat or too thin, too short or too tall to operate the required equipment. He or she must be able to function with and without corrective lenses (for the eyes), have a minimum level of education (most often high school, but some college work and even a college degree is required in a few agencies), perhaps live in the community, have no felony convictions, and have a driver's license. Once these minimum criteria are met, as determined by examining and checking the candidate's initial application (assuming truthfulness), other factors are considered. In general, these factors include intellectual ability, healthfulness, psychological and emotional stability, maturity, physical ability, character, and interpersonal style.

**Intellectual ability.**    A candidate's intelligence is measured by some form of testing, although some police departments exempt candidates if they have a college or university degree. As noted previously, the trend has been to make these examinations more valid; however, not all agencies have followed or have been forced to follow this trend. Some agencies still use tests that measure general intelligence (IQ tests), which may be culturally biased;

that is, they may have questions that are specific to cultural experiences and not a measure of basic intelligence. A test that assesses the intellectual content of the job is more appropriate.

**Medical requirements.**   A candidate's health is determined by a general or a specific medical examination. This may only be a general physical given by the police agency's designated physician or a physician of the candidate's choice. In some departments, the physical exam is very exact; there is an attempt to determine general health status and to identify specific problems, including heart, back, and knee problems. Any "weakness" that may be aggravated by the requirements of police work will often eliminate applicants. The rationale for this is that the costs of losing an officer to injury or illness, often with a long-term disability salary, are too great.

**Psychological testing.**   Another phase of the selection process used by some police agencies is psychological screening to determine emotional and psychological stability and maturity. These tests may be written, oral, or both, and the written part may be evaluated by a police officer or psychologist. Psychologists are looking for serious emotional and psychological problems that will disqualify candidates or for a profile of what type of person the psychologist believes is a potentially good police officer. Testing to eliminate individuals with obvious problems requires the use of rather broad psychological parameters, while testing for a particular psychological profile narrows the parameters somewhat. Using a profile of potentially "successful" recruits tends to eliminate more applicants; it also suggests that the profile predicts who will and who will not become a good police officer. Such a decision is problematic because agencies have different styles of policing. Research in this area suggests that psychologists do not always agree on who is and who is not qualified to be a police officer (Schoenfeld and Kobos 1980). In addition, it is questionable whether psychological testing can predict who will become an effective police officer (Costello, Schoenfeld, and Kobos 1982; Spielberger 1979).

Perhaps one of the most serious problems in psychological screening is who administers and evaluates the tests. In the last two decades, a substantial number of psychologists have developed expertise in screening applicants and providing other services to police organizations. Most states, if not all, have at least a few police experts available, yet many departments continue to rely on psychologists who have limited (if any) experience in the police field. Consequently, the types of evaluation and resulting recommendations may not be as meaningful as desirable. Psychological evaluations of applicants and of officers (e.g., for reassignment, promotion, and suitability to return to work after a traumatic experience) are potentially effective tools if properly used by knowledgeable persons.

**Polygraph examination.**   Some police departments utilize the polygraph or "lie" detector to check the accuracy of background information and to discover any inappropriate behavior, past or present (e.g., criminal acts, drug use). The polygraph is touted by police as an effective tool in discovering problems with some applicants (Swanson, Territo, and Taylor 1988, pp. 201–203). However, research suggests that it is not a reliable method to determine the truth or falsehood of an individual's statements (Hodes, Hunts, and Raskin 1985; Kleinmuntz and Szucko 1982; Rafky and Sussman 1985; Spielberger 1979). The polygraph may have some public relations benefits (e.g., the community thinks only those whose character is above reproach are employed). In addition, it may result in some applicants' confessing wrongdoing out of fear that the "lie" detector will discover the "truth" or in discouraging others with problems from applying (Swanson, Territo, and Taylor 1988, pp. 201–203). What is not known is how many applicants lie successfully and are employed, and how many other applicants are wrongly eliminated because of the use of this device.

**Physical fitness.**   It is also important to determine the physical ability and agility of candidates. Some police tasks require physical endurance, strength, and coordination. Five areas of physical ability have been related to police work in general: upper-body strength, leg strength, grip strength, balance and coordination, and quick reactions. It is possible to generally test for these abilities or to do so in a more valid manner. As noted, the trend has been toward using the most direct measurement by simulating actual physical activities of police officers like body dragging (using a dummy or a sack of sand, etc.), running a certain distance in a given time, and climbing a fence (Swanson, Territo, and Taylor 1988, pp. 197–200). However, the more general physical ability testing is still used. This test may include sit-ups, push-ups, chin-ups, and running. One of the problems with this type of testing is that it tends to eliminate applicants who can successfully pass a more valid test.

One of the problems of job-valid tests is the tendency to measure for only *median abilities*. For example, some agencies require applicants to drag or carry a 150-pound dummy or sack of sand a certain distance. This simulates dragging or carrying an adult person of median body weight to safety, that is, away from a wreck or fire. However, adult males often weigh more than 150 pounds. Presumably, those individuals who could barely drag or lift the 150-pound dummy would have difficulty with heavier persons. Perhaps, as some agencies argue, those officers would be so "psyched up" in actual stressful events that they would be much stronger than "normal." In addition, the practice of testing in this, and other areas, for the most demanding aspects of the job, rather than the general median ability, or most frequently performed task, would probably eliminate too many candidates and might have an adverse impact on certain groups of applicants (e.g., women).

**Background investigations.**   Another step in the selection process is the assessment of character and general suitability for police work as determined by past experience and lifestyle. Is the person honest, reliable, and dependable? The background investigation, based on the extensive personal history provided by the applicant, is an examination of character and suitability. Family background, employment history, criminal and possibly juvenile records, credit history, personal and employment references, friends and neighbors, military records, and education records are all checked to develop a general assessment of how a person has lived his or her life prior to applying for police work.

**Oral interview.**   Most police departments utilize some form of oral interview in the selection process. Some departments use more than one inter-

HUMAN RESOURCE MANAGEMENT **245**

view (e.g., an interview with both an oral board and a manager or executive in the organization). Applicants' *interpersonal style, decision-making* skills, and *communication ability* are assessed during the oral interview process. In many agencies the interview is highly structured, using specific questions and evaluation forms. Just as in other phases of the selection process, this phase has become increasingly job-valid.

The interview often includes three or four persons. Some of the interviewers may be from outside the police department. Candidates are measured on attributes such as confidence, candor, presentation, communication skills, and overall demeanor. The interviews are not usually substantive (i.e., require the candidate to know something specific about police work), but they can be. Oral interviews can also be stressful or more relaxed. Some oral interview boards designate a certain member to give applicants a difficult time by asking questions such as: "Why are all manhole covers round?"

Many agencies use oral interviews to rank candidates for selection. Where this occurs, the other steps in the process are used only to qualify candidates on a pass/fail basis. To some degree, this has been done to enhance the employment of minorities and women who may have passed but did not do well in one or more of the other steps in the selection process. While this approach to selection is more flexible, it also tends to be more subjective. The selection of board members, organization pressures to employ certain types of candidates, or the candidates' personal contacts can influence the rankings.

**Selection summary.** Table 7-1 presents a summary of the general steps of the police selection process and the most important concerns at each step. The selection of candidates for police organizations is time-consuming and expensive. Given the costs associated with selection, the steps of the process are usually arranged from least costly/most likely to eliminate the most candidates to most expensive. As a result, the written test and physical agility test are usually given at the beginning, followed by the medical exam, polygraph (if used), psychological test (if used), oral interview, and finally, the background investigation. Although all agencies do not use the same sequence, many tend to follow a similar path.

**Table 7-1**  Steps and Issues in the Police Entry-Level Selection Process

| Steps | Related Issues |
|---|---|
| Attracting Candidates | Advertising and personal contacts |
| Selection Criteria | Age, size, weight, eyesight, criminal record |
| Intellectual Ability | General intelligence or job content |
| Medical Requirements | General health and specific problems |
| Psychological Testing | Emotional stability and psychological profiles |
| Polygraph | Character and background |
| Physical Fitness | Agility and endurance |
| Background Investigation | Character, employment, family credit, criminal record |
| Oral Interview | Interpersonal style and communication skill |

Once the candidates are selected, they are usually ranked and employed based on need. This ranking lasts for a given time period—six months to two or more years—before retesting is undertaken. In cases where minority employment has been a problem, there may be two lists, one with nonminorities and one with minorities. Selection from these lists is often based on the degree to which a certain percentage of minorities has been employed. These goals or quotas will be discussed more in chapter 9. Once selected, most individuals attend a training program.

## Preparation

The first step in preparing the successful applicant for police work is *initial training*. An effective career development program will already have identified those abilities and skills that are required for entrance to the occupation, those that must be enhanced, and those that must be taught to new officers during training. In many states, the training program content is determined by a state standards organization, although some departments provide more training than is minimally required.

Historically, until the late 1950s, training was primarily the responsibility of cities and counties and a few colleges and universities. However, in the late 1950s, statewide standards and training organizations began to be established. These organizations were created to standardize selection and training of police and, for the most part, have been successful in improving training. College and university involvement also grew rapidly in the 1960s, but the programs being created were not always designed to train police officers in specific skills; rather, some, and eventually most, became more educationally oriented (i.e., emphasized concepts, theories, and understanding rather than specific methods, skills, and techniques [Sherman 1978; Ward and Webb 1984]).

As these changes took place, training also tended to become more *extensive*. Nineteenth- and early-twentieth-century training, where it existed, might have been only two or three weeks in length. By the 1960s, some agencies had initial training of four to six months or longer. This greater length tended to be accompanied by greater *diversity* in subject matter and training methods. More knowledge was being developed and new subjects were added as role conceptions and models changed. There was also an attempt to improve instruction through the use of media and role playing; that is, by developing simulated situations to help officers respond to domestic disturbances, crimes in progress, shootings, and so on.

What has not changed is the *stress orientation*. From the outset, many entry-level programs had a "boot camp" philosophy. Recruits were expected to be obedient and were subjected to both intellectual and physical demands in a highly structured, militarylike environment. Discipline, even harassment, was an integral part of many training programs. However, this has usually not been the case for training after employment. As a general rule, training for experienced officers is nonstressful.

A recent development in some states is the requirement that prospective employees complete a basic training program before being considered for

**Recruits attend a basic police training academy.**

employment. By doing this the police agency does not have to pay the cost of training, including the recruit's salary. For example, in California many police agencies currently require candidates to have completed basic police training prior to employment. It is not uncommon to have regional or county-wide recruit training programs with both individuals employed by agencies and others who are "paying their own way" in hopes of later finding a job.

## Police Role Conception

The role conception of the police is influential in determining the length and diversity of the training program. A political-craftsman view of the role does not emphasize the importance of training as much as a bureaucratic-professional perspective. The latter tends to stress the importance of preparation and requires extensive training. The crime fighter–social service role debate does not concern itself primarily with length of training; rather, it focuses on both content diversity and training orientation. The crime-fighter perspective tends to value a stress-oriented approach to training with subject matter that emphasizes physical conditioning, criminal law and procedure, criminal investigation, and tactics in making arrests and using nondeadly and deadly force.

A social service view of the role does not discount the importance of these subjects but would include material on the social and behavioral sciences (e.g., knowledge about human behavior, the educational and counseling roles of police officers, and alternatives to making arrests and using force). The stressful nature of training may also be deemphasized. Recruits might not be required to stand inspections, march in formation, run "laps" (or exercise) for mistakes, or endure general harassment. Nonstress training is more like an academic environment and less like military basic training.

## Training Reality

Another important aspect of initial training is the degree to which *reality* is presented and discussed. What image of police work is to be provided? What lessons are actually taught? A training program tends to represent the formal organization's view of police work. There is also an informal organization or culture that represents a different reality for officers. Is the reality of both organizations being presented or only an idealized view of the nature of the work? Does an unrealistic presentation of police work make occupational adjustments more difficult?

An example helps illustrate this point. One of the authors taught a class on deadly force in a recruit training program. Recruits were asked to decide what to do in several situations that might require the use of deadly force. The situations presented required the recruits to utilize departmental policy as a basis for their decisions. After class, a senior officer, who was an adviser to the new recruits, called them all outside the classroom. He told them what they should do in those situations. In some instances, what he told the recruits would require them to lie and to violate departmental policy. The recruits were attentive to the instructor and the senior officer but whom did they believe? This incident exposed them to the formal and informal organization's view of the use of deadly force. However, one was not discussed "officially" in the training program.

*Program Development*

Initial training is influenced by *developmental assumptions* and *program design* and *delivery*. Developmental assumptions are concerned with stress versus nonstress training, the relative merits of classroom versus on-the-job experience, and how individuals learn. Some considerations in program design are task-subject relationships, instructional methods, instructors, time in training, and delivery system. The delivery of the training program includes an evaluation mechanism for making the necessary adjustments to increase the program's effectiveness. Figure 7-2 depicts important considerations in the development of initial training programs.

**Developmental assumptions.**   As noted earlier, one of the important issues in police training is whether it should be *stressful* or *nonstressful*. Stressful training is like a military boot camp or basic training, whereas nonstressful training has a more academic environment. Although many police training programs are stress oriented, there is no evidence to indicate that this approach is any more or less effective than a nonstress approach. Stress-related training is the result of an experiential judgment by police managers and it is related to a crime-fighting and bureaucratic role conception. Arguments that stress-related training produces disciplined, well-conditioned individuals can be offset by equally logical arguments that such training produces rigid, inflexible autocrats who are ill equipped to cope with the diverse reality of police work. Perhaps the most comprehensive study in this area found that nonstress training produced officers who received higher performance evaluations, liked their work more, and got along better with the public (Earle 1973). Given the trend toward foot patrol and the rational-contingency model in some departments, a stress-oriented training approach may be counterproductive. However, since police behavior is probably determined more by what happens after the officer is "on the job," training program experiences may have little long-term impact on adjustments to the work.

    Another important aspect of training development is to consider assumptions about how learning takes place. How do adults learn? This phase

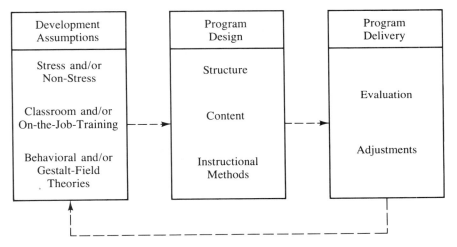

**Figure 7-2** Initial Training Program Development

of training program development is often explicitly overlooked; however, it cannot be avoided because developing instruction methods incorporates learning assumptions. There are two schools of thought in this area: behavioral and Gestalt.

*Behavioral theorists* essentially believe that learning is a function of stimulus and response or trial and error. Desired behavior or the learning of knowledge and skills is rewarded and the failure to learn is punished or ignored. Trainees are given points or some form of credit for desirable behavior like attendance, promptness, or performance. *Gestalt-field theories* do not support the stimulus-response approach; they maintain that learning is more cognitive in that it should emphasize knowledge, skills, and understanding. Learning involves gaining or changing insights, points of view, or thought patterns. More emphasis is placed on analytical processes like reasoning and problem solving (Roberg 1979, pp. 255–260). Stress-oriented police training or any training with a vocational or occupational emphasis tends to be based on behavioral assumptions, while nonstress, academically oriented programs are based more on Gestalt assumptions.

Another important philosophical debate concerns assumptions about the relative importance of *classroom or formal* versus *on-the-job or apprentice-like* training. As previously noted, formal police training has become more extensive in recent decades. However, on-the-job or apprentice-type training has remained important and has become even more structured in the past decade or so. The assignment of new officers to experienced "old timers" to "break in" has given way to highly structured Field Training Officer (FTO) or similar programs.

In *FTO programs* well-qualified, experienced officers are selected and trained to act as mentors for new recruits. The "break-in" or probationary period is a highly structured experience for new officers, in which they must demonstrate specific knowledge and skills. Frequent evaluations are made of rookies' performance, often by several FTOs who supervise their work in different areas and on different shifts.

Field Training Officer programs tend to be based on certain common guidelines that have proved successful. These guidelines suggest a task-analysis study prior to program development, placement of the program in the patrol division, well-planned and organized training, standardized evaluation of all recruits, frequent feedback on performance, and periodic program evaluation. Individuals selected to be FTOs should be competent, experienced, and mature, and they should receive specific training on the development of new officers (McCampbell 1986).

**Program design and delivery.**   In the design and delivery of training programs, the factual/conceptual nature of the material, the subjects to be taught, the instructor, and the instructional methods to be employed must be considered. In addition, during and after the program there must be a method to evaluate the degree of effectiveness in order to make any necessary adjustments.

To what degree is the material to be treated *factually* or *conceptually*? For example, when discussing traffic accident investigation, one elaborate procedure may be taught to officers or alternative procedures may be given and their relative merits discussed. The approaches are ones of training (i.e., dealing with specific facts and procedures) or of education (i.e., dealing with theories, concepts, issues, and alternatives). Most police training is oriented toward teaching facts and specific procedures rather than theories and concepts. As a result, the identification of the body of knowledge and skills to be included as subject matter becomes extremely important because police officers are being taught precisely how to perform.

Recently, in a training program (with which we are familiar) a police instructor told recruits that placing a paper bag over an unruly prisoner's head was an effective control technique. Later, two officers in the class used this technique and a prisoner suffocated to death. The paper bag technique was taught as fact, even though it is medically dangerous. When developing training programs that emphasize specific facts and procedures, the accuracy and completeness of the information provided is critical, as is monitoring those who provide the information.

Another important concern in program design is related to the *subject matter*. Ideally, training program subject matter is based on a task analysis of the jobs the recruits will perform; however, this is not always done. Some agencies and some states have attempted to identify police tasks and responsibilities through job analysis, but this is more the exception than the rule. More common is to have training based on legal requirements and the wisdom and insight of experienced officers. In many states, these requirements are determined by standards organizations or commissions, whose employees are mostly former or retired police officers.

Whether the training is based on task analysis or experience, the organization must determine what subject matter is most important because most, if not all, programs are constrained by time and resources. For example, one task police officers might have to perform is to fire their guns at suspects. Training police officers to accurately fire their weapons under conditions of stress is extremely difficult to do, costly, and time-consuming. Multiply the time and costs of training officers in how to respond to this complex task by the time and cost of other complex tasks like high-speed pursuit driving, intervening in violent situations without using force, and having a thorough understanding of criminal law and you have an idea of the constraints under which these programs operate.

Once the basic subject structure of a training program is determined, the *content* of the subjects must be identified by developing outlines or handouts or by identifying the textbooks to be utilized. We have observed police training in which the best available information was not used. At times, some of the information given to police officers is inaccurate. This is quite easy to do in a field that changes so rapidly; therefore, it is incumbent on those responsible for program development to ensure the accuracy and completeness of program content. Calling on "experts" (e.g., persons currently active in practice and research) in subject areas is one way to ensure accurate content.

Course content is often determined by the instructor. Selecting an instructor is a sensitive area because of the importance of the training and the roles that prestige and politics play. In many police agencies, serving as a trainer is a prestigious assignment. Unfortunately, in some cases, training programs are used as "dumping grounds" for the incompetent, injured, or lazy. Politically, decisions about eliminating poor instructors can also be a problem. Should politically influential persons be selected and retained as instructors regardless of knowledge and teaching ability? Who is going to tell the chief of police or sheriff that he or she is a poor instructor?

Finally, what *instructional methods* are to be utilized? In part, this is governed by both the instructor and training program manager, but it is also influenced by teaching philosophies. Two contrasting philosophies are pedagogy and andragogy. *Pedagogy* involves the one-way transfer of knowledge, usually by lecturing on facts, in which "absolute solutions" are expected to be memorized. *Andragogy* stresses analytical and conceptual skills and promotes the mutual involvement of instructor and student (Roberg 1979, pp. 257–260).

Pedagogy is closely related to behavioral theories and factual orientation, whereas andragogy is more in line with a Gestalt and conceptual approach. The former involves lectures, use of visual aids, student note taking, rote memorization, and factual test taking. The latter involves more problem analysis, role playing, group discussion and projects, independent student

learning, and exercises requiring recruits to "act out" required skills in simulated situations. However, while many training programs currently use
more role playing, simulations, and problem analysis, conceptual understanding and insight development are rarely emphasized. Even in
community-service and rational-contingency approaches to policing, the
training emphasizes how to do a job rather than why the job is necessary or
why one method is more effective than another.

How effective is the training provided to the recruits in law enforcement? One means of evaluating this training is to follow up on field performance to determine the areas in which recruits are having the most difficulty.
Once problems are identified, a determination can be made as to how to improve the program. In addition, as new knowledge and skills become available, they should be incorporated into the program. Finally, if a department
undergoes fundamental changes, the entire training program may change as
assumptions and delivery systems are examined.

## Performance and Evaluation

Once employees are selected and initially trained, they must perform. This
performance and its evaluation are the third phase in the career development
model. *Evaluation* involves comparing employees' activity and behavior
with *standards of performance*. Who has expectations about police activity
and behavior that formally or informally become standards? What are the
standards of performance? Are these standards valid? What types of standards are there? Who does the evaluation? How is it done? How often is it
done? How are the evaluations used? What are the problems in performance
evaluations? Table 7-2 presents an overview of some considerations in performance evaluation.

The expectation-integration model provides a useful means of looking
at sources of expectations that may become standards of police performance.
The diverse groups in a community have expectations, there are legal expectations, and the organization has expectations. Community expectations
may be translated into organizational policies and procedures that provide

**Table 7-2**   Police Personnel Evaluation

| Evaluation Categories | Standards and Measurement | Evaluation Problems |
|---|---|---|
| Attitude<br>Appearance<br>Methods<br>Product or service | Quality<br>Quantity<br>Validity<br>Absolute<br>Comparative | Too strict/lenient<br>Halo effect<br>Central tendency<br>Who does it?<br>When is it done?<br>How is it utilized? |

officers with guidance and requirements for their performance. However, the organization does not explicitly reflect all these expectations. For example, assume a police officer uses force against a minority juvenile in questionable circumstances. While a police investigation may find that the officer was legally and organizationally justified, the minority community expectation may result in the perception of inadequate police performance. One or even a few such "performance failures" might not create problems for the organization, but a substantial number may result in drastic changes.

Historically, performance evaluation has gone through several identifiable trends, although it is difficult to determine how the most current developments apply to departments in general. The management and personnel practices are too diverse to provide accurate assessments that apply to most police departments. However, general changes can be noted, including (1) from subjective to more objective criteria, (2) from an emphasis on quantity to an emphasis on both quality and quantity, and (3) from a criteria checklist approach to using goals and objectives.

As in the selection process, there has been a tendency toward the development of more *valid and reliable evaluation measures*. The assessment of personnel, particularly since the 1960s, has gradually become more concerned with specific performance requirements other than attitudinal (e.g., positive and conscientious) and appearance (e.g., well groomed, well dressed) measurements. While an officer's attitude and appearance are rarely discounted, they are essentially indirect measures of performance and not necessarily directly linked to effectiveness.

The second major trend has been a *decline in an emphasis on quantity,* although a concern for quantity is still important. The legalistic-professional model emphasized production as measured by quantifiable activities such as the number of investigations, arrests, traffic tickets, citizen contacts, or buildings inspected. By the 1960s, and particularly in the 1970s and 1980s, a concern for quantity began to be balanced with a concern for quality; for instance, the quality of the investigation became as important as the number of arrests made.

The third trend in evaluation is a movement away from *listing evaluative criteria* to identifying and evaluating performance based on *goals and objectives*. Prior to the 1970s and even now in many police organizations, evaluation procedures at most organizational levels involved developing a list of criteria to use as a basis for evaluating performance. These criteria include a mix of qualitative and quantitative factors, often with attitudinal and appearance factors included. Officers are rated by category, either a general one or in comparison to other officers. For example, on appearance, an officer might be rated "excellent," "good," "average," or "below average" or perhaps in the "highest 10 percent," "next highest 20 percent," and so on. The former is a general classification scheme, and the latter requires a comparison with other officers. Several performance evaluation methods are shown in table 7-3.

In a goals and objectives approach (sometimes called management by objectives), performance is measured by the accomplishment of specific purposes. Goals are usually broad, general statements of purpose that identify an organization's mission; for example, to prevent or reduce or control crime. Objectives are quantifiable, measurable, and time-bound, if possible. A unit of the police department, like patrol, might have as an objective a 10 percent reduction in the citizen's fear of crime in the next six months. Since fear levels can be measured objectively with citizen surveys, this is a quantifiable objective. Each subunit's objectives are related to the unit's objectives and the organization's goals to provide a unity of purpose. While this system is not without flaws (it is difficult to quantify many police activities), it does change the basis for performance evaluation from subjective checklists to specific performance accomplishments.

**Table 7-3**  Performance Evaluation Methods

| Method | Definition |
|---|---|
| 1. Discrete category scale | Identification of personal or job traits that are evaluated in terms of a series of categories such as:<br><br>| Needs Improvements | Standard Performance | Outstanding Performance |<br><br>The number of categories usually ranges from two to five, but there can be more. |
| 2. Graphic scale | Identification of traits, but evaluated on the following type of scale:<br><br>Unsatisfactory    Poor    Good    Superior    Excellent<br><br>This is a more flexible version of the discrete category scale. Responses can be placed anywhere on the continuum. |
| 3. Adjective scale | Identification of traits that are more complete in evaluative response. An example is<br><br>Handles situations clumsily; ignores policy, etc.    Judgment often illogical; tends to overlook policy, etc.    Acts judiciously under most circumstances, etc.    Judgments impartial and logical, etc.    Thinks soundly and logically, etc. |
| 4. Simple ranking:<br>a. Simple order | Ranking of "best" to "worst" employee. |
| b. Alternative ranking | Employees halved into "highest" and "lowest" performing groups. Highest half ranked from top down; lowest half from bottom up. |
| c. Group ranking | Criterion groups established to represent specific levels of performance. Employees being evaluated are placed in a group appropriate to their level of performance. |
| 5. Paired comparison | Every employee compared with all others being evaluated. Employee receiving highest number of favorable comparisons is ranked highest; conversely, fewest favorable comparisons results in lowest ranking. |
| 6. Forced distribution | The bell-shaped curve or normal frequency distribution is employed; an example would be allocating 10% for highest and lowest rankings, 20% for next highest and lowest groups, and 40% for the middle group. |
| 7. Free response | Evaluation of employee in "rater's own words." |
| 8. Performance checklists | Checklist of desirable traits, behavior provided. Rater checks those that apply to employee. Items checked can be given different weights to determine total rating. |
| 9. Forced choice | Sets of descriptive statements concerning performance are used and the rater selects those that best describe the employee's performance. |

## Role Conceptions and Police Models

This phase of career development is also influenced by role conceptions. The political-craftsman view of police work tends to be less formal and more subjective in its evaluation of personnel. The bureaucratic-professional perspective is just the reverse; evaluations tend to be formal and attempts are made to make them objective.

Because of the styles associated with them, police models are also very important in the evaluation of police officers. The political-watchman model tends to be haphazard. The legalistic-professional, community-service, and rational-contingency models have different priorities relative to police tasks. In the legalistic-professional model, officers are judged on rule compliance and quantitative output, such as number of reports, investigations, tickets, and arrests. The community-service model evaluates officers based on quality of citizen contacts, advice given, and decisions made. In the rational-contingency model, the accomplishment of specific goals or objectives, quantitative or qualitative, is often the basis of evaluation. These goals and objectives may represent either enforcement or nonenforcement activities.

## Measurement Theory

Performance evaluation is essentially a *measurement problem* like that involved in any analytical or research endeavor. As previously noted, one of the important trends in this area has been the attempt to make selection standards valid. To a lesser degree, this has also applied to evaluation of police officers. Moreover, such a trend is probably desirable because it will most likely improve organization effectiveness.

To understand how to develop a valid performance evaluation system, one must first understand *construct validity*. A construct involves a mental image of something such as intelligence or effectiveness in a particular type of situation. Construct validity is concerned with the relationship between the definition of the construct and some measure of it; the purpose is to make the measure match the definition of the construct as closely as possible. For example, after a task analysis of the requirements of police work, it is decided that candidates for the job must be able to read and understand certain types of written material. The construct is reading ability and the definition specifies a given level of desired reading ability (e.g., at the twelfth-grade level). To have construct validity, the measure of reading ability must match the desired level of ability. For reading, this is not particularly difficult to do because fairly precise measures of reading ability already exist. However, what is not clear is the level of reading ability that should be required. Should police officers be required to be able to read and understand complex legal decisions or only memos and other materials from the police department?

It is not always possible to have a perfect match between the construct and the measurement device, as is often the case in performance evaluation. Two problems exist: measurement deficiency and measurement contamination. A *measurement deficiency* involves, in effect, an incomplete measurement; for example, only the quantity and not the quality of the work is measured. *Measurement contamination* involves an evaluation process that takes into consideration factors that are not intended to influence the process; for example, a measure can tap into the rater's personal likes and dislikes of the person being evaluated (Roberg 1979, pp. 229–231).

In developing performance standards, it is important to remember that they must be valid. The construct, or performance standard, must be related to the tasks to be performed, and the measure of the standard must be related to the construct in such a way that both measurement deficiencies and contamination are minimized.

## *Performance Standards*

The standards, goals and objectives, and policies and procedures developed by police departments are the basis for performance evaluations. As noted, the degree to which these *performance criteria* are measurable and meaningful is important to the evaluation's success. *Qualitative* standards are more subjective and difficult to utilize. For example, suppose a performance standard required officers to be courteous when interacting with citizens. This standard, like appearance, requires constant interpretation. *Quantitative* standards are more precise but are also binding. A certain number of traffic tickets or arrests per month is specific; however, is that number too small or too large? Are specific standards, goals, and objectives achievable or do they demand too little of employees? Are specific quantitative accomplishments sufficient to determine good work? Do they, or should they, guarantee a favorable evaluation? These are some of the questions that must be addressed in this area.

The standards of performance created by an organization can usually be grouped into some combination of the following categories: *attitude*, *appearance*, *product or service*, and *methods*. Within each category, the standards can be placed on a general to specific continuum and measured qualitatively, quantitatively, or both. Attitude and appearance standards were briefly discussed earlier and are not addressed here.

The product or service category includes behavior and work activity that can be defined vaguely as "volume of work" or, more specifically, as "will write ten moving traffic violations a month." The general standard requires a subjective assessment by the rater, usually compared with the activity of other officers or average activity within a group (e.g., what is the average or mean number of tickets written by all officers on a shift). The more specific standard identifies precisely what is expected in productivity and what should be the result of systematic analysis concerning what is both reasonable and possible for officers to accomplish.

The methods category includes all standards that identify a process or procedure that an officer must go through when performing an activity. For example, assume an organization has an elaborate procedure for "traffic stops" when issuing tickets. A general methods standard would be "follow organizational procedures," while a more specific standard, or standards, would include steps like "parks vehicle in proper position when making traffic stops," "approaches vehicle in the proper manner," and so on. Note, however, that in this example even the more specific standards are qualitative, based on departmental norms or expectations.

Whether performance standards are attitudinal or concerned with appearance, product-service, or methods, the standards should be valid or directly related to the performance to be measured. If they are not valid, the standards may be too vague and too likely to be interpreted differently by raters. Quantitative standards, often stated as goals or objectives, have measurement built in. Accomplishing a certain number of investigations or arrests is a measure of performance. If this measure meets the standard, goal, or objective, then the performance meets or exceeds acceptable levels. Qualitative standards require more explicit definitions. For example, for the performance criterion "acceptable public contacts," what is an acceptable public contact? This might include definitions of courtesy, use of discretion, tone of voice, accuracy of information, supportive behavior, and attitudes toward and response to the citizen. By itself, "acceptable public contacts" is too vague, but with definition it becomes more measurable.

## *Methods of Evaluation*

Once standards are identified, a process for rating employees must be developed. Generally, the standards are measured by either a *comparative* or *absolute* method and are usually applied in the evaluation by the employee's immediate supervisor. Comparisons involve measuring one person against another or comparing all members of a group and then ranking them. Absolute evaluations utilize categories such as "well above standard," "above standard," "standard," and "below standard" or "excellent," "good," and "fair."

Another form of evaluation involves the *critical incident* approach that analyzes performance in a situation. For example, an evaluator might actually observe an officer's performance in a "critical" situation like a traffic stop or investigation. (*Critical* refers not to danger but to incidents considered important by the organization.) The rater then compares the officer's performance with the standards developed by the organization for a response in that situation. This approach is a useful developmental tool for managers because it often promotes a meaningful discussion about the employee's actual performance in important situations. FTO programs, for example, are based in part on this method. Organizational expectations can be clarified, employee concerns can be discussed, and areas of required improvement can be noted.

In addition, some organizations also use *peer evaluations or self-evaluations*. Peer evaluations, supplemented by a managerial review, can provide useful information. This approach is inevitably comparative because peers tend to base their evaluations on how the person being evaluated stacks up with other employees. To be most effective, peer evaluations should be done anonymously. Self-evaluation can also be a useful tool in determining how the employee thinks he or she is doing. When compared with managerial or peer reviews, it provides an interesting picture of the different perceptions of that employee's performance.

## Problems in Evaluation

In conducting performance ratings, a number of common problems must be addressed. One problem is the tendency for some raters to be either *too strict* or *too lenient*. Usually this occurs when performance standards are vague and not valid. The more general the standard, the more it is open to a number of interpretations; consequently, the rater's values, priorities, and expectations may become more important than the actual performance.

Other possible rating problems are central tendency and the halo effect. *Central tendency* rating problems are those in which a rater tends to give everyone average ratings, not really distinguishing each individual's performance. The *halo effect* occurs when the same rating is given to an employee on all performance standards, based on knowledge of the employee's performance in only one area. Other possible problems include differences between raters and differences over time. Obviously, only managers who are familiar with an employee's performance should evaluate that employee. Ratings should be based on specific, valid standards of performance and should be used by trained raters who are given guidance on what the standards mean and who are responsible for recognizing the differences in performance based on those standards. Most performance evaluation problems can be successfully resolved if standards are precise, valid, and applied by well-trained managers.

Some additional police managerial problems in performance evaluation include who conducts evaluations, when and how often officers are evaluated, and how the evaluations are used. In police organizations, evaluations tend to be more frequent during the officer's probationary period, perhaps even daily in some agencies, and to occur much less frequently (e.g., every six months) once the officer is off probation. After the evaluations are made, their use varies. Some agencies use them to chart changes over time and to make reassignment and promotion decisions. However, many departments treat evaluations as little more than a required activity (e.g., a civil service requirement), acting only when serious performance problems are noted; some agencies do not even evaluate an employee's performance.

Performance evaluation at all levels of the organization has tremendous potential to improve performance and productivity. An effective appraisal system requires the organization to systematically analyze its goals and objectives, the positions and roles of its employees, the activity and behavior taking place, and how this contributes to its goals and objectives. Finally, it requires the organization and its managers to make decisions about what is the most effective, and acceptable, activity and behavior (Kuykendall and Unsinger 1979; Roberg 1979).

## Development

This final phase of career development is concerned with the career long-term growth of employees in the organization. Once a person is recruited, selected, trained, and completes probation in a police department, his or her career begins and his or her development becomes important to the organization. The problems and issues discussed in the section on initial training apply here as well and are not discussed again. However, some additional unique aspects of postemployment development are addressed. Development of employees can be for the individual as well as for a specific position within the organization; it can involve training within or outside the organization, and it requires continuous information about the current and possible future status of employees (Leibowitz, Farren, and Kaye 1986).

Police employees have outside interests that are not related to their careers, such as recreational or vocational interests or interests in emotional and psychological growth. Even when such development is not specific to a position within the organization, it does influence a person's sense of well-being. Having information about individual growth opportunities and providing assistance in seeking them out is an important part of a developmental program.

Research has identified three career stages that employees pass through during their working life: the *establishment stage*, the *maintenance stage*, and the *stage of decline*. From their twenties to their forties, persons are usually getting established in their careers. The degree to which they will be successful in the organization is largely determined during this period. From about age forty to age fifty-five, many individuals reassess their lives. They may change their lifestyles and even their values as they examine their lives and career status. Finally, from the midfifties through retirement and beyond, individuals prepare for an adjustment to a different type of life without work or with reduced involvement in their work. Effective career development planning takes into consideration all phases of the employee's career (Schultz and Schultz 1986).

## Role Conception and Police Models

As in the other phases of the model, police role perception is an important factor in determining how enhancement, or employee development, is treated. Generally speaking, the more bureaucratic, professional, and social service–oriented the role perception, the more career development is valued. However, within the democratic models, there is a distinct relationship between a specific model and career enhancement.

Managers tend to emphasize the value of human resources more in the rational-contingency and community-service models than in the political-watchman or legalistic-professional models. Consequently, there is a greater concern about enhancing the growth of the employee throughout his or her organizational life. As managers become more competent, they increasingly realize that if an organization is to be as productive as possible, a substantial majority of its employees must also be competent and motivated. An organization may survive without effective career development, but performance is often inadequate. As contingency theory would suggest, career development requires the continuous monitoring of new knowledge, skills, and technology that may be applicable to the mission of the organization, and this must be compared with the positions' requirements to ensure that employees are effectively equipped.

*Career Path Enhancement*

Not only must individuals in existing positions be upgraded as knowledge and skills change, planning must be undertaken to incorporate employee interests with career paths that involve position enhancement, new assignments, and promotion. For example, assume Officer Janet Smith works in a police department for twenty-five years and her career path is

- patrol for five years
- transferred to traffic enforcement specialist for two years
- promoted to sergeant and transferred back to patrol for two years
- transferred to the detective unit for four years, where she works as a burglary and homicide investigator
- promoted to lieutenant and transferred to a training and personnel unit, which she supervises for three years
- promoted to captain and serves as a supervisor in charge of patrol for four years
- transferred to the detective unit again and placed in charge for three years
- promoted to deputy chief and serves for two years before she retires

An effective career development program must upgrade this officer's knowledge and skills while she is in each of these assignments, plus it must prepare her for each change in her career, including retirement. In addition, supervisors need to be alert to declining officer interest during an assignment in order to take action, if possible, before this lack of interest adversely affects morale and performance.

## Continuous Updating

Officers and managers must be kept up-to-date on changing laws, police methods, and technologies and must be prepared for reassignment or promotion. Some agencies have sufficient resources that allow them to develop their own programs. Other agencies must find programs outside the organization. Many states, as a result of statewide training and standards commissions, have developed extensive career-development training programs for police. For example, in many states it is possible to attend training programs that assist in preparing an officer for almost any assignment or promotion. Many agencies also use private training groups and colleges and universities. A substantial number of private trainers are available to assist police organizations, and many colleges and universities offer useful programs or courses.

Experienced older officers and managers are more difficult to train than recruits. They tend to want to be treated more as a peer than as a student and they usually do not want a stress-related orientation, preferring a more academic approach. This suggests that experienced officers might prefer, and benefit from, an andragogical approach to training. Experienced officers also tend to have more precise expectations about training and to be more critical of training program subjects, methods, and instructors.

Perhaps the most problematic aspect of career development training is the evaluation procedures used. Whereas recruits in initial training are often rigorously evaluated, experienced officers and managers rarely attend programs designed specifically for police that include a meaningful evaluation of performance. In other words, it is highly unlikely that an experienced officer will ever be "flunked" based on training program performance, regardless of how inadequate the officer's performance might be. Such a training program flaw is a serious defect in police career development because too often program participants do not take the training seriously.

## Summary

In order to have an effective career development program, an organization must have a personnel management system that addresses the problems and issues described in this chapter. Personnel practices are concerned with the management of human resources in the organization. Employees must be selected, trained, evaluated, and developed throughout their careers.

The construction of an effective career development system requires an understanding of the community's social, political, economic, and administrative environment. It also requires an awareness of the tasks employees perform and their attributes and interests. The development of programs should integrate task requirements with employee skills and expectations. Career development includes essentially four phases: selection, preparation, performance and evaluation of performance, and development or enhancement of employees through their work life.

Historically, the selection of police personnel has passed through three phases: subjective-political, subjective-merit, and objective-merit. Essentially, as selection moved through these phases, it became more reliable and valid and excluded fewer persons who were qualified to be police officers. The training of police has also changed; training programs are more available and longer and their content is more diverse.

Currently, the selection of police personnel involves attracting candidates through a variety of means (e.g., use of media, brochures, visitations to college campuses), assessing the intellectual ability of the candidate, determining his or her medical, psychological (in a minority of agencies) and physical qualifications, and inquiring into the candidate's character using the polygraph or background investigation. In addition, candidates usually go through an oral interview designed to assess their interpersonal style, judgment, and communication ability.

In training, decisions must be made about methods of instruction, instructors, the amount of time to be given to training, and how the subject matter will be presented. A fundamental part of program development is concerned with assumptions made about learning. Should training be primarily trial and error (behavioral theory) or should it emphasize understanding as well as specific knowledge and skills (Gestalt-field theory)? To what degree should material be treated factually or conceptually? What subjects, or content, should be emphasized? What instructional methods should be utilized? These are some of the questions that need to be answered.

Once trained, officers can be evaluated in terms of attitudes, appearance, methods used to accomplish a task, and the product or service provided. However they are evaluated, the standards or goals or objectives utilized should be job-related, important to the job, observable, and measurable. When conducting evaluations, supervisors and managers must be careful to avoid giving only average ratings (central tendency problem) or the same rating based on a single evaluation criteria (halo effect). Decisions must also be made concerning who will conduct the evaluation, when and how often it will be done, and how the results will be used.

Throughout their careers, police officers must be prepared for changes in job assignments and promotions. The growth or development of officers can involve training inside and outside the organization. The body of knowledge, technology, and skills required to be an effective police officer changes over time and according to position. For optimal performance, officers need continuous updating in all these areas to ensure individual and organization success.

## Discussion Questions

1. Define the concept of career development. Discuss the issues and problems associated with career development in organizations.
2. Identify the four phases of the career development process and discuss, in general, what happens in each phase.
3. Identify and explain the three selection decision models.
4. How does occupational status and the applicant pool influence the selection process?
5. Identify and explain each stage in the entry-level selection process. Explain the problems that may exist in each stage.

6. Discuss the important issues in preparing recruits for their work in policing. Particular emphasis should be given to concerns in program development.
7. How has performance evaluation of officers changed historically in police organizations?
8. How does measurement theory relate to performance evaluation?
9. Identify and explain the different types of performance standards, methods of evaluation, and evaluation problems.
10. Why is the career long-term growth of employees important? What are the types of problems that must be addressed in the development of employees throughout their careers?

# References

Chapman, S. G., "Personnel Management," in *Local Government Police Management*, 2nd ed., ed. Bernard L. Garmire (Washington, D.C.: International City Management Association, 1982), pp. 241–273.

Costello, R. M., Schoenfeld, L. S., and Kobos, J. C., "Police Applicant Screening," *Journal of Clinical Psychology* 38, no. 6(1982):212–221.

Dunnette, M. D. and Motowidlo, S. J., *Police Selection and Career Development*, National Institute of Law Enforcement and Criminal Justice (Washington, D.C.: Government Printing Office, 1976).

Earle, H. H., *Police Recruit Training: Stress vs. Non-Stress* (Springfield, Ill.: Charles C Thomas, 1973).

Gordon, J. R., *Human Resource Management: A Practical Approach* (Boston: Allyn & Bacon, 1986).

Hodes, C. R., Hunt, R. L., and Raskin, D. C., "Effects of Physical Countermeasures on the Physiological Detection of Deception," *Journal of Applied Psychology* 70, no. 1(1985):177–187.

International City Management Association, *Municipal Yearbook* (Washington, D.C.: International City Management Association, 1986).

Kleinmuntz, B. and Szucko, J. J., "Is the Lie Detector Valid?" *Law and Society Review* 16, no. 2(1982):105–125.

Kuykendall, J. and Unsinger, P. C., *Community Police Administration* (Chicago: Nelson-Hall, 1979).

Leibowitz, Z. B., Farren, C., and Kaye, B. L., *Designing Career Development Systems* (San Francisco: Jossey-Bass, 1986).

Los Angeles County Sheriff, *Career Development in Law Enforcement* (Washington, D.C.: Law Enforcement Assistance Administration, 1973).

McCampbell, M. S., *Field Training for Police Officers: State of the Art* (Washington, D.C.: National Institute of Justice, 1986).

Rafky, J. and Sussman, F., "An Evaluation of Field Techniques in Detection of Deception," *Psychophysiology* 12, no. 1(1985):121–130.

Roberg, R. R., *Police Management and Organization Behavior: A Contingency Approach* (St. Paul: West, 1979).

Schoenfeld, L. S. and Kobos, J. C., "Screening Police Applicants," *Psychology Reports* 47, no. 2(1980):419–425.

Schultz, D. P. and Schultz, S. E., *Psychology and Industry Today*, 4th ed. (New York: Macmillan, 1986).

Sherman, L. W., *The Quality of Police Education* (San Francisco: Jossey-Bass, 1978).

Spielberger, C. D., ed., *Police Selection and Evaluation* (New York: Praeger, 1979).

Swanson, C. R., Territo, L., and Taylor, R. W., *Police Administration*, 2nd ed. (New York: Macmillan, 1988).

Ward, R. H. and Webb, V. J., *Quest for Quality* (New York: University Publications, 1984).

Werther, W. B., Jr. and Davis, K., *Personnel Management and Human Resources*, 2nd ed. (New York: McGraw-Hill, 1985).

# CHAPTER 8

# Police Operations:
# Patrol and Investigations

Police operations consist of two major functions: patrol and investigations. Although many departments have other operational activities (e.g., traffic and juvenile, community relations, crime prevention), a substantial majority of all personnel work is either patrol or investigations. These two operational units contend with the widest array of problems and have the most influence on the public's perception of the police.

In small departments, patrol and investigations do not exist as separate units or specializations because the police tend to be generalists. However, in most moderate-size or larger departments, there is a tendency to specialize. This specialization takes place between the initial and follow-up phases in a crime investigation. After a crime is reported to police, a patrol officer is often dispatched to investigate. This officer conducts the initial or preliminary investigation and then forwards a report to investigators or detectives for follow-up and case development. While patrol officers do much more than investigate crimes, the criminal act connects the patrol and investigation functions in police departments.

This chapter is divided into three sections: a description of a criminal act continuum, including a discussion of the alternatives available to police in responding to crime, and sections on patrol and investigations that discuss the development of each operational function and analyze related concerns. In addition, chapter 10 discusses other important patrol and investigation issues.

## The Criminal Act Continuum

Willmer (1970) suggests that a criminal is an "emitter of signals" as a crime is contemplated and committed. Both Willmer (1970) and Unsinger (1977) identify phases or stages of a crime (Kuykendall 1982). Figure 8-1 depicts a criminal act continuum that has several stages set in a time frame. Each stage of a crime presents intervention opportunities for the police. The various stages, and the implications for investigative techniques and information sources, are discussed in the following paragraphs.

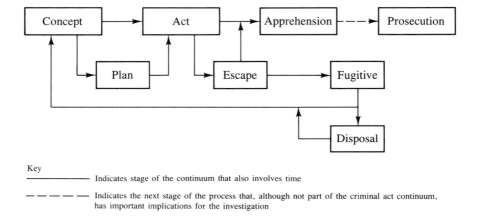

Key
——————— Indicates stage of the continuum that also involves time

— — — — — Indicates the next stage of the process that, although not part of the criminal act continuum, has important implications for the investigation

**Figure 8-1**   Criminal Act Continuum
*Source*: Adapted from J. Kuykendall, "The Criminal Investigation Process: Toward a Conceptual Framework," *Journal of Criminal Justice* 10, no. 2 (1982): 131–145.

## Concept and Plan

In the first stage, the idea for the crime is formulated. The act may immediately follow the *concept* or there may be a *planning phase*. Any planning that follows the concept phase may involve others who have knowledge about the act and unusual behavior by the planner and any associates, including persons from whom necessary supplies or equipment are purchased. Planning relationships establish links that may increase the number of signals the planner emits; the more links, the greater the planner's vulnerability. In addition, persons already suspected of recurring criminal activity may emit signals (e.g., behave suspiciously or tell others of their plans) of impending criminality. If so, the police may focus on the persons or locations that might be involved.

## Criminal Act, Escape, and Fugitive Status

The actual *crime* may last for only a few seconds or for an extended period. The "cast of characters" usually includes the suspect and victim, which may be an individual, an organization, or the state. There may also be witnesses and informants who have important information. Those involved may be able to assist the police in determining the identity and location of the person or persons involved in the crime. In addition, there may be physical evidence that proves useful. After the crime, and assuming there is no apprehension, the *escape* phase begins. The effectiveness of the police during this phase depends on information available about the suspect(s) (e.g., vehicle description, weapons, items stolen), the rapidity with which the information is transmitted to the police, and the speed and tactical competency of their response. After refuge is reached, the *fugitive* phase begins. Depending on whether or not a suspect has been determined, the police will either attempt to identify a suspect or locate and arrest the individual(s) involved. If an arrest is made, the police often assist in preparing the case for possible prosecution. An alternate intent is to secure enough information to be able to use the suspect as an informant.

## "Fruits" Disposal and Repeat Cycle

In some crimes, there are "fruits" such as stolen property that may be sold or bartered away. This *disposal process* recycles criminals through the criminal act continuum and exposes them to additional risks, and it provides the police with unique opportunities. The police may establish a "sting operation," in which officers work undercover to purchase stolen property. In addition, some individuals are *recurringly involved in crime*; this increases police opportunities to apprehend them because as more crimes are committed, the police are often able to collect additional information.

## Information Sources

The signals emitted at any point of the criminal act continuum are possible sources of information, which may be obtained from people, physical evidence, and information systems. There are four roles played by *people* in criminal investigations: victim, suspect, informant, and witness. Victims, if they survive, may have information about the criminal, property stolen, time of occurrence, and so on. Suspects may be willing to provide information about the crime and their involvement. Informants have information that pertains to "suspicious" events or behavior, impending crimes, individuals recurringly involved in criminal activity, and the specific identification and location of suspects.

Witnesses can be grouped into three categories: primary, secondary, and location. *Primary* witnesses have direct knowledge about the crime. *Secondary* witnesses have knowledge about events that may have transpired just before or after the crime. For example, a primary witness might see the crime being committed, and a secondary witness might see a "suspicious" person before the crime occurred or a vehicle leaving the scene. *Location* witnesses have information about the location of identified suspects. Police officers are also potentially important sources of information. As a result of investigating crimes and associating with criminals, officers acquire knowledge that proves useful in their work.

*Physical evidence* includes all material objects, pictures, drawings, and measurements related to a crime scene; tools used in the crime; any property, fingerprints, and blood samples connected with the crime; and the individuals who might be involved. This type of information may prove useful in determining if a crime was committed, identifying the suspect and where he or she might be, helping to convince a suspect to confess, and if there is a trial, providing corroborating evidence of a suspect's involvement.

*Data systems* include recorded information concerning activities, individuals, property, and other types of possible leads and evidence. Law enforcement organizations maintain record systems about crime, persons suspected and convicted of crimes, criminal networks and relationships, methods of operation (modus operandi), stolen and recovered property, and aliases and "nicknames." Many other organizations—such as public utilities, credit companies, and the military services, to name a few—also have information that may prove useful in investigations.

## Intervention Considerations and Investigative Techniques

Police intervention is determined by the type of crime and crime analysis. There are basically two types of crimes from an intervention point of view: those involving a *criminal and a victim* and those with, in effect, *two criminal parties*. The second type usually involves the buying and/or selling of illegal goods or services (e.g., prostitution, drug transactions). In such crimes, police intervention often takes place during the commission of the crime. For other crimes, the police response may occur after commission, or a patrol (visibility) or educational response may be specified, or both may be used. The more that is known about the problem (crime analysis), the more precise the response.

Two important considerations in intervention are related to the prevention-apprehension and proactive-reactive role debates. A decision may be made either to intervene prior to the act in order to prevent the crime or during or after the act in order to make an apprehension. As noted in chapter 2, this decision is influenced by a number of factors. When police intervene during the concept or criminal act phase, they are responding proactively; when they conduct investigations after the crime, they are responding reactively.

Police managers must also decide whether the police response will be overt or covert, that is, visible or invisible. *Covert* or clandestine police activity is fraught with risk—to democracy, to criminals, and to officers. Some crimes (e.g., drugs, prostitution) must be investigated in a clandestine manner; however, the use of stakeouts and decoy programs involves covert police intervention when there are other alternatives available (e.g., routine investigations, intensified overt patrol, career criminal targeting).

In responding to crime, there are five basic investigative techniques: interviewing, role playing, scientific analysis, pattern analysis, and monitoring. *Interviewing* involves a communication process in which one person attempts to obtain information (e.g., by talking with victims, witnesses, suspects, and informants). When *role playing*, police assume a fictitious identity to obtain information; this is the clandestine or "undercover" dimension of investigative work. *Scientific analysis* is concerned with physical evidence and how it is gathered, processed, stored, and used. *Pattern analysis* is concerned with the structure of crimes, the relationship between crimes and criminals, and crime targets. Crime is analyzed by time and location, criminal links and behavior, and modus operandi (that is, the criminal's method of operation) in an attempt to identify criminals, criminal relationships, and possible locations of future criminal activity. Finally, *monitoring* involves observing persons and/or locations suspected of involvement in criminal activity. This monitoring may include the use of technological devices (e.g., eavesdropping equipment) to assist in listening, following, and taking pictures.

The relationship between the crime continuum, sources of information, and investigative techniques is identified in table 8-1. As noted at the beginning of the chapter, patrol officers do much more than just respond to crime; nevertheless, a crime is the organizational link between patrol and investigations. Consequently, the stages of a criminal act and the alternatives and techniques used in the police response need to be understood before discussing more specific aspects of the patrol and investigation functions.

## The Patrol Function

The major *goals* of patrol include (1) crime prevention and deterrence, (2) apprehension of criminals, (3) recovery of stolen property, (4) creation of a sense of community security and satisfaction, and (5) provision of noncrime-related services. As noted in chapter 2, officers tend to utilize four strategies (visibility, apprehension, counseling, and education), either formally or informally, in attempting to accomplish these goals. Patrol activities

**Table 8-1**   Relationship of Information Sources and Investigative Techniques to the Criminal Act Continuum

| Stages of the Continuum | Information Sources Emphasized | Investigative Techniques Emphasized |
|---|---|---|
| Concept | People (i.e., informants and police officers), information systems | Role playing<br>Pattern analysis<br>Monitoring |
| Plan | Same as above | Same as above |
| Act | All sources except the suspect | All techniques |
| Escape | Same as above | Monitoring |
| Fugitive | Same as above | Monitoring<br>Interviewing<br>Pattern analysis<br>Role playing |
| Disposal | Same as above | Pattern analysis<br>Monitoring<br>Role playing |

*Source:* Adapted from J. Kuykendall, "The Criminal Investigation Process: Toward a Conceptual Framework," *Journal of Criminal Justice* 10, no. 2 (1982):137.

can also be grouped into law enforcement, order maintenance, and service categories. *Law enforcement* activities involve problems in which police conduct investigations, make arrests, or issue citations. *Order maintenance* problems may or may not involve a violation of the law (usually minor), in which officers tend to use alternatives other than arrest. Examples include loud parties, teenagers' drinking beer, and minor neighborhood disputes. *Service activities* involve taking reports and providing information and assistance. The deterrence and prevention, apprehension, and recovery of stolen property goals are related to the *law enforcement* category. The other two goals—creation of a sense of community security and satisfaction and provision of noncrime-related services—are related to the order maintenance and service activities.

The workload of patrol officers can be divided into four basic categories: administrative duties, calls for service or reactive activities, self-initiated or proactive activities, and preventive patrol. Although the percentage of time spent in each of these categories varies among police departments, a typical distribution is about 20–25 percent for administrative duties, 20–25 percent for calls for service, 30–40 percent for preventive patrol, and 10–15 percent for self-initiated activities (Gay, Schell, and Schack 1977).

## Historical Development

Two of the most important activities of patrol officers are *watching* and *being watched*. Natural watching took place in preindustrial societies as a means of social control. The nightwatch was originally the responsibility of the private citizen, who served as a community obligation. Eventually, the citizen watcher became the paid watchman who became the nineteenth-century patrol officer. Patrol officers in the political-watchman model were dispersed throughout the community in the hopes of preventing crime. However, given their availability, the lack of other government services, and political expediency, the patrol function became an all-purpose governmental service. Patrol remained, even into the 1980s, the least specialized and the most diverse part of police work.

In the political-watchman model, the patrol officer was essentially a *"neighbor,"* although how good a neighbor remains a subject of controversy. One scenario is that the "friendly neighborhood cop" knew and was known by the inhabitants of a beat or area. Supposedly, officers became aware of who was trustworthy, who was dangerous, and who was neither. Officers were also more concerned with "quality of life" order maintenance problems, such as vandalism and disruptive juvenile activities, and with providing a sense of neighborhood security, rather than being preoccupied with crime fighting and law enforcement. A less favorable perspective concerning neighborhood cops is that they were corrupt, inefficient, and indifferent to basic responsibilities. This is the neighbor who was a lazy, discriminating, dishonest bully. Recently, however, the possible positive aspects of the neighborhood cop have been stressed as a basis for suggesting a reorientation for patrol officer's behavior.

As previously discussed, concepts known as community and problem-oriented policing have recently emerged as a possible new direction for police. These are examples of our community-service and rational-contingency models. Community policing is defined by Trojanowicz and Carter (1988, p. 17) as: "A philosophy and not a specific tactic, . . . [it] is a proactive, decentralized approach, designed to reduce crime, disorder, and . . . fear of crime, by . . . involving the same officer in the same community on a long-term basis" in order to increase trust and cooperation. Goldstein (1987) says that community policing involves assigning officers permanently to a specific neighborhood, establishing police priorities based on community desires, and systematically analyzing problems. However, community policing is not without critics, particularly among individuals who think that the patrol officer in the political-watchman model was more a bum than a hero (Haller 1983; Sherman 1983; Walker 1977, 1984).

The legalistic-professional model, which gradually replaced the political-watchman approach, produced a patrol officer who was like a *soldier*, in sharp contrast to the often unruly and undisciplined "neighborhood cop." For patrol, the hope was that officers would become more disciplined and professional in responding to police problems and citizens, particularly in the area of crime control. This model also stressed the importance of making the police less political by making them more impersonal and more responsive to organizational authority. This process was enhanced by the development of the Uniformed Crime Reports, a national reporting system for crime that became increasingly popular as a means of measuring police effectiveness. This system tended to stress the crime-fighting dimension of the police role as organizations and officers became less interested in what they defined as noncrime-related activities.

As this model became increasingly influential in the twentieth century, the informal watching of citizens and neighborhoods by police began to change. In the nineteenth century, industrialization took men away from home to work. In the twentieth century, the car took men farther away as less densely populated suburbs developed. In addition, as more women be gan to enter the workforce, there was less supervision of children at home. Reduced supervision, primarily of teenage boys, and less informal watching by neighbors in densely populated cities placed an increasing burden on the more formal watching done by police, particularly from a car. The nature of watching from a car is different from watching while walking. As Sherman (1983, p. 149) notes, "what the . . . officer sees is familiar buildings with unfamiliar people [while] what the public sees is a familiar . . . car with an unfamiliar officer." Consequently, officers may not develop the neighborhood contextual knowledge that helps them determine who is doing what to whom and when they are doing it.

Along with the car, although not simultaneously, came the radio and the telephone. Being able to contact police and dispatch them to help citizens changed patrol from essentially watching to prevent crime to waiting to respond to crime. Citizens tended to request police assistance more often (the recent development of an emergency telephone number—911—has significantly contributed to this tendency), and this reinforced the all-purpose service orientation of the patrol function. In particular, poor people used the police as lawyers, doctors, psychologists, and social workers. The "soldiers" of the legalistic-professional model were forced to work somewhat as a neighborhood cop, but they knew less about the neighborhoods and people, were often ill-equipped to perform noncrime-related functions, and did not tend to like the order maintenance and public service aspects of police work (Sherman 1983; Walker 1984)).

The community-service model, related to the community and problem-oriented approaches described earlier, attempted to remedy the problems associated with patrol in the legalistic-professional model. An effort was made to overcome perceived problems of police isolation from citizens and to better prepare officers to respond more effectively to order-maintenance, public service, and law enforcement problems. In the rational-contingency

model, systematic research and analysis became the basis for the police response, although public and police preferences still play an important role.

## Police Patrol Issues

In this section, we discuss resource determination and allocation, selected
research findings, and guidelines for the development of the patrol function.
The first issue is concerned with how many officers a police department
should have and how patrol resources should be allocated. The second part
identifies and briefly discusses some of the more important patrol-related research. The third issue involves guidelines for developing the patrol function
based on these research findings.

### Resource Determination and Allocation

Essentially, there are three ways to determine the "appropriate" number of
police personnel: intuitively, comparatively, and by workload. The *intuitive
approach*, which is an "educated guess," involves the experience and judgment of police managers. The *comparative method* involves comparing one
or more communities, using the ratio of police officers per 1,000 population
unit, with the one attempting to justify additional personnel. For example,
assume a community of 50,000 (50–1,000 population units) has 100 police officers, which is a ratio of 2.0 officers per 1,000 persons. If the ratio for the
comparative group of communities was 2.2, the apparent disparity would be
10 officers (2.2−2.0 = 0.2 times 50 = 10). Although often used, comparing ra-
tios is not very reliable since departments tend to be diverse with respect to
managerial effectiveness, use of technology, competency of officers, public
expectations, and policing styles.

 The last approach, *workload*, is rarely utilized for an entire department
because it requires an elaborate information system, standards of expected
performance, well-defined community expectations, and prioritization of
police activities. To determine workload, the organization must be able to

identify precisely what the community expects the police to do, which calls must be processed (and which calls can be ignored or given only a minimum response), and an expected level of service. Given the number of possible tasks to be performed, and the time and effort that can be spent on those tasks, police work is virtually a "bottomless pit" of human resource needs. Consequently, police departments, using whatever method, rarely have difficulty justifying additional resources.

The two most important variables in allocation of personnel are location and time. Knowing the *location* of problems assists departments in dividing up a community into geographic beats or sectors of approximately equal workload. *Time of occurrence* is important because it determines how personnel will be grouped into working time periods or shifts. As a rule, the more problems, the more officers will be assigned. The *time it takes to respond* to problems is equally as important because the resource being allocated is a skilled officer's time. The resources, or person-hours, available to police organizations are governed by a number of factors: the workweek, the number of vacation days, sick time taken, training time, and overtime. Generally, a police organization must have about five patrol officers to put one officer "on the street," 24 hours a day, 7 days a week, 365 days a year. In police agencies, only about 20–25 percent of the personnel provide direct service to the public at any one time (Cawley, Miron, and Araujo 1977).

*Mobility* is also an important aspect of allocation. Police officers walk, use bicycles, horses, motor scooters, motorcycles, dogsleds, snowmobiles, cars, boats, helicopters, and planes. In deciding what form of mobility should be used, police managers need to consider speed, access, density, visibility, and community consequences. Walking officers can go places cars cannot. Cars have limited mobility in densely populated areas with traffic congestion but they can get to many problems quickly. Walking officers can see things officers in cars cannot, who can see things officers in helicopters cannot, who can see things neither the walking officer nor the squad car officer can see. Of course, the community may have an opinion about the different forms of mobility. For example, some communities consider helicopters unnecessarily intrusive, because of noise and invasion-of-privacy issues.

**Bicycle patrol allows not only for good mobility but for close interaction with the public as well.**

## Selected Research Findings

Prior to the 1960s, there was only limited research about the patrol function. However, in the last two decades, there have been numerous studies concerning various aspects of patrol. Except for team policing, addressed in chapter 11, some of the most important studies are presented and discussed in this section.

**Kansas City preventive patrol experiment.**   In the early 1970s, Kansas City conducted an experiment to assess the impact of the effectiveness of random patrol, which means that patrol officers are allowed to patrol where they want in their districts when not on assignment. Fifteen similar geographic areas were selected and three different levels of patrol were utilized. Five beats had about three times normal patrol, five maintained normal patrol levels, and five had almost no patrol (i.e., no beat was left unattended because police units had to respond to calls in those areas). The findings indicated that the different levels of random patrol had no impact on crime rates, services provided, or citizen feelings of security. Since many police departments routinely based requests for personnel and resource allocation decisions on having a certain percentage of an officer's time devoted to random patrol, this research raised important questions about random patrol effectiveness and the resource needs of police (Kelling, Pate, Dieckman, and Brown 1974).

The primary impact of this study was that police patrol became more directed and specialized, which will be discussed later in this chapter. The findings may also indicate that the problem of random patrol is not that it has so little impact on crime because criminals are not watching for police, but that police, particularly in cars, may do little effective watching themselves (Sherman 1983). Other considerations are the resource range implications of the findings and the definition of normal patrol. The patrol levels measured were about one-third to three times "normal" patrol. What would have happened, for instance, if there had been absolutely no patrol or levels higher than three times normal patrol? Other research has clearly indicated that "saturation" of areas with visible police units has a dramatic impact on certain types of crime, even if this impact is short-lived and may result in time, area, or crime displacement. In other words, the crime rate may stay down only as long as the police are present or shortly after they leave, or the crime rate may go up in other time periods, in other areas, or for other types of less deterrable crimes (Caiden 1977). One study suggests that five times normal patrol at night does have an impact on the crime rate (Currey 1983). In addition, there is no standard definition of normal patrol. The size of a beat (geographic area), the number of problems in the typical beat, and the number of officers available to respond varies from community to community. Consequently, what is considered normal patrol for one city may not be the same for other cities.

**Directed patrol.**   Directing what patrol officers do rather than randomly employing unused patrol time became increasingly popular after the Kansas City research. Directed patrol is more proactive, uses noncommitted time in specified activity, and is based on crime and problem analysis. In this approach, police tend to use a broader range of strategies and tactics. They may conduct education programs and engage in more field interrogations. Directed patrol can also include a covert and/or a career criminal approach, which are forms of specialized patrol.

In general, the results of the evaluations of directed patrol are positive (Cordner 1981). Of particular importance is the proactive dimension of the directed activity, be it making arrests, issuing citations, conducting field interrogations, or educating the public about crime. Proactivity produces more information, heightens citizen awareness of police, perhaps creates an impression of greater police watching, and most certainly requires police to be more alert and active.

**Covert patrol.**   Patrol officers (and detectives) working undercover (covertly), has always been a police activity. Police wearing civilian clothes designed to blend into the environment can walk, ride bicycles or motorbikes, or drive around in unmarked cars. They can concentrate in a certain area or on a type of crime, act as a possible decoy in hopes of being victimized, or look for or follow individuals suspected of criminal activity. This can be done randomly or in a directed manner by focusing on a specific problem, area, or person.

These covert patrol tactics, whether general or specific, have had mixed results. They tend to be widely utilized by police organizations; and while some programs have had positive results in increasing arrests (which is the purpose of this approach), there has been minimal impact on crime rates. This approach is costly and in some communities has resulted in increased allegations of police entrapment and actual increases in the number of injuries and deaths among police officers and citizens (Caiden 1977; Sherman 1983; Webb 1977).

**Field interrogation.**   What is the impact of conducting field interrogations on crime rates and citizen attitudes? Field interrogations involve stopping and talking with "suspicious" persons. This proactive patrol tactic not only produces information about persons who may be wanted or who have committed a crime, it also clearly indicates that police are watching. Neither citizens nor criminals can be sure of this when police only ride around in cars. While this activity can be associated with any type of patrol, it is often a part of directed patrol efforts. In one study that compared areas with a different frequency of field interrogations, a slightly lower crime rate was found in areas in which it was used most often. And when police conducted the interrogations, even in minority communities, with civility and by explaining the reasons for the interview, there was no adverse impact on citizen attitudes (Boydstun 1975).

**Response time.**   One criterion historically used to assess patrol effectiveness has been the rapidity of the police response to calls for service, particularly those involving crimes and injuries. It was assumed that the faster the response, the more satisfied citizens would be, and the more likely suspects would be apprehended. Research concerning these assumptions does not generally support the importance of response time because citizens tend to delay too long in calling the police (Pate, Bowers, Ferrara, and Lorence 1976; Sherman 1983). In addition, citizens are often more concerned about when police are coming than how fast they arrive. However, response time is important to assist injured parties or sick persons, for crimes in progress, and for those that are reported quickly and that include information about suspects. When actual response time is short (that is, citizens do not delay in reporting the crime and the police respond quickly), there may be some investigative benefits relative to evidence and the likelihood of a successful apprehension (Cordner, Greene, and Bynum 1983).

**Foot patrol.**    Another trend that developed in the 1960s, but became more prevalent in the 1970s and 1980s, was a return to foot patrol, or police officers walking beats. Many cities, particularly those that were older and densely populated, had never totally abandoned foot patrol. For other communities, however, the return was a departure from essentially motorized patrol, which was criticized as having further isolated police officers from citizens. Foot patrol, it was argued, would improve community relations, reduce fear of crime, decrease crime rates, and result in more arrests.

The most comprehensive evaluations of foot patrol or "walking a beat" suggest that foot patrol may result in only a slight reduction in crime, but it does reduce the citizens' fear of crime and it also changes the nature of police–citizen interaction (Trojanowicz 1982; Police Foundation 1981). There is also some evidence that officers who walk beats tend to have a higher level of job satisfaction because of the increased variety in their work (Trojanowicz 1983). Perhaps the most striking feature of foot patrol is how it appears to change the police–citizen relationship. Foot patrol officers tend to have more nonadversial, or positive and constructive, exchanges. To be successful, however, foot patrol must be in an area in which officers can interact with citizens (e.g., shopping centers, neighborhoods, or areas with businesses or outside citizen activity) and see those citizens frequently. The size of a foot patrol beat should not be so large that it cannot be traversed once or twice per shift even while performing other duties. This aspect is necessary to obtain the benefits of improved police–citizen interaction and a reduction in the fear of crime (Greene 1987; Payne and Trojanowicz 1985; Trojanowicz and Banas 1985; Sherman 1983).

**One- and two-person cars.**    Historically, when police first began to use automobiles, two or more officers were often assigned to one car. However, by the 1940s, some departments began to utilize one-person cars. Since then there has been considerable controversy surrounding this issue. Do one- or two-person cars do more work? Which is safer for the officer? Which is safer for the citizen? Perhaps the most comprehensive study occurred in San Diego in the 1970s (Boydstun, Sherry, and Moelter 1977). The findings indicate that there is little difference between one- and two-person units in calls for service or in officer-initiated or proactive activity. One-person units pro-

The role of the foot patrol officer can take many forms, including lending a "helping hand" to those in need.

duced more arrests, filed more formal crime reports, received fewer citizen complaints, and were clearly less expensive. The only apparent advantage of two-person units was that they required less time to process calls for service.

One-person units also had a safety advantage. Even considering the danger of the area and shift assignment, one-person units had fewer resisting-arrest problems and about equal involvement in assaults on officers. The driving safety records were about the same. The study concluded that one-person units or cars are at least equal to and are often safer than two-person cars, and they are also more effective and more efficient. However, these findings do not match the preferences of many police officers, who tend to want to work in two-person units. The perception that they are safer, even though they are not, tends to influence officer attitudes. This belief suggests that police managers may need to educate their employees about the research findings and why the department uses certain practices.

**Management of demand.**    Given the problems police departments have in responding to requests for service, their attempts to structure or control demand have been predictable. While managing demand has been done for decades in many departments, it has become increasingly important in the last five to ten years. Essentially, managing demand requires categorizing requests for service and matching those requests with differential police responses. Which calls for service require an immediate response and which can wait? Can some calls be handled by persons other than sworn officers? Which calls can be answered by telephone or mail or by asking the citizen to come to the police station?

Differential police responses to demands include dividing the patrol force, called *split-patrol*, by designating some units to respond to calls for service (possibly by appointment) and some to patrol and to respond to more serious calls (Tien, Simon, and Larson 1977). Calls for service can be categorized by importance or emergency nature. Such categories might include crimes in progress, serious and recent felonies where apprehension seems possible, sick and injured persons, persons who might be harmed, and categories for calls that do not require an immediate response by a patrol unit.

Less serious matters can be handled by nonsworn personnel, volunteers, reserves, and by appointment, telephone, or mail.

In general, the evaluation of attempts to manage demand have been positive. Time can be saved for crime prevention, patrol, and other activities without loss of citizen satisfaction. In the long term, there may be considerable savings because fewer personnel may be required (National Institute of Justice 1986). In the twentieth century, however, police have been essentially a reactive force in the community. This means that they are controlled by the public because most police–citizen interactions result from citizen requests. Attempts to manage demand, along with other directed patrol responses, make the police more proactive, which may result in less police accountability to the community. As police further define what problems they will respond to and how they will respond, they may become more efficient and effective while becoming less open, responsive, and democratic (Mastrofski 1986).

## Patrol Development Guidelines

Given the research to date, the patrol function in a police department is probably most effective if developed using the following guidelines:

1. Except in cases of obvious adverse impact on officer morale, only one-person units should be utilized.
2. In neighborhoods with dense population and/or an active citizenry (businesses, outside social interaction, and recreational activities), small walking beats should be established.
3. There should be a mix of covert and overt patrol activity with an emphasis on the overt. Police should use stakeouts and decoys only as a last resort because they are too dangerous to justify the results (if any) obtained in arrests and reductions in crime.
4. Directed patrol is preferable to random patrol; therefore, police departments need to have a systematic crime analysis capability.
5. Patrol officers should utilize as many strategies (visibility, apprehension, education, and counseling) as possible to balance the positive and

negative contacts in the community. This will prevent the development of a predominantly adversarial relationship between police and citizens.
6. Patrol officers should be polite and proactive; when appropriate and legally justified, they should conduct citizen stops in an informative and civil manner.
7. Police should have the capability of matching different police responses with various categories of calls for service, but this should never be done to the extent that citizen satisfaction is ignored in favor of other police objectives.

The difference between a police department that follows these guidelines and one that does not will probably be reflected in only minor differences in the crime rate, a slight improvement in number of arrests, and a substantial impact on both the citizens' fear of crime and citizen satisfaction concerning police activities. Police should not engage in activities designed to influence the crime rate if the activities are destructive to community expectations or concerns. As long as it is legally permissible and not discriminatory, citizen satisfaction should be the highest priority.

## The Investigative Function

Investigators or detectives—the terms will be used interchangeably—are essentially specialists in responding to crimes serious enough to warrant an investigation. The major *goal* of the criminal investigation function is to increase the number of arrests for crimes that are prosecutable and that will result in a conviction. As a by-product of this goal, investigators recover stolen property and produce information that may be useful in other crimes, often through the development and manipulation of informants (Cawley, Miron, and Araujo 1977; Forst 1982; Waegel 1982; Wycoff 1982).

As discussed previously, crime investigation is usually divided in many police departments. Patrol officers conduct the initial or preliminary investigation and investigators follow up and develop the case. In some jurisdictions, the development phase involves working with the prosecuting attorney to prepare a case for trial. In others, this phase is the responsibility of investigators employed by the prosecuting attorney's office. An investigator's basic responsibility is to establish a case, identify a suspect, locate the suspect, possibly obtain a confession, and then dispose of the case (Sanders 1977). The disposal phase may or may not involve a prosecution or a conviction. Investigations can be terminated if the police determine no crime has been committed, if they have insufficient evidence to proceed, or if there is no longer a suspect (e.g., a murder–suicide).

In the 1970s, as a result of the research of Greenwood and Petersilia (1975), investigative units in police departments were criticized as ineffective and inefficient. This research reported that detectives rarely produced information, not provided by patrol officers, that resulted in an arrest and spent more time in processing information than in looking for suspects. Subsequent research suggests that detectives do, in fact, "solve" some cases by their own investigative efforts, but only in about 8 percent of those cases in which arrests are actually made (Eck 1984).

The types of cases detectives investigate can be divided into three categories: "whodunits," "walk throughs," and "where are they." *Whodunits* are those cases in which there are initially no suspects and, unless they involve very serious crimes, they are rarely investigated thoroughly. *Walk throughs* are cases in which a suspect is easily determined and police officers must only observe legal guidelines to reach a successful conclusion. Interestingly, one of the major management problems for investigative units is to ensure that "walk throughs" are processed adequately. It is not uncommon for such cases to be rejected for prosecution as a result of incomplete or inappropriate investigations. In *where are they* cases, the suspect is known but not his or her location. These cases may have simple solutions or may be complex mysteries. Often, persons wanted by the police are determined to avoid capture, which makes the police task even more difficult (Kuykendall 1986).

## Historical Development

When the constable-nightwatch system of policing began to be replaced in the 1840s, crime detection was the province of both the new police and private detectives. Private detectives were hired to recover stolen property, not apprehend criminals. They often had a close association with criminals, were aware in advance of criminal activity, worked for a fee, and would not return stolen property until they were paid. People were easily taken advantage of in this system. However, a greater concern for the recovery of stolen property than for prosecution was a major factor in development of the private detective's role.

The transition of detective work to essentially a public rather than a private matter began in the 1840s, but was not substantially complete until the early 1900s. The major reasons for this transition were related to the methods employed by private detectives and the desire to prosecute suspected criminals. In addition, the emergence of insurance companies tended to gradually lessen the victim's concern about return of their property.

The public detectives of the political-watchman model were like secretive rogues. Although some of their exploits were romanticized, they were mostly inefficient and corrupt. They often had a close association with criminals, used and manipulated "stool pigeons," and even had "deadlines" that established areas of a city in which detectives and criminals agreed that crimes could be committed. Nineteenth- and early-twentieth-century detectives believed that their work should be essentially clandestine. They were considered to be members of a "secret service," whose identity should remain unknown lest the criminal become wary and flee. Some detectives wore disguises, submitted court testimony in writing, and even used masks when looking at suspects. Although they did investigate crimes, detectives functioned primarily as a nonuniformed patrol force. They tended to go where persons congregated (e.g., station house landings, steamboat docks, beer gardens) to look for pickpockets, gamblers, and troublemakers.

Just as police reformers of the early twentieth century hoped to replace the "neighbor" patrol officer with the "soldier" crime fighter, they also hoped to replace secretive rogues with a scientific criminal investigator. The relationship with criminals and stool pigeons was criticized as corrupting and undesirable for a professional police officer. It was also believed that the use of science would make the relationship unnecessary. As reformers stressed the importance of the detective as a perceptive, rational analyst, much like

Sherlock Holmes, they also emphasized reorganization of departments to improve efficiency.

As with patrol officers, detectives gradually began to be more reactive than proactive. By the 1920s and 1930s, detectives were mostly investigating crimes after the fact rather than using clandestine tactics. Although many were ill equipped to utilize the newly developed scientific methods, this was not as significant a problem as it first appeared because the use of scientific evidence proved to be valuable in few cases and rarely aided police in identifying suspects. Consequently, the information that became most important in making arrests and ensuring successful prosecutions was derived from witnesses, informers, and, perhaps most important, suspects. As detectives stopped being secretive rogues, they gradually became inquisitors who often coerced information from suspects to make cases.

By the 1960s, changes in criminal procedural laws—known as the due process revolution—and the continuing emphasis on reorganization and efficiency in police departments had created a detective who was essentially a clerk or bureaucrat. While some detectives continued to work undercover, the majority were reactive and only infrequently identified suspects who were not obvious. These detectives spent substantially more time processing information and coordinating with other criminal justice agencies than looking for suspects.

Of course, all elements of the detective's role described in this section are present to some degree. Some detectives are secretive, some are skillful in obtaining confessions without coercion, and all must invest considerable time in processing information. While the emergence of the legalistic-professional type of police organization did tend to produce a detective who was more bureaucrat than sleuth, subsequent models (community-service and rational-contingency) tend to have a broader view of the detective's role. These models use the detective in both clandestine and educational activities. As a result of crime analysis techniques, the detective has continued to evolve, becoming somewhat less reactive (since the 1960s) and more proactive, with an emphasis on criminals rather than on crimes. This, of course, is not a new role for the detective, and so far police departments have been able to make these changes without the extensive corruption problems historically associated with them (Kuykendall 1986).

Currently, detectives have multifaceted roles: They work undercover; they operate sting operations designed to buy or sell stolen property; they may be involved in career criminal programs that target individuals suspected of recurring criminal involvement; they may be assigned as part of an investigative group to "bust up" organized activity like violent juvenile gangs; and they may be involved in intelligence-gathering activities. However, the investigators or detectives involved in these activities constitute only a small percentage of those in detective work, and the substantial majority of detectives function more as clerks than sleuths. To characterize the detective as a clerk is not intended to demean the role, rather it simply suggests the perspective from which most detectives should be viewed. They are primarily information processors, not Sherlock Holmes, Mike Hammer, or Dirty Harry.

## Investigative Issues

Several important investigative issues are discussed in this section, including the democratic context of investigations, resource determination and allocation, case management, target selection, and incitement and entrapment. Of course, other possible areas could be explored, but they are either too technical to be treated adequately in one chapter (e.g., maintenance of documentation, statistical reporting, competence of individual investigators) or they are treated more generally elsewhere in the text (e.g., recognition of employees, work environment, competence, and so on).

### The Democratic Context of Investigations

One of the more important issues is an understanding of the democratic context within which investigations take place. In democratic societies there is a concern for freedom, privacy, and individual rights, and the possibility of the abuse of power by the police. Three important aspects of the police response to crime are *secrecy*, *response mode*, and *investigative focus*. Each of these investigative dimensions can be divided as follows: visible or invisible (or overt and covert), reactive or proactive, and event or individual. The most democratically sensitive aspects of an investigation are secrecy or invisibility; and second, those aspects that are individually (i.e., directed at a specific individual rather than a case or an event) focused. An invisible response makes it difficult to hold the police accountable and may result in legal problems of entrapment (to be discussed later). Further, when the police begin to focus on an individual as a possible suspect, that person's freedom and individual rights are in potential jeopardy. Managers need to be aware of the process associated with conducting criminal investigations, the different types of investigations that are possible, and the ones that are the most democratically sensitive (Kuykendall 1982).

## *Resource Allocation and Determination*

The number of personnel to be assigned to investigative units has never been precisely determined. It depends on whether detectives work in pairs or alone; the extent of patrol participation in investigations; the training, experience, and competency of the investigators; and the technological assistance available. In practice, some agencies use a "10 percent of total sworn personnel" criterion. The range in moderate to large police departments is from about 8 percent to over 20 percent of all personnel.

In terms of assignment (either in pairs or alone), one-person assignments, as in patrol, generally seem to be more appropriate for most situations. Exceptions include particularly dangerous assignments, some interrogations, and meeting suspicious informers. However, even in these areas, as in investigations in general, there is less direct evidence concerning the relative efficiency or effectiveness of one- and two-person assignments in crime investigation (Bloch and Weidman 1975).

## Case Management

Case management is concerned with the decision to either investigate or not investigate a crime, the monitoring of those decisions, and the process involved. It includes consideration of the initial investigation, case screening, the continuing investigation, and relationships between investigators and patrol officers, detectives and prosecutors, and police and witnesses. Since the Greenwood and Petersilia (1975) study on investigative effectiveness, police organizations have become increasingly concerned with formalizing what has long been an informal practice; namely, deciding which cases to investigate, which cases require only a minimal effort, and which cases can be ignored. This has become known as *case screening* or *case management*. In general, the basis for decision making is crime "solvability." Although extremely serious or sensitive (for political or economic reasons) crimes will usually be investigated regardless of the likelihood that a suspect will be identified, many crimes are given only cursory consideration.

**The initial investigation.** In this phase of case management, it is important to prescribe the role of patrol officers so that they can identify the most important evidentiary factors in solving a case and to ensure some participation by the officer in the continuation of the investigative process. The reporting process for the patrol officer should include a form that identifies the most important factors in solving each type of crime and the sequence in which the officer should look for these factors. The patrol officer should clearly note which factors are present and which are not and he or she should indicate the effort required to determine the presence or absence of each one. The police agency will then be able to more accurately estimate the time required for each case, the likelihood of a successful result (if one has not already been achieved), and the effort that should be invested in a continuing investigation.

**Case screening.** Some police departments have adopted a mathematical formula that weights evidentiary factors. Follow-up decisions are based on achieving a certain number of points based on the formula. However, the key element is always evidence that provides a direct, meaningful connection to a suspect. Without such information, police usually do not solve crimes unless they invest considerable resources, and they can rarely do this except in serious crimes.

Case screening models should take into consideration the following:

1. A system to eliminate predictably unsolvable crimes.
2. Flexible criteria to allow, if necessary, political and situational factors to be considered.
3. Individuals, acting as case screeners, who will ensure the adequacy and completeness of the investigations of both patrol and detectives, and who will determine the appropriateness of the resources expended in each case.
4. For large departments, or any that have decentralized investigations, co-ordination to ensure that screening criteria are applied consistently.
5. A system to inform victims and witnesses of the status of investigations.
6. A method to ensure that any additional information discovered about suspended cases will be recorded and considered in possibly changing the status of a case.

**The continuing investigation.** The manager's role in supervising ongoing investigations involves several important considerations. In some cases, depending on the workload, the investigation may be given to patrol officers. Progress must be reviewed to determine if the continued allocation of resources, given the results, is appropriate. This managerial decision should be based, at least in part, on predetermined guidelines governing how much investigative time should be given to each case. Managers must also be alert to the emergence of linkages of crimes that may result from the analysis of suspended investigations. There should be some investment of resources in an attempt to develop such linkages and, when appropriate, suspended cases should be reopened.

The careful utilization of resources in investigations allows the manager to assign more resources to other crimes of organizational concern. In addition, other types of specialized investigative efforts may be developed. Managing the continuing investigation requires the creation of a monitoring system that provides adequate documentation of the activities and results of the investigative unit. This will permit an assessment of performance and a determination of the adequacy of the decisions made relative to resource utilization (Greenberg and Wasserman 1979).

**Investigator–patrol relationships.**  The relationship between detectives and patrol officers is potentially one of conflict. It is important to address this potential conflict because effective communication is vital to the success of many investigations. Investigators should make an effort to develop and maintain a good rapport with patrol officers. Managers should encourage and reward, both informally and formally, the development of this type of relationship. This relationship should be based on frequent personal contacts, the acknowledgement of the patrol officers' contribution in investigations, seeking patrol officer advice when appropriate, and keeping officers informed as to the status of cases.

One of the major problems that may exist between patrol officers and investigators is related to status differentiation. Investigators dress differently, may be perceived to have more status, and may even be of higher rank or receive a higher salary. These problems are not always easy for managers to resolve. Often the solution is found in the basic organizational design of the agency (e.g., using team or community policing). Another way to address this problem is to a create a personnel system that gives equal status and financial rewards to both patrol officers and investigators. Managers also need to be alert to the manner in which investigators and patrol officers are treated. It is essential that patrol officers not be given the impression that, when compared to investigators, they are "second-class" citizens (Bloch and Weidman 1975).

**Detective–prosecutor relationships.**  Investigators and prosecutors depend on each other; consequently, it is mutually beneficial for both to communicate and cooperate effectively. In many departments, the acceptance of cases for prosecution is one key measure of investigative productivity. To achieve this type of relationship, there needs to be an atmosphere of mutual trust and respect. Just as in the patrol–investigator relationship, it is important to avoid the problems that might result from perceived status differences.

Cooperative arrangements need to be developed that include how cases will be handled, the role, if any, the prosecutor's office will play in evaluating investigative effectiveness, the type of information required for that evaluation, and the handling of physical evidence. This latter area is crucial in many criminal cases. A cooperative relationship between investigators and prosecutors will often increase both the number of cases accepted for prosecution and the number of convictions. Investigators develop a more complete understanding of what is necessary to prosecute a criminal case and prosecutors become more aware of the resource and investigative problems and constraints of the police agency (Bloch and Weidman 1975).

**Police–witness relationships.**   Witnesses, including victims, are vital to the successful resolution of many criminal cases; consequently, they should not be inconvenienced unnecessarily. Efforts should be made to avoid unnecessary requests for repetitions of the witnesses' story; unnecessary and unproductive trips to the police station, prosecutor's office, or the court system; and unnecessary delays in prosecuting cases or demands on the witnesses' time during trial.

Other areas of concern include the following: importance of keeping witnesses informed of the status of cases; inadequate protection in cases in which a witness may be at risk; and failure to recognize the witnesses' willingness to participate in the process. Police managers must be sensitive to the needs and concerns of witnesses to ensure the most productive result possible in criminal investigations. In addition, this may have positive benefits in other aspects of police work. Citizens may become more cooperative and supportive of police activities in the community (Bloch and Weidman 1975).

## Target Selection

Target selection is concerned with who will become the subject of a police investigation. Most, if not all, police departments that have investigative units engage in proactive investigations, and often in a covert manner. Since proactive investigations usually have an area or an individual as a target, managers must decide who will and who will not be investigated or selected as a target. In some proactive investigations, individual selection can be random; they are "targets of opportunity." This frequently occurs in vice-related activities when police spot a person who may be engaged in prostitution, selling or buying drugs, or perhaps gambling. In other proactive investigations, the targets are usually selected on the basis of presumed involvement in criminal activity.

This type of investigative activity is often associated with career criminal or repeat offender programs. Police departments often make an effort to identify individuals suspected of recurring involvement in criminal activity, using warrants for arrests, analyzing police records, and using informants or intelligence data. Since the 1970s, one of the most popular and widely publicized approaches to "catching criminals" involves proactive investigations that focus on so-called career criminals (Gay 1985; Martin and Sherman 1986; Sherman 1982).

Despite the emphasis given to such programs, proactive, individually oriented apprehension programs are not new; rather, they represent only the organizational formalization of informal, individual efforts long practiced in many police departments. "Good" police officers, either on patrol or in investigations, have often monitored or focused on individuals they suspected of criminal activity. In most of the nineteenth century, the primary thrust of detective activity was covert and individually-oriented investigations.

The results of research in this area concerning effectiveness are mixed. Some programs have had favorable results (Martin and Sherman 1986), while others have failed, often for rather obvious reasons: placing white, middle-aged undercover officers in a black neighborhood; resentment from other officers who were not informed of the activities of officers in special programs; inadequate or nonexistent training of patrol officers or detectives in how to pursue or watch criminals; and the lack of competence and skill on the part of managers in charge of the programs. On balance, these special programs may have minimal long-term impact on crime in a community. According to recent research in this area (Gottfredson and Hirschi 1986, pp. 231–232), "the evidence is clear that the career criminal idea is not sufficiently substantial to command more than a small portion of the time . . . of the criminal justice practitioner . . . [because] when [career criminals] are captured it . . . [is] for mundane public-order offenses more suggestive of failure [in crime] than success."

Managers must carefully scrutinize career criminal programs to decide if they should be utilized or maintained. To be considered successful, such programs should meet the following criteria:

1. Suspects should be apprehended, prosecuted, and convicted more rapidly than they would be without such programs.
2. Persons apprehended should be currently active in committing serious crimes.
3. The convictions obtained should be for more serious crimes that are equal to or greater in number than the convictions that would have been obtained had the officers in the program investigated crimes in a more routine manner.

## Incitement and Entrapment

Do certain police investigative activities *incite* individuals; that is, by their existence, do they encourage the commission of crimes? When are individuals *entrapped*; that is, when are they provided, by the police, both the opportunity and intent to commit a crime? Covert police investigations, whether the police play the role of victim or criminal, have the potential of doing both. Do sting operations (in which undercover police purchase stolen property) encourage sellers, who now have a ready outlet for stolen property, to steal more? Does the random selection of targets for selling drugs provide the intent to buy drugs? These are some of the questions that police managers must ask themselves when supervising criminal investigations. Fortunately, legal guidelines are extensive in these areas, so acceptable procedures are often well defined.

More troublesome, however, is the issue of incitement, particularly when police purchase illegal goods or services. Can such programs actually result in more victims? If criminals can easily sell stolen property for a competitive or higher price, will they steal more while the outlet is available? Should this be a matter for police concern given the potential benefits of the undercover operation (e.g., more arrests, more useful information, and development of informants)?

Unfortunately, the results of incitement cannot be precisely measured; however, it is a political issue of potentially serious consequences. There may be an adverse community reaction to any police action or inaction that is believed to result in more victims. It seems plausible, if not probable, that sting operations may do precisely that. To prevent improprieties if used, sting undercover operators should never pay more than the "going rate" for stolen property, they should never encourage suspects to steal specific items, and they should actively discourage repeat business. This latter recommendation may be difficult to follow, but it is necessary to keep criminals from stealing primarily because they have somewhere to sell what they steal.

## Summary

The patrol and investigations functions in police departments have the greatest number of personnel, respond to the widest array of problems, and have the most impact on public perceptions of police. In most departments of moderate or larger size, the patrol and investigations functions are divided at the follow-up phase in the investigation of a crime. Patrol officers conduct the initial investigation and investigators or detectives follow up to develop the investigation.

The police have a number of alternatives that influence how patrol officers and investigators respond to crime. These alternatives can be explained through the use of a criminal act continuum, which has five stages and two repeat cycles. At any point on the continuum the police may choose to intervene, acquiring information from people or data systems or collecting physical evidence. Where the police choose to intervene on this continuum determines whether they are proactive or reactive, overt or covert; it also determines the most appropriate investigative techniques.

The purpose of the patrol function is to prevent or deter crime, apprehend suspects, recover property, provide services, and enhance citizens' feelings of security and safety. Historically, the role of patrol officers changed as they became less attuned to the community and more legalistically and bureaucratically oriented. However, in recent years, there has been some movement back to a neighborhood orientation in an attempt to improve community satisfaction and support.

Substantial research has been conducted on the patrol function since the 1960s. As a result, some of the most important beliefs about patrol have been challenged, such as the importance of random patrol and response time. However, research findings can be utilized to develop guidelines for the patrol function in police departments. The guidelines suggested in this chapter tend to emphasize the importance of community satisfaction, within legal limits, as the most important measure of patrol effectiveness.

Since the middle of the nineteenth century, the role of the detective has changed dramatically from secretive rogues to bureaucrats or clerks. While some detectives currently are proactive, function in a covert manner, and focus on individual criminals rather than on criminal cases, the majority conduct reactive, overt investigations. These changes have resulted in most detectives' becoming involved in crimes after the act rather than before. Consequently, they have become more case and information processors than sleuths.

In the last two decades, the management of the criminal investigation function has received substantial attention. This has resulted in a number of changes in the activities of investigators and in how investigative units should be managed. One important trend is that police have become more oriented toward criminals rather than toward case investigations. In reality, this trend is a return to the practices of the nineteenth and early twentieth centuries. While the evidence on the effectiveness of career criminal programs is mixed, there is some doubt as to the value of this approach.

In managing the criminal investigation function, attention must be focused on resource allocation and determination and case management, including case screening, the initial and continuing investigation, and relationships between those involved (e.g., patrol officer, investigator, victim, witness, prosecutor). Finally, police managers must be alert to the problems associated with investigative endeavors that may incite additional crime or entrap individuals.

## Discussion Questions

1. Describe the criminal act continuum and explain what happens at each stage, including the types of police intervention that are possible.
2. Explain the two basic types of crimes from an intervention point of view. Identify and define the five possible investigative methods used in responding to these crimes.
3. How has the patrol function in police departments changed since the middle of the nineteenth century?
4. What are the most important considerations in the allocation of patrol resources in police organizations?
5. Discuss the Kansas City Patrol Experiment and explain its importance to changes in the patrol function.
6. Define and distinguish between *overt* and *covert* and *random* and *directed* patrol.
7. Identify and explain the advantages and disadvantages of foot patrol.
8. Identify and discuss the three types of cases in which investigators become involved.
9. Discuss how the role of the detective has changed since the middle of the nineteenth century.
10. Develop a case management system for the investigations function in a moderate-sized police department. Identify and explain each part of the system and why you would include it in your system.

# References

Bloch, P. B. and Weidman, D. R., *Managing Criminal Investigations*, National Institute of Law Enforcement and Criminal Justice (Washington, D.C.: U.S. Government Printing Office, 1975).

Boydstun, J. E., *San Diego Field Interrogation: Final Report* (Washington, D.C.: Police Foundation, 1975).

Boydstun, J. E., Sherry, M. E., and Moelter, N. P., *Patrol Staffing in San Diego* (Washington, D.C.: Police Foundation, 1977).

Caiden, G. E., *Police Revitalization* (Lexington, Mass.: D. C. Heath, 1977).

Cawley, D. F., Miron, H. J., and Araujo, W. J., *Managing Criminal Investigations: Trainer's Handbook* (Washington, D.C.: University Research Corporation, 1977).

Cordner, G. W., "The Effects of Directed Patrol," in *Contemporary Issues in Law Enforcement*, ed. J. J. Fyfe (Newbury Park, Calif.: Sage, 1981), pp. 37–58.

Cordner, G. W., Greene, J. R., and Bynum, T. S., "The Sooner the Better: Some Effects of Police Response Time," in *Police at Work: Policy Issues and Analysis. Perspectives in Criminal Justice* 5, ed. R. R. Bennett (Beverly Hills, Calif.: Sage, 1983), pp. 127–144.

Currey, G. H., "Police Research Technology," *Journal of Criminal Justice* 11, no. 1(1983):15–26.

Eck, J., *Solving Crimes* (Washington, D.C.: Police Executive Research Forum, 1984).

Forst, B., *Arrest Convictability as a Measure of Police Performance*, National Institute of Justice (Washington, D.C.: Government Printing Office, 1982).

Gay, W. G., *Targeting Law Enforcement Resources*, National Institute of Justice (Washington, D.C.: Government Printing Office, 1985).

Gay, W. G., Schell, T. H., and Schack, S., *Improving Police Productivity: Routine Patrol*, vol. 1, National Institute of Law Enforcement and Criminal Justice (Washington, D.C.: Government Printing Office, 1977).

Goldstein, H., "Toward Community-Oriented Policing: Potential, Basic Requirements, Threshold Questions," *Crime and Delinquency* 30, no. 1(1987):6–30.

Gottfredson, M. and Hirschi, T., "The True Value of Lambda Would Appear to Be Zero," *Criminology* 24, no. 2(1986):213–234.

Greenberg, I. and Wasserman, R., *Managing Criminal Investigations* (Washington, D.C.: Department of Justice, 1979).

Greene, J. R., "Foot Patrol and Community Policing: Past Practices and Future Prospects," *American Journal of Police* 6, no. 1(1987):1–15.

Greenwood, P. and Petersilia, J., *The Criminal Investigative Process* (Santa Monica, Calif.: Rand, 1975).

Haller, M. H., "Chicago Cops: 1890–1925," in *Thinking About Police*, ed. C. B. Klockars (New York: McGraw-Hill, 1983), pp. 87–99.

Kelling, G. L., Pate, T., Dieckman, D., and Brown, C., *The Kansas City Prevention Patrol Experiment* (Washington, D.C.: Police Foundation, 1974).

Kuykendall, J., "The Criminal Investigation Process: Toward a Conceptual Framework," *Journal of Criminal Justice* 10, no. 2(1982):131–145.

———, "The Municipal Police Detective: An Historical Analysis," *Criminology* 24, no. 3(1986):175–201.

Martin, S. E. and Sherman, L. W., "Catching Career Criminals," *Justice Quarterly* 3, no. 2(1986):171–192.

Mastrofski, S., "The New Autonomy of American Police," unpublished paper, 1986.

National Institute of Justice, *Evaluation of the Differential Police Response Field Test: Research Report* (Washington, D.C.: National Institute of Justice, 1986).

Pate, T., Bowers, R. A., Ferrara, A., and Lorence, J., *Police Response Time: Its Determinants and Effects* (Washington, D.C.: Police Foundation, 1976).

Payne, D. M. and Trojanowicz, R. C., *Performance Profiles of Foot Versus Motor Officers*, National Neighborhood Foot Patrol Center (East Lansing: Michigan State University, 1985).

Sanders, W., *Detective Work* (New York: Free Press, 1977).

Sherman, L. W., "From Whodunit To Who Does It." (New York: John Jay College, 1982), unpublished paper.

———, "Patrol Strategies for Police," *Crime and Public Policy*, ed. J. Q. Wilson (San Francisco: ICS Press, 1983).

*The Newark Foot Patrol Experiment* (Washington, D. C.: Police Foundation, 1981).

Tien, J. M., Simon, J. W., and Larson, R. T. *An Alternative in Police Patrol: The Wilmington Split-Force Experiment* (Cambridge, Mass.: Public Systems Evaluation, Inc., 1977).

Trojanowicz, R. L. *An Evaluation of the Neighborhood Foot Patrol Program in Flint, Michigan* (East Lansing: Michigan State University, 1982).

———, "An Evaluation of a Neighborhood Foot Patrol Program," *Journal of Police Science and Administration* 4, no. 11(1983):410–419.

Trojanowicz, R. C. and Banas, D. W., *Job Satisfaction: A Comparison of Foot Patrol Versus Motor Patrol Officers*, National Neighborhood Foot Patrol Center (East Lansing: Michigan State University, 1985).

Trojanowicz, R. C. and Carter, D., *The Philosophy and Role of Community Policing*, National Neighborhood Foot Patrol Center (East Lansing: Michigan State University, 1988).

Unsinger, P. C., "Utilizing the Entire Criminal: A Continuum to Deter and Detect Crime," *Crime Prevention Review* 4, no. 2(1977):8–12.

Waegel, W. B., "Patterns of Police Investigation of Urban Crimes," *Journal of Police Science and Administration* 10, no. 4(1982):452–465.

Walker, S., *A Critical History of Police Reform* (Lexington, Mass.: D. C. Heath, 1977).

———, "Broken Windows and Fractured History: The Use and Misuse of History in Recent Patrol Analysis," *Justice Quarterly* 1, no. 1(1984):75–90.

Webb, K. W., *Specialized Patrol Projects*, National Institute of Law Enforcement and Criminal Justice (Washington, D.C.: Government Printing Office, 1977).

Willmer, M., *Crime and Information Theory* (Edinburgh: University of Edinburgh Press, 1970).

Wycoff, M. A., "Evaluating the Crime Effectiveness of Municipal Police," in *Managing Police Work*, ed. J. R. Greene (Newbury Park, Calif.: Sage, 1982), pp. 15–36.

# CHAPTER 9

# Critical Issues
# in Management

The purpose of this chapter is to address important police managerial issues that have not been previously discussed. Chapter 10 presents critical operational issues. The management–operations separation is used for purposes of organization, but it does not mean that operational issues have no managerial significance and vice versa. The issues to be discussed in this chapter include legal aspects of management, equal opportunity employment (including affirmative action and women and minorities), corruption, career paths, civilianization of police work, higher education, labor relations, compensation, private employment of police, stress and officer health, and family problems.

# Legal Aspects of Management

The law provides an important framework for police organizations. In addition to the substantive and procedural laws that govern police officers as they carry out their duties in the community, there are also other important legal considerations for police managers; for example, how to discipline and fire officers, whether or not officers can work part-time, when they have to retire, whether there can be restrictions on off-duty conduct, and whether or not departments can establish a residency requirement. Three of the most important issues in this area—civil liability, sexual and racial discrimination after employment, and drug testing of employees—will be discussed in this section. In writing this section, we decided to focus on issues rather than legal cases because of the large number of relevant cases involved and because we believe that an issues emphasis is more appropriate for this book.

## Civil Liability

In the last decade, police officers and organizations have increasingly become targets for civil suits. Police officers who violate laws, departmental policies, procedural custom (i.e., routine way of functioning), or act in what might be considered an unreasonable manner that harms an individual may be sued civilly. Additionally, of course, there may be criminal conduct to consider (e.g., illegal use of force may involve a crime). Even managers can be held responsible if they are found to be negligent in the employment or training or retention of an officer or if they are aware of inappropriate conduct by subordinates and do nothing to correct the conduct. As a rule, the organization (or insurance company) pays any monetary damages that are assessed because the officer probably was acting within the scope of his or her employment. However, if an officer acts in a "reckless, wanton, or grossly negligent manner," he or she may be held liable and be personally responsible for any damages (Swanson, Territo, and Taylor 1988, pp. 333–363).

Many police officers and organizations consider civil suits an unwarranted intrusion into their activities. In large agencies, considerable resources have to be used to respond to the numerous civil suits filed against the organization. Some communities implicitly encourage such suits because they are quick to "settle" out of court, even when the plaintiff does not have a good case, in order to avoid the publicity and the risk of the courts granting a larger settlement. Of course, some civil suits are settled because the plaintiff has an excellent case.

On balance, civil suits are probably one effective method of controlling police behavior. The threat of civil action encourages responsible organizational, managerial, and officer behavior. In other words, it is much more difficult for police organizations to tolerate, or cover up, inappropriate activity. Even individual officers must be thoughtful, cautious, and reasonable in their actions. While the threat of a civil suit may result in some officers' taking fewer risks in the name of public safety, the more likely consequence is that a larger number of officers will be encouraged to behave themselves. We think this bodes well for the police–democratic relationship.

## Sexual and Racial Discrimination

Another important legal consideration is the possibility of discrimination against women and minorities inside the police organization. Examples include racist and sexist remarks and behavior, harassing activities, limited assignments, limited opportunities for promotion, and special assignments. For women, sexual discrimination also includes sexual innuendo and pressure. This includes touching in an unwanted manner, creating unwanted situations or discussions that are sexual in nature, or using the authority of position to attempt to obtain sexual favors. Women should not be subjected to sexual stereotypes, denigrated, or made to feel that their organizational success depends on dispensing sexual favors or catering to men's stereotypical views. There are specific legal guidelines in this area and managers should become aware of those that are appropriate to their assignment.

All organizations should have policies and procedures governing racist and sexist behavior, a mechanism to report such practices, and a requirement that a thorough investigation be made when problems exist or allegations are made. Offensive language, jokes, gestures, or behavior should not be tolerated. Furthermore, any distinction based on race or sex in the organization should not be made unless it is legally supportable and it is done within the context of integrating expectations.

## Drug Testing of Employees

The increasing use of drugs by prospective and existing police officers has resulted in some organizations' conducting tests to determine drug usage. Individuals who support drug testing believe that it is necessary to ensure dependable judgment, to obtain public trust and cooperation, to minimize the potential for corruption, to enhance the credibility of officers' testimony in criminal trials, to improve officer morale, to enhance officer productivity, and to avoid civil suits. Opponents of drug testing argue that drug tests may not be valid, that tests may prove difficult to interpret (e.g., how much is used, when, and how often), and that they do not determine the extent of drug use among officers.

There appear to be two divergent legal trends in this area. The first is that drug testing is considered legal when reasonable suspicion exists that a specific police officer is using drugs. The second trend suggests that reasonable suspicion is not necessary under certain circumstances; for example, when an officer transfers into a sensitive law enforcement position and the drug test is only to be used administratively. In addition, if it is known that a drug test is part of a selection process, then individuals who apply for a transfer to the position are, in effect, consenting to the test.

One of the most important aspects of this issue is the future of random testing of police employees. While proponents believe that random testing is necessary to "wage war" successfully on the drug problem and police corruption, it also tends to presume guilt. However, if a truly random selection process (i.e., everyone has an equal chance of being selected for the test) is used, even this argument may be discounted. How widespread random testing of police becomes is open to speculation but there is little doubt that it is a major issue with important legal implications (Dunham, Lewis, and Alpert 1988).

# Equal Employment Opportunity

The most recent political concern about racial, ethnic, and sexual discrimination in the United States culminated in the passage of the Civil Rights Act of 1964. This act was amended in 1972 and the Equal Employment Opportunity Commission (EEOC) was established to investigate allegations of employment discrimination. The purpose of the EEOC is to prohibit discrimination based on race, color, religion, sex, and national origin (Swank and Cosner 1983, pp. 56–60). The commission's mandate includes any employment decision, including selection, demotion, promotion, termination, layoff, and transfer. Any performance standard or expectation, process, or procedure related to these decisions is subject to EEOC review (Swanson, Territo, and Taylor 1988, pp. 190–191). This section discusses two important aspects of equal opportunity employment: affirmative action, and women and minorities in police work.

## Affirmative Action

Police organizations have a long history of employment discrimination against women and minorities. Prior to the early 1970s, the number of women in policing was minimal. Even when employed they were limited to specialized roles like matron, juvenile specialist, sexual assault investigator, or some clerical or minor administrative role. Blacks, while employed in police work since at least the 1860s, are still not employed in proportion to their numbers in the population and neither are Hispanics, Asian Americans, Native Americans, or homosexuals.

Attempts to prohibit employment discrimination in the United States began to influence law enforcement in the early 1970s. In 1971, a U.S. District Court ordered the Alabama Department of Public Safety to employ a certain percentage of black police officers. This class action lawsuit was brought by the National Association for the Advancement of Colored People. Since that time, a number of lawsuits directed at police agencies have resulted in mandated quotas or goals in police employment and promotions (Weston and Fraley 1980, pp. 29–32).

Most agencies have not been subjected to legal action to eliminate employment discrimination; however, faced with both the possibility of legal action and political pressure, many agencies have developed voluntary programs to attract and promote more women and minorities. In 1985, of 223 cities with a population of 50,000 or more, 116 had either court-imposed or voluntary plans to improve the employment and promotion of women and minorities (International City Management Association 1986, p. 28).

These programs have had a substantial impact on the number of minorities and women employed in law enforcement. Precise estimates are difficult to make; however, it is reasonably accurate to speculate that between the 1960s and 1980s, the number of women and minorities increased from about 5 or 6 percent of the total sworn officers (not including clerks or other noncommissioned personnel) to between 15 and 20 percent. Although promotions to higher ranks have not correspondingly increased, there have been gains in this area, particularly in the highest position. In 1986, the chiefs of police in four of the five largest U.S. cities were black. It is difficult to predict

**Effective affirmative action programs have resulted in a greater representation of women and minorities in policing.**

at what rate the number of women and minorities will increase, but one important factor is interest in police work. Even if discrimination is completely eliminated in employment and promotion processes, there is no guarantee of continued increases.

Police agencies' attempts to remedy past discrimination in employment and promotions are reflected in an affirmative action plan. The agency must make an affirmative or positive effort to redress past practices. These plans have been developed either voluntarily, voluntarily but with political pressure, or by court order following legal action. Some departments vigorously resisted the attempt to change employment and promotion practices, although their efforts usually failed because they had such a poor record in employing women and minorities. Additionally, police organizations have had difficulty establishing the validity of the criteria used to select and promote employees. This latter issue resulted in one of the most important changes that many departments had to make as a result of affirmative action—the requirement that selection and promotion standards be directly related to the task requirements of the job. As discussed in chapter 7, this is when selection criteria changed from being essentially merit-subjective to merit-objective.

A number of complex legal issues involved in the affirmative action area are best left to a more complete analysis (Hochstedler, Regoli, and Poole

1984). This subject is politically controversial and the legal bases for affirmative action programs, particularly in terms of how discrimination is determined and what organizations may be required to do, are subject to change. In addition, charges of "reverse discrimination" are commonplace in police agencies that have established goals or quotas in the employment of women and minorities. However, the job-valid selection and promotion criteria that many police agencies have adopted are unlikely to change. From the standpoint of developing an effective personnel management system, this is a positive development. A well-managed organization needs to be aware of precisely what tasks its members perform and what is necessary to prepare and enhance that performance.

## Women and Minorities

It is important to understand conceptually that the United States has been and, in some instances, continues to be a racist and sexist society. Consequently, many persons believe that it is necessary for affirmative action programs to exist in order to protect minority groups and to facilitate their economic integration into society. Victims of employment discrimination have had, and continue to have, problems in integrating police departments for essentially two reasons: (1) the lingering sexist and racist attitudes and behavior of some citizens, officers, and managers, and (2) the resentment that has been created among nonminorities based on the perception that less-qualified women and minorities have been given preferential treatment as a result of affirmative action programs.

The perception that affirmative action programs, particularly ones with numerical goals for selection, assignment, or promotion, give minorities and women preferential treatment is commonplace among white male police officers. While many police officers are aware of the long history of sexism and racism in the United States and may be neither racist nor sexist themselves, they believe that programs that require the hiring and promotion of a certain number of women and minorities perpetuates discriminatory practices. This is a particularly sensitive matter, because some white males have either been denied a police job, or promotion once employed, that women and minorities received even though the white male's performance was better during the selection, or promotion, process.

While attitudes do not always determine behavior, racism and sexism are difficult to hide if interaction is extensive, particularly under stressful conditions. The degree of overt racism that exists in police organizations is difficult to determine, but it has probably declined since the 1960s and before when it was commonplace. On the other hand, overt sexism of male officers is still a flagrant problem. Many male officers, possibly the majority, do not believe that women as a group are suited for most aspects of police work.

This perspective is reflected in the following types of practices: (1) some women are stared at, insulted, and harassed; (2) some women are limited in the assignments and work shifts they are given; (3) some women are excluded from "serious" or "critical" calls for service; (4) some male officers are more protective of women than they are of other men; (5) women are resented, if not challenged, when placed in supervisory roles; (6) women are "tested" by being asked to "prove" they can perform in areas where their ability is suspect (e.g., fighting); (7) women are not allowed to work alone or with a female partner; (8) women are not assigned to high crime areas; and (9) women are more closely supervised. Historically, other minority groups also have had similar problems, and in some, if not many, instances still do.

One of the most important aspects of the involvement of women and minorities in police work is *cultural matching*. Can or should the persons functioning as police officers be "matched" to the persons being policed? Does more effective policing result when "like polices like"? This issue first emerged in modern policing with a debate over who would make the "best" police officer, locals or outsiders. Locals, it was argued, would be more familiar with the community and its citizens, would have more knowledge about problems, and would be more empathetic. This is essentially an argument for *individualization* of police treatment through the flexible use of police discretion. On the other hand, by being unfamiliar with community inhabitants, outsiders would be more objective in their responses and more likely to fairly and consistently enforce the law. This is an argument for *standardization;* its intent is to reduce the discretionary behavior of officers.

The next phase in cultural matching came in the mid-nineteenth century with an argument in favor of hiring the Irish to police the Irish. The Irish, it was argued, understood the "Irish problem" better and would be more effective and more accepted by Irish citizens. For the remainder of the nineteenth century and throughout the twentieth century, this issue has continued to be of significant concern. Arguments have been made that individuals from the working-class culture make better police officers because they have associated with the type of "street people" they will deal with as officers. Individuals from a military background have also been supported as prospective "good" police officers, based on the assumption that they would be disciplined, mature, and effective in stressful situations.

The most current example of cultural matching is the emphasis that has been given to employing more minorities and women. Advocates are essentially making a cultural matching argument—blacks for blacks, Hispanics for Hispanics, Asian Americans for Asian Americans, homosexuals for homosexuals, and women for women. There are, of course, other arguments to be made for these groups; most important, to provide equal opportunity in employment to redress past discrimination. Nevertheless, when anyone makes or attempts to make an argument that the police officers should be from the groups being policed, it is a cultural matching issue.

If women and minorities have special qualities by virtue of their cultural identity and awareness, perhaps they can make a unique contribution. While there is considerable testimonial evidence to support this argument, empirical evidence is scant. Given the adjustment made by many women and minorities to police work (that is, they often adopt the values of the police culture), the sexual and racial makeup of a police department may not make a substantial, long-term difference in the quality of policing a community receives (Davis 1984; Decker and Smith 1980; Decker and Wagner 1982; Lester, Gronan, and Wondrack 1982; Martin 1980; Morash and Greene 1984; Rodgers 1987; Siche 1978; Walker 1983). The gender or race of the officer may be less important than the community's expectations concerning how tasks should be performed and how citizens should be treated. In this regard, the officer's style, strongly influenced by the police culture and socialization process, may be more important than other factors.

Women and minorities are obviously an integral part of the makeup of police organizations. Their numbers will most likely increase, although the rate is unpredictable. Almost all persons entering law enforcement in the future will have to work with, probably supervise, and be supervised by males, minorities, and women. The more successful managers are in integrating the diverse expectations of these groups, the more productive the organization will become.

## Corruption

Allegations of corruption in a police organization usually result in a crisis of substantial magnitude. Corruption scandals are a "double-edged sword"; they provide the opportunity for reform while damaging, if not destroying, the careers and perhaps the lives of the individuals involved. The term *corruption* has been utilized to describe a wide array of deviant police behavior, including taking gratuities (e.g., free coffee and meals), physical brutality, violating suspects rights, criminal activity like robbery, and being "on the take." The last type of corruption usually involves receiving something of value, most often money, not to enforce certain laws. The emphasis in this section is on this aspect of corruption.

Historically, corruption has been a chronic problem in many police organizations. Policing, as a position of public responsibility and trust, provides widespread opportunity to deviate. Many citizens are willing to give officers money or other items of value to escape apprehension and prosecution. Others, victims for example, may want to reward the police for services and assistance provided. Or perhaps a business owner appreciates the officer "coming in" to provide more security and protection. All of these activities can involve giving something of value—from a free cup of coffee or discount purchase, to thousands of dollars—with the intent of influencing the officer's discretion. Although taking money to allow drug sales or gambling or prostitution to take place is obviously more serious than taking a free cup of coffee, the latter creates a climate conducive to the development of more serious corruption problems.

Sherman (1985, p. 259) suggests that a "developmental ladder" may exist in police corruption. He identifies four possible career stages in an officer's moral development:

Stage    Activity

1     Accepts minor "perks" like free coffee or meals.
2     Allows bar closing to be extended for money or other valuable consideration.
3     Does not cite traffic violators in lieu of monetary consideration.
4     Takes money to allow gambling, prostitution, and ultimately, perhaps, narcotics.

Some officers may stop at taking gratuities, others at fixing traffic tickets, and others at helping drug pushers. At some point in the moral development of an officer, a decision is made that this is "as far as I go," because to do more makes the behavior unacceptable to that officer's moral standards. Even corrupt police officers have things they will not do (e.g., they may take gambling payoffs but not drug money, or they may take money from cocaine dealers but not heroin dealers).

Two theories have been suggested to explain police corruption: the "rotten apple" and environmental. The *rotten apple* theory blames corruption on a few bad apples in the barrel, who probably had character defects prior to employment. This is compatible with the predispositional theory of police behavior. The *environmental theory*, related to the socialization theory of police behavior, suggests a more comprehensive explanation of corruption. Supposedly, corruption is a function of the political environment of a community and police activities. Politically corrupt cities, aided by public tolerance if not participation, create an environment in which police corruption flourishes (Sherman 1985).

The environmental theory of corruption is implicitly pessimistic about the possibility of police organizations' controlling corruption scandals. However, since the 1960s, some police leaders have attempted to respond to corruption by taking a more systematic perspective; that is, if corruption is endemic to a police system, then solutions must be based on a systemwide response (Caiden 1977). This perspective includes the belief that corruption can be substantially controlled even if the political environment is corrupt.

Control of corruption requires that leaders create a moral climate that encourages honesty and that discourages and punishes the corrupt officer. There must also be a managerial commitment to strict accountability throughout the organization, a mechanism to investigate allegations of corruption, including providing opportunities (e.g., undercover police try to get out of traffic tickets by giving money or offer bribes to allow gambling to take place) to determine if officers are corrupt.

Police leaders must stress the importance of integrity in all activities, both inside and outside the organization. Perhaps the most difficult problem in responding to corruption is that many officers believe that their job is difficult and dangerous and not appreciated by the public. Police officers who think of themselves as both special and deprived often have little difficulty in rationalizing inappropriate behavior. Although police work is a job to be proud of, it is not necessarily more important than other jobs. Further, individuals in the field of policing are special only in the sense that everyone is special and not because their work is so unique that they are above the law and deserve more than other persons in our society. It should be emphasized, especially to recruits, that if they cannot accept the ethical responsibilities, frustrations, and rewards that go along with the role of the police in a democratic society, they should seek another occupation.

## Career Paths

The career paths available to police officers are influenced by organization size, structure, and managerial practices. Small departments have few opportunities for a career path because the number of positions is limited. However, the range of tasks to be performed may be similar to those of large departments. Officers in small departments tend to be generalists; that is, a "career" involves becoming increasingly proficient at performing numerous tasks while functioning in a limited number of positions, perhaps only one. In larger departments, a "career" involves performing a number of specialized tasks in different positions, possibly with promotion to higher rank.

The structure or design of the organization is important because the more specialization and the smaller the span of control, the more positions are available for employees to pursue. Narrow spans of control tend to result in more levels in the organizational hierarchy. The degree of specialization creates the number of different roles or types of positions. However, if these jobs are too specialized, they may not be particularly interesting or challenging. Nevertheless, careers often include working in several jobs, as the employee attempts to "move up" the organizational hierarchy. The less specialization and the fewer levels in the hierarchy, the fewer the jobs. Instead of performing few tasks in numerous positions, the officer performs more tasks in fewer positions. Both represent career paths that may be part of an officer's career development.

The management practices of a police agency also influence career paths because a particular conception of the police role is influential in determining how departments are organized. Typically, moderate to large police departments have patrol and investigations functions and numerous other types of operational specializations like traffic, crime prevention, undercover activities, intelligence gathering, and related administrative activities (e.g., research and development, planning, training, recruitment, and selection).

Most commonly, a career path would involve beginning as a patrol officer and possibly working in one or more of the other specializations, before being considered for promotion. Depending on success in subsequent promotions, the officer would move up in the organization while functioning as a manager in patrol or investigations and possibly in one other specialized area (e.g., traffic). Some officers do not get promoted, some move up only one or two organizational levels, and most never become middle- or top-level managers.

In police departments, salary and status are often associated with position in the organization. Usually, to make more money and enjoy more prestige, an employee must move up in the hierarchy. Most departments have pay ranges for their employees. For example, a patrol officer may make an annual salary of approximately $20,000 to $30,000, depending on years of experience and perhaps other considerations like education; middle- and upper-level managers usually have a higher pay range. In other words, a "successful career path" in police work is typically connected to being promoted.

It is possible to create a personnel system in which pay ranges overlap so that excellent patrol officers and investigators make as much or more money than lower-level managers. This approach encourages competent patrol officers and investigators to make a career in these specializations, getting better with training and experience while getting paid for it. Higher salaries can be related to unique distinctions for patrol officers, such as giving them a title that signifies a special status: senior officer, lead officer, field training officer, police agent. This can be done for investigators as well. However, such distinctions should be based on differences in task proficiency, as determined by experience and testing (Whisenand 1973).

A career path includes the sequence of experiences a person has during his or her organizational life. What can managers do to structure a series of experiences that will sustain employee interest? To a substantial degree, this is related to the conscious effort by managers to identify employee preferences in general, to match those preferences to the tasks to be performed, and to create a system that prepares employees to become increasingly proficient while rewarding them for their accomplishments. Career development, through the use of career paths, is linked to expectancy theory and the expectation-integration model. It is also related to job design and motivation. Effective patrol officers who must strive for promotion primarily to obtain a higher salary may not be as satisfied and productive as managers as they were in patrol (see chapter 5).

## Civilianization

Historically, one of the most often made personnel recommendations is that the police should hire more civilians. The traditional argument is that civil

ianization "frees up" officers to perform "more important police tasks."
Some police jobs may require skills few, if any, police officers possess. In addition, if the civilians employed have diverse backgrounds, the police organization may become more representative of the community and perhaps more responsive and less isolated. Adding more civilians may also have some cost-savings benefits. Often, civilians are paid less money and may receive fewer benefits than police officers. Of course, the opposite may also be true because highly qualified and specialized civilians, such as computer analysts, may be paid more.

However, if civilians are given the least demanding and interesting work, as is often the case, there may be more productivity and absenteeism problems. If so, any cost savings that might be obtained could be offset. In addition, there is the matter of officer acceptance: Will police officers accept civilians as equal partners in the police enterprise? If not, what are the implications for cooperation, mutual trust and respect, and effective communication?

Despite these possible problems, the use of more civilians in clerical, communication, technical, and some managerial jobs is a well-established practice. What is not clear, however, is the degree to which more civilians make any difference in what happens in the organization, either in terms of costs or productivity (Harring 1981; Heininger and Urbanek 1983; Schwartz 1975). Once again, as contingency theory would suggest, each department must determine the needs or duties of civilian personnel based on an assessment of its own environmental circumstances.

## Higher Education

Since the early twentieth century, there have been advocates for college-educated police officers. However, fewer than one-hundred crime and justice-related education programs (counting community colleges) were established prior to the early 1960s. In that decade the federal government began to provide monies to improve police agencies, first through the Office of Law Enforcement Assistance, which became the Law Enforcement Assistance Administration and was the predecessor of the National Institute of Justice. The first two agencies attempted to encourage educational attainment by giving grants to colleges to start criminal justice programs and by giving loans and grants directly to students and police officers to attend college. The number of programs and students grew rapidly between the mid-1960s and mid-1970s, declined sharply in the latter half of the 1970s, and began to stabilize in the early 1980s. By then there were hundreds of well-established academic programs in law enforcement, criminal justice, or criminology in two- and four-year colleges and universities (Kuykendall 1977).

The assumption on which program development was based was that higher education would improve police performance. Requiring a college education also strengthens the argument that the occupation is a profession, which means that the police can demand higher wages and benefits. However, not everyone in police work wanted more education for officers. Opponents argued that college-educated persons would find the work boring, expect too much from the job, and demand too much autonomy; they also argued that a college education was not necessary to be effective. By the 1970s, many minorities were also opposed because they believed the requirement would discriminate against them.

Proponents of higher education argued that managers and organizations must become more flexible in responding to the talent and ability of educated persons, that police work can be an intellectually stimulating and challenging occupation, and that even if higher education is not directly related to task requirements, it indirectly contributes by improving writing skills and self-discipline and providing an understanding of human behavior and the causes of crime, among other things.

In an attempt to respond to the issues involved in this debate, a number of research studies have been conducted to determine the relationship between higher education and police performance. Such research was particularly critical because of the need to validate the selection and promotional criteria that agencies utilized. Concern about validation has abated somewhat since 1985 when the 5th Circuit Court of Appeals, in *Davis v. City of*

*Dallas,* upheld the right of the Dallas Police Department to require applicants to have completed forty-five semester units (i.e., one and one-half years) of college.

Research findings concerning the relationship between education and police performance are mixed; however, the preponderance of evidence supports a positive relationship. This does not mean that all officers with a college degree perform more effectively than all officers who do not have one; rather, it means that the typical, or average or mean, level of performance of the college-educated officer will probably be better (Bae 1980; Daniel 1982; Lynch 1976; Murrell 1982; Roberg 1978; Vernon 1980). Despite these findings, few community police agencies in the United States require any college education for entrance to, or promotion within, their agencies (Alpert and Dunham 1988, p. 186). The reasons include the arguments noted earlier: affirmative action programs, job interest, and fear.

Some police agencies have not created, or have modified, higher education requirements (even if only a few college courses), because it made employment of minorities more difficult. In addition, police selection is always limited by those interested in the work. Interest among college-educated persons has not always been high because, for many persons, police work is a less desirable job than other types of available employment. This is particularly true for college-educated minorities. This means that the available labor pool might not include a sufficient number of college-educated persons interested in police work. Finally, there is fear of change. Many individuals in law enforcement who do not have a higher education are afraid of those who do and of the changes that educated persons might foster. Most often this fear results in comments like "college kids don't have any common sense" or they are "too theoretical." This is why, overall, there have been few gains in changing educational requirements for police officers since the 1960s (*Law Enforcement News* 1987).

Despite the apparent lack of progress in this area, at least in terms of establishing minimum requirements, many agencies have made substantial gains. Many individuals who apply for a police job have some college education, if not a degree. Many police departments have a substantial number of officers who have college degrees. One reason for this is that it may be necessary to have a four-year degree in order to be competitive for promotion.

Many practical problems are associated with requiring some college education for selection and promotion. How much education will be required? How will this be measured—in units or years or by degree? What types of education or degrees will be allowed? Does the institution or college have to be accredited; if so, by whom? What is the quality of the institution and the program? Will officers be allowed to adjust their work schedule so that they can go to college? Will agencies pay their expenses? Will officers be paid more money if they attain a certain level of education? Will education of a certain type exempt them from part of their initial or subsequent training? These are some of the questions that must be answered if police agencies are to become serious about increasing educational requirements.

## Labor Relations

The police labor movement has gone through several stages. Fraternal police organizations were evident as early as the 1890s. Attempts were made to organize workers between 1917 and 1919 and again between 1943 and 1947, without success. During these periods, there was little public or political support for a labor movement among public safety employees. However, since the mid-1960s, the police labor movement has had greater success. During the 1960s and 1970s, the United States went through a period of social unrest. The perception of a rapidly increasing crime rate, the civil rights movement, and demonstrations about the Vietnam conflict focused public attention on police. They were harshly criticized, particularly by political liberals. Feelings of isolation intensified, which strengthened in-group solidarity, and the police rank and file became more militant. These developments plus an ongoing frustration about inadequate economic benefits and, in many agencies, the arbitrary treatment of employees by management resulted in a rapidly growing labor movement (Johnson 1981, pp. 191–192; Walker 1977, pp. 110–120).

The police employee organizations, called police associations, that were established demanded higher salaries, better fringe benefits, more participation in how, when, and where they worked, and more elaborate disciplinary procedures designed to protect employees. They also tended to fight back against changes suggested by critics. In many police organizations, employee organizations have become a major obstacle in effecting change. What began as an attempt to improve the lot of the working police officer often became a barrier to improving performance. Of course, members of police associations do not always agree with this perspective. From their point of view, they may be acting to preserve "hard won" gains and prevent a decline in professionalism. In addition, some police associations are vocal proponents of organizational changes that will enhance productivity. In some cases, police associations may be more "progressive" than police managers.

The issues that are negotiated between police employee organizations and management tend to fall into one of three categories: salary and benefits, conditions of work, and discipline and grievance procedures. *Salaries and benefits* are influenced by a number of factors, such as the economic health of a community, the inflation rate, salaries in other police agencies (or salaries of comparable positions in other occupations), management's resistance, the militancy of the police association, and public support, or lack thereof, for either labor or management.

The *conditions of work* category includes a broad range of possible issues. In fact, legal action has been necessary, in some instances, to establish the parameters in this area. For example, what might be included are the procedures to be utilized for evaluation, reassignment, and promotions; equipment and uniforms; the number of persons assigned to a car or even to a section of the community; the use of civilian employees; how seniority will be used in assignments and promotions; and when officers may and may not work off duty.

*Grievance procedures* are concerned with the process to be used in accusing an officer of a violation of organizational policies and procedures, or law. Usually, this involves an identification of officer rights (which may even be codified in state law), how the complaints must be filed, how evidence is obtained and processed, who will make disciplinary decisions, and what ap-

**Police on the picket line for increased pay, an example of labor-management conflict.**

peals, if any, will exist. Quite often, police employee organizations, in an effort to protect employees from arbitrary treatment by managers, will demand elaborate grievance mechanisms that frustrate attempts to respond to almost any type of inappropriate police behavior. However, grievance procedures may also be a useful way of clarifying work rules or, said another way, of understanding and agreeing on performance expectations.

Prior to reaching a labor–management agreement, there may be strikes, job actions (e.g., work slowdowns or speedups), refusals to negotiate, required or voluntary intervention by outside mediators or arbitrators, and, in general, much unpleasantness. However, as police managers become more effective in dealing with employee groups, labor–management conflict often decreases.

*Police labor–management relations* involves the recognition of shared governance in police agencies. It makes police departments more democratic than autocratic in managerial style. Although both sides, labor and management, may try to infringe on each other's "rights," the management rights–labor rights tension is probably more healthy than harmful to police departments. Dealing with formalized labor groups makes the manager's job more difficult, but the manager also becomes more effective because the process results in more constructive participation. The labor–management relationship creates the most serious problems when one group gains too much power and then focuses on narrow objectives; for example, a police association that tries to protect inadequate or illegal police performance, that makes monetary demands communities cannot pay, or that creates a climate in which employees are not held accountable for their behavior for fear of the reaction of the police association.

Managers must become familiar with a detailed body of facts, laws, and procedures in order to understand the police labor movement and their role in working with police employee groups. Viewed negatively, it is a time-consuming, frustrating, and unnecessary process. Viewed positively, it is a way to improve communication, clarify performance expectations, and ensure responsible employee behavior.

# Compensation

How much money should police employees be paid and what retirement benefits should they receive? The answers to these questions vary considerably throughout the United States. Historically, police departments have stressed salaries and retirement systems in an attempt to attract well-qualified candidates. This section addresses both issues.

## Salaries

In general, police officers in the East and West are paid more than those in the Midwest and South. Also, as a rule, the larger the city the higher the salaries; however, there are certainly exceptions. Of cities with a population of 250,000 and over, starting salaries for patrol officers vary by 100 percent or more. In 1985, excluding Alaska, the salary range for patrol officers was from $7,000 to $32,000. For chiefs of police, the range was about $23,000 to $112,000 (International City Management Association 1986, pp. 94–150).

The factors that determine police salaries include tradition, area cost of living, community support, economic health of the community, inflation, taxation philosophy, and crises incidents and reform movements. In communities that support the police, have high expectations concerning their performance, are willing to pay to provide good public services, and are economically healthy, police are usually well paid.

One of the more important factors in determining salary is any reform movement that takes place. Generally, when a police organization, or police in general, go through a reform period following a major crisis (e.g., a corruption scandal), there are usually suggestions to improve the quality of personnel. The suggestions often include a recommendation for increases in salaries and other benefits. The most recent national crisis and police reform movement came in the 1960s, when police were criticized as responding inadequately to crime and civil unrest. Consequently, in the 1970s, salaries were increased substantially in many police organizations in hopes of attracting better-qualified personnel.

The specific salary of a position is often determined comparatively. The patrol officer salaries of one agency are compared with the mean or average salary of a group of similar agencies (i.e., usually in the same area and of a similar size). Another comparison method is to determine the salaries received by similarly qualified individuals in other occupations. Assume that the typical employee of a police agency is twenty-five years old, of above average intelligence, with two years of college. What types of jobs are available for this type of individual and how much do they pay? Determining salaries in this way assumes that the police agency must be competitive to attract candidates from a particular labor group.

Of course, salary determination is also part of the collective bargaining process that occurs in many police agencies. Once basic, entry-level salaries are established, the salaries of civilian specialists and management personnel and others can be established. There is usually a 3 to 7 percent differential between ranks in police organizations. Other compensation concerns include pay for merit performance, seniority, shift differential (e.g., greater pay for working in the evening or late at night), overtime, retirement, medical, disability, insurance, uniforms, and equipment. While this listing is not inclusive, it does provide some idea of how extensive compensation packages can be.

Managers, except at the highest level, usually have little influence in determining salary and benefits. More often, they can only administer the procedures associated with taking sick time or other approved time, vacations, and overtime. Thus, managers must resort to other techniques to motivate employees to be more productive. Does this make management more difficult? Most likely, in that it also requires police managers to be more creative, to emphasize other motivational techniques, and to demonstrate more effective leadership.

## Retirement Systems

Since the 1970s, an increasing number of police organizations, particularly large ones, have had problems with their retirement systems. During the twentieth century, extremely liberal retirement benefits were given to police officers as one means of attracting well-qualified applicants. This has resulted in some communities' having one or two officers on retirement for every two or three who are working. It is not uncommon in those cities to have approximately one-half of personnel costs going to pay retired officers. Many cities support two police departments—one working and one retired.

The solutions to this problem are painful and will be difficult to implement. Some cities have already started by requiring increased officer contributions and by reducing benefits. Unless more cities take such actions, some communities may have to declare bankruptcy as a result of this and other fiscal problems. When that happens, the pension benefits of the police in that community may be lost forever.

Another possibility is to integrate police systems with Social Security; however, this is not a popular alternative as it would probably result in officers' having to work longer. This is perhaps the most perplexing problem associated with police retirement. The earlier police are allowed to retire, the more it costs to fund their retirement years (Fogelson 1984). If officers are unable to be effective into their fifties and sixties, as many proponents of early retirement argue, then early retirement will remain necessary. However, an emphasis on healthier lifestyles and improved medical knowledge may offset this problem somewhat. In addition, there is no reason that police officers, if proven too old to function in police work, cannot assume other responsibilities in government.

Another important aspect of this problem is disability retirement, which is the practice of allowing individuals who are physically or psychologically disabled to receive a retirement income. Disability retirements are controversial because they are given on questionable grounds in some instances (e.g., drinking problems, limited physical injuries). In addition, in many police departments, if a police officer is considered to be incapable of performing any police task, he or she is considered incapable of performing all police tasks. For example, it is not uncommon to place on disability retirement officers who are capable of performing any number of administrative or investigative tasks but are unqualified for patrol work. Consequently, these officers may be excluded from all police tasks and be placed on disability, even though they may not want that. In some instances, it is even possible for an officer to receive a disability retirement from one police organization yet work full time for another police agency.

## Private Employment of Police

Private police (i.e., security guards and private detectives) have long outnumbered public police in the United States. In police departments, many officers have worked part-time in a law enforcement capacity for extra money. Examples of such work include routine security work at businesses, traffic control and pedestrian safety, and maintenance of order and security at major sporting and recreational events (e.g., football games, rock concerts) and at parks, airports, and malls.

Police departments tend to use one of three approaches to manage the private employment of police: officer contract, department contract, or union brokerage. In the *officer contract* approach, each officer finds his or her own work independently and then obtains the organization's permission to do the work. The *department contract* system is the same, except prospective employers go through the police department. The department approves the work, assigns officers, and takes care of reimbursements after being paid by employers. In the *union brokerage* approach, the union takes care of finding jobs and placing and paying officers.

There are a number of possible problems that may develop, regardless of the managerial approach taken. Conflicts of interest may arise if an officer works as a process server, bill collector, or bail bondsman. Some work may be seen as lowering the professional status of officers (e.g., working as a bouncer at a bar). There may also be problems related to the risks of the private employment. If an officer is injured in a private position, he or she may not be able to work. Departments must also take into consideration a limit on time worked. Excessive private employment can impair an officer's productivity when performing regular police duties (Reiss 1988).

One of the interesting, and unexplored, aspects of the private employment of public police is the impact on crime and public safety. It is possible that widespread involvement of police in this role might have a substantial impact on the crime rate and citizens' perceptions of safety. This is an area that deserves additional exploration because the practice of public police working in a part-time job is commonplace in many communities.

## Stress

Even though police work can be an exciting and rewarding experience, it is also a demanding job for several reasons: emotional and psychological strain, occasional physical danger, boredom, uncertainty, and shift work. Recurring involvement with human suffering may result in emotional and psychological adjustment difficulties. This problem in police work is often discussed under the heading of stress and stress management. When a person is required to adapt to any experience, he or she is under stress. Obviously, some experiences are more demanding than others, and the greater the pleasure or apprehension produced, the greater the stress. Some stress is positive, known as *eustress*, while other stress is negative, known as *distress*. There is the stress associated with general living (e.g., school, friends, marriage, divorce, raising children, unpreventable health problems); the stress associated with any occupation (e.g., interesting, valuable, enjoyable, rewarding, or none of these); and the stress associated with the unique aspects of police work.

Police officers, at times, work with individuals who are suffering greatly. In addition, the apprehension associated with being injured or killed is very real, despite the low probability that either will occur. Police officers are trained to believe that if they can anticipate danger, they may be able to prevent it. This concern for survival has tended to exaggerate the real danger of the work, but the perception is nevertheless influential in work-related strain.

Police work is more likely to be boring and routine than dangerous. This creates the same work-related problems that occur in any occupation where repetitive tasks (e.g., driving, giving tickets, taking reports), are involved. Routine work punctuated by physical, emotional, or psychological demands and danger requires extraordinary coping ability. Lastly, shift work in law enforcement has an adverse impact on officer health, particularly if officers rotate shifts too frequently. The inability to establish and maintain a routine sleeping pattern and social activities outside work may be a major factor in poor officer productivity, accidents, and health problems.

In general, police work is considered to be a high-stress occupation for these reasons. Whether police work is one of the more stressful occupations is not really known, but stress has nevertheless become an important issue. Some police agencies attempt to determine a police recruit's stress coping capability during the psychological phase of the selection process. Many police agencies have attempted to educate officers and managers about the causes, consequences, and indicators of stress-related problems. Interestingly, apart from potentially dangerous situations, officers have identified the perceived arbitrary and unfair behavior of police administrators and organizations as the major cause of stress (Territo and Vetter 1981; Terry 1981). This research underscores the dichotomy that exists between management and labor and the disparate police cultures previously discussed.

It is important for managers to be alert to the possible signs of stress (e.g., any officer who is marginal or below in performance or any officer whose performance becomes erratic or changes suddenly), because there may be negative consequences for both the individual and the organization. Individuals in unusually stressful occupations are also more likely to have a variety of health problems and may have poor coping habits. Several health problems often associated with police work are briefly discussed in the following section.

## Officer Health

Jack Jones is in his late twenties and has been a police officer for five years. He is assigned to patrol and works from midnight to eight. He is twenty pounds overweight, does not exercise regularly, eats a diet high in sugar, fat, and processed foods, drinks eight to ten cups of coffee per day, smokes a pack and a half of cigarettes each day, drinks several beers daily, and two or three times a month gets drunk with his "buddies." Sarah Smith is also in her late twenties, has been working for five years, and is assigned to the midnight shift. She doesn't smoke or drink coffee. She rarely drinks anything with alcohol in it, exercises regularly three or four times each week, is not overweight, and has a well-balanced high-fiber diet that is low in sugar, fat, and processed foods.

Which officer has the lifestyle that is more likely to produce a healthy, energetic, and alert police officer? Which officer is more likely to be absent from work more often? Which officer is likely to have the higher level of productivity? Which officer is likely to receive fewer citizen complaints? Assuming that Officers Jones and Smith are similar in their emotional and psychological makeup, intellectual ability, and interest in and commitment to the job, Sarah Smith is likely to be the more productive employee.

The most serious health problems for police are related to diet, exercise, smoking, drinking, and drug use. A well-balanced diet, adequate exercise, no smoking, limited drinking, and no drug use will improve officer health and probably improve productivity, and will assist in coping with job-related stress. Other effective and positive stress-coping methods include relaxation training (e.g., meditation) and peer counseling (e.g., talking with other officers about problems).

The consequences for failing to effectively manage health and stress-related problems can result in serious organizational consequences. In addition to alcoholism and drug abuse, both of which are serious police problems, there is the possibility of a job-related disability, suicide, and premature death. As previously discussed, many police agencies pay a substantial amount of money every year to officers who are disabled due to physical injury or emotional or psychological problems. Other officers commit suicide or die prematurely before or shortly after retirement. Many of those who die early have a history of poor health habits.

Of particular concern in many agencies is the growing use of drugs by police officers. This has become increasingly critical in recent years. As discussed earlier in this chapter, more and more police organizations are testing applicants and officers to detect drug use. In some communities, the problem is so widespread that police organizations have had to relax selection standards concerning the use of drugs in order to employ sufficient personnel (*Law Enforcement News* 1985, 1986).

As a personnel issue, employee health is perhaps the most important problem (second only to selecting good candidates) confronting police organizations. Promoting effective stress-coping behavior and a healthy lifestyle is directly related to an organization's effectiveness and productivity. Even more important, it has positive benefits for the longevity and well-being of employees.

## Family and Lifestyle

In addition to these health-related issues, family and general lifestyle are also important personnel matters. Because of the nature of police work and the sometimes negative public reaction, spouses and children may have adjustment problems. Officers may have difficulty in communicating their feelings about the job or they may go through personality changes as a result of their experiences. This can result in serious marital problems and divorce. Many departments have provided training and counseling programs for police families to help them understand their spouse's role.

Because of their stature in the community, all police organizations must confront the issue of regulating the off-duty behavior of police officers. For example, should cohabitation be allowed? Should high-risk activities like motorcycle racing be prohibited? What about dress, hair length, off-duty drinking, places frequented, and so on? Are officers allowed to have another job? If so, what type and when can they work? What legal standing does a police organization have in attempting to regulate this and other off-duty lifestyle behaviors? These are examples of the types of issues that managers may have to address in this area. Some of the more important factors are the mores of the local community, their expectations of the police, the values of the police leaders, and the strength and aggressiveness of employee groups. Making and enforcing rules in these areas can create some interesting management–labor and legal conflicts.

## Summary

The managerial issues identified and discussed in this chapter include legal aspects of management, career paths, civilianization, equal employment opportunity (i.e., affirmative action and women and minorities), the impact of higher education, labor–management relations, compensation, private employment of police, stress and health, and family-related problems.

A number of legal issues are of concern to police managers, but three of the most important are civil liability, sexual and racial discrimination after employment, and employee drug testing. Increasingly, police organizations have been sued in civil court in an attempt to hold officers accountable for inappropriate behavior. This has become an important means of regulating police behavior. As police departments have employed more women and minorities, they have been confronted with problems of sexual and racial discrimination. Police managers need to be alert to such problems and to take rapid action to prevent or confront them. Finally, whether and under what circumstances police officers should be tested for drug use has become important. The use of drugs by police applicants and officers is a problem of major importance; consequently, departments have attempted to test officers to eliminate or reduce drug use.

Traditionally, the career paths available to police officers took them out of operational activities and into management. However, it is possible to structure an organization so that officers can stay in patrol or investigative work and yet receive higher salaries and achieve greater status. Civilianization has also had an important impact on career development in policing. It is a persistent reform theme in police work as many agencies have attempted to employ more nonsworn officers to fill either the less demanding, or the more technically difficult, jobs.

The emphasis on affirmative action has resulted in the employment of more women and minorities in police departments. However, this trend has not been without critics who believe that affirmative action results in preferential treatment or reverse discrimination in the selection and promotion processes. An important part of employing women and minorities is cultural matching. Supposedly, individuals with a certain cultural background will be more effective in policing individuals with the same background (e.g., black police for the black community).

While the preponderance of evidence suggests that a college education, in general, results in more effective police performance, few agencies require any college units for either employment or promotion. However, some police organizations have a substantial number of officers who have a college education.

The growth of police unions or associations is a relatively recent event in law enforcement. While some police organizations have had serious labor–management conflict, the debate and negotiations that have taken place have also had some positive benefits, the most notable being the greater involvement of the rank and file in the management of the organization.

One important labor–management issue involves the salaries and benefits that officers receive. There are many factors that influence salary and benefits, including cost of living, economic health of the community, and police services expected. For some police organizations, one of the more serious problems in this area is retirement benefits, which have become very expensive. Historically, many police organizations have promised excellent retirement benefits in order to attract well-qualified applicants.

Another important trend in police work is the increasing use of police officers who work part-time in a private capacity. The type of work is administered in a number of ways, but the problems remain essentially the same; what type of work, how much time can be spent, and what happens if the officer is injured. The final personnel problem discussed was stress. This has become increasingly important to police organizations and officers in the last decade. A supportive family, healthy lifestyle, effective coping habits, and a quality work environment are all important parts of controlling the destructive consequences of stress.

## Discussion Questions

1. When is it legally appropriate to hold police officers liable for their action? Do you think the increasing number of civil suits filed against police organizations and officers is a positive or negative development? Why?
2. Should police departments test either applicants or officers, or both, for drug use? Explain the reasons for your answer.
3. How has affirmative action changed the police selection process and the racial makeup of the personnel of police departments? Explain why you believe affirmative action is or is not a good idea.
4. What is cultural matching? Do you think that cultural experiences make any difference in the effectiveness of police officers? Give the reasons for your answer.
5. Explain the two theories of police corruption. Why has corruption been a problem of such significance in the history of police departments? How can corruption be controlled?

6. What is a career path? How does a career path influence the career development of officers?
7. Discuss the impact of higher education on the development of police. Do you think individuals with college degrees are more effective police officers than persons without degrees? Give the reasons for your answer.
8. Why is the police labor movement essentially a recent development? What are the most important areas for discussion in police labor relations?
9. How are police salaries determined? Do you think police officer salaries are too high? Do they receive too many benefits? Explain your answer.
10. What is stress and how is it related to officer health? Think about your lifestyle relative to diet, exercise, and stress-coping ability. Would it be conducive to the most effective performance as a police officer?

# References

Alpert, G. P. and Dunham, R. G., *Policing Urban America* (Prospect Heights, Ill.: Waveland Press, 1988).

Bae, R. G., "The Influence of Higher Education on the Utilization of Police Discretion in a Southern Indiana City." Unpublished Ph.D. diss., University of Southern Mississippi, 1980.

Caiden, G. E., *Police Revitalization* (Lexington, Mass.: D.C. Heath, 1977).

Daniel, E. D., "The Effect of a College Degree on Police Absenteeism," *Police Chief* 49, no. 9(1982):70–71.

Davis, J. A., "Perspectives on Policewomen in Texas and Oklahoma," *Journal of Police Science and Administration* 12, no. 4(1984):395–403.

*Davis v. City of Dallas,* 777 F. 2d 205 (5th Cir. 1985), cert. denied 476 U.S. 1116 (1986).

Decker, S. H. and Smith, R. L., "Police Minority Recruitment," *Journal of Criminal Justice* 8, no. 6(1980):387–393.

Decker, S. H. and Wagner, A. E., "Race and Citizen Complaints Against the Police," in *Managing Police Work. Perspectives in Criminal Justice*, no. 4, ed. J. R. Greene (Newbury Park, Calif.: Sage, 1982), pp. 107–122.

Dunham, R. G., Lewis, L., and Alpert, G. P., "Law Enforcement: Testing the Police for Drugs," *Criminal Law Bulletin* (March–April 1988), pp. 155–166.

Fogelson, R. M., *Pensions: The Hidden Costs of Public Safety* (New York: Columbia University Press, 1984).

Harring, S., "Taylorization of Police Work: Prospects for the 1980s," *Insurgent Sociologist* 10, no. 11(1981):25–32.

Heininger, B. L. and Urbanek, J., "Civilianization of the American Police: 1970–1980," *Journal of Police Science and Administration* 11, no. 3(1983):200–205.

Hochstedler, E., Regoli, R. M., and Poole, E. D., "Affirmative Action in Policing: A Fourteen Year Review." Paper presented at the annual meeting of the Academy of Criminal Justice Sciences, 1984.

Johnson, D. R., *American Law Enforcement: A History* (St. Louis: Forum Press, 1981).

International City Management Association, *Municipal Yearbook* (ICMA: Washington, D.C., 1986).

Kuykendall, J., "Criminal Justice Programs in Higher Education: Course and Curriculum Orientations," *Journal of Criminal Justice* 5, no. 2(1977):149–163.

*Law Enforcement News*, "Drug Use by Cops Seen as Growing Problem," September 23, 1985, p. 1.

——, "Police Eye Leniency on Applicants' Drug Use," October 28, 1986, p. 1.

——, "College Requirements for Cops Gain No Ground," February 24, 1987, p. 1.

Lester, D., Gronan, F., and Wondrack, K., "The Personality and Attitudes of Female Police Officers," *Journal of Police Science and Administration* 10, no. 3(1982):357–360.

Lynch, G. W., "The Contributions of Higher Education to Ethical Behavior in Law Enforcement," *Journal of Criminal Justice* 4, no. 3(1976):285–290.

Martin, S., *Breaking and Entering: Policewomen on Patrol* (Berkeley: University of California Press, 1980).

Morash, M. and Greene, J. R., "Evaluating Women on Patrol: A Critique of Contemporary Wisdom," *Evaluation Review* 10, no. 2(1984):230–255.

Murrell, D. B., "The Influence of Education on Police Work Performance." Unpublished Ph.D. diss., Florida State University, 1982.

Reiss, A. J., "Private Employment of Public Police," *NIJ Reports* (Washington, D.C.: National Institute of Justice, 1988).

Roberg, R. R., "An Analysis of the Relationships Among Higher Education, Belief Systems, and Job Performance of Patrol Officers," *Journal of Police Science and Administration* 6, no. 3(1978):336–344.

Rodgers, C. J., "Women in Criminal Justice." Paper presented at the annual meeting of the Academy of Criminal Justice Sciences, 1987.

Schwartz, A. I., *Employing Civilians for Police Work* (Washington, D.C.: The Urban Institute, 1975).

Sherman, L. W., "Becoming Bent," in *Moral Issues in Police Work*, eds. F. A. Elliston and M. Feldberg (Totowa, N.J.: Rowan and Allanheld, 1985), pp. 253–265.

Siche, J. L., *Women on Patrol: A Pilot Study of Police Performance in New York City*. National Institute of Law Enforcement and Criminal Justice (Washington, D.C.: Government Printing Office, 1978).

Swank, C. J. and Cosner, J. A., *The Police Personnel System* (New York: Wiley, 1983).

Swanson, C. R., Territo, L., and Taylor, R. W., *Police Administration*, 2nd ed. (New York: Macmillan, 1988).

Territo, L. and Vetter, H. J., eds., *Stress and Police Personnel* (Boston: Allyn & Bacon, 1981).

Terry, W. C., "Police Stress: The Empirical Evidence," *Journal of Police Science and Administration* 9, no. 1(1981):61–75.

Vernon, P., "Developing and Field Testing a Procedural Model for Examining the Effectiveness of Academic Involvement for Police Officers." Unpublished Ph.D. diss., Georgia State University, 1980.

Walker, D. B., "Black Police Values and the Black Community," *Police Studies* 5, no. 4(1983):20–28.

Walker, S., *A Critical History of Police Reform* (Lexington, Mass.: D. C. Heath, 1977).

Weston, P. and Fraley, P. K., *Police Personnel Management* (Englewood Cliffs, N.J.: Prentice-Hall, 1980).

Whisenand, P. M., *Police Career Development* (Washington, D.C.: Law Enforcement Assistance Administration, 1973).

# CHAPTER 10

# Critical Issues
# in Operations

This chapter is concerned with operational issues that are important in the major functional units of police departments, namely, patrol and investigations. While the issues addressed are certainly not exhaustive, they are among the most important, including the "good cop," police–citizen encounters, use of force, pursuits, domestic violence, crimes in progress, drugs and crime, bias-related crime, and AIDS.

## The "Good Cop"

Attempts to define the *good cop* include the style distinctions noted in chapter 2 and the democratic models of policing. Is a legalistic style of policing better than a service style? Perhaps a legalistic style is better in a legalistic-professional department but not necessarily in a department that is community-service oriented. To a substantial degree, the prevailing model of policing advocated by the community and police determines what constitutes a "good cop." It is possible to be considered a "good cop" in one city and a "poor cop" elsewhere; a "good cop" in an urban area may be a failure in a smaller community and vice versa.

Other aspects of the "good cop" issue emphasize one or more of the following criteria: the *degree to which police work within the law*, *organizational productivity*, and *minimization of mistakes*. Are "good cops" always the ones who work within the law? The movie *Dirty Harry* with Clint Eastwood provides a useful illustration of this point. Harry was interrogating a prisoner who had kidnapped a young girl and buried her alive. Unless she was found quickly, she would suffocate. In order to obtain information about her location, Harry tortured the suspect—an action that is clearly illegal. Is Harry a good cop or a bad cop? Ethically, what is the right and wrong decision in this situation?

In the area of organizational productivity, the issue is to determine to what degree an officer is productive relative to organizational objectives. Often this measurement of effectiveness is quantitative, for example, miles patrolled, buildings checked, crimes investigated, traffic citations issued, and arrests made. Obviously, these accomplishments can also have a qualitative dimension, but not always. Is the best officer the one who does the work most valued by the organization? Organizations often reward performance on this quantitative basis.

The last criterion considered—minimization of mistakes—has always been an important aspect of law enforcement. In attempting to integrate community and individual expectations, police managers have often been more concerned about avoiding mistakes (that is, not engaging in controversial activities) than being productive or effective. In such organizations, those officers who do the least may be considered the best. This "don't rock the boat" or "don't make waves" attitude is rather typical of the political-watchman model of policing and some older officers in all types of departments.

## Police–Citizen Encounters

One of the most extensive studies of police–citizen encounters was conducted by Reiss (1971). He reported on over 5,000 police–citizen interactions that took place in areas that were racially diverse and had different crime rates. Reiss discovered that approximately 86 percent of the encounters were reactive; that is, they resulted from citizen requests. About 14 percent of the encounters were proactive; that is, they were initiated by police officers.

Approximately 60 percent of citizens behaved in either a detached or civil manner toward police, about 20 percent were agitated (mildly upset), and about 10 percent were antagonistic. Almost all antagonism toward officers came from suspects. Police officers behaved in a businesslike or routine manner in about 74 percent of the encounters, were personal (jovial, expressed humor) in about 15 percent, and were hostile or derisive in about 11 percent. Police were more likely to be hostile or derisive when citizens were agitated or antagonistic than when they were calm or detached. As might be expected, police were more likely to experience antagonism and be injured in proactive rather than in reactive encounters.

Reiss further found that police officer behavior was closely related to citizen behavior; if a citizen was antagonistic, the officer would most likely respond in the same manner. Only about 20 percent of suspects arrested were cooperative with police, while about 50 percent openly challenged police authority, most often verbally. Of the 225 citizens arrested, 9 percent were handled with gross force and 42 percent were treated "firmly."

This research suggests that police–citizen encounters are more the result of citizen requests for intervention than police-initiated activities. In most cases, police behavior toward citizens is businesslike or routine, if not friendly. Most encounters are not unlike those of any business providing a service to a client; they involve exchanges of information in a friendly and/or civil manner. Police are rarely antagonistic toward citizens; when they are, however, it is usually when dealing with suspects who are first antagonistic toward them. Police infrequently make arrests; when they do, they rarely have to use physical force that involves fighting.

Reiss's findings are useful and provide a benchmark for the study of police–citizen encounters, but he does not address the different types of situations police encounter and the dynamics of those encounters. Sykes and Brent (1983) analyzed over 3,000 police–citizen encounters in an attempt to address these and other issues. Three of the situations they used in their research are defined as follows:

1. Hazardous. These are the types of calls that officers believe are potentially risky and personally rewarding but they may also be depressing. Examples include domestic fights, assaults, and purse snatchings.
2. Annoying. These calls tend to be neither risky nor personally rewarding, but they may be depressing. Examples are unwanted guests, loud parties, disturbances involving children, and failure to pay a bill.
3. Boring. These calls may be slightly depressing for some officers, but they are neither risky nor rewarding. Examples are taking reports and persons drinking.

Sykes and Brent identified three possible police responses in each situation: definitional, imperative, and coercive. Police officers want to regulate, assert authority, or "take charge" of any situation and achieve three objectives: (1) secure the information that is needed to define the problem and the role of those involved, (2) deal with the overt behavior of the individuals involved in order to get the citizens to respond in an orderly and civil manner, and (3) obtain an appropriate outcome.

The *definitional* approach in police–citizen encounters involves asking questions. By doing this, the officer obtains information and focuses the attention of those involved on the problem. By asking a question, the officer directs the exchange of information, may discover more about the problem, and requires the intellectual attention of participants. A second part of the definitional response that is sometimes used is an accusation. Once the officer has established the roles of those involved in the problem (i.e., offender, victim, witness), he or she may assume control by accusing a person of a criminal or regulatory violation. The definitional approach determines the information exchange and, by the participants' involvement, intellectually controls their behavior.

The second police response is *imperative*, which involves issuing a command or giving an order. When neither the definitional (questions) approach nor the imperative (orders) approach is effective, the officer may try *coercion*. Coercion involves the threat of using force, utilizing restraining force, perhaps actually striking someone, and ultimately, using deadly force.

The research further found that the most common initial police response (about 83 percent) was definitional. Police almost always speak first in police–citizen encounters, thus they have the opportunity to initially direct the discussion. The second most common initial response was imperative (about 17 percent). The coercive response was not used initially in any type of situation, but it was used eventually if citizen cooperation was not obtained. However, when a citizen did not cooperate, the police most often repeated the initial approach, usually definitional. Sometimes the imperative was also utilized when cooperation was not forthcoming.

Sykes and Brent (1983) provide an interesting analysis of police–citizen interaction. However, there are at least two other important factors they do not consider: interpersonal style and escalation pattern. For purposes of discussion, a simple characterization of an officer's *interpersonal style* is provided below:

*Friendly*: Smiles, displays humor, affection, and/or personal knowledge of the individual; for example, "Hi, how are you? Nice day, isn't it. Do you realize you were speeding?"

*Formal*: Businesslike, bureaucratic, routine exchange between professional and client; for example, "Hello, I'm Officer Smith. You were speeding. May I see your driver's license, please?"

*Forceful*: Domineering, autocratic, assertive, aggressive; for example, "Where's the fire, buddy?"

Police officers may attempt to obtain information, compliance and respect, and a successful outcome by utilizing a definitional, imperative, or coercive approach. They may behave in a friendly, formal, or forceful manner when using these approaches. Some styles are more compatible with certain responses than others. Friendly coercion is almost a contradiction, although a smiling, jovial officer who threatens bodily harm is not unheard of in police organizations.

A second important consideration is *escalation pattern*. Which approaches and styles do officers initially utilize, and when and why do they change the approach or style? In potentially disruptive or dangerous situations, the officer may initially be forceful and coercive, skipping the other approaches and styles. Managers need to be aware of what happens in police–citizen encounters so they can attempt to influence the officer's style, response, and escalation pattern. To do this, managers need to address the following questions:

1. Given the type of situation, what is the most appropriate initial police style and response?
2. If initial styles or responses are unsuccessful in obtaining desired information and orderly behavior, how many attempts should be made using the same approach and style before changing?
3. Is the most effective approach to change style and then response, or response and then style? For example, should the sequence be friendly-formal-forceful in a definitional mode, or should the officer as he or she moves from formal to forceful also move from definitional to imperative?

Extensive training and police guidance are essential if police organizations are to effectively manage police–citizen encounters. Too often police officers are left to their own discretion concerning both the style and the approach in dealing with citizens. Police officers should be trained in the styles that will achieve a successful result with minimal reliance on a forceful style or coercive response. However, coercion and forceful behavior cannot always be avoided; therefore, police managers must also prepare officers to use them effectively when necessary. The next section focuses on one aspect of coercion, the use of force.

# Force

When police officers employ coercion, it may include the use of force, that is, the use of physical control like handcuffing or other physical restraints (e.g., arm or finger holds, choke holds) to subdue suspects, or the use of non-lethal (clubs, mace, tasers) or lethal weapons (guns). The decision to utilize force is one of the most critical for police officers. Some community groups—particularly minorities—are often greatly concerned with the possible excessive use of force by the police, and police officers tend to have a continuing concern, if not an unhealthy preoccupation, about their own survival.

Public expectations concerning the police use of force, as compared with the police perspective about when and how much force is appropriate, may be the most important issue in police–community relations. A police organization distrusted by a community for perceived excesses in the use of force will have chronic relationship problems. Therefore, it is essential that managers understand some of the more important factors in this area.

## Police Use of Force

Friedrich (1980) suggests that research concerning the use of force by police can be divided into three categories.

1. The individual approach explains the use of force in terms of officer characteristics.
2. The situational approach explains the use of force by relating it to the characteristics of situations in which police encounter citizens.
3. The organizational approach explains the use of force as a result of the police organization or some aspect of the officer's work.

While much of the research in this area is flawed by research design problems, Friedrich was able to reach some tentative conclusions. In terms of *individual* explanations, he found that experience seems to make little difference in whether officers use force either reasonably or excessively. However, officers who really like or dislike their job tend to use force more, both when it is used reasonably and when it is used excessively. In other words, how long officers have been working tends to make little difference in the use of force, unless it results in the officers' either really liking or disliking their work, in which case they are more likely to use force, including excessive force. Another important factor is prejudice. The more prejudiced an officer is against a particular group, the more likely that officer is to use force against that group.

Friedrich further discovered that *situational* factors are more influential than individual factors in determining the use of force. The most significant situational factors are citizen attitude, use of alcohol, age, class differences, two-person police units, and the total number of officers involved in a situation. When citizens fail to respect the authority of the officer or are overtly antagonistic, and/or have been drinking, and/or are between eighteen and twenty-five years of age, and/or are perceived to be of lower-class status, and/or two or more officers are involved, police are more likely to use force. Interestingly, gender seems to make little difference and the race of the citizen is less important than perceived class distinction. The most important factor appears to be the citizen's attitude. Less information was found on *organizational* factors, but it does seem clear that more progressive or professionally managed police departments can influence the use of force.

In concluding his analysis, Friedrich argues that the results are far from definitive; however, some important factors and relationships can be identified. Perhaps the most important factor is the behavior of citizens. Individuals who are cooperative rarely are targets of police force, whereas those who are not, particularly suspects, are much more likely to suffer at police hands. This stresses the importance of the effective training of police officers in responding to noncooperative citizens with means other than the use of force.

## Deadly Force

The use of deadly force by both police and citizens is a national tragedy and a problem of critical importance. Since 1949, when data first began to be collected by the National Center for Health Statistics, an estimated 15,000 citizens, and possibly more, have been killed by police. About half of these mortalities were minorities (mostly black). The center has not reported this many deaths, however, research conducted by Sherman and Langworthy (1979) suggests that the center's statistics are approximately 25 to 50 percent low. The estimate of 15,000 citizen deaths takes into account their research. Although there is no accurate way to determine the number of citizen deaths since the 1840s when modern police departments were first established, it is not unreasonable to assume that 30 to 40,000 citizens or more have been killed by police.

As for the killing of police by citizens, the long-term picture is equally bleak. Van Raalte's (1986) research identifies as many as 30,000 officers killed in the line of duty. However, he does not separate those killed in accidents from those killed by citizens. Based on a comparison of officers killed since 1960 with citizens killed, it would appear that there is about a 1:5 ratio; that is, about one police officer is killed by a citizen for every five citizens killed by police (Kuykendall 1981). However, in the last few years, there has been an apparent decline in both areas. When comparing changes between 1981 and 1984, this decline may be as much as 50 percent (*San Francisco Chronicle* 1986).

In recent years, there has been substantial research concerning the police use of deadly force. Some of the more prominent authorities in this area are Geller (1983), Fyfe (1978, 1980, 1982, 1985), Scharf and Binder (1983), and Blumberg (1985). A summary of their most important findings follows:

1.  While police use of force is a rare event, there is considerable variation in how often it occurs in different neighborhoods and cities. The number of citizens shot tends to vary based on the crime rate in general (and on violent crime in particular), the number of arrests, and gun density (i.e., the ratio of gun ownership to population). In general, the greater the lack of social cohesion and the more violence, the greater the use of deadly force.

2.  The number of times police shoot and hit their targets also tends to vary among departments, based on restrictiveness of shooting policies, training, and skill levels of the officers.

3.  Minorities are shot disproportionately to whites when compared to their numbers in the population, but not when compared with the minority arrest rate or number of police contacts. However, in some cities, minorities are shot at in situations (e.g., running away) in which whites are not. The decline in the use of deadly force in recent years is largely attributable to the decreasing number of minorities being shot.

4.  Historically, a substantial number of citizens have been shot who posed no threat to officers, but this is changing as more police departments adopt restrictive "defense of life" shooting policies. These policies have limited when police can use their weapons, often only to protect their lives, or someone else's. Training of police in how and when to use deadly force has also probably reduced the number of shootings, but this is less clear.

5.  Those situations that have the greatest probability of officer injury or death involve crimes in progress and any arrest situation. These account for over 50 percent of all officers killed. Contrary to popular belief, domestic disturbances are not particularly dangerous. Police officers are also likely to be killed off duty, especially if they perceive their responsibilities to include aggressive intervention rather than passive observation.

6.  Black officers are more likely to use deadly force and to be shot than white officers because black officers are assigned more frequently to high-crime-rate, black neighborhoods.

7.  Police officers who utilize deadly force may experience a decline in productivity and performance afterward, are more likely to shoot again

(than nonshooters), and may suffer from postshooting psychological trauma. In a few cases, this trauma is so severe that the officer becomes disabled.

8. The decision to shoot or not to shoot largely appears to be the result of the officer's perception of a threat—to the officer, to others, or to the public in general. The age, race, or experience of the officer does not appear to significantly influence who shoots and who does not.

9. Women may utilize deadly force less frequently than men because they have no ego involvement with suspects. Men may tend to personalize violent encounters to such a degree that the encounter becomes a survival competition governed more by "macho" rules than by organizational training and policy (Grennan 1987).

## Managing Police Use of Force

The management of the use of nondeadly and deadly force presents different problems for the organization, because the use of nondeadly force tends to be influenced more by individual and situational variables (other than a direct threat to the officer or someone else). In general, however, the important considerations are situational understanding, policy and procedural guidance, training, and supervision.

With nondeadly force, police managers need to be aware of the factors identified earlier. In addition, the manager must be alert to a personal or a career crisis that may predispose an officer toward the use of force. One police agency found that many of their unnecessary-use-of-force problems came from officers who had worked three to five years. These officers had become disenchanted with police work and were more cynical about, and less patient with, citizens (Roberts 1985). Of course, as pointed out in the previous chapter, stress, lifestyle, drinking, and drug use also contribute to behavioral problems.

In the use of deadly force, situations can be classified as deliberate, sequenced, or spontaneous. In the *deliberate* situation, the officer has the time to consider alternatives. Shooting at "fleeing felons" is an example of the de-

liberate use of deadly force. In *sequenced* situations, the officer makes a series of decisions that may result in the use of deadly force. For example, the
decision to pursue an armed suspect may result in a deadly confrontation.
The decision to draw a weapon or take an exposed position may provide an
impetus toward the final, ultimate decision. Finally, the *spontaneous* situation literally "explodes" as the officer is suddenly and, perhaps unexpectedly, confronted with a perceived threat. This is the situation that is most
difficult to manage because the police response is more a function of instinct
than of other factors.

The deliberate use of force can be reduced, if not eliminated, by developing more restrictive policies and enforcing them. Many police departments have done this by adopting a restrictive shooting policy. For example,
as noted earlier, officers may be permitted to shoot only when their life or
another person's life is in danger or to capture or recapture a violent felon
when all other means have failed; this is known as a defense-of-life policy.

Sequenced situations are also manageable because procedures and
training can provide the officer with guidelines and methods that may reduce
the need to use force. Officers can be taught when to aggressively intervene
or passively observe and use other alternatives (e.g., call in specialists like
special weapons teams or hostage negotiators). Officers can also be taught
how to pursue suspects to minimize the risk to themselves and others.

As noted, the spontaneous situation is the most difficult to manage.
However, the type of police programs that are emphasized may have some
influence. Decoy programs, stakeouts, and undercover drug purchases all
have the potential for spontaneous violence. When suspects are confronted
with the reality that they are "caught," they may resist. The training and procedures police use in these situations must be carefully considered.

The role of training in the use of force is somewhat problematic because
the impact is difficult to determine. What type of training is best in preparing
officers to decide when to use force? Providing skills is largely a function of
resources and repetition; unfortunately, training in decision making is more
difficult. While some agencies have attempted this kind of training, there is
little evidence available concerning the effectiveness of various types of
training programs.

**Role playing in police training may help to improve decision making in the use of deadly force.**

Finally, supervision may be the most important factor because managers are, or should be, aware of officer characteristics and problems, the degree to which policies and procedures are followed, and the proficiency of officers in making decisions and performing basic police tasks. A critical factor in managing the police use of force, as it is in most areas of police performance, is the manager.

## Pursuits

When and under what circumstances police officers are to pursue suspects, either on foot or by car, is another important managerial concern. The decision to pursue a suspect requires that an officer balance the risks involved to the officer, to the person being pursued, and to others who might become involved. The police rationale for pursuits is that (1) the person has violated the law, (2) the person may be guilty of a serious crime and/or dangerous to the public, and (3) not to pursue will encourage others to run away to avoid the police. A fourth reason not often mentioned is that pursuits are exciting, even fun, for some officers. Many police officers simply like chases. It is one of the most dramatic and adventurous parts of police work, and pursuits may become the substance of valued "war stories."

## Foot Pursuits

Little is known about the foot pursuits made by police officers. Although they may be less risky for bystanders, it is not clear that they are less risky to officers and suspects. In chases, both officer and suspect may have to run through streets, yards, alleys, up stairs, and over or around other obstacles (e.g., fences). The physical condition, and vulnerability to injury or illness (e.g., heart attack), of both parties is an important consideration. In addition, when the suspect is apprehended or "cornered," there may be a tendency to resist police authority.

It is difficult to find specific police policies or procedures in this area. Training is usually limited to improving the officer's general physical condition. Police need to explore when and how to conduct foot pursuits. If suspects run away for the same reasons they usually do in automobile chases (i.e., for minor violations of the law), it may be pointless to risk the possibility of physical injury to the officer. Also, there is no point in engaging in a pursuit that the officer is unlikely to win. An adult police officer who is overweight and/or out of condition probably cannot "run down" a teenager. Some of the questions that should be considered before beginning a foot pursuit are: What is the likelihood that the suspect will be caught? What is the likelihood that the officer will be injured? What is the likelihood that others will be injured? What is the seriousness of the alleged crime?

## Automobile Pursuits

Alpert and Anderson (1986) provide an interesting analysis of automobile pursuits in the United States. They identify several possible conclusions to automobile pursuits:

1. The vehicle stops and the suspect surrenders.
2. The vehicle crashes by itself or with other vehicles, which may or may not involve injuries and/or death.
3. The vehicle or police car or another vehicle hits a pedestrian with or without injuries or death.
4. A vehicle not involved in the chase is "run off the road" and crashes with or without injuries and/or death.
5. The police use some type of force to stop the vehicle, which might include firearms, roadblocks, ramming, bumping, boxing in, and so on, which may or may not involve injuries and/or death.
6. The police car crashes with or without injuries and/or death.

Alpert and Anderson report on one study conducted by the California Highway Patrol in 1983 that analyzed 683 pursuits involving the Highway Patrol and ten urban police departments. Most pursuits resulted from a traffic violation, took place at night, lasted for one mile or one or two minutes, involved two patrol vehicles, and ended when the offender stopped. The offender was usually male and about twenty years of age. Approximately 77 percent of suspects were apprehended, 70 percent of the pursuits ended without accident, and 68 percent lasted less than five miles. Other research in this area suggests that police pursuits are potentially very dangerous. For example, injuries and fatality rates may be as high as 23 percent and 3 percent, respectively (*Time* 1988). Given the possible risks involved and the fact that few chases result in apprehending persons who have committed dangerous crimes, it seems appropriate to provide strict policy guidelines in this area.

In deciding whether to engage in a pursuit and in developing policy guidelines, the following factors should be taken into consideration:

1. Tactical preparation of officers, including the training to operate a police car under the high-speed conditions of a chase.
2. Familiarity with the area in which the pursuit is taking place.
3. Type and condition of vehicles involved in the pursuit.

4. Likelihood of successful apprehension (can the person be arrested later?).
5. Knowledge of the offense (does the seriousness of the crime warrant risk given other conditions?).
6. Traffic, road, and weather conditions.
7. Geographic area (hills, mountains, school district, and so on).
8. Time of day or night.
9. Pedestrian traffic.
10. Visibility.

Once the police pursuit begins, other important considerations must be addressed, including speed of the police vehicle, use of lights and sirens, number of police vehicles involved, tactics to be utilized to secure a stop, obtaining clearance, if necessary, from the pursuing officers' manager, coordination with other agencies, the use of air support, if available, and coordination of communication. When several vehicles are involved, particularly when two or more police agencies are concerned, there is a tendency for officer discipline to "break down." These breakdowns must be anticipated by mangers, who should intervene to prevent practices inconsistent with organizational policy and procedure, such as the tendency of unauthorized police units to become involved. In areas with two or more police agencies, there should be joint planning and policy development.

One possible problem in a pursuit is the behavior of officers at the end. Suspects may become the targets of unwarranted physical abuse because the officers may be so "psyched up" that they "take it out" on the suspect. Historically, it was not uncommon for suspects who ran from police to be physically abused after being apprehended. Managers must be alert to this possibility.

Finally, and of considerable importance, is the training required for pursuits. The training received by police for driving a vehicle may be inadequate to prepare them for high-speed chases. While costly and time-consuming, special training is necessary if police are to minimize the risks involved in vehicle pursuits. Officers who might become involved in a pursuit should be required to qualify in pursuit driving just as they are usually required to demonstrate proficiency in the use of firearms.

## Domestic Violence

Domestic violence, or family fights or disturbances, is a serious problem for police organizations. Such problems are numerous, have the potential for violence, and are usually perceived to be dangerous by the officer and the organization. Statistically, the probability of an officer being killed responding to a domestic disturbance is quite low, among the lowest of all police problems (Garner and Clemmer 1986). However, this low probability of being killed may be the result of officers' taking greater precautions (e.g., at least two or more officers are assigned to such calls in many agencies) because they believe the calls to be potentially dangerous.

The perception that domestic disturbance calls are particularly dangerous is probably the result of those officers killed, the larger number that are assaulted, the emotional tension and anger evident in many of these calls, and the police culture that perpetuates the perception of danger by telling "war stories." Police officers like to tell stories about the humorous and exciting things that happen to them and other officers. Probably the most frequent, tension-filled (although not necessarily dangerous) call officers respond to is a domestic disturbance. Consequently, officers may develop a greater number of stories about this type of incident. In calls where the officer becomes excited or tense, or there is verbal or physical resistance, officers usually conclude that the call is potentially dangerous.

Historically, police departments have utilized four approaches in responding to these problems: officer discretion, separation, mediation, and arrest. Until the 1960s, almost all police departments allowed officers to exercise discretion or had a policy of separation. Beginning in the 1960s, and into the 1980s, some departments established training programs that were designed to develop officer's mediation skills. By the mid-1980s, the arrest alternative became increasingly popular. However, prior to this, arrests were often made when the victim was willing to "file charges" and testify against his or her spouse. In 1987, of 176 cities with a population over 100,000, 62 allowed officers to exercise their own discretion, 9 had a preferred policy of separation, 22 suggested mediation, and 78 wanted arrests made, if possible (*Law Enforcement News* 1987).

Where officer *discretion* is utilized, it means that the officer is free to make an arrest, suggest a temporary separation (e.g., one party is encouraged to spend the night elsewhere), or give advice. This advice is often the result of the officer's values concerning marital relationships and what causes marital problems. The content of the advice varies among officers and its effectiveness is unknown. When *separation* is the preferred policy, officers are encouraged to have the parties in question "separate" for a time, allowing them to reflect before deciding what to do. This is the result of the belief that decisions made in the "heat of the moment" will be regretted and that the disputants will probably reconcile. *Mediation* is based on crisis intervention or violence prevention training in which officers defuse the situation, may act as mediators to help the parties resolve their dispute, and/or refer them to professional counselors for prolonged assistance.

Recently, more departments are emphasizing the *arrest* alternative in domestic disturbances. This is required in some states (e.g., California, Oregon, Washington) where there is evidence of harm to one party in the dispute. Changing legal requirements reflect a concern for the violence associated with family disturbances (i.e., it may result in a homicide), the influence of the women's movement, and research that suggests that an arrest is the most effective of the alternatives described earlier (Steinman 1987). However, this research (Sherman and Berk 1984; Berk and Newton 1985; and Jaffe, Wolfe, and Austin 1986) is not without its problems; the most notable are how effectiveness was defined (that is, no callbacks in a relatively short period, usually six months) and the fact that officers may not have been adequately trained to use other alternatives in the study (e.g., counseling). In addition, arrests do not always result in a prosecution. The person arrested may be referred for some type of counseling, and perhaps the counseling and not the arrest is the most important factor. There are other potential problems associated with making arrests. It limits officer discretion, it may be more costly and time-consuming, and it may have long-term, possibly negative, consequences (e.g., increased divorces, increased single-parent households, increased welfare and child care costs).

## Crimes in Progress

Intervening in a crime in progress is among the riskiest and most dramatic aspects of police work. Consequently, both the officer and the organization should carefully consider the type of response to be made. First, the organization must decide who will respond. This decision depends on a number of factors, including time and resources available and the seriousness of the crime. Some agencies have specialists for certain types of problems (e.g., special weapons and tactical teams, hostage teams, and so on). However, time or resources do not always allow for such a specialized intervention nor does the seriousness of the crime always warrant this type of response. A bank robbery in progress is distinctly different from a prowler. Some of the important considerations in planning a response for crimes in progress are as follows:

1. Identify locations and types of buildings and/or businesses where the more serious types of crimes in progress may occur, develop detailed maps of these areas, and obtain plans of the buildings.
2. Develop scenarios of how crimes might develop and how the parties in the crimes might behave—including the criminal, victim, bystanders, and officers.
3. Communication procedures for receiving in-progress calls must be developed that are effective in relating information to, and among, officers.
4. If specialized units are available, the person responsible for the decision to utilize these units must be identified.
5. As much information as possible must be secured about the persons involved in the crime and their motives and intentions.

6. The police should be careful how they approach the crime locations lest they alert those involved. Procedures should be established concerning how officers are to approach the scene of a crime, including the number to come to the scene, those to be located in the surrounding area, and so on. Officers should also be alert because they may see possible suspects leaving the crime location or area. The first officers to arrive should carefully determine if the crime is still in progress and keep other officers and managers fully informed.

7. If plainclothes officers are involved, they must be easily identifiable lest they be mistakenly injured or killed.

8. Unless the life of a victim is in immediate danger, the police should probably not aggressively intervene. The police should take risks only to save lives or avoid serious injury. Otherwise they should wait, observe, and negotiate (Adams 1985).

The police must remember that intervention decisions should balance risk with possible harm to the victim. Where there is little or no danger, there should be no aggressive intervention because this may increase the risk to victims, police, and suspects, However, one of the most problematic aspects of decision making in this area is to assess risk to victims based on the presumed intent of suspects. Will armed suspects hurt or kill the victims if they have not already done so? There is no clear answer to this question but, generally speaking, the police should probably not intervene aggressively unless the suspect has harmed victims or they are convinced that harm is imminent. Often trained specialists (e.g., hostage negotiators) will be able to predict with reasonable accuracy when this possibility becomes apparent.

## Drugs and Crime

Perhaps the most serious problem confronting urban police departments in the 1980s is the use of drugs and related crimes. Many people experiment with illegal drugs, some people become addicted, and some commit crimes to support their addiction. Many criminals are under the influence of alcohol or drugs when they commit crimes. In addition, there is extensive violence associated with the distribution of drugs. Further, the massive amount of money involved contributes to the development of corruption in police departments. The annual cost of these and related problems has been estimated in the vicinity of $59 billion (Graham 1987).

Police departments need a multi-faceted response to this problem. First, to decrease the demand for drugs, potential users must be targeted. This can be done through the development of school-related education programs and advertisements and education programs on the radio or television, in newspapers, in community groups, in churches, and so on. Users and distributors must also be targeted, especially any systematically organized distribution in a community. Such an organization may develop around existing gang structures and has the potential for tremendous violence. It is not uncommon for competing gangs, or drug organizations, to commit numerous murders to control drug trafficking in their area. Police must act aggressively to curtail such violence by providing the necessary resources to disrupt drug distribution and break up gang activities.

While police departments can have some impact on the drug problem in their community, other levels of government must also be involved. Drug trafficking is an international problem; therefore, it requires both a national and international response from the federal government (Graham 1987), and, although a governmental response at all levels is desirable, perhaps the most effective long-term solution will be a decrease in demand. There is so much money involved in the sale of illegal drugs that as long as there is a demand, there will be individuals willing to provide drugs to users.

## Bias-Related (Hate) Crime

Racially or sexually motivated crime is a long-standing problem for police departments. However, there is little information about this kind of crime. Blacks, Hispanics, homosexuals, and other minority groups that are targets of criminal activity because of their race, ethnicity, or sexual preference are included in this category. The type of crime includes, but is not limited to, harassment, assault, and murder. Police organizations need a mechanism to identify these crimes, record them, and develop a specific response. The training of officers about the possibility of such crimes is an important first step. When these crimes occur, the organization must make a concerted response that involves traditional patrol and investigative methods and also includes the group that may be the target. Both police and community education, and a police and community response, are necessary (*Law Enforcement News* 1987).

## AIDS

As the number of persons who have Acquired Immune Deficiency Syndrome (or AIDS) has increased, the concerns of police officers have become an important managerial problem. Patrol officers, the most likely police personnel to be exposed to AIDS, tend to have the most concern. They are afraid of any contact with AIDS victims that might transmit the disease. However, AIDS involves high-risk behavior and is transmitted as a result of unprotected sexual contact, sharing of needles, and any activity that includes the exchange of vaginal secretions, semen, or blood. Although it may be possible for AIDS to be transmitted through other means (e.g., bites, urine, feces), research indicates that it is highly unlikely and no such cases have thus far been reported. Police organizations should provide training in this area, develop the necessary procedures, and provide the equipment that will lessen officer concerns. For example, officers should protect any wounds on their own bodies, cover open wounds on victims, use rubber gloves when necessary, and use masks/airways when giving cardiopulmonary resuscitation (Hammett 1987).

## Summary

This chapter identifies contemporary police operational issues. The major operational problems of a police organization have a significant influence on the motivation, behavior, and well-being of officers. These issues include police–citizen encounters, use of force, pursuits, domestic violence, crimes in progress, drugs and crime, bias-related or hate crimes, and AIDS. All of these operational problems can be addressed through adequate information about the problem, the development of appropriate policy and procedures, and effective training.

When police officers and citizens interact, it is most often a reactive encounter that is routine and businesslike. Police officers most often control situations simply by asking questions. However, when there is a lack of citizen cooperation, police officers may give orders or make threats. Resistance to police authority is most likely to come from suspects who, in turn, are most likely to be abused by police. Police use of force is influenced by a number of factors, but perhaps the most important is the attitude of the citizen. Cooperative citizens are rarely the victims of police force, excessive or not.

One of the most important concerns in the use of force is the killing of police by citizens and vice versa. Tens of thousands of citizens and officers have been killed since the middle of the nineteenth century, which underscores the magnitude of this problem. What is promising, however, is that restrictive policies concerning when police use force and improved safety procedures can reduce the number of deaths and injuries of both officers and citizens.

One police situation that sometimes results in accidents or the use of deadly force is a pursuit, either on foot or in a motor vehicle, most often a car. Although little is known about foot pursuits, these may be potentially dangerous for officers for health and safety reasons. Many risks are involved in car pursuits, particularly when the evidence suggests that they involve only minor violations of the law in most cases. This underscores the importance of strict policy guidance and training in responding to this problem.

Similar to pursuits in the potential danger for officers are crimes in progress. All agencies need a preconceived plan for responding to these types of problems. Domestic disturbances, although probably not as potentially dangerous, present their own operational difficulties. A number of alternatives have been used historically by police but the trend in some states is toward arrest. While initial research in this area is positive, it is too early to judge the effectiveness of arrest policies as solution to this problem.

Finally, drugs and crime, bias-related crimes, and AIDS were considered. The tremendous increase in drugs and the relationship to violent crime may be the most significant problem confronting police in recent decades. Bias-related crime, while often unreported, is an issue of importance in some communities. When women or minorities are victims of crime because of their sex or race, this suggests serious relationship problems in a community. Finally, AIDS is also becoming a problem for many communities as patrol officers, and other police, must prepare to respond to individuals who are infected with this deadly disease.

## Discussion Questions

1. What are the different ways that can be used to define a "good cop"?
2. Based on the research presented, explain what tends to happen during police–citizen encounters. What is the most likely police approach in dealing with citizens? Why?
3. Explain the difference between police officer approaches and interpersonal styles and how these relate to escalation patterns.
4. What are the most important factors in determining when police use force?
5. Identify and explain the most important considerations in the police use, and management, of deadly force. Summarize the major research findings in this area.
6. Develop an automobile and foot pursuit policy for a police department. Explain why you would have such a policy.
7. Explain the alternatives police organizations have used historically to respond to domestic disturbances. Which alternative do you think is most effective? Why?
8. Discuss how drugs, bias-related crime, and AIDS have influenced the police in your area.

# References

Adams, T. F., *Police Field Operations* (Englewood Cliffs, N.J.: Prentice-Hall, 1985).

Alpert, G. P. and Anderson, P. R., "The Most Deadly Force: Police Pursuits," *Justice Quarterly* 3, no. 1(1986): 1–14.

Berk, S. and Newton, P. J., "Does Arrest Really Deter Wife Battery?" *American Sociological Review* 50, no. 2(1985): 253–262.

Blumberg, M., "Research on the Police Use of Deadly Force," in *The Ambivalent Force*, eds. A. S. Blumberg and E. Niederhoffer (New York: Holt, Rinehart & Winston, 1985), pp. 340–350.

Friedrich, R. J., "Police Use of Force: Individuals, Situations and Organizations," *The Annals* 435 (November 1980): 82–97.

Fyfe, J. J., "Shots Fired: An Examination of New York City Police Firearms Discharges." Ph.D. diss., University of New York at Albany, 1978.

———, "Administrative Interventions on Police Shooting Discretion," *Journal of Criminal Justice* 7, no. 4(1980): 309–323.

———, "Blind Justice," *Journal of Criminal Law and Criminology* 73, no. 2(1982): 707–722.

———, Interview. *Law Enforcement News*, June 24, 1985, pp. 9–12.

Garner, J. and Clemmer, E., *Danger to Police in Domestic Disturbances—A New Look*. Research in Brief. (Washington, D.C.: Government Printing Office, 1986).

Graham, M. E., "Controlling Drug Abuse and Crime: A Research Update," *NIJ Reports* (March/April 1987), pp. 2–7.

Geller, W. A., "Deadly Force: What We Know," in *Thinking About Police*, ed. C. Klockars (New York: McGraw-Hill, 1983), pp. 313–331.

Grennan, S. A., "Findings on the Role of Officer Gender in Violent Encounters with Citizens," *Journal of Police Science and Administration* 15, no. 1(1987): 78–85.

Hammett, T. M., "AIDS and the Law Enforcement Officer," *NIJ Reports* (November/December 1987), pp. 2–7.

Jaffe, P., Wolfe, D., and Austin, G., "The Impact of Police Charges in Incidents of Wife Abuse," *Journal of Family Violence* 1, no. 1(1986): 37–49.

Kuykendall, J., "Trends in the Use of Deadly Force by Police," *Journal of Criminal Justice* 9, no. 5(1981): pp. 359–366.

Law Enforcement News, "Spouse Abuse Arrests Grow," March 10, 1987, p. 1.

———, "Bias-Related Crime: The Police Response," April 28, 1987, p. 1.

Reiss, A. J., Jr., *The Police and the Public* (New Haven: Yale University Press, 1971).

Roberts, M., "Police Management Training Program." Lecture, San Jose State University, 1985.

*San Francisco Chronicle*, "Big Decline in Killings of Citizens by Police," October 20, 1986, p. 23.

Scharf, P. and Binder, A., *The Badge and the Bullet* (New York: Praeger, 1983).

Sherman, L. W. and Berk, R. A., "Deterrent Effects of Arrest for Domestic Assault," *American Sociological Review* 49, no. 2(1984): 261–271.

Sherman, L. W. and Langworthy, R. H., "Measuring Homicide by Police Officers," *Journal of Criminal Law and Criminology* 70, no. 4 (1979): 546–560.

Steinman, M., "Arrest Policies and Spouse Abuse: Putting a New Policy Direction in Perspective," *American Journal of Police* VI, no. 2(1987): 11–26.

Sykes, R. E. and Brent, E. E., *Policing: A Social Behaviorist Perspective* (New Brunswick, N.J.: Rutgers University Press, 1983).

*Time* Magazine, "The Perils of Hot Pursuit," November 19, 1988, p. 96.

Van Raalte, R., Interview. *Law Enforcement News*, March 24, 1986, pp. 9–12.

# CHAPTER 11

# Planning, Change, and Innovation

As we have emphasized throughout the text, the police operate in relatively unstable environments. Thus, if police agencies are to stay abreast of community needs and expectations, as well as those of the criminal justice system, they will need to adapt to changing external environmental conditions. Of course, the same holds true for internal environmental conditions. The organization must be willing to adapt to administrative, personnel, or technological changes as well. Accordingly, the processes of planning, change, and innovation are of vital importance to the field of policing. In this chapter we will discuss planning as it relates to organizational change, why change is frequently resisted, ways to overcome such resistance, and requirements for successful innovation in police organizations.

## The Process of Planning

*Planning* is the process of deciding in advance what is to be done and how it is to be done (Kast and Rosenzweig 1985, p. 478). Planning is essentially an intellectual process. This process not only identifies the sequence the organization must go through to accomplish goals and objectives, it also identifies alternatives. The creation of both this sequence and the alternatives in problem solving is the intellectual component of planning. Creativity can come in a variety of forms. One is *imitation*, or using plans developed by others. Before this is done, however, the organization must make sure the circumstances that resulted in the development of the plan are similar. Other forms of creativity used by law enforcement agencies are inductive and deductive reasoning. *Inductive reasoning* means moving from the *specific* to the more *general*, or examining specific data and making generalizations about what it might mean. For example, this might include analyzing crime data and noting a trend or pattern in certain types of crime that might require a special police response. *Deductive reasoning* is just the reverse, moving from the *general* to the *specific*. For example, if an organization assumes that the primary role of the police is to maintain order, what specific policies and procedures are necessary to implement this role conception?

**Police managers in the process of developing strategic and operational plans for the organization.**

Another form of creativity is *idea linking*, often done in a process of *free association*. Planners are encouraged to identify any ideas, without limitation or inhibition, that might relate to the problem or plan at hand. This intellectual process of freely associating ideas may result in innovative solutions. This is particularly true when those involved in the process come from different backgrounds and have different perspectives on the problem. For example, having individuals from several levels in the organization adds ideas and perspectives to a free-association process (Kuykendall and Unsinger 1979, pp. 98–99).

There are essentially two main types of plans: strategic and operational. *Strategic plans* are designed to meet the long-range, overall goals of the organization; *operational plans* are designed to meet the specific tasks required to implement the strategic plans. Strategic plans focus on *external* environmental factors that affect how the goals and objectives of the organization will be defined and achieved. Thus, important environmental factors that the police should consider in developing strategic planning include personal, family, and business demands; crime problems; and community attitudes, especially regarding the provision of social services and how order-maintenance activities are handled (Roberg and Kirchhoff 1985). Criteria used to measure these factors may include population trends and geographic dispersion, number of businesses and geographic dispersion, retail sales trends, employment trends, crime analysis (e.g., Uniformed Crime Reports, victimization surveys), and citizen attitudes as measured through surveys and interviews (p. 137). Strategic planning is important to police managers because it allows them to prepare for and deal with the changing environmental conditions in which their organizations operate.

There are three main types of operational plans: standing, time-specific, and functional. *Standing plans* are for recurring problems and situations. These plans provide the basic framework for responding to organizational problems. A general mission plan, encompassing organizational goals and objectives, policies, procedures, methods, and rules and regulations, is an example of a standing plan. *Time-specific plans* are concerned with a specific purpose and conclude when an objective is accomplished or a problem is solved. Examples include a specific program, project, or the budget. *Functional plans* include the framework for the operation of the major functional units in the organization, such as patrol and investigations. Functional plans include how resources are to be allocated and how to respond to crimes in progress (Kuykendall and Unsinger 1979, pp. 106–107). This planning process, including creativity and the two major types of plans, is depicted in figure 11-1.

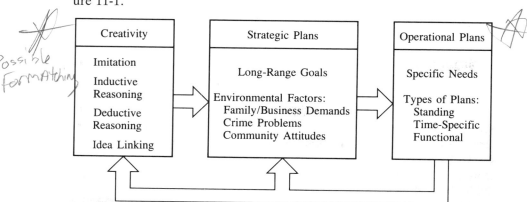

**Figure 11-1**   The Planning Process

Planning should be based on relevant research and should attempt to take into consideration the elements of different types of plans, including those that are relatively permanent (e.g., a general mission statement), those specific to a particular problem (e.g., an increase in burglaries in a certain area), and those related to the major functional units (e.g., allocation of patrol officers). However, action research planning is more than a process, it is a way of thinking about organizational problem solving. The results of the process are always viewed as only a temporary solution that requires periodic reexamination. Managers and employees need to establish a mind-set that planning leads to temporary solutions to problems, that the solutions will have problems that require adjustments, and that the problems for which the solutions are proposed are likely to change with some regularity. Thus, planning is a continual process and an integral part of the organization's and employees' work life.

## Planning for Change

Planning for change involves a *futuristic* orientation. Problems regarding operational practices and procedures are identified and, based on a diagnosis of these problems, recommendations for change are made. Such recommendations specify certain actions to be taken by the organization in order to enhance organizational performance. For such changes to occur in an orderly manner, employees (especially those directly affected by the change) must be involved in the planning process from beginning to end. Specific strategies and methods that can be used to involve employees in developing and implementing organizational change are the focus of chapter 12.

A planning model, shown in figure 11-2, indicates that planning for change is a continual process. Additionally, the process must be viewed from a systems perspective, in which the relationship between the organization and its environment is taken into consideration. Thus, planning allows the organization to adapt to internal and external environmental demands in a timely fashion. The model relies on an *action research* orientation; that is, data are collected, diagnosed, and fed back to organization members prior

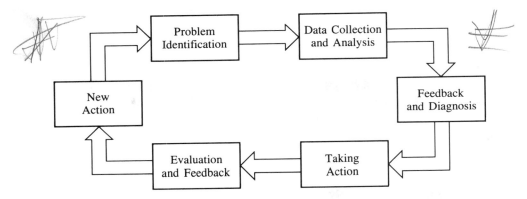

**Figure 11-2** A Planning Model

to action being taken. Once the plan for action has been implemented, results are carefully evaluated and new action (modification) takes place if necessary. The *purpose* of action research in planning is twofold: (1) to produce knowledge to improve the performance of the organization under study, and (2) to be able to generalize the findings to other organizations operating under similar conditions and circumstances. In other words, it is hoped that the findings of the research will be applicable to other organizations attempting to improve their performance. Each of the six stages of the planning model is discussed in the following paragraphs.

**Problem identification.** In the initial stage, someone in the organization, generally a top-level manager or someone with influence and power, recognizes that a problem exists that requires corrective action. Once the problem is identified, the person responsible for developing and implementing the remainder of the plan must be determined. In general, this can be accomplished in one of three ways: with an external change agent, with an internal change agent, or with a combination of external-internal change agents. While each of these approaches is discussed in the next chapter, the choice usually depends on the nature of the problem and the degree of expertise required to solve the problem. Because police organizations frequently do not employ personnel with the expertise required to conduct action research, they often must use either an external or a combination of external-internal change agents.

Managers' role perspectives strongly influence the identification of a problem situation and the method of solution. For example, seeing police work as order maintenance influences the types of problems that the organization will identify and plan for. Domestic disturbances, for instance, were not considered to be a police problem requiring systematic planning until the 1960s.

Problem identification can also be the result of mechanisms that exist in the planning process. The organization can develop guidelines that determine when a problem exists. For example, if officers receive a certain number of complaints about their activities or behavior, there may be a need to reexamine the policies, procedures, and methods and training in that area. Problem identification can come from data analysis, employee grievances, community expressions of concern or need, and managerial perception and insight. The latter, obviously, is strongly influenced by the manager's perception of the police role.

**Data collection and analysis.** The collection of relevant data is crucial to the planning process, since a plan for action can only be as good as the information on which it is based. The change agent must decide which type(s) of data to collect in order to best diagnose the problem(s) under investigation. The methods for gathering data that are generally the most useful to police agencies include:

1. Review of the literature: Reviewing pertinent literature on the subject, including books, journal articles, and reports, will usually be an effective first step in data collection.

2. Records, reports, and documents: Statistical and analytical interpretations of internal records and reports are necessary to predict the operational needs of a department and to develop a systematic plan. External documents and reports can also provide valuable information and direction

for planning activities. Such documents include federal and/or state legislation, consultant surveys, annual reports and studies conducted by other agencies, as well as material prepared by public and private sector organizations.

3. Personal data collection: Organizational members closest to the problem at hand should be interviewed for their opinions, ideas, and suggestions regarding appropriate planning activities. Potential outside interview sources should not be overlooked; both public and private organizations may have experienced managerial problems similar to those found in policing. Local college and university faculty members may be able to serve as valuable resource persons, either formally as consultants or informally by directing the department to useful reference materials. It may also be necessary for the change agent to observe a situation or operation directly in order to acquire information not otherwise available.

4. Questionnaires: When a quantity of information is needed from many individuals or from individuals who are widely dispersed geographically, a formal questionnaire can be an effective means of data collection. A questionnaire is most useful when it can be answered with reasonable convenience, is not vague or ambiguous, and will obtain the information necessary to be able to adequately respond to the problem at hand.

5. Experimentation: Experimentation is the most advanced method of data collection since it creates new information. Because experimental designs offer the greatest degree of control in the collection of data, they offer the most significant and potentially useful information. However, because they are often time consuming, costly, and disruptive of operations, experiments are not widely utilized by police organizations for planning and change purposes (Galvin and LeGrande 1971, pp. 211–213).

Once the data are collected, they must be analyzed for interpretation. Because a manager most likely will determine the relative importance to be assigned to the interpretation and use of the data, it is crucial that the data are properly analyzed and understood. Therefore, if the data are sufficiently complex, the manager may need to consult with someone well versed in statistical applications.

**Feedback and diagnosis.**  Since action research is based on a mutual effort between the change agent and organizational members, the data are fed back to the members, usually in a group meeting. With assistance from the group (which in some instances might include citizens) regarding the analysis or meaning of the data, a final interpretation of the findings is made. The group's input is necessary, because the results may have been influenced by "hidden" or informal activities that the data may not reflect. The purpose of the feedback is to help the group diagnose the strengths and weaknesses of the organization or unit under study. In this way, specific plans for action can be identified and their likelihood for success or failure can be debated from a knowledgeable perspective. "Deviant" or contrary views are often of great benefit in this phase and should not be dismissed from consideration.

Because there are usually several feasible courses of action, the alternatives must be evaluated and the most appropriate selected. A number of guidelines may be used to evaluate each of the alternatives:

1. Which alternative best accomplishes the specific objectives of the plan?
2. Which alternative is most practical when the available resources (i.e., manpower, time, and equipment), both present and future, are realistically appraised?
3. Which alternative may be most effectively implemented, considering the time available before action must be taken?
4. Which alternative will be the most acceptable to the political leadership and the various segments of the community?
5. Considering all factors, which alternative has the best chance of successfully solving the problem (Galvin and LeGrande 1971, p. 213)?

**Taking action.**  The next stage is to take action or implement the plan that has been formulated. Of course, management must formally agree with the plan before any action can be taken. Some "bargaining" with management may need to take place before certain aspects of the plan can go forward. Because employees have been active participants in the planning process from the beginning, resistance to change should be greatly reduced.

**Evaluation and feedback.** The cyclical nature of action research is evident at this stage, since data must again be collected after the action has been implemented. Once the plan has been in operation long enough for valid measurements to be taken, results of the evaluation are then fed back to organization members for their information and input regarding modification.

**New action.** The final stage is concerned with modifying the original action, based on the information provided by the evaluation. An initial action is seldom effective without some change, which is best accomplished when planning is viewed as a continual process, and actions are thus modified to meet current as well as future conditions.

The planning process involves programs for change in what an organization does or how it operates. When planning for organizational change, police managers need to determine how behavioral changes in employees can most effectively be brought about. Our attention now turns to a discussion on change in organizations.

## Organizational Change

*Organizational change* occurs when new ideas or behaviors are adopted by an organization (Pierce and Delbecq 1977). Usually, an innovative idea, such as a new method of management or a new patrol strategy, is introduced and behavioral changes are supposed to follow. Consequently, the ultimate success of any organizational change effort depends on how well the organization can alter the behavioral patterns of its employees. Employee behavior is influenced by factors such as leadership styles, motivational techniques, informal relationships, and organization and job design. Any change in the organization, regardless of how it is introduced, involves an attempt to persuade employees to change their behavior and their relationships with one another. In order to bring about timely change in the organization, managers need to consider why people resist change, how resistance can be overcome, and the effects of pace on change.

## *Resistance to Change*

Probably the most common characteristic of change is people's resistance to it. Generally, individuals do not like to change their behavior. Adapting to a new environment or learning a new method or technique often results in feelings of stress or other forms of psychological discomfort. Following is a brief discussion of the major reasons people tend to resist change in organizations (Kerr and Kerr 1972, pp. 4–6).

**Sunk costs.** "Sunk costs," which include such factors as time, energy, experience, and money, are extremely influential forces in resisting change. Individuals or groups with many such "investments" sunk into a particular organization or job may not want changes to occur, regardless of their merit. For example, many police agencies are attempting to remove seniority from the promotional process in order to base promotions solely on those activities and skills required for a particular position. Resistance to such change is usually strongest from the older, more experienced employees who feel that their vested interests in the organization, and the reward structure, are threatened. This may also explain why older people tend to resist change most strongly; they simply have more invested in the system as it exists and potentially more to lose if the status quo changes.

This is especially problematic for police organizations. Often major changes in police organizations require a change in the style, activities, and behavior of officers. Police departments frequently have two or more "generations" of officers, each group wedded to a particular philosophy of policing. For instance, officers who were developed in a political-watchman model may have trouble adjusting to a legalistic-professional model; those who are crime fighters in the legalistic-professional model may have problems adapting to the social service perspective required by the community-service approach. Perhaps most difficult is changing the intuitive, action orientation of police, in general, to the more scientific, systematic perspective required of the rational-contingency model.

**Misunderstandings.** Resistance to change is likely when organization members do not clearly understand the purpose, mechanics, or potential consequences of a planned change because of inadequate or misperceived communication. A critical problem that frequently develops in this area is the uncertainty about consequences of change. If employees are not told how they will be affected by change, rumors and speculation will follow and the resulting resistance may be strong enough to severely limit the change process. When change is imposed on employees, instead of occurring as a result of participation by those involved in the changes, misunderstandings are more likely to occur.

**Group norms.** Groups have a tremendous impact on the behavior and attitudes of organization members. Group norms (i.e., expected behavior from group members) may be a powerful factor in resistance to change. If an individual follows the norms strictly, he or she may not easily perceive the need for adaptation or change. If significant organizational changes are to occur, police managers must consider group norms and influences and involve group consensus and decision making in planning for change. The manager's and worker's cultures in police organizations illustrate the importance of taking group norms into account.

**Balance of power.** One source of equilibrium in organizations is the balance of power among individuals, groups, and organizational units. Changes that are perceived to threaten the autonomy, authority, power, or status of a group or unit will most likely encounter resistance, regardless of their merit. Such resistance is documented by the case study presented later in this chapter. A police organization attempted to decentralize its operations by using a neighborhood team policing concept. Since this approach provides more control and autonomy for lower-level management (sergeants), middle-level management (lieutenants) resisted any changes because of their perceived loss in authority and prestige. The department's detectives also felt demeaned by the new system because they were forced to work alongside patrol officers as a team.

## Reducing Resistance

The following discussion focuses on methods police managers can use to lessen resistance and institute change in a beneficial and constructive fashion. Because of individual differences, the same method(s) will not reduce resistance in every organization member. In general, however, several methods are valuable in reducing resistance to organizational change: sharing expectations, avoiding coercive tactics, using group decision making, and making changes tentative.

**Sharing expectations.**   A mutual sharing of expectations, as espoused by the expectation-integration model, between the organization (especially top-level management) and the individual can greatly facilitate understanding and reduce dysfunctional conflicts. Much of the misunderstanding that may precede organizational change results from too little open communication between the two parties; distrust develops and the change process becomes a traumatic experience, strongly resisted by the rank and file. On the other hand, if two-way communication and shared expectations are encouraged, specific reasons for resistance can be discovered and additional explanation, or a change in strategy, can be made.

**Avoiding coercive tactics.**   Those who resist change are sometimes coerced into accepting the change. Strauss and Sayles (1980, p. 251) accurately interpret the use of coercive tactics as *overcoming* resistance, in contrast to *reducing* resistance. Due to the paramilitary, mechanistic design of many police organizations, management often assumes that whatever is communicated from the top of the pyramid will be readily accepted by the lower echelons and put into practice. When questions arise or policies are not carried out enthusiastically, "uncooperative" members may be threatened with sanctions such as transfers from an immediate peer group, suspensions, demotions, and even termination.

Such coercive tactics only exacerbate the situation. Although this approach may be immediately effective and lead to compliance with the change, the long-range results will certainly be harmful. Resistance may actually become stronger over time, followed by resentment and possibly sabotage. The related decrease in morale will most likely result in lowered levels of performance and increased employee turnover. Thus, while coercive tactics may initially suppress resistance, the long-term effects for both the organization and the individual are likely to be inflammatory and counter-productive.

Changes in police organizations, particularly major changes, are often characterized by the use of centralized decision making and coercive tactics. Both methods are associated with the mechanistic model. Management and workers often have an adversarial relationship in police organizations because coercive tactics are used to manage employees and implement change. This management perspective seems to suggest that since many employees do not understand the need for change and will resist it anyway, there is no need to involve them in the process. Instead they must be forced to go along with the change. Some police managers even hope that the use of coercive tactics will result in the retirement or resignation of those officers and managers who are opposed to the change. Not only is this approach inhumane, it assumes that only the proponents of change have the "right" vision for the future of the organization, and that opponents can add nothing to the process. This conception of organization and management is essentially political in nature; as noted later, it is a reflection of segmentalism.

However, even given that change is usually more effective if coercive tactics are not utilized, they may be necessary under some circumstances. Even when there is substantial consensus on the direction an organization should take, there will most likely be resistance. In such instances, changes in activity and behavior may have to be mandated. It is important to remember, however, that this should be a "last resort" technique and not the basic perspective from which managers should function.

**Using group decision making.** Kurt Lewin's (1958) initial studies on the development of group methods in decision making revealed that behavioral change is more likely to occur and persist when based on a group, rather than an individual, decision. This is especially true when the group is important to an individual, who will change attitudes and behavior in order to conform. Lewin further stated that the basis for successful change involves: (1) *unfreezing* existing habits and stereotypes, (2) *changing* to new behavioral patterns and attitudes, and (3) *refreezing* or reinforcing the new patterns and attitudes to ensure future conformity. The key to this method is group pressure, which will be especially strong if the participants feel they "own" the decision and are responsible for it.

According to this analysis, it would appear that a participative management style can reduce much of the conflict and resistance to change that may otherwise occur. Through the use of task forces, ad hoc committees, group seminars, and other participatory techniques, organization employees can become directly involved in planning for change. By thoroughly discussing the issues, a more accurate understanding and unbiased analysis of the true situation is likely to result. While the group may still reject a particular decision for change, resistance based on misunderstanding will nevertheless be reduced.

**Making changes tentative.**   In general, changes should take place on a tentative or trial basis, particularly in those organizations that are mechanistic in character. If employees do not perceive changes as irreversible, they will feel less threatened by any change and their resistance will be reduced. Strauss and Sayles suggest two distinct advantages to this method:

1. It enables employees to test their own reactions to the new situation, and provides them with more facts on which to base their decision.
2. It helps to "unfreeze" their attitudes and encourages them to think objectively about the proposed changes (1980, p. 212).

## Pace of Change

Planned organizational change should occur at an appropriate pace, neither too rapid nor too gradual. The pace is critical; if change is forced through abruptly, it could cause severe resistance that could disrupt the organization over a long period. On the other hand, if change is so gradual and slow that the employees cannot really see anything "happening," they may return to the more familiar and comfortable ways of the past. Change should be introduced quickly enough to show that something is happening and slowly enough to prevent it from totally disrupting the status quo and being rejected.

Contingency factors play an important role in determining the pace for organizational change, since organic organizations can withstand more rapid change than mechanistic organizations. For mechanistic police agencies, a gradual or medium pace would be the least disruptive route to change and, therefore, the most beneficial. In those agencies or units that are more organic in design and whose employees may be more amenable to change, change should be introduced rapidly. Quick change reduces the need for the series of adjustments required by slow change, since slow change may leave the organization in a continual state of confusion.

Because it is hard to grasp the difficulties and "unforeseen" problems that frequently accompany organizational change efforts, the following case study highlighting several problem areas is presented. In this example, presented by psychologists Morton Bard and Robert Shellow,* a large urban police department attempted a radical change, from a relatively bureaucratic, mechanistic design to a more flexible, organic design. An analysis of the project's planned change efforts, and the resulting implications, follows the case study.

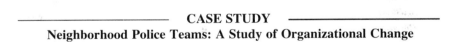

——————————— **CASE STUDY** ———————————

**Neighborhood Police Teams: A Study of Organizational Change**

*Historical background.* *New York City has one of the most tradition-bound police departments in the country. Its organizational problems are serious and enormous and crusted over with a time-hardened protective shell. When the then new Police Commissioner arrived on the scene in 1971, he took the job with the aim of inducing major change in the Department. He knew the Department very well and decided that one of the major needs was for some kind of transitional model for delivering better services to the unique neighborhoods that constitute New York City. For example, within*

*\*Source:* Extracted from Bard, M. and Shellow, R., "Neighborhood Police Teams," in *Issues in Law Enforcement—Essays and Case Studies*, eds. R. Shellow and M. Bard (Reston, VA: Reston Publishing, 1976), pp. 171–182. Reprinted by permission of the authors.

a two-square block area, there may be an enclave of Greeks; then one of Mohawk Indians in another three- or four-square block area; and of Syrians in still another. Nevertheless, the NYPD policy had traditionally served these diverse areas uniformly. Regardless of the numerous special qualities in these culturally different neighborhoods, operating procedural orders read as if written by a single mimeograph machine. They were applied literally everywhere, despite the differing problems encountered increasingly in different neighborhoods. The Commissioner thought this was wrong. He felt that there must be some way to relate the unique character of each "Little Italy" or Chinatown or whatever without enfeebling the police or disturbing the general order of the city as a whole.

***Introduction of the plan.*** The new Commissioner now introduced a plan somewhat like the British in policing style since it was oriented toward service to neighborhoods. The Department's response was at first primarily negative because of normal resistance to change and because the Department had not been consulted. But the public's response was enthusiastic. Suddenly every effective community organization began to put political pressure on the Commissioner to implement the neighborhood team plan in their neighborhoods. So the Commissioner had to move more rapidly than originally planned. While speedy organization was politically expedient, it was organizationally dangerous to proceed before the groundwork had been carefully laid. Both the men in the ranks and the department executives had to understand and participate in the decision if it were to work. In addition, the proper organizational structure and training had to be set up to support the operation.

Even before any team training began, some changes were made in the organizational structure. The Commissioner himself directed the work of "decentralizing" some police functions in the command structure. The initial plan called for establishment of small police departments within each precinct. Certain sergeants were to be designated "team commanders" with responsibilities similar to that of the chief of a small town police force. In that way, each team commander had a force of 35 police officers, and each team would cover one neighborhood. Roughly, that meant five neighborhood teams per precinct.

In effect, this restructuring eliminated the traditional patrol sergeants who, strictly speaking, were accountable to no one on a day-to-day basis. It also re-involved the precinct C.O.'s who had generally been remote from the daily operational problems in the various neighborhoods of their areas.

Under the Commissioner's plan, the newly designated team sergeants were given great flexibility. They could assign manpower according to the priorities they judged had problems in their areas. They could also assign officers to work in uniform or in plain clothes, whatever suited the developing needs of the neighborhood. The sergeant's new flexibility strengthened his authority, but above all it acknowledged responsibility and his accountability to the people in his neighborhood.

Where in the past everything had been done uniformly, sergeants were now given freedom to make decisions. Depending on the type of relationship he had worked out with the community, the sergeant could set up a neighborhood office, develop ways of getting information from the community people, and supervise his men in a way that permitted both individual freedom and team participation. It was meant to be a marked departure procedurally from the highly mobile, centrally dispatched, controlled police force which had until then been organized in precincts for administrative simplicity and efficiency.

Seen from a broad perspective, this team concept was a shift away from the highly centralized and remote management of police services that had developed in large cities. It was also an effort to decentralize certain functions rationally and shift the point of accountability from the captains to sergeants at the line level.

Initially, one neighborhood in each section of the city was chosen, quietly and without fanfare for the experiment. But word soon got out, and a wholly unexpected public clamor for neighborhood police teams spread throughout the city. It was as if the general public hungered for a return to that closer relationship with police that was virtually impossible so long as unit mobility remained a primary concern of headquarters. As a partial response to the pressure, the words "Neighborhood Police Team" were quickly lettered on patrol cars. Launching this program in this manner be-

*fore it was thoroughly understood gave it a public relations quality that was potentially destructive. Initially five neighborhoods were designated as team areas but before very long there were over forty-five. The authors joined in an effort to put the brakes on before the expectations of citizens far outstripped the Department's ability to deliver the new type of service that everyone was eager to get.*

***Preparation for training.*** *After the first teams had been in existence for some time, the Commissioner turned to the problems at hand: the men didn't know what their roles were supposed to be and the organizational structure was vague. The authors were brought in during the early stage to help put together the training program itself. They made two inputs: one was to get them to hold off on proliferating the program; the other was to gain a commitment to move toward establishing precinct-wide conversion to the neighborhood program.*

*Responding to public demand for Neighborhood Police Teams, the Department originally set up approximately forty-five teams in almost as many precincts. In other words, in more than half of the city's seventy-seven precincts, there was only one neighborhood team operating while the rest of the precinct operated as usual. So the competition, the rivalry, the who-takes-calls and who-doesn't confusion were predictably unsatisfactory and irresponsible. The authors suggested the establishment of neighborhood teams entirely in five precincts. They were concerned that sector men and sector squads in the same precincts but outside the teams might sabotage or otherwise undermine the efforts of any "foreign" neighborhood teams in their midst. Indeed, it was seen that it would be extremely difficult to preserve the integrity of those neighborhood teams and give the program a real test unless whole precincts were fully converted to the new system.*

*A parallel development during this reorganization was the creation of an "Operations Lieutenant" in each of the five precincts. Traditionally in the NYPD a lieutenant occupied what was basically a more-or-less honorific position. It was wasteful; they were virtually high-class clerks. The new operations lieutenant was sent back out on the street and given responsibility for shift supervision. With the team commanders fully responsible for their area and the operations lieutenant responsible for the whole precinct during a given shift, there was not only a potential, but a very real probability, that horns would be locked, particularly on tactical issues. To head off trouble the operations lieutenant was converted into a neighborhood team coordinator. He oversaw the operations of the teams in his precinct. The theory was he would no longer need to vie with the team commanders, but become a vital part of the team program.*

**Operational phase.** *The first neighborhood team was operating by early September 1971. By late December and early January, forty teams were operating. During this two-month period, two things became increasingly evident; first, the men did not know what was expected of them; and secondly, there was highly variable performance on the street.*

*In response to a profound policy shift, the implementation now followed almost a classic course. The first news came in a TOP (temporary operating procedure) memo which was distributed to all commands. In three single-spaced pages the disturbingly vague TOP was to serve only as a guideline. Using this discretion in setting policy, the Police Commissioner held that in order to deliver services more meaningfully to the many and varied neighborhoods of the city the normal precinct structure would have to change.*

*Very quickly, the issue of interpreting policy through a training program of some sort became crucial. Should the bulk of training be directed at the brass, the sergeants, or the men? Several of those involved believed that the sergeants had the greatest need to understand neighborhood policing concepts because they were the ones who were to serve as models for the men. It was decided to devote intensive training time to the sergeants and then assist them in training their team members, but also provide some kind of training for the precinct commanders, their executive officers, and the lieutenants. While the sergeants may have known very well what they were supposed to do and how they were to do it, and while their men may also have understood their roles clearly, the lieutenants could disrupt the entire organization by jerking men from shifts, giving them special assignments, and floating them off here and there.*

The training plan evolved from a joint effort of the Police Department and some doctoral candidates who attended one of the authors' seminars in 1972. The seminar group consisted of ten students and ten police officers. Ranging from sergeant to captain and representing three divisions in the New York Police Department, the officers were there to keep the social scientists informed of the realities of police work. The graduate students were there to contribute their insights and knowledge of human behavior, of changing social systems, and of educational methodology.

The seminar agreed at the outset that the Neighborhood Police Team Concept had several profound implications:

1. It acknowledged the importance of community participation in crime control.
2. It acknowledged the need for new skills and competencies in the delivery of police services.
3. It acknowledged the need for change in organizational behavior from authoritarian military uniformity to democratic team flexibility.

The planning group concerned with the reorganized approach now decided that the most effective strategy would call for a period of intensive training for approximately thirty team commanders in the experimental precincts. Beginning with a brief orientation with patrol personnel and experimental teams, one of the team commanders together with civilian and police trainers conducted field training over a one-year period. One each of five pairs of trainees (a civilian and an officer) was assigned to the five experimental precincts. Along with the five or six team commanders, the civilian and police trainees would serve as a resident field training faculty within each precinct.

Such assignments were a world shaking opportunity for many team commanders. It is a kind of freedom that can be mind-boggling to those who have been operating in a very tight, authoritarian organization. Some of those selected for training couldn't really handle it. From those who could, we hoped to learn a lot. Certain of those team commanders have done fantastically innovative and unusual things particularly relevant to their areas. Others were *not able to rise to the occasion. From them we did learn what kind of person makes a good team commander.*

*After the basic concepts were decided, we held training sessions for personnel from the planning division and the Police Academy. Together we designed a consecutive five-day training program for the team commanders. It was calculated to project a new concept of supervision. It was hoped that we could thus expose the men to a range of options for use in their ongoing educational role in those precincts. Each one of the precincts was planned to become what a teaching hospital is to a medical student. Further, each of those precincts would be related to the Police Academy. In addition, the team commanders, whose roles are at least partly educational, would be part-time training faculty.*

*To promote continuous training sessions, we encouraged team commanders to hold them not only on unusual subject matter and in unusual ways, but also at unusual times and places. If Sunday morning is quiet, a team commander should be able to pull everybody off the street. With modern communication and response capability, why not? If the public doesn't see officers on the street and gets upset, then the public has to be educated too. That's another police responsibility. If you are doing relevant work and delivering service, the public will buy your approach. Communities will support efforts that are relevant and effective in the service they provide.*

*The neighborhood approach collided, of course, with the traditionalists both in the precincts and in the Department as a whole. As mentioned earlier the lieutenants were originally jealous of the new authority given to the team commanders. The detective division and special squads needed reorientation too. In precincts where the neighborhood model was operative, many detective and special squad functions were already performed by neighborhood teams. As a result, the team commander had to be consulted before any officers external to his team were brought into the neighborhood. If a special unit did go in, the team responsible for that area had to go right along with them and serve as a guide, thus heading off a possible sabotage of the team effort.*

*In general, there is a very serious clash between the mobile patrol philosophy and the neighborhood police philosophy in most departments. Mobile patrol emphasizes rapidity of response and rapidity of return to service.*

In effect: get to the assignment, get it over fast, get back to service ready for the next assignment. On the contrary, with the neighborhood team approach: try to increase contact between police and citizen, and provide a higher quality of service, perhaps spend more time on some problems, get to know people better, be available within the neighborhood. The team commander was expected to monitor reactions of people in the areas he serviced and to identify those who might be considered spokesmen for the various factions of the community. Such spokesmen were (and are) not formally designated. For example, gang leaders can be as important as administrators or block captains. The team commanders had to discover those people and relate to them in such a way as to get their input. Then the stage was (and is) set for providing police services adjusted to the needs and problems of each neighborhood.

None of these basic organizational changes were accomplished simply by the Commissioner's original decision to implement a neighborhood police program. Training and retraining and training again was necessary to accomplish changes of the scope contemplated by the neighborhood approach. But even before training could start, it had to be funded. A proposal for funding was submitted in 1971 to the Law Enforcement Assistance Administration, a federal agency. After months of delay, it was approved for eighteen months. The grant was for a one-shot study with provision for possible extension, and it was to be augmented by Police Academy funds. The Academy was also to oversee the performance of the contract. By the time training began and civilian staff was hired, three full precincts and a number of scattered teams had been trying to operate on the neighborhood model without any training at all.

The fate of the training teams differed greatly within each precinct. In only two of the five precincts did the training really get off the ground. Even then, it was often not under optimal conditions. The single most critical factor was, of course, the attitude of the precinct commanding officer. For example, in the 24th Precinct only two men from each team were allowed to leave street patrol for training during the same hours. This attacked the very heart of the team training concept since it prevented the trainees from organizing well-coordinated, smooth-functioning groups. Eighty percent of this same precinct was comprised of rookie policemen who were transferred there during the training. While these coincidental transfers were an attempt to reduce corruption in the precinct, they produced a rapid turnover that directly opposed the Neighborhood Police Team [NPT] concept of fostering neighborhood police ties. Add to this the fact that all training sessions were held early on Sunday morning and you can begin to get the feel of some of the obstacles to training in a precinct where the NPT program was given low priority.

In the two precincts which understood and supported the NPT concept, the commanding officers were responsible for the positive reception. In fact, even before the arrival of the trainers, one precinct was operating according to the commanding officer's conception of the spirit of the NPT concept. The C.O. held a forum for the men in his command to explain the kinds of innovation that would be introduced. The precinct sergeants also made contacts with 140 block associations and then assigned particular policemen to deal with the various problems brought to light. The C.O. also met with heads of the Parks Department, the Sanitation Department and other local service agencies so as to coordinate their efforts with the police in serving the community. When we pressed this commanding officer for his opinion of the value NPT trainers had been to his precinct, he conceded that they had made some contributions, such as suggestions for rumor control and improved understanding of varying reactions to standard police procedures. Among ethnic groups the Hispanics react particularly negatively to being touched by a policeman when being questioned, for instance. Also the NPT trainers had helped in pointing out the paternalistic attitude of many police toward the people whom they serve. The necessity of treating fellow citizens as adults was stressed.

Even in those instances where training seemed to proceed fairly effectively, many problems were not resolved. For example, during training one team examined a problem in their neighborhood that involved public reaction to police handling of robbery investigations. Often citizens were annoyed when patrolmen completed robbery reports without taking clearly evident fingerprints. After some brainstorming, the trainees suggested that one of the team pairs could carry a fingerprint kit so that this pair could be sent over to take prints when the next such robbery report was being made. A *simple enough plan, it was an outcome of team work that would certainly have improved police/community relations and might have aided in crime solving as well. But the plan was squelched at higher precinct levels and the team was told that the $12.00 purchase price for the kit was not available.*

*Throughout the field training there was ongoing conflict between the Neighborhood Police Team trainers and their supervisors at the Police Academy. While both the civilian and police trainers as staff members were, in effect, in the paramilitary structure of the Police Academy, they operated semi-autonomously. Because most of their funding was external they were not accountable to the Police Academy in the traditional sense. Thus, their very existence was viewed as a threat to the authority of the Academy. In addition to this, the Police Project Director was changed ten or more times in the course of two years. This accentuated the sense of isolation within the Academy structure. Also, the cooperative joint decision-making style of the training team was antithetical to the traditional bureaucratic chain of command of the Police Academy personnel and the Department in general. This stylistic difference and its implications resulted in various disagreements. From the beginning the training team was criticized for its casual dress and flexible hours. Police trainers among the NPT (who were detailed to the project) wore civilian clothes, not uniforms.*

*By the spring of 1972 the conflict between the police training team and the Police Academy supervisors was intense. The NPT training team was not keeping up with the initial quota set for training hours and was under pressure to proceed with training so as to justify its existence. So the Police Academy initiated an investigation of the training team's progress. That included the sending of evaluation forms on the trainers to the five NPT precincts without the trainers being informed. The Police Academy also demanded a strict account of the hours worked. At first the NPT trainers refused to comply because they resented the imposition of traditional structures. Later they agreed to comply, although they viewed stringent requirements for time and activity reports as harassment. Their morale was at an all-time low.*

*It became clear that the Police Department would not request that the training grant be refunded. A new administrator was appointed to take charge of all training programs including NPT training. He came with the* avowed purpose of "shaping up" the NPT training team, and there were several hostile confrontations. The Police Project Director was released shortly afterwards when his initial contract ran out. Then the trainers were pulled out of the precincts and given training assignments within the Academy. Some members of the team left; the team ceased to function as a team at that point.

***Program evaluation.*** In evaluating the NPT training program as innovative change, we must first use the goal of the program as a criterion. The goal was to set up a training program in each NPT precinct that, first, could continue after the trainer had moved on and, second, could meet the needs of the specific teams involved. Obviously, this also meant as these teams, their neighborhoods, and their problems changed the programs had to be flexible so as to change with them. Measured against this criterion, the NPT training cannot be considered a success. Only a few precincts have any program at all at this point; the one precinct with both an ongoing program and training had it underway before the NPT trainers arrived on the scene.

It is clear to us from this review of the NYPD experiment that innovation which originates at the top, as was the case with the NPT training program, tends to lose its innovative character as it filters down to the lowest levels of the organization. Two NPT police officers in the precincts that favored the program said that they did not feel that their ways of carrying out their duties had been much affected by the NPT program. When pressed, one admitted that in certain ways his performance had been facilitated. He appreciates the flexible duty hours and the fact that he can now wait to see a case through to the end rather than have to rush on to the next call. He said that not much has changed in work time away from the station house, but that the atmosphere at headquarters is more open to the public. For others, the training may even have had a negative effect to the extent that it increased some patrolmen's already cynical attitude toward training programs in particular and change in general.

Prospects are not totally bleak, however. There have been a number of innovations as a result of the training program, although they are not necessarily those that were delineated in the goals of the specific training pro-

*gram. First, the introduction of civilians in the institutional police depart-*
*ment was a radical change from previous policy; and some of them are still*
*working there. Second, some of the training techniques developed by the*
*NPT trainers have been incorporated into the curriculum at the Police Acad-*
*emy and into the functional management training. This might be considered*
*the institutionalization of some of the innovative aspects of the NPT training*
*program. Third, the even temporary toleration by the police structure of the*
*group decision-making style of the trainers can only be viewed as an inno-*
*vation when seen in the context of the traditional, military-style decision*
*making of the police. The fact that some civilian trainers are still employed*
*by the Police Department also indicates some degree of acceptance.*

## Neighborhood Police Teams Study: An Analysis

In the NPT study, management did not alter employee behavior to the extent
necessary for effective implementation of the planned change. Although the
commissioner was undoubtedly correct in assuming that traditional patrol
operations were not serving the unique needs of many neighborhoods, the
desired changes were unfortunately not communicated to the department as
a whole. As noted previously, when employees are not consulted in the planning for change, resistance is likely to be strong. This frequently happens
when top management attempts to introduce change rapidly; employees feel
that they are being forced into something that may not be to their advantage.

If the organization's membership had been involved in the change process from the beginning, the results would most likely have been more favorable. The amount of employee resistance could have been substantially
reduced by applying the methods described earlier: sharing expectations,
avoiding coercive tactics, using group decision making, and making changes
tentative. Through shared expectations, the anticipated advantages (to both
the individual officer and the community) could have been communicated,
along with possible disadvantages perceived by the officers who had to carry

out the program. Perceived problems and misunderstandings could have been dealt with openly. In spite of initial turbulence, it is better to meet resistance head-on and deal with it, rather than ignore possible signs of trouble and hope that they will disappear.

Participatory management devices (such as ad hoc committees, task forces, and group seminars) used early in the change process would most likely have reduced resistance to the NPT by allowing discussion on what the program involved and what was needed for its implementation. This is not meant to suggest that all department members would have been suddenly converted, but resistance can be reduced through discussions based on facts rather than misperceptions. As the expectation-integration model would suggest, members of the community should also have been invited to participate in making decisions that would affect policing in their neighborhoods. Had this been done, the tremendous public pressure for the program could have been anticipated. Also, department staff would then have been aware of the public's desire for such change (and the reasons for it); this could have helped lessen resistance.

Finally, because of the "unforeseen problem" of public acceptance, the program, which was to have been tentative, was implemented very rapidly before the concept was totally understood, giving it a public relations quality that was potentially destructive. It would have been wiser to introduce NPT only in the experimental districts (as originally intended), evaluate the results, and implement the program throughout the organization only if the results indicated that the program was more effective than traditional patrol. In this way, the change would have been tentative, and all departmental members would have had a chance to objectively evaluate the proposed change. In short, the NPT case study offers an excellent example of what can happen when organizational change is not properly planned and is introduced too rapidly, especially in an organization that is mechanistic in design.

There are several possible explanations why attempting change in police organizations is problematic. First, police managers may not be aware of effective methods to implement change. For example, extensive attempts to change the Dallas police department (Wycoff and Kelling 1978) probably failed because the architects of change were unaware of how to effectively implement change (Kuykendall and Roberg 1982). Second, managers may not trust employees to participate in the change process because they believe they will not understand the need for change or that the employee is not competent enough to offer useful suggestions. Third, the manager's experience may suggest that the process of soliciting employee involvement is time-consuming and will probably result in modification of the manager's agenda for change. Of course, change is time-consuming. However, encouraging participation at the outset usually saves time, especially if the alternative is potential lost productivity and lost time required to correct problems brought on by those who resist the change. In addition, the manager's vision may not be the most effective approach or plan for change. Other well-intentioned members of the organization may be able to add substantially to the process and plan for change.

## Change and Innovation

If constructive and timely change is to take place in police organizations, mid- and top-level managers must develop an *organizational climate* that fosters and encourages innovation. *Innovation* refers to the ability to develop and use new ideas and methods. Such an organizational climate would need to be relatively open, trustworthy, and forward-looking. Although managers frequently espouse this kind of climate in all types of organizations, the rhetoric may outweigh the action when it comes to lower-level employees. As Moss-Kanter explains in her influential book, *The Change Masters* (1983): "the message behind the words of the top is that those below the top should stay out of the change game unless given a specific assignment to figure out how to implement a decision top management has already made" (p. 100).

## Rules for Stifling Innovation

Moss-Kanter goes on to point out that often top management behaves as if they were following a set of "rules for stifling initiative." She proceeds to establish a set of ten rules that are frequently followed in organizations today:

1. Regard any new idea from below with suspicion—because it's new, and because it's from below.
2. Insist that people who need your approval to act first go through several other levels of management to get their signatures.
3. Ask departments (units) or individuals to challenge and criticize each other's proposals. (That saves you the job of deciding; you just pick the survivor.)
4. Express your criticisms freely, and withhold your praise. (That keeps people on their toes.)
5. Treat identification of problems as signs of failure, to discourage people from letting you know when something in their area isn't working.
6. Control everything carefully. Make sure people count anything that can be counted, frequently.
7. Make decisions to reorganize or change policies in secret, and spring them on people unexpectedly. (That also keeps people on their toes.)
8. Make sure that requests for information are fully justified, and make sure that it is not given out to managers freely. (You don't want data to fall into the wrong hands.)
9. Assign to lower-level managers, in the name of delegation and participation, responsibility for figuring out how to cut back, lay off, move people around, or otherwise implement threatening decisions you have made. And get them to do it quickly.
10. And above all, never forget that you, the higher-ups, already know everything important about this business (p. 101).

Rules such as these, according to Moss-Kanter, reflect *segmentalism* in action; that is, a culture and attitude that make it unattractive and difficult for people in the organization to develop innovative solutions to solve problems. Such a segmentalist approach is a real handicap, because most organizations have people that are potential innovators, capable of change. The problem, therefore, is that organizations may not suffer from a lack of potential innovators, so much as they do from a failure to provide the necessary power and means to allow their employees to innovate.

## Requirements for Successful Innovation

In their report on police innovation in six American cities, Skolnick and Bayley (1986, pp. 220–225) made several recommendations they believe are necessary to improve police effectiveness. The belief that innovation is necessary stems from the negative findings produced by research that has evaluated traditional policing methods over the past several decades. Results of this research, as noted by Skolnick and Bayley, indicate that (1) increasing the number of police does not necessarily reduce crime rates or raise the proportion of crimes solved; (2) random motorized patrolling does not appear to reduce crime or reduce citizen's fear of crime; (3) two-person patrol cars are not more effective than one-person cars in reducing crime or catching criminals (and tend to be less safe); (4) police on patrol rarely encounter serious crime; (5) rapid response to emergency calls has no impact on arrest rates or citizen satisfaction; (6) criminal investigations by departments do not solve crimes in the sense of finding unknown offenders, instead detectives are primarily responsible for the prosecution of known suspects (pp. 4–5).

The impact of these results is substantial; they suggest that the traditional methods of policing in America are not contributing to crime prevention or reassuring the public. From this background, Skolnick and Bayley set out to "locate innovation and to understand why and how it happens;" their "findings" are set forth below.

First, and most important to successful innovation, is effective and energetic leadership from the office of the chief. While executive leadership is vital to any enterprise, it is essential to the traditional paramilitary, mechanistic character of police organizations. Since police departments tend not to be democratically run, most members are aware of the chief's preferences, demands, and expectations. However, it is not enough to simply espouse certain ideals and values; the chief* must become an active, committed expo-

---

*When referring to the position of police chief in their discussion, Skolnick and Bayley use the gender-specific term *he*; we have taken the liberty of referencing the chief's position in non-gender terms. While it is true that essentially all police chiefs in this country are male, it seems

nent of them. To paraphrase Selznick in his book, *Leadership in Adminis-tration* (1957), the chief must build a sense of purpose into the structure of the enterprise.

The second requirement for successful innovation is that the chief must be able to motivate, even manipulate, department personnel into enlisting in the service of the values that he or she espouses. In attempting to change values and norms in police organizations, some resistance from the "old guard," who have strong ties to the status quo, is likely. Because these in-dividuals may retain much influence, police executives often attempt to keep or enlist their support. As a result, chiefs may actually affirm conflicting norms, telling different audiences what they want to hear. As a result, no-body in the department knows what the chief stands for and everyone is con-fused. Preferably, a majority of the officers can be brought along by persuad-ing them that the new values are superior. This is seldom easy, however, especially in departments that have associations and unions that are resistant to change and innovation. Nevertheless, Skolnick and Bayley maintain that an innovatively inclined chief can gain the support of the rank and file. Some of the tactics they observed included:

1. Concentrating on influencing younger members of the department, then promoting them to positions of influence.
2. Urging retirement of members of the old guard, coupled with hiring of new officers—the more the better.
3. Discerning who among older officers might be attracted to the new val-ues, some out of genuine commitment, others perhaps because they see that's the way the wind is blowing.
4. Employing the chief's office as a training ground for middle manage-ment.
5. Sending trained middle managers into the field as team leaders or pre-cinct or patrol captains and lieutenants, spreading the word.
6. If all else fails, using the power of the chief's office to sanction those fighting innovation. (As one chief commented after coping with a bit of

appropriate, especially when discussing innovation, to promote the ideal of equal access to the top executive position in policing.

rebellion against the new values, "In the absence of respect, fear will do nicely.") (pp. 222–223).

Once established, the integrity of innovation must be defended. This simply means that once a new value system (one dedicated to the development and use of new concepts and methods) has been established, it will need to be defended from the pull to return to the status quo. This is especially necessary in policing, since police departments are heavily tied to traditional ways of doing things.

Finally, innovation is unlikely to happen without public support. Innovative crime prevention programs that were instituted and implemented with community input enjoy strong, and often unexpected, support from the public. If properly introduced and explained to the community, police innovations will most likely be widely and popularly supported.

Taking into consideration these recommendations for successful police innovation, effective executive leadership is clearly essential, at least in the six cities Skolnick and Bayley studied. Top-level leadership is undoubtedly necessary before a climate of innovation can start to be developed in policing; however, unless new values and norms (and, in some instances, increased skill levels) are inculcated by middle- and lower-level managers, innovation and change will not be forthcoming. As we have noted previously, the primary reason for the failure of team policing was the reluctance of midlevel managers to adopt the new philosophy and value system required to sustain such a program. Chapter 12 discusses the importance of the manager's role in the change process and how he or she might become actively involved in implementing constructive change.

## Summary

Since police organizations operate in relatively unstable environments and need to adapt to changing circumstances to be effective, police managers should have an understanding of the processes relating to planning, change, and innovation. Planning was defined as the process of deciding in advance what is to be done as well as how it is to be done. Based on action research, a planning model containing six stages was developed. The stages include problem identification, data collection and analysis, feedback and diagnosis, taking action (implementation), evaluation and feedback, and new action (modification).

Organizational change occurs when the organization adopts new ideas or behaviors. The ultimate success of any organizational change effort depends on how well the organization can alter the behavioral patterns of its employees. In order to implement timely and constructive change, police managers need to understand why people resist change, how resistance can be reduced, and the effects of pace on change. People have a tendency to resist change in organizations because of "sunk costs," misunderstandings relating to the nature of the change, group norms, and threatened changes in the balance of power. Resistance to change may be reduced by sharing expectations, avoiding coercive tactics, using group decision making, and making changes tentative.

Determining the appropriate pace of change is critical if the change is to be properly implemented. If the pace is too gradual, employees may feel that nothing is happening and return to the more familiar ways of the past; on the other hand, if the pace is too rapid, members may feel threatened and strongly resist the change. Consequently, change should be introduced quickly enough to show that something is happening, but slowly enough to prevent rejection. Since most police organizations tend to be mechanistic in design, a gradual or "medium" pace would be the most beneficial; although for those agencies or units that are more organic in nature, a rapid pace is likely to be more beneficial.

If organizational change is to be successful, police managers must attempt to establish a climate for innovation throughout the organization. Innovation refers to the ability to develop and use new ideas and methods. Rules for stifling innovation and requirements for successful innovation were discussed. Probably the most important requirement for promoting innovation in a police organization is effective and energetic leadership from the top in espousing new ideas and values and in motivating organizational members to adopt them as well.

# Discussion Questions

1. Describe the process of planning and why it should be viewed from a systems perspective.
2. What is action research and how does it relate to the process of planning?
3. Describe the six stages of the planning model.
4. Discuss at least three reasons for employees' resisting organizational change.
5. Discuss at least three methods that may be useful in reducing resistance to organizational change.
6. Why is the pace of change so critical to the success of organizational change efforts?
7. What do you think were the primary reasons for the resistance encountered in the NPT case study, and do you think such resistance was justified?
8. Discuss some of the possible explanations why attempting change in police organizations might be problematic.
9. Define innovation; discuss several reasons or "rules for stifling" innovation that are frequently followed by top management.
10. Discuss several factors that appear necessary if innovation in policing is to occur.

# References

Bard, M. and Shellow, R., "Neighborhood Police Teams," in *Issues in Law Enforcement—Essays and Case Studies*, eds. R. Shellow and M. Bard (Reston, Va.: Reston Publishing, 1976).

Galvin, R. T. and LeGrande, J. L., "Department Goals and Planning," in *Municipal Police Administration*, eds. G. D. Eastman and E. M. Eastman (Washington, D.C.: International City Management Association, 1971), pp. 209–216.

Kast, F. A. and Rosenzweig, J. E., *Organization and Management: A Systems and Contingency Approach* (New York: McGraw-Hill, 1985).

Kerr, S. and Kerr, E. B., "Why Your Employees Resist Perfectly 'Rational' Changes," *Hospital Financial Management* 26(1972): 4–6.

Kuykendall, J. and Roberg, R. R., "Mapping Police Organizational Change: From a Mechanistic Toward an Organic Model," *Criminology* 20(1982): 241–256.

Kuykendall, J. and Unsinger, P. C., *Community Police Administration* (Chicago: Nelson-Hall, 1979).

Lewin, K., "Group Decision and Social Change," in *Readings in Social Management*, eds. T. M. Newcomb and L. Hartle (New York: Holt, Rinehart & Winston, 1958), pp. 197–211.

Moss-Kanter, R. A., *The Change Masters: Innovations for Productivity in the American Corporation* (New York: Simon & Schuster, 1983).

Pierce, J. L. and Delbecq, A. L., "Organization Structure, Individual Attitudes and Innovation," *Academy of Management Review* 2(1977): 27–37.

Roberg, R. R. and Kirchhoff, J. J., "Applying Strategic Management Methods to Law Enforcement: Two Case Studies," *American Journal of Police* 4(1985): 133–153.

Selznick, P., *Leadership in Administration: A Sociological Enterprise* (New York: Harper & Row, 1957).

Skolnick, J. H. and Bayley, D. H., *The New Blue Line: Police Innovation in Six American Cities* (New York: Free Press, 1986).

Strauss, G. and Sayles, L. R., *Personnel: The Human Problems of Management*, 4th ed. (Englewood Cliffs, N.J.: Prentice-Hall, 1980).

Wycoff, M. A. and Kelling, G. L., *The Dallas Experience: Organizational Reform* (Washington, D.C.: Police Foundation, 1978).

# CHAPTER 12

# Enhancing Organizational Performance

The importance of timely change in responding to environmental demands placed on the police was discussed in the last chapter. The purpose of this chapter is to explore how police managers can help facilitate constructive and enduring change within their organizations in order to enhance performance. To this end, the role of organization development and specific strategies or methodologies used for introducing change will be the focus of our discussion. The role played by change agents, a process of "mapping" police organizational change, a set of cooperative goals for organic policing, and the manager's perspective in organization development are considered integral aspects of the change process.

## Organization Development

Some specific strategies or methods that have been used to develop and change organizations in nonthreatening ways will now be considered. *Organization development* (OD) is a process by which intervention strategies, based on behavioral science research, are utilized to enhance organizational effectiveness through planned change. It consists of an *organization-wide* effort to *enhance performance* by improving the quality of work environments and by positively affecting employee beliefs and attitudes and levels of motivation. This process differs from other planned change efforts, such as purchasing new equipment or changing uniform design, by focusing on human resources (Huse and Cummings 1985, p. 1).

Organization development, then, is a program for introducing planned, systematic change in an organization. Typically, organization members must interact and collaborate with one another in introducing change; this process is directed by a change agent. The change agent uses behavioral science techniques, including questionnaires, interviews, group discussions, and experimentation, to diagnose problem areas and to design appropriate change responses. Several characteristics guide change agents in their choice of intervention strategies:

1. The basic building blocks of an organization are groups (teams). Therefore, the basic units of change are groups, not individuals.
2. An always relevant change goal is the reduction of inappropriate competition between parts of an organization and the development of a more collaborative condition.
3. Decision making in a healthy organization is located where the information sources are, rather than in a particular role or level of hierarchy.
4. One goal of a healthy organization is to develop generally open communication, mutual trust, and confidence between and across levels.
5. "People support what they help create." People affected by a change must be allowed active participation and a sense of ownership in the planning and conduct of the change (Beckhard 1969, pp. 26–27).

Next we will discuss the role of the change agent in the organization development process.


## The Role of Change Agents

There are three primary forms of change agents in organization development. The first and generally most common is the *external* change agent brought in by the organization to diagnose problem areas and make recommendations for change. Second, the organization may provide an *internal* change agent, who has a good working knowledge of the organization and is aware of its problems. Third, the *combination* external-internal change agent involves a team approach that attempts to utilize knowledge and resources that exist inside the organization and outside as well.

Each form of change agent has particular advantages and disadvantages. The external agent is generally a professional OD consultant, who has appropriate academic credentials and is well grounded in the theory and practice of organizational change and behavioral interventions. These individuals usually have some experience in developing public sector agencies, including the police. External agents are frequently viewed as outsiders who do not understand the "real" workings of police organizations, particularly if they have not had "police experience" and therefore may not be trusted. Consequently, it is crucial that external agents establish a high degree of rapport with both management and rank-and-file employees if they are to have an impact. Additionally, because external agents tend not to have extensive knowledge about internal relationships and behavior, they can approach the organization with an "open mind" regarding change strategies and directions they deem appropriate.

Internal agents, on the other hand, are usually not trained as OD specialists, but they have a good working knowledge of the department. Individuals used in this capacity would normally include mid- to upper-level managers (e.g., lieutenants through assistant chiefs), who have wide-ranging experiences in the organization. Their knowledge can contribute substantially to the change process if used in an objective fashion. Insiders, however, are often viewed as being more closely associated with certain groups or individuals who approach the change process with preconceived notions and/or hidden agendas about what should be done. There may be suspicion that the agent's recommendations further his or her personal gain or are "what the chief wants," rather than what is best for the organization. Consequently, internal change agents may actually have a more difficult time establishing rapport within the organization than external agents. Therefore, if management decides to use insiders, the people who are chosen must be widely respected throughout the organization for their integrity, knowledge, and objectivity.

The combination external-internal change agents, although difficult to coordinate, offer advantages over both of the other forms. The objectivity and behavioral knowledge of the professional OD consultant is combined with the insider's insights into how the organization is actually run, including both formal and informal relationships and group behavior. This blending of knowledge can substantially contribute to successful change by helping specify appropriate change strategies and identifying where in the organization the process should begin and at what pace it should proceed. Finally, using this team approach may develop even greater rapport throughout the organization, thus reducing resistance to recommended changes. Of course, in such an arrangement, both cooperation and "turf" problems can develop, actually decreasing the potential for implementing change. Careful attention must be paid to this potential problem in police organizations, since there is often a built-in suspicion between civilian (outsider) and sworn (insider) personnel. However, if management carefully selects external and internal change agents who complement each other, this approach provides a high probability of success.

Selection of an appropriate change agent is of considerable importance to successfully implementing organizational change. Since the agent is responsible for diagnosing the organization's problems (i.e., selecting, collecting, and interpreting data), if the diagnosis is faulty, the OD intervention will probably have little chance of ultimately being successful. Based on this diagnosis, the change agent must select the most appropriate intervention strategy for implementing organizational change.

## Organization Development Intervention Strategies

*Organization development interventions* are particular types of strategies that change agents and managers use to help improve levels of organizational effectiveness. They can focus either on structural changes, which emphasize organizational outcomes, or on behavioral changes, which emphasize individual outcomes. Changes that focus on the organization's structural characteristics are formal and readily observable, such as span of control, hierarchical levels, and job descriptions. On the other hand, changes dealing with behavior (both individual and group) are more informal and include attitudes, values, and belief systems. Because behavioral changes require more emotional involvement than structural changes, managers need to deal with these issues in a more in-depth, intense manner.

### Intervention Depth

In general, *intervention depth* can be defined as the extent of an individual's emotional involvement in the change process (Harrison 1970). While emotional involvement is present at any level of intervention, the concept of depth is concerned with the degree to which the intervention is related to one's involvement. As Harrison explains:

> Strategies which touch the more deep, personal, private, and central aspects of the individual or his relationships with others fall toward the deeper end of this continuum. Strategies which deal with more external aspects of the individual and which focus upon the more formal and public aspects of role behavior tend to fall toward the surface of the depth dimension (p. 183).

In other words, strategies that deal with the formal aspects of the organization, including structural characteristics and job descriptions, are relatively open and easily manipulable. However, an organization's informal aspects, including individual beliefs and attitudes and interpersonal and group relationships, are relatively hidden and take considerable emotional involvement if they are to be changed. Accordingly, strategies attempting to change individual behavior must be at a deeper level of emotional involvement if they are to have lasting impact than strategies dealing with structural considerations.

## Typology of Organization Development Interventions

The following discussion of OD strategies will be based on the level of intervention depth required to bring about successful change. The strategies will be grouped according to two *change targets*: (1) *structural*, which emphasizes tasks, activities, and role relationships and is concerned with the formal organization and data that are readily available; and (2) *behavioral*, which emphasizes emotional and psychological reactions, is related to the informal organization and the individual, and has private or hidden data.

Because certain OD strategies require deeper levels of emotional involvement if they are to be successful, we have classified several relevant strategies into four levels of "depth," from relatively impersonal (i.e., structural) to highly personal (i.e., behavioral). The OD strategies and their degree of intervention depth are depicted in figure 12-1.* It is important to keep

---

*The four levels of intervention depth have been adapted from Harrison (1970), who discussed five levels of depth.

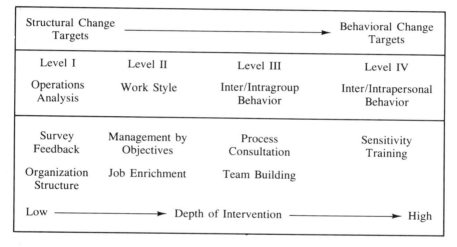

**Figure 12-1** Organization Development Strategies and Intervention Depth

in mind, however, that all of these levels overlap to some degree and should not be viewed as mutually exclusive. The OD strategies presented, while by no means an all-inclusive list, provide a sample of available methods that are likely to be of value in implementing change in a police organization.

## Level I: Operations Analysis

The first level is concerned with the roles and functions to be performed within the organization, generally with little regard for individual characteristics (e.g., beliefs and attitudes) or for the persons occupying the roles. The change strategy focuses on determining and specifying resources, tasks, authority and power, and other structural characteristics important to the formal operations of the organization. Examples of intervention strategies at this level include survey feedback and structural design changes.

**Survey feedback.** This strategy uses questionnaires to collect information from the employees regarding their feelings about the organization. Once collected, the data are fed back to managers and employees so that they can evaluate and define problems and develop plans of action; this is also known as action research. Feeding the information back to employees is generally accomplished through groups, starting with top management and systematically moving down through the lower organizational levels.

**Organization structure.** In this strategy, the structural characteristics of the formal organization are changed through the manipulation of role relationships and the redistribution of tasks and resources, or the power attached to various roles. This would include changing reporting and decision-making relationships between and among individuals and units, as well as increasing or decreasing the span of control and the number of hierarchical levels in the organization. Oftentimes, the need for such changes is determined through survey feedback techniques.

Examples of such structural changes were provided by the NTP case study (see chapter 11), where role relationships were substantially altered. For instance, certain sergeants were designated "team commanders" with responsibilities similar to those of the chief of a small town department. Additionally, the honorific position of lieutenant was upgraded to that of an "operations lieutenant," with added responsibility for shift supervision. Although such changes are structural in nature, it is obvious, based on the results of the NTP study, that deeper levels of intervention may be necessary if these changes are to be accepted and implemented. When apparently structural changes require task or responsibility adjustments on the part of employees, the possibility of behavioral consequences is likely. In other words, managers must keep in mind that even surface intervention levels may require additional deeper methods of intervention if they are to be successful.

## Level II: Work Style

The second level is concerned with the selection, training, counseling, and evaluation of individuals in accord with job design and other structural characteristics of the work they perform. While this strategy is deeper than the preceding one, the focus is on observable performance rather than on the personal characteristics of the individual. Attempts to facilitate change at this level can include both external rewards (e.g., transfers and promotions) and internal rewards (e.g., greater satisfaction and feelings of accomplishment). Two frequently used strategies at this level are management by objectives (MBO) and job enrichment.

**Management by objectives.**   This is an attempt to help resolve conflicts and increase understanding of organizational and individual goals by increasing communications between the two parties. To this end, MBO requires mutual planning by managers and employees in establishing goals and objectives, in measuring job performance in terms of goals and objectives, and in deciding whether performance measures have been met. Additionally, periodic reviews of progress and accomplishments and mutual problem solving occur in the course of work performance. The MBO process frequently goes beyond the manager–employee relationship and deals with work teams in an effort to solve problems.

The potential advantages of evaluating employees in terms of mutually set measures include greater ego involvement, increased motivation, and increased planning behavior, all of which can affect performance. At least three aspects of MBO affect its success: (1) goals and goal setting, (2) participation and involvement of subordinates, and (3) feedback and performance evaluation. Each of these aspects is described by Tosi and Carroll as follows:

> **Goals and goal setting.**   A number of studies have clearly demonstrated that when an individual or group has a specific goal, there is higher performance than when the goals are general, or have not been set. Generally, high performance can be associated with higher individual or group goals. A number of studies also suggest that performance improvement occurs when an individual is successful in achieving past goals. When there is previous goal success, the individual is more likely to set higher goals in future periods, and he is more likely to attain them.

> **Participation.**   There have been a number of diverse findings about the relationship of participation in decision making and productivity. These apparently

contradictory findings have been resolved by concluding that if the subordinate perceives the participation to be legitimate, it will have positive effects on productivity. In addition, participation does seem to have an effect on the degree of acceptance of decisions reached mutually. There is also evidence that involvement and participation are positively correlated with the level of job satisfaction.

**Feedback.** Both laboratory and field research have demonstrated that relatively clear, unambiguous feedback increases problem solving capacities of groups and improves the performance of individuals. Positive attitudes, increased confidence in decisions, and greater certainties of superior's expectations were found to be related to communications which clarified roles and role expectancies with more and better information . . . Positive actions are more likely to be taken by subordinates when feedback is viewed as supportive and is objectively based (1970, p. 45).

A recent study of 141 police agencies that reported using some form of MBO over the past three years (Hatry and Greiner 1986) found that such processes can help departments motivate managers to improve efficiency and service outcomes. However, the researchers discovered several major problem areas that frequently crop up during implementation of MBO programs, including vagueness in defining objectives, excluding lower-level personnel from the process, not regularly comparing performance with goals, not regularly providing performance feedback, and not providing sufficient training opportunities. These problem areas are major components of successful MBO interventions; therefore, if they are not implemented properly, the resulting changes are likely to be dysfunctional in nature.

**Job enrichment.** Enriching work through job redesign is based on the premise that work satisfaction and efficiency can be increased if jobs include high levels of variety, autonomy, and feedback. Steps that can be taken to enrich jobs (based on the job characteristics model) were discussed in chapter 5. Further, employees who have relatively high growth-need strength are more likely to benefit from job redesign. Two of the more recent strategies used to enrich police jobs (although not originally intended for this purpose) are community and problem-oriented policing.

## Level III: Inter/Intragroup Behavior

The third level of intervention is concerned with the processes through which performance is achieved within and among work groups. This level involves factors such as how the individual perceives his or her role, what is or is not valued, and how the individual acts toward others (e.g., delegating authority or reserving decisions, communicating or withholding information, and collaborating or competing with others on work-related issues). Strategies are oriented toward attempts to structure work behavior and working relationships among individuals and groups. Group processes are diagnosed and change strategies often involve bargaining and negotiating between group members and among groups. Changes in group norms, communications, behaviors, and methods of resolving present and future conflicts often result. Two of the more common OD strategies at this level include process consultation and team building.

**Process consultation.** This strategy focuses on the "human processes" that occur in an organization, including individual, interpersonal, and intergroup levels (Schein 1969). In process consultation (PC), the major assumption is that the group is the building block of the organization and little can be changed without group participation and effort. Consequently, intervention efforts are directed at helping group members diagnose functioning problems (including dysfunctional conflict and competition and lack of cooperation and poor communication) and develop and implement solutions to these problems.

Process consultation typically uses an outside change agent as a group facilitator to help group members learn the necessary skills to diagnose problem areas. One of the most influential writers in this area, Edgar Schein, defines PC as "a set of activities on the part of the consultant which help the client to perceive, understand, and act upon process events which occur in the client's environment" (p. 9). As such, the change agent, in this case referred to as a process consultant, does not attempt to provide his or her own solutions to group problems. Instead, the consultant spends time observing groups in action and then "guides" them in diagnosing and learning how to alleviate the problems they are experiencing. The consultant withdraws when group members have maintained the capacity to diagnose and deal with similar problems that may develop in the future.

Process consultation would likely have been useful in lessening the chaos and improving the chances for successful change in the NTP project. By requiring the various work groups that were of particular importance to the change process, including patrol and investigation, lower- and mid-level managers (sergeants and lieutenants), and training (civilian and sworn), to work together, it is likely that communication and cooperation would have increased while dysfunctional competition would have been reduced. By allowing the work groups themselves to identify problems and work through solutions, commitment to the program is also likely to have increased. Of course, by utilizing PC, the change process would have taken a substantially longer time. As we have noted previously, however, time is usually required if lasting changes are to be implemented, especially in relatively mechanistic agencies.

**Team building.** This strategy includes utilizing intervention methods that will develop effective teamwork both within and among work groups. The purpose of team building is to improve work performance by enhancing interpersonal and problem-solving skills of group members. This process normally begins with diagnostic meetings that enable each group member to share his or her perceptions with other members. The purpose is to obtain the views of all members and to make their views known; such diagnosis implies the value of openly confronting certain issues and problems that may only have been discussed privately in the past. Once problems are identified, the group attempts to reach a consensus on their priorities and develop an action plan to solve the problems. It is important that each group member takes part in the action plan. In this way, each member has contributed to the decision and is involved in carrying out those decisions; increased levels of motivation and commitment are likely to result from such a high degree of participation.

Team building can also help facilitate other OD interventions, including organization structure, MBO, and job enrichment. These change programs are usually implemented through various committees and work groups. The use of team building can help such groups plan high-quality change programs and ensure that the programs are accepted and implemented by organization members (Huse and Cummings 1985, p. 113). This strategy is also closely associated with process consultation. In fact, most team-building methods incorporate PC by attempting to help the group diagnose and understand its own process. However, it goes beyond this process focus and may include examination of the group's task or problem, role and power influences, and relations between people and their work roles (p. 114). Additionally, the change agent often acts as a resource person and lends his or her expertise to help the group define and solve its problems.

Team-building techniques could also have been useful in preventing the chaos that occurred in attempting to implement the NTP program. Officers who understood the culture best could have helped clarify role relationships, not only within the patrol and investigative units, but also between sergeants and lieutenants, thus reducing dysfunctional competition and power influences. Much wider participation by group members, and possibly the public, in problem identification and plans for action could have led to a greater understanding, commitment, and acceptance of the program. Furthermore, the change agent could have identified additional OD strategies, including structural changes (e.g., toward more organic characteristics) and job redesign (e.g., formally recognizing and developing work enrichment activities), that could have been useful in implementing timely change.

## Level IV: Inter/Intrapersonal Behavior

The final and deepest level of intervention focuses on the feelings, attitudes, values, and perceptions that organization members have about one another. Personal feelings, including warmth and coldness, acceptance and rejection, love and hate, and trust and suspicion, are directly confronted and dealt with in this strategy. Interventions are directed toward helping members feel more comfortable in being themselves with one another. The degree of mutual caring and concern is expected to increase.

**Sensitivity training.** The basic strategy at this level is concerned with individual and individual–group problems and attempts to increase the "sensitivity" of self and others in the workplace. Sensitivity training or T-groups (*T* for training) generally consist of ten to fifteen members who meet with a professional trainer, who facilitates group dialogue, at a site away from the job. Participants may include organizational "cousins" (people from different work groups in the same organization), members from the same organizational "family" (people from the same work group), or "strangers" (people from outside the organization). Police departments, for example, have used strangers in T-groups designed to improve police–community relations, especially with respect to minorities. According to Campbell and Dunnette (1968), the basic objectives of sensitivity training include:

1. To increase self-insight concerning one's behavior in a social context— to learn how others see and interpret one's own behavior and to gain insight into why one acts the way he does in different interpersonal situations.
2. To increase sensitivity to the behavior of others . . . and the development of the ability to infer accurately the emotional bases for interpersonal communications.
3. To increase awareness of the types of processes that facilitate or inhibit group functioning. For example, why do some members participate actively while others do not? Why do different groups, who may actually share the same goals, sometimes create seemingly insoluble conflict situations?
4. To increase diagnostic and action oriented skills in social, interpersonal, and intergroup situations.
5. To teach a person to learn how to learn—continually to analyze his own interpersonal behavior in order to reach and engage in more effective interpersonal interactions with others.

These objectives are applicable to many T-groups, however, a particular training program may emphasize certain objectives over others. For instance, one trainer may emphasize understanding group process as applied to organization development, another may focus on group process as a way of developing individual insight and functioning, and a third trainer may emphasize improving interpersonal and intrapersonal learning (Huse and Cummings 1985, p. 96).

Due to the highly personal nature of T-groups, their use and level of effectiveness is strongly debated in the OD field. Research on these programs is difficult to conduct and the findings are mixed. After reviewing much of the research in this area, Huse and Cummings (p. 98) suggest there are three conditions under which T-groups can improve both individual and group functioning: (1) the T-group must be structured in order that learning can be transferred back to the organization; (2) the closer the T-group is tied in with an ongoing OD program, the greater its effectiveness appears to be; and (3) when applied to organization behavior, T-groups are more effective in organizations supporting information sharing, openness, and conflict resolution. Since these characteristics are generally not found in police organizations, this approach should be used with an appropriate degree of caution and employed only by exceptionally qualified experts.

In the typology of OD interventions presented, the deeper the level of intervention (from level I through level IV), the more significant the impact, either positive or negative, on organization members. For this reason, Harrison (1970, p. 187) suggests two criteria that should be considered in choosing an appropriate intervention strategy: (1) It should intervene at a level no deeper than that required to produce lasting solutions to the problems at hand, and (2) it should intervene at a level no deeper than that at which the energy and resources of the client can be committed to problem solving and to change. With these important considerations in mind, we next discuss how the methods presented in the OD typology can be used to bring about constructive change in police organizations.

## Mapping Police Organization Change

Based on the core characteristics of mechanistic and organic systems of policing, described in chapter 4, Kuykendall and Roberg (1982) have developed a process for "mapping" change in police organizations. This change process is based on the level of intervention depth required to implement enduring change in police organizations, depending on the particular department's characteristics. In addition, the process is based on the proposition that many police organizations can benefit by moving toward a more organic approach to police organization and management. Such an approach, which we will term *organic policing*, has relatively flexible organizational characteristics, especially with respect to organization structure, job design, and leadership styles. Organic policing, by its very nature, allows departments greater latitude in responding to changing internal and external environmental conditions.

In order to properly describe the mapping process, a brief review of the five characteristics representing extremes on a continuum of both mechanistic and organic organizations is necessary (see table 4-2 for a synopsis, p. 131). *Mechanistic systems*, in general, have the following characteristics: (1) organization positions and tasks are *specialized*; (2) interactions between members tend to be *hierarchical* in nature; (3) knowledge and influence are derived from *authority*; (4) the organization is *rule-oriented* and means (or the proper ways to do a job) are emphasized; and (5) accountability and rewards are *position-oriented* and tied to following instructions. Common characteristics of *organic systems* include: (1) there is a *generalist* approach to jobs and tasks; (2) interactions between members tend to be *collegial* in nature; (3) status and influence are derived from ability and reputation, referred to as *power*; (4) the organization is *situation-oriented* and ends (or getting the job done) are emphasized; (5) accountability and rewards are *goal-oriented* and tied to excellence of performance.

The purpose of mapping organizational change is to aid police organizations in moving along the continuum toward the organic characteristics. This mapping process, depicted in table 12-1, delineates appropriate intervention depth and change strategies for a targeted change. The basis for selecting the most appropriate intervention level is determined by examining whether the organizational characteristics targeted for change are essentially *structural* (formal and readily observable) or *behavioral* (informal and relatively hidden) in nature.

**Table 12-1**   Mapping Police Organization Change from Mechanistic Toward
Organic Policing

| Mechanistic Organization Characteristics | Organic Organization Characteristics | Intervention Depth | Intervention Strategy |
|---|---|---|---|
| Specialization (Structural) | Generalization (Structural) | Operations Analysis Work Style | Survey Feedback/ Organization Structure Management by Objectives/Job Enrichment |
| Hierarchical (Structural) | Collegial (Behavioral) | Inter/Intragroup Behavior Inter/Intraper- sonal Behavior | Process Consultation/ Team Building Sensitivity Training |
| Authority (Structural) | Power (Behavioral) | Inter/Intragroup Behavior Inter/Intraper- sonal Behavior | Process Consultation/ Team Building Sensitivity Training |
| Rule-Oriented (Behavioral) | Situation-Oriented (Behavioral) | Inter/Intragroup Behavior Inter/Intraper- sonal Behavior | Process Consultation/ Team Building Sensitivity Training |
| Position-Oriented (Structural) | Goal-Oriented (Structural) | Operations Analysis Work Style | Survey Feedback/ Organization Structure Management by Objectives/Job Enrichment |

*Source:* Adapted from Kuykendall, J. and Roberg, R. R., "Mapping Police Organizational
Change: From a Mechanistic Toward an Organic Model." *Criminology* 20(1982): 249.

According to table 12-1, when both organizational characteristics are structural, the intervention should be at one of the first two levels, either operations analysis or work style. When one or both of the characteristics are behavioral, a deeper level of intervention directed at inter/intragroup or inter/intrapersonal behavior will most likely be required. As indicated, all but one of the mechanistic characteristics are structural, whereas two of the organic characteristics are structural and three are behavioral.

Many characteristics of the mechanistic and organic systems are interactive. In other words, a change in one characteristic (e.g., movement along the specialization–generalization continuum) may result in the need to change another characteristic (e.g., movement along the hierarchical–collegial continuum), which would require a deeper level of intervention. An organization attempting a job redesign toward team policing would be an example of this interactive effect. Since an important aspect of this form of job enrichment is to combine investigative and patrol functions, patrol officers and detectives need to work more closely together. Consequently, although a change is primarily structural in nature (i.e., level I or II), team building (level III) may also be necessary to bring about constructive change.

Taking into account Harrison's criteria for choosing the most appropriate intervention depth, the map hypothesizes the lowest intervention levels believed necessary to introduce lasting change, from mechanistic toward organic policing. In attempting to move toward an organic approach, change agents and managers must take departmental differences into account. For example, police departments that operate in relatively turbulent environments will need to become more organic in nature than those departments whose environments are relatively stable. In addition, some units within departments may need to become more organic than others, especially those in which the majority of the members are highly educated and have higher-order need strengths and high skill and ability levels. All this suggests that each department must determine where it falls on the mechanistic–organic continuum and, depending on current environmental conditions, it must determine how far it needs to move (assuming some movement is necessary) toward the organic end to maximize efficiency and effectiveness.

The mapping process allows for individual differences in police organizations. Once it is determined that movement toward organic policing would be beneficial, departments can begin the change process at different levels, based on their particular characteristics and needs.

## Improving the Quality of Work Life

In the late 1960s, the concept of *quality of work life* (QWL) was introduced in the United States and focused on the prevailing poor quality of life in the workplace (Davis 1977). A current definition of QWL includes two distinct elements: (1) a concern for the well-being of workers as well as for organizational effectiveness, and (2) the promotion of employee participation in important work-related problems and decisions (Huse and Cummings 1985, p. 202). Therefore, the quality of work life (i.e., the work environment) pertains not only to the well-being, satisfaction, and participation of the worker, but also to the overall effectiveness of the organization as well.

A set of "cooperative" goals has been prescribed that should help police managers improve the quality of work life in their organizations (Roberg, 1981). Each of these goals has been designed to increase the integration of individual (worker) and organizational (manager) expectations and needs. In light of the Reuss-Ianni (1983) findings that indicated the presence of both a manager's and worker's or street cop's culture that would mitigate against individual–organization integration, it is especially important to attempt to build cooperative work arrangements. We believe that a certain degree of cooperation is desirable and necessary, if the quality of police work environments is to be noticeably improved.

Figure 12-2 presents the hypothesized and sequential relationships among the "cooperative" goals. If these five goals are to be achieved, approximately equal contributions must be made by the individual and the organization. However, because organizations are "organized," the initial impetus toward establishing an atmosphere of cooperation will most likely need to originate from the organization itself. Of course, in attempting to meet these goals, the OD intervention strategies described throughout the

**Figure 12-2** Cooperative Goals for Improving the Quality of Work Life

chapter should prove useful. Each goal is considered to be a valuable end in itself; however, before the ultimate goal of revitalization can occur, each of the preceding goals must reach high degrees of attainment. Furthermore, each goal develops and depends on the others; if the first goal of sharing expectations is not realized, the others will most likely not be achieved to the degree necessary to have a substantial impact on improving the work environment.

**Initial Sharing of Expectations**

This all-important first goal is related to the expectation-integration model developed in the first chapter. If the individual and the organization are to truly complement one another in achieving mutually desirable and beneficial ends, they must initially share their expectations about one another. The individual asks: Why is the organization interested in me? What does the organization perceive my role to be once I am inside the organization? What types of objectives and goals does the organization expect me to pursue? What does the organization expect from me in the future? Conversely, the organization asks: Why is the individual interested in this organization? What does the individual perceive his or her role to be once inside the organization? What types of objectives and goals does the individual expect to pursue? What does the individual expect from this organization in the future? These questions must be dealt with by both parties if a satisfactory relationship is to develop.

This expectation-sharing process should begin during the initial employment interview and continue through recruit training and beyond. This makes it possible for both parties to accurately assess one another and determine if each feels comfortable enough with the other to establish an ongoing association.

Expectations should be mutually shared, particularly about the police role and appropriate police behavior, so that each party knows what to expect from the other. Prior to employment, individual and organization expectations will seldom be exactly the same. In most situations there will be differences, some of them substantial. However, if these differences are known, each party can work constructively toward "bridging the gap" and establishing a high-quality work environment. On the other hand, if such differences are not shared, each party may work against the other in an attempt to satisfy selfish ends. Both the individual and the organization become discontent with each other, which produces dysfunctional consequences and a low-quality work environment.

The importance of this first step toward improving the quality of the work environment cannot be overstated. By rigorously promoting expectation-integration, both the individual and the organization start off in step and clear the path for fulfilling each of the remaining goals.

## Developing Humane Relationships

This goal follows naturally from the first and is a vital ingredient to the definition of management provided in chapter 1. Because of the preoccupation with hierarchical status and power in many police organizations (i.e., "don't ask questions, simply follow orders"), humane and trusting relationships frequently are not established between the organization and the individual. Humane relationships are possible, however, if the parties are willing to share their expectations from the beginning of their association. In this way, mutual problems can be communicated and the level of humane dealings can be enhanced. Although it is difficult to specify exactly what this level should be, it will involve a climate of trust; neither party will take advantage of the other.

This second goal transcends individual–organization interactions, for humane relationships should be built throughout the organization. In other words, individual reactions to the ideas of other organization members and groups should be compassionate and charitable. The more persons, particularly managers, who have this basic orientation, the more likely that discretionary judgments will reflect concern for others. This does not mean, however, that inappropriate or ineffective performance should not be confronted, only that it should be responded to in a humane fashion.

Establishing humane relationships throughout the organization is an extremely difficult task. As discussed previously, most OD strategies attempt to develop an environment of mutual trust and confidence between and across organizational levels. However, such efforts may take several years or longer to accomplish. The problem stems from the nature of complex organizations; the number of differentiated functions works against the development of high levels of humane and trusting relationships among all organization members and units. Because not everyone is equally concerned with the operation of certain units (i.e., those inside are more concerned than those outside), it is difficult to establish humane relationships over wide areas. Also, only a few instances of inhumane behavior (such as deception, animosity, or back stabbing) can reduce carefully built-up positive relations to negative ones. Nevertheless, if the remaining cooperative goals are to be achieved, at least a moderate level of humaneness must be developed throughout the organization.

## Developing Open Communication

The achievement of a moderate level of humane relationships should also help create open levels of communication throughout the organization. This basically means that individual–organization and individual–individual communications should be straightforward and above board; facts are not distorted for personal and selfish purposes. People can "say what they mean" accurately and forthrightly, without fear and damaging or vengeful reprisals.

An organization can be judged to have a high degree of openness when neither party to a communication is afraid to send or receive information that may be negative, provided that it is sincere. In turn, such information is internalized constructively and used for purposes of improvement. This does not imply that positive information is not communicated; it is, but the main problem in cultivating openness usually concerns the communication of negative but accurate information. Consequently, open communication means that critical information can be dealt with maturely. If individuals or groups are considered deficient in certain areas of work, they can be approached openly about the subject, and methods of improving performance can be discussed. Conversely, if the organization is perceived to have certain policies that are too rigid and thus needlessly confine the individual or group, the policies can be openly discussed and suggestions offered for their revision.

If open communication is to be developed throughout the organization, some movement toward organic policing is most likely necessary. The current preoccupation with hierarchical status and power severely inhibits open communication, which may not be possible in those agencies that adhere to a rigid, paramilitary design and all the sanctions that accompany it. In such agencies, for example, the differentiation between individuals in high-status positions and those in low-status positions (particularly patrol officers) is a monumental roadblock to open communication. Under such conditions, simple dialogue is often difficult and open communication is usually not possible. It is clear, therefore, that much less emphasis should be placed on hierarchical status and power if this goal is to be realized.

Channels of communication must not only be opened in the formal sense, but informally as well; the informal organization plays a crucial role in the achievement of open communication. Consequently, the honest opinions of informal leaders should be actively solicited in an attempt to avert potential problems and conflicts. For example, because police associations and unions tend to play an important role in the lives of many department members, frank discussions should take place between management and association leaders, in an effort to prevent conflicts that could prove harmful to both members and nonmembers. The stifling of open communication may lead to severe conflict and even hostility in the long run, thus producing a climate of "working against" rather than "working for" one another. Such an attitude can lower employee morale and motivation, which leads to decreased levels of initiative and performance.

The inability to bring conflict "out in the open" where it can be confronted is one of the major problems facing police managers. Conflicts are an inevitable part of organizational life and they should be recognized and dealt with at an early stage, so that they do not reach crisis levels and undermine individual and organizational performance. If conflicts are openly confronted early enough, the prospects for preventing harmful consequences are substantially improved.

The goal of open communication is similar in many respects to the second goal of establishing humane relationships, for it is not realistic to believe that individuals and units throughout the organization can be equally affected. Openness also can be destroyed by only a few instances in which individuals or groups are treated unfairly or punished after communicating in a forthright and honest manner. The organization can help ensure open communication by giving positive rewards for this desired behavior. Once organization members realize that management is serious about open communication, the attainment of this goal is possible.

### Developing Participative Decision Making

The fourth goal capitalizes on the strengths of individual members through participation in decisions affecting their work environments. The extent to which participation in decision making can be developed stems directly from each of the preceding goals, especially from developing open communication, and failure to sufficiently achieve them will greatly inhibit the potential benefits of this approach. Some of the anticipated advantages of widespread participation include:

1. A more thorough understanding of what the organization is, where it is going, and how it will get there.
2. A more thorough understanding of how the individual fits into the organization and contributes to it and vice versa.

3. A greater understanding of the "worth" of other organization members.
4. An increased emphasis on cooperation between organization members and groups, leading to decreased levels of dysfunctional competition.
5. Increased control by the individual over his or her own destiny within the organization, leading to greater "ego" involvement and commitment.
6. Higher levels of motivation, leading to increased effort and performance.

One method that has been gaining favor in police management regarding participation in decision making and problem solving has been the use of quality circles. A *quality circle* consists of a group of employees from the same work area, who volunteer to meet on a regular basis for the purpose of identifying and solving problems affecting common work activities. Team members often receive some training in problem identification, problem solving, data collection and analysis, and team building in order to help them function more effectively. A facilitator is usually available to help formulate and guide the discussion. Quality circles are not used to air personal gripes and problems, but are oriented toward improving the quality of the work product and enhancing employee participation.

Originally developed in Japan in the mid-1950s to accentuate the Japanese emphasis on participatory management and decentralized decision making, the use of quality circles has blossomed in recent years in American organizations, including the police. However, quality circles were designed to enhance a managerial philosophy based on strong participation by lower-level employees in the decision-making process. Consequently, mechanistic organizations that tend to emphasize centralized decision making and an autocratic managerial philosophy will undoubtedly not be as successful with quality circles as the Japanese.

The use of quality circles in policing can be highlighted by the Dallas Police Department (Melancon 1984), which has one of the more extensive programs in the country. A full-time facilitator is responsible for the orientation, implementation, and overall operation of the quality circle program. Team leaders, generally sergeants who have attended three-day seminars to learn about the philosophy, techniques, and fundamentals of the operation, supervise their respective work groups. Team members are volunteers from specific work groups, who are required to attend at least three meetings before determining whether they wish to participate. Members attend meetings in both on-duty and off-duty status and may drop out at any time. Since quality circles are considered a part of the job, the members receive either overtime pay or compensatory time off for attendance during their off hours.

Team members receive training in areas such as brainstorming techniques, cause-and-effect analysis, problem definition, and data collection and sorting techniques. Work problems are then identified and possible solutions suggested; many of the recommendations made by the department's quality circles have been implemented. At one time or another, the department has had fifteen to eighteen quality circles in operation covering a great variety of organizational units, including patrol, detectives, traffic, dispatching, property, records, legal services, community services, training, vehicle services, the tactical unit, and personnel (Hatry and Greiner 1986, p. 10).

Melancon (1984) reports enhanced morale and quality of work life improvements for the participating employees. A survey of team leaders indicated that quality circles were beneficial in solving problems in the work area and that management supported the program. The survey further indicated that officers felt that through the program, the organization exhibited more openness, trust, and support toward the employees. To ensure the success of a quality circle program, certain key elements should be included:

1. In-depth training, which includes orientation, quality circle philosophy, and operational techniques.
2. Management participation in and open support of the program. This includes a willingness to listen to suggestions and a commitment to encourage and use worker input in decisions.
3. Feedback through chain-of-command channels and proper follow-up on recommended changes or solutions.
4. Publication of quality circle team achievements in departmental newsletters, activity reports, or graphic displays using bulletin boards or other postings (Melancon 1984, p. 55).

A national survey of three hundred police departments found that 16 percent (forty-eight) were using quality circles (Hatry and Greiner 1986). Over 80 percent of the programs had begun in 1980 or later; only two departments had terminated their programs. The researchers discovered that although police departments probably have greater difficulty implementing quality circle programs due to their more authoritarian management style and hierarchical rank structure, a surprising number of police officials were willing to try participatory techniques. Thus, management style appears to be less of a problem than originally anticipated.

For an interesting portrait of a manager who adheres to a participatory style of management, see the case study of MacGregor later in this chapter. Notice how MacGregor develops within his subordinates those values and conditions that lead to effective participation in decision making. Such an approach may be difficult for police managers to utilize given their reluctance to delegate (see chapter 6); however, the unwillingness to take "risks" in management undoubtedly discourages the active participation of employees. MacGregor's approach illustrates both the potential costs and benefits of a style of management designed to create candor, openness, and responsible and motivated employees.

Although quality circles appeared to improve employee morale in the affected work groups, Hatry and Greiner (1986) have been unable to demonstrate significant improvements in agency performance, in part because the topics selected have been too narrow in scope and in part because the circles involved a very small proportion of the work force in any one agency. If police quality circles spent some time focusing on the more substantive service delivery problems facing the individual work units, their long-term viability would be greatly strengthened.

## Capability for Revitalization

The other cooperative goals culminate in the development of the capability for revitalization or self-renewal. The achievement of this ultimate goal depends, as have the others, on the mutual contributions of both the individual and the organization. According to Bennis, who has written extensively on the future of organizations, revitalization includes the following elements:

1. An ability to learn from experience and to codify, store, and retrieve the relevant knowledge.
2. An ability to "learn how to learn"; that is, to develop methodologies for improving the learning process.
3. An ability to acquire and use feedback mechanisms in performance, to develop a "process orientation"; in short, to be self-analytical.
4. An ability to direct one's own destiny (1967, p. 10).

Revitalization is especially important to police organizations and their employees since they operate in environments that are relatively unstable and require constant attention to changing external and internal conditions. Also, this goal is as crucial to the individual as it is to the organization, since an individual's skills and abilities may become obsolete if he or she is unwilling to learn and adapt to current conditions. Such a situation may lead not only to stagnation on the job, but to other unhealthy outcomes as well, including losing influence in the organization, transfer to an undesirable location or job, and possibly, termination.

As discussed in the last chapter, the organization can do much to encourage greater receptivity to change by reducing the threatening aspects often associated with the change process. Even though the organization can make allowances for the development of this goal, it is up to the individual and group to carry through and actually permit the process of revitalization to take place.

This capability, then, is significant because of the decay that will inevitably occur without it. As Bennis astutely noted; "Growth and decay emerge as the penultimate conditions of contemporary society. Organizations, as well as societies, must be concerned with those social structures that engender buoyancy, resilience, and 'fearlessness of revision' " (p. 10). While police organizations have not generally been known for their "fearlessness of revision," they will need to move in this direction if they are to keep pace with their constantly changing environments.

**Warren G. Bennis (1925– ), an important contributor to the understanding of
the future of organizations and their need for revitalization.**

In sum, by moving toward the accomplishment of cooperative goals,
managers can have a vital impact on the quality of work life in their organizations. As a result, it is likely that motivation and performance levels will
increase, along with overall effectiveness of the organization.

CASE STUDY

**MacGregor: A Case Study of Participatory Decision Making**

*No question about it—some managers are better organized than others, but how often have you run into a really well organized manager—I mean really well organized? Not too often, I bet! In the course of my work I run into hundreds of managers a year, yet I can think of only one who managed to be super-organized—to the point where he had time to play an enormous amount of golf. As further proof of his organization, consider this: About two years after I ran into MacGregor, which incidentally is not his real name, he was promoted to the post of chief of operations at the corporate level—a fact I discovered when I saw his face looking out at me from the financial section of my newspaper above the announcement of his new executive assignment.*

*My encounter with MacGregor came about during the course of a study of the extent to which operating managers actually use participative management techniques in their dealings with subordinates. The problem with an inquiry of this nature is that nearly every manager either says he uses a participative approach (because isn't that what every good manager does?) or maybe honestly believes that this is his preferred* modus operandi; *in any event, what I was interested in was information about behavior, not about beliefs (pious or otherwise). So I had to develop an indirect approach for use with the managers being interviewed and follow it up with some questions directed at the subordinates they supervised. Accordingly, I developed a questionnaire that I used in interviewing more than 100 managers in ten major U.S. and Canadian firms. The first item on the questionnaire asked whether the interviewee held regular meetings with his subordinates; if so, how often; and what was the nature of the matters discussed. Finally, it tried to determine whether subordinates were offered the opportunity to initiate discussion and actively participate in the decision making process or were merely afforded the opportunity to hear about decisions the boss had made.*

*MacGregor, who at the time was manager of one of the largest refineries in the country, was the last of more than 100 managers I interviewed in the course of the study. Although the interview had been scheduled in advance,* the exact time had been left open; I was to call MacGregor at his office early in the week that I would be in the vicinity and set up a specific date and time.

Here's how that phone call went: The switchboard operator answered with the name of the refinery. When I asked for MacGregor's office, a male voice almost instantly said, "Hello," I then asked for MacGregor, where-upon the voice responded, "This is he." I should have recognized at once that this was no ordinary manager; he answered his own phone instantly, as though he had been waiting for it to ring. To my question about when it would be convenient for me to come see him, he replied, "Anytime." I said, "Would today be all right?" His response was "Today, tomorrow, or Wednesday would be O.K.; or you could come Thursday, except don't come between 10:00 A.M. and noon; or you could come Friday or next week — anytime." I replied feebly, "I just want to fit in with your plans." Then he said, "You are just not getting the message; it makes no difference to me when you come. I have nothing on the books except to play golf and see you. Come in anytime — I don't have to be notified in advance, so I'll be seeing you one of these days," and he then hung up. I was dumbfounded. Here was a highly placed executive with apparently nothing to do except play golf and talk to visitors.

I took MacGregor at his word and drove over immediately to see him without any further announcement of my visit. MacGregor's office, in a small building at one corner of the refinery, adjoined that of his secretary — who when I arrived, was knitting busily and, without dropping a stitch, said to me, "You must be Mr. Carlisle; he's in there," indicating MacGregor's office with a glance at a connecting door.

MacGregor's office was large and had a big window overlooking the re-finery, a conference table with eight chairs arranged around it (one of which, at the head, was more comfortable and imposing than the rest), an engineer's file cabinet with a series of wide drawers, two easy chairs, a sofa, a coffee table with a phone on it, and a desk. The desk had been shoved all the way to the corner; there was no way a chair could be slipped in behind it, and it was covered with technical journals. A lamp stood on the desk, but its plug was not connected to an outlet. There was no phone on the desk. MacGre-gor, a tall, slender man with a tanned face, stood by the window, peering ab-

*sently into space. He turned slowly when I entered his office and said, "You must be Carlisle. The head office told me you wanted to talk to me about the way I run things here. Sit down on the sofa and fire away."*

## *MacGregor's* Modus Operandi

*"Do you hold regular meetings with your subordinates?" I asked.*

*"Yes I do," he replied.*

*"How often?" I asked.*

*"Once a week, on Thursdays between 10:00 A.M. and noon; that's why I couldn't see you then," was his response.*

*"What sorts of things do you discuss?" I queried, following my interview guide.*

*"My subordinates tell me about the decisions they've made during the past week," he explained.*

*"Then you believe in participative decision making," I commented.*

*"No—as a matter of fact, I don't," said MacGregor.*

*"Then why hold the meetings?" I asked. "Why not just tell your people about the operating decisions you've made and let them know how to carry them out?"*

*"Oh, I don't make their decisions for them and I just don't believe in participating in the decisions they should be making, either; we hold the weekly meetings so that I can keep informed on what they're doing and how. The meeting also gives me a chance to appraise their technical and managerial abilities," he explained. "I used to make all the operating decisions myself; but I quit doing that a few years ago when I discovered my golf game was going to hell because I didn't have enough time to practice. Now that I've quit making other people's decisions, my game is back where it should be."*

*"You don't make operating decisions any more?" I asked in astonishment.*

*"No," he replied. Sensing my incredulity, he added, "Obviously, you don't believe me. Why not ask one of my subordinates? Which one do you want to talk to?"*

*"I haven't any idea; I don't even know how many subordinates you have, let alone their names. You choose one," I suggested.*

*"No, I wouldn't do that—for two reasons. First I don't make decisions, and second, when my subordinate confirms that I don't make decisions, you'll say that it's a put-up job, so here is a list of my eight immediate subordinates, the people who report directly to me. Choose one name from it and I'll call him and you can talk to him," said MacGregor.*

*"OK—Johnson, then. I'll talk to him if he's free." I said.*

*"I'm sure he's able to talk to you. I'll call him and tell him you're on the way over." Reaching for the phone, he determined that Johnson wasn't doing anything either, and would be happy to have someone to talk to.*

**Subordinate's view of MacGregor.**    *I walked over to Johnson's unit and found him to be in his early thirties. After a couple minutes of casual conversation, I discovered that MacGregor and all eight of his subordinates were chemical engineers. Johnson said, "Suppose MacGregor gave you that bit about his not making decisions, didn't he? That man is a gas."*

*"It isn't true, though, is it? He does make decisions, doesn't he?" I asked.*

*"No, he doesn't; everything he told you is true. He simply decided not to get involved in decisions that his subordinates are being paid to make. So he stopped making them, and they tell me he plays a lot of golf in the time he saves," said Johnson.*

*Then I asked Johnson whether he tried to get MacGregor to make a decision and his response was:*

*"Only once. I had been on the job for only about a week when I ran into an operating problem I couldn't solve, so I phoned Macgregor. He answered the phone with that sleepy 'Hello' of his. I told him who I was and that I had a problem. His response was instantaneous: 'Good, that's what you're being paid to do, solve problems,' and then he hung up. I was dumbfounded. I didn't really know any of the people I was working with, so because I didn't think I had any other alternative, I called him back, got the same sleepy 'Hello,' and again identified myself. He replied sharply, 'I thought I told you that you were paid to solve problems? Do you think that I should do your*

*job as well as my own?' When I insisted on seeing him about my problem,
he answered, 'I don't know how you expect me to help you. You have a technical problem and I don't go into the refinery any more; I used to, but my
shirts kept getting dirty from the visits and my wife doesn't like washing all
the grime out of them, so I pretty much stick in my office. Ask one of the
other men. They're all in touch with what goes on out there.'*

"*I didn't know which one to consult, so I insisted again on seeing him.
He finally agreed—grudgingly—to see me right away, so I went over to his
office and there he was in his characteristic looking-out-the-window posture.
When I sat down, he started the dirty-shirt routine—but when he saw that
I was determined to involve him in my problems, he sat down on the sofa
in front of his coffee table and, pen in hand, prepared to write on a pad of
paper. He asked me to state precisely what the problem was and he wrote
down exactly what I said. Then he asked what the conditions for its solution
were. I replied that I didn't know what he meant by that question. His response was, 'If you don't know what conditions have to be satisfied for a solution to be reached, how do you know when you've solved the problem?'
I told him I'd never thought of approaching a problem that way and he replied, 'Then you'd better start. I'll work through this one with you this time,
but don't expect me to do your problem solving for you because that's your
job, not mine.'*

"*I stumbled through the conditions that would have to be satisfied by the
solution. Then he asked me what alternative approaches I could think of. I
gave him the first one I could think of—let's call it X—and he wrote it down
and asked me what would happen if I did X. I replied with my answer—let's
call it A. Then he asked me how A compared with the conditions I had established for the solution of the problem. I replied that it did not meet them.
MacGregor told me that I'd have to think of another. I came up with Y,
which I said would yield B, and this still fell short of the solution conditions.
After more prodding from MacGregor, I came up with Z, which I said would
have C as a result; although this clearly came a lot closer to the conditions
I had established for the solution than any of the others I'd suggested, it still
did not satisfy all of them. MacGregor then asked me if I could combine any
of the approaches I'd suggested. I replied I could do X and Z and then saw*

that the resultant A plus C would indeed satisfy the solution conditions I had set up previously. When I thanked Macgregor, he replied, 'What for? Get the hell out of my office; you could have done that bit of problem solving perfectly well without wasting my time. Next time you really can't solve a problem on your own, ask the Thursday man and tell me about it at the Thursday meeting.' "

I asked Johnson about Mr. MacGregor's reference to the Thursday man.

"He's the guy who runs the Thursday meeting when MacGregor is away from the plant. I'm the Thursday man now. My predecessor left here about two months ago."

"Where did he go? Did he quit the company?" I asked.

"God, no. He got a refinery of his own. That's what happens to a lot of Thursday men. After the kind of experience we get coping with everyone's problems and MacGregor's refusal to do what he perceives as his subordinates' work, we don't need an operating superior any more and we're ready for our own refineries. Incidentally, most of the people at our level have adopted MacGregor's managerial method in dealing with the foremen who report to us and we are reaping the same kinds of benefits that he does. The foremen are a lot more self-reliant, and we don't have to do their work for them."

I went back to see MacGregor. His secretary was still knitting. The garment she was working on was considerably more advanced that it was on my first visit. She motioned me into MacGregor's office with her head, again not dropping a stitch. MacGregor was in his traditional office posture, looking vacantly out of the window. He turned and asked, "Well, now do you believe that I don't make any decisions?"

I said, "No, that could have been just a fluke." He suggested I see another subordinate and asked me to pick another name from the list. I picked Peterson who, when phoned to see whether he was available, said that he had nothing to do. So I went to Peterson's office.

Peterson was in his late twenties. He asked me what I thought of MacGregor. I said I found him most unusual. Peterson replied, "Yes, he's a gas." Peterson's story paralleled Johnson's. MacGregor refused to make decisions related to the work of his subordinates. When Peterson got into a situation he could not deal with, he said he called one of the other supervisors, usually Johnson, and together they worked it out. At the Thursday meetings, he reported on the decision and gave credit to his helper. "If I hadn't," he added, "I probably wouldn't get help from that quarter again."

In reply to a query on what the Thursday meetings were like, he said, "Well, we all sit around that big conference table in MacGregor's office. He sits at the head like a thinned-down Buddha, and we go around the table talking about the decisions we've made, and if we got help, who helped us. The other guys occasionally make comments—especially if the particular decisions being discussed was like one they had had to make themselves at some point or if it had some direct effect on their own operations." MacGregor had said very little these past few meetings, according to Peterson, but he did pass on any new developments that he heard about at the head office.

**Head-office assessment of MacGregor.** By the time I had finished with Johnson and Peterson, it was time for lunch. I decided to go downtown and stop at the head office to try to find out their assessment of MacGregor and his operation. I visited the operations chief for the corporation. I had wanted to thank him for his willingness to go along with my study, anyway. When I told him I had met MacGregor, his immediate response was, "Isn't he a gas?" I muttered something about having heard that comment before and asked him about the efficiency of MacGregor's operation in comparison with that of other refineries in the corporation. His response was instantaneous. "Oh, MacGregor has by far the most efficient producing unit."

"Is that because he has the newest equipment?" I asked.

"No, as a matter of fact he has the oldest in the corporation. His was the first refinery we built."

"Does MacGregor have a lot of turnover among his subordinates?"

"A great deal," he replied.

Thinking I had found a chink in the MacGregor armor, I asked, "What happens to them; can't they take his system?"

"On the contrary," said the operations chief, "Most of them go on to assignments as refinery managers. After all, under MacGregor's method of supervision, they are used to working on their own."

***More pointers on MacGregor's style of managing.***   *"How do they run their own operations—like MacGregor's?" I asked.*

*"You guessed it. More and more of our operations are using his system."*

*I went back to the refinery with a few last questions for MacGregor. His secretary had made considerable progress on her knitting and her boss had resumed his position by the refinery window.*

*"I understand you were downtown. What did they tell you about this place?"*

*"You know damn well what they said—that you have the most efficient operation in the corporation."*

*"Yup, it's true." he replied, with no pretense at false modesty. "Periodically, I get chances to go to work for another major oil company—but I've gotten things so well organized here that I really don't want to take a job like the one I faced when I came here five years ago. I guess I'll hang on here until something better comes up."*

*"Let me ask you a couple of questions about the Thursday meeting," I continued. "First of all, I understand that when you are away, the 'Thursday man' takes over. How do you choose the individual to fill this slot?"*

*"Oh, that's simple, I just pick the man who is most often referred to as the one my subordinates turn to for help in dealing with their problems. Then I try him out in this assignment when I'm off. It's good training and, if he proves he can handle it, I know I have someone to propose for any vacancies that may occur at the refinery manager level. The head-office people always contact me for candidates. As a matter of fact, the Thursday-man assignment is sought after. My subordinates compete with each other in helping anyone with a problem because they know they'll get credit for their help at the Thursday meeting. You know, another development has been that jobs on the staff of this refinery are highly prized by young people who want to get ahead in the corporation; when junior management positions open up here, there are always so many candidates that I often have a tough time making a choice."*

*"Sounds logical," I said. "Now let me focus a bit more on your role as refinery manager. You say you don't make decisions. Suppose a subordinate told you at a Thursday meeting about a decision he'd made and you were convinced that it was a mistake. What would you do about it?"*

*"How much would the mistake cost me?"*

*"Oh, I don't know,"* I answered.

*"Can't tell you, then. It would depend on how much it would cost."*

*"Say, $3,000,"* I suggested.

*"That's easy; I'd let him make it." said MacGregor.* I sensed I'd hit the upper limit before MacGregor either would have moved in himself or, more likely, would have suggested that the subordinate discuss it with the Thursday man and then report back to him on their joint decision.

*"When was the last time you let a subordinate make a mistake of that magnitude?"* I asked skeptically.

*"About four weeks ago,"* said MacGregor.

*"You let someone who works for you make such a serious mistake? Why did you do that?"*

*"Three reasons,"* said MacGregor. *"First, I was only 99.44 percent sure that it would be a mistake and if it hadn't turned out to be one, I'd have felt pretty foolish. Second, I thought that making a mistake like this would be such a tremendous learning experience for him that he'd never make another like that again. I felt it would do him more good than signing him up for some of the management-development courses that are available. Third, this is a profit center. It was early in the budget year and I felt that we could afford it."*

*"What was the result?"* I asked.

*"It was a mistake—and I heard about it in short order from the controller downtown by phone." (I realized suddenly during the whole time I had been in the office, neither MacGregor's phone nor his secretary's had rung.)*

*"The controller said, 'MacGregor, how could you let a stupid mistake like that slip through?' "*

*"What did you say?"*

*"Well, I figured a good attack is the best defense. I asked him which refinery in the organization was the most efficient. He replied, 'You know yours is. That has nothing to do with it.' I told him that it had everything to do with it. I added that my people learn from their mistakes and until the rest of the plants in the organization started operating at the same degree of efficiency as this one, I wasn't going to waste my time talking to clerks. Then I hung up."*

*"What happened?"*

*"Well, relations were a bit strained for a while—but they know I'm probably the best refinery manager in the business and I can get another job anytime, so it blew over pretty quickly," he said, not without a degree of self-satisfaction.*

**Uniqueness of MacGregor.**   *MacGregor was unique among the managers I interviewed in the course of my study. Presumably his approach was a distinct possibility for each of the refinery managers I talked to, and certainly with adaptations it could have been used by many of the 100 executives I interviewed—but it wasn't. He had taken management by objectives to its logical limits by concentrating his efforts on formulating and negotiating objectives and had divorced himself from direct involvement in solving problems his subordinates came upon in carrying out their responsibilities.*

*MacGregor's frequency of regularly scheduled meetings with his subordinates was typical of the managers interviewed in the study; ten percent met less frequently and about five percent more often. But his focus on discussion of completed decisions was unique. Slightly less than three-quarters of the executives with whom I talked saw the purpose of their meetings as a combination of information communication and problem solving; the balance were split evenly between a primary focus on communication of information and a primary emphasis on problem solving. Interestingly, the majority of those who emphasized problem solving were refinery executives.*

*When describing the degree of reliance they placed on the contributions made by subordinates in the determination of final decisions, half of the managers felt that it was considerable, a quarter that it was heavy, and the balance that it was either not too significant or that it varied with the individuals involved. Only MacGregor left the actual decision making (except in rare circumstances) to the subordinates themselves.*

*All of the managers, except MacGregor, either stated explicitly or made it clear during the course of the interviews that all important decisions arrived at in these meetings were made by themselves. They received suggestions, considered their sources, and either compared the proffered solutions with solutions they had developed on their own, or considered them carefully before reaching a final solution. In using this approach to group decision making, the managers were obviously manifesting their deeply held convictions that one of the key responsibilities of an upper-level executive is to act as chief decision maker for those who report to him. They believed that, after all, the superior is ultimately responsible for the quality of the decisions made in his organization and the only way to carry out this task is to become directly involved in the decision making process itself.*

*Most of the managers I have encountered—both organizational superiors and outside managers involved in the studies I've conducted or the consulting assignments I've carried out—pride themselves on the extent to which they invite their subordinates to participate in organizational decision making; but their perceptions of this process and its organizational impact often differ sharply from those of the subordinates involved. For many of the latter, the participative management routine is just that—a routine acted out by the boss because it evidences his espousal of a technique that is supposed to increase the likelihood that subordinates will accept and commit themselves to decisions; he may even believe the decisions were jointly determined. However, most participative management is seen by lower-level participants as, at worst, a manipulative device and at best an opportunity for them to avoid decision making responsibility and assure that if a wrong solution is reached, the boss himself was a party to the decision.*

*MacGregor avoided this trap by refusing to give managers reporting to him the opportunity to second-guess the solution he would be most likely to choose. Although he allowed himself some margin in case emergency action on his part should become inevitable, he made it clear that he wanted to hear about problems only after they had been solved and about decisions only after they had been made.*

---

## The Manager's Perspective

If police organizations want to move toward organic policing, the manager's perspective will need to become that of a change agent, at least to some degree. If organization development efforts are not promoted by police managers, change efforts cannot effectively be carried forward and implemented. This is not to suggest that police agencies may not need the help of external change agents in assessing needs and developing strategies for change—most will—but that managers must get involved in the developmental process if constructive changes are to be brought about. We feel that if police managers are to succeed as effective change agents for their organizations, three major recommendations will require their careful consideration.

The first recommendation calls for *increased emphasis on the use of research findings*. Although in the past there was little empirical research to guide police managers in their quest to effectively run their organizations, this is no longer the case. During the past several decades, police organizations have quite possibly been the most studied public organizations in the country. The findings presented throughout this text are testimony to the increased level of attention that has been given to the field of policing by researchers. Furthermore, the results of this research are readily available in journals, books, governmental records, and other publications. There is no longer any viable excuse to continue to use dated practices that have never been tested, may not be effective, and are based solely on tradition and inertia.

Of course, additional research remains to be conducted in many areas of police management and organization in order to improve the quality of work life. Accordingly, police managers need to develop a "spirit of scientific inquiry" and encourage researchers to study their organizations for the mutual benefit of adding knowledge to the field and improving their organization's performance. This does not preclude the notion that police organizations may wish to hire and use their own researchers; most agencies could readily profit from improved or newly created research and development units. Police managers need to understand the contributions that researchers can make toward improving organizational performance, and thus make more significant the role of research in policing. This knowledge will help managers upgrade their status within the organization.

The second recommendation calls for *increased recognition of the significance of patrol work*. If motivational and performance levels of patrol officers are to be improved, increased attention must be paid to recognizing the importance of patrol work. Steps need to be taken to enhance the quality of work life for patrol personnel, especially since they are considered the "backbone" of the organization. Hence, organizational performance cannot improve until patrol officer performance improves. Job enrichment, increased participation in decision making, and rewards based on performance are but a few strategies that would most likely improve the morale and performance of patrol personnel. Although we have sufficiently covered each of these topics elsewhere, we would like to reiterate that it is time to recognize the important role played by patrol in police organizations.

In many police agencies, for example, the only way patrol officers can obtain increased job satisfaction and flexibility, and increased status and pay, is through promotion to another job (detective) or to management (sergeant). This situation may force outstanding performers to compete for a limited number of positions, even though they may not really wish to leave patrol. Consequently, those employees who are the most vital to the successful operation of the organization may feel compelled to seek another job in order to fulfill their needs or to feel justly recognized and rewarded. However, if the significance of patrol work is sufficiently recognized and enhanced, individuals will not feel that they must leave the position to gain certain types of rewards.

The third recommendation calls for *increased levels of initiative and innovation on the part of managers*. Many police managers have fallen into a "complacency rut" or "doing things as they have always been done before" attitude. If working environments are to be improved, these patterns and attitudes will need to be altered. Whenever traditional management concepts and practices are faithfully followed, inertia sets in and the decaying process begins. Future managers will need to thoroughly question the effectiveness of traditional policing practices. They can do this by promoting and utilizing research findings, from within their organization and from the outside as well, to create policy changes and implement new practices where and when they are called for. This does not mean that all traditional concepts and practices are obsolete and ineffective, but practicing managers must be willing to look to the future for new ways of adapting to change, rather than to the past and the status quo.

Pursuing this final recommendation will be no easy task for many managers. For example, one recent study of lower- and middle-level police managers from a diverse number of agencies indicated that they differed from managers in general and from "ideal" managers in that they have a much greater need for security (Rawlins and Daumer 1987). While we must be careful not to overgeneralize these findings, they are not surprising given the relatively mechanistic nature of many police organizations. Managers who have such strong needs for security are not likely to have high levels of initiative and a desire for innovation. While this situation has been allowed to develop and even flourish, it is not irreversible. However, as discussed in the last chapter, strong and innovative leadership from top-level management is necessary to establish a path in this direction. If police leaders utilize properly the types of OD strategies presented throughout this chapter to move their organizations toward organic policing, increased levels of initiative and innovation should become a permanent staple of police organization and management.

## Summary

Organization development was defined as a process by which intervention strategies are utilized to enhance organizational effectiveness through planned change. It differs from other planned changed efforts in that it focuses attention on an organization's human resources. The important role played by change agents in the OD process was also discussed. The different types of change agents that can be used in police organizations include external, internal, or a combination of both; each form carries particular advantages and disadvantages associated with it. Since the change agent is responsible for diagnosing an agency's problems and then making recommendations for change based on the diagnosis, it is crucial that the organization select an appropriate type of change agent.

Change agents use many types of OD interventions or strategies to help implement change and improve organizational effectiveness. The interventions can focus either on structural changes, in which case organizational outcomes are emphasized, or on behavioral changes (both individual and organizational), in which case attitudes, values, and beliefs are emphasized. Intervention depth, or level of emotional involvement required by the employee in the change process, is also an important consideration; the deeper the level of emotional involvement, the greater the impact on the individual, either positive or negative. In general, behavioral changes require deeper levels of intervention than structural changes.

A typology of OD interventions was presented based on four levels of "depth," from relatively impersonal (i.e., structural) to highly personal (i.e., behavioral). The strategies presented provide a sample of available methods that are likely to be of value in implementing constructive change in police organizations. The first level, operations analysis, includes survey feedback and organization structure; the second level, work style, includes management by objectives and job enrichment. The succeedingly deeper third level, inter/intragroup behavior, includes process consultation and team building. The final and deepest level of intervention, inter/intrapersonal behavior, includes various forms of sensitivity training. A process for "mapping" police organization change toward organic policing was also presented. Such an approach allows for adaptability in responding to changing internal and external environmental conditions.

Quality of work life was defined as a concern for worker well-being and organizational effectiveness, as well as the promotion of employee participation in work-related problems and decisions. A set of cooperative goals was promoted for improving police work environments. These goals are aimed at enhancing individual–organizational interactions and include the initial sharing of expectations, development of humane relationships, development of open communications, development of participative decision making, and a capability for revitalization.

The manager's perspective in contemporary policing was analyzed. It was noted that if constructive changes are to occur, managers must become adept at the role of change agent, at least to some degree. Finally, if police managers are to succeed in their role of change agent and thus promote constructive change, three recommendations should be considered: namely, placing increased emphasis on the use of research findings, placing increased recognition on the significance of patrol work, and increasing their own levels of initiative and innovation.

## Discussion Questions

1. Define organization development.
2. Describe the three forms of change agents used in OD. List several advantages and disadvantages associated with each form.
3. Discuss the meaning of intervention depth with respect to the change process.
4. Describe four levels of OD interventions and provide an example of at least one strategy that can be used at each level.
5. List the two major criteria that should be considered for choosing an appropriate OD intervention strategy.
6. How would "mapping" enhance police organizational change?
7. What is meant by the quality of work life?
8. Discuss five cooperative goals that may help managers improve the QWL in their organizations.
9. With respect to the MacGregor case study, explain why you feel such a participatory style would or would not be beneficial in policing.
10. Describe organic policing. What recommendations might future police managers follow if they wish to move their organization in this direction?

## References

Beckhard, R., *Organization Development: Strategies and Models* (Reading, Mass.: Addison-Wesley, 1969).

Bennis, W. G., "Organizations of the Future," *Personnel Administration* 30(1967): 1–19.

Campbell, J. P. and Dunnette, M. D., "Effectiveness of T-Group Experience in Managerial Training and Development," *Psychological Bulletin* 70(1968): 73–104.

Carlisle, A. E., "MacGregor," *Organizational Dynamics* 5(1976): 50–60.

Davis, L., "Enhancing the Quality of Work Life: Developments in the United States," *International Labour Review* 116 (July–August 1977): 53–65.

Harrison, R., "Choosing the Depth of Organizational Intervention," *Journal of Applied Behavioral Science* 6(1970): 181–202.

Hatry, H. P. and Greiner, J. M., *Improving the Use of Quality Circles in Police Departments* (Washington, D.C.: National Institute of Justice, 1986).

Huse, E. F. and Cummings, T. G., *Organization Development and Change*, 3rd ed. (St. Paul, Minn.: West Publishing, 1985).

Kuykendall, J. and Roberg, R. R., "Mapping Police Organizational Change: From a Mechanistic Toward an Organic Model," *Criminology* 20(1982): 241–256.

Melancon, D. D. "Quality Circles: The Shape of Things to Come?" *The Police Chief* (November 1984), pp. 54–55.

Rawlins, C. L. and Daumer, H.-J., "Police Manager Life Style Choices: A High Need for Security," *Journal of Police Science and Administration* 15(1987): 145–152.

Reuss-Ianni, E., *Two Cultures of Policing: Street Cops and Management Cops* (New Brunswick, Conn.: Transaction Books, 1983).

Roberg, R. R., "Improving the Quality of Police Work Environments: Toward the Development of Cooperative Goals," *The Police Chief* (April 1981) pp. 52–55.

Schein, E., *Process Consultation: Its Role in Organization Development* (Reading, Mass.: Addison-Wesley, 1969).

Tosi, H. L. and Carroll, S. J., "Management by Objectives," *Personnel Administration* 33, no. 4(1970): 44–48.

# CHAPTER 13

# Police Organization and Management: Future Considerations

What does the future hold for the police in the United States? Trends in police organization and management are not always easy to identify, particularly in periods of a decade or less. In general, changes in police practices tend to be evolutionary rather than revolutionary. *Evolutionary* change occurs in small, incremental steps. *Revolutionary* change occurs when significant adjustments are made in a relatively short period. The latter is usually the result of a major crisis or scandal; for instance, when extensive corruption is uncovered.

The four models discussed in chapter 2 indicate a continuum of change in policing that has had a significant impact on organization and management. The next logical step on this continuum is for more police departments to move toward either a community-service or a rational-contingency model. Any changes that occur must take into consideration the expectation-integration (E-I) model and the importance of attempting to balance and integrate expectations of employees, the organization, and the community. There are two major expectation-integration problems in this regard: employees and the organization, and the organization and the community. Both are discussed in this chapter along with the possible implications and problems of community/problem-oriented policing (what we call the community-service and rational-contingency models) and possible future trends concerning managerial perspectives.

## Integrating Employee and Organization Expectations

When attempting to integrate employee and organization expectations, one of the most significant problems is the absence of a humanistic orientation. While some managers may have this type of relationship with individual employees, a humanistic approach is not a predominant characteristic of police management. Since the reforms of the early twentieth century created increasingly bureaucratic police departments, the concerns and needs of the employee have been deemphasized in favor of organization goals and objectives.

Also since this reform period, many police managers have considered inappropriate behavior as one of the most important managerial issues. Klockars (1985) notes that organization reforms were intended to eliminate the "lazy, the stupid, the brutal and the corrupt" from police organizations. Instead, the mechanistic system (also called paramilitary or bureaucratic), which was the basis for reform, produced many officers who were cynical, did as little work as possible, "covered their ass" (often by lying) to avoid getting into trouble, and, at times, were indifferent to their responsibilities.

To be fair to reformers, the mechanistic system, and its associated design features (i.e., specialization, hierarchical control of communication and authority, strict chain of command, well-defined jobs, elaborate rules, regulations, policies, and procedures), was the conventional wisdom for well-managed organizations in both the public and private sectors until the 1940s and 1950s. However, police departments tended to cling to it well after behavioral science research indicated that a more humanistic approach might improve performance. Although some departments have experimented with "new" management techniques since the 1960s, police management continues to be characterized by a mechanistic approach. Until police departments adopt a more organic policing approach, the development of a humanistic perspective is unlikely.

While we recognize that a mechanistic orientation may be needed in some activities, situations, or even in an entire organization in some communities (e.g., for a time after a corruption scandal), there needs to be an alteration in managerial philosophy. The basic assumption that police organizations should be mechanistic in nature should be changed to police organizations can have *variable* orientations depending on the degree of stability in the environment (i.e., the greater the degree of environmental instability, the greater the need for an organic approach). This assumption requires that managers believe that employee expectations are just as important, if not more so, than organizational goals. Furthermore, managers must recognize that if employee expectations are not met, organizational goals will not be accomplished either. In general, some movement toward organic policing will most likely improve employee performance and reduce behavioral problems.

Movement toward organic policing will undoubtedly be difficult since prolonged adherence to a mechanistic orientation has created substantial divisiveness between police managers and employees. This is reflected in the previous discussions concerning the manager's and worker's cultures in police departments. Each culture has a somewhat different conception of the police role, appropriate strategies and styles of behavior, how discretion should be exercised, and in general, what is required to be a "good" cop. Until these two cultures with their diverse values can be integrated, there is little hope that employee and organization expectations can be highly integrated. To a great extent, police behavior is determined by the socialization process recruits go through. While this process is influenced by management through formal organizational activities like training and the development of policy and procedures, it is probably influenced more by the employee's or worker's culture.

Police work remains an essentially political endeavor clothed in bureaucratic and professional rhetoric; consequently, it will be subject to both the rational and irrational realities of the political process. As a result, police managers will not stop being as concerned about avoiding problems as accomplishing results. Since the problems are likely to come from the perceived inappropriate behavior of officers, many managers will continue to consider officers more a potential liability than a productive, intelligent resource.

We believe the initial attempt to more completely integrate individual and organizational expectations should be to adopt a more *humanistic managerial philosophy* and, depending on environmental circumstances, to move toward an *organic policing philosophy*. After this is accomplished, the techniques concerning organizational change and development, identified in chapter 12, will prove useful. However, we also believe that if any progress is made in this area (in other than a few departments) over the next decade or two, it will be a slow and painful process. Police managers, organizations, and employees do not change basic perspectives in such a short period. This is an area where incrementalism is probably the most likely trend.

Interestingly, an important recent development in attempting to accredit police organizations may potentially limit substantial gains in this area. The Commission on Accreditation for Law Enforcement Agencies (CALEA), initiated in the late 1970s, wants to standardize police organizations and behavior in the United States. While CALEA has not yet had a substantial impact, more and more agencies are attempting to achieve accreditation. The standards established by CALEA will most likely perpetuate an essentially mechanistic approach in police departments (CALEA 1984). For some departments, accreditation may initially be a desirable improvement; however, it will make the development of organic policing more difficult. Although accreditation is intended to make the police more professional, it is primarily based on managerial concerns, is designed to control and structure officer behavior, and largely ignores employee expectations. In this regard, it continues a well-established trend that began early in this century; that is, organizational expectations are preeminent and employees must fit into a system based on this perspective.

## Integrating Organization and Community Expectations

Attempts to balance and integrate employee–organization expectations must occur concomitantly with attempts to balance and integrate organization–community expectations, because the employee is the primary organizational link with the community. What employees believe, how they behave, the strategies utilized, and methods employed influence community expectations. Of course, managers also interact with the community, individual citizens, community groups, and elected and appointed officials, but the worker and his or her activities and behavior are the primary interactive element.

As noted previously, communities are often quite diverse. As diversity in expectations increases, so does the number of expectation-integration problems. This is of particular concern in urban areas. When expectations become too diverse, police managers may not be inclined to listen attentively to the community. To a substantial degree, police professionalism in management has been associated with police-initiated or proactive programs and activities, which has resulted in the development of a "professional knows best" attitude among the police. Thus, community concerns are always "interpreted" within the context of professional expertise. Of course, the police occupation, while it may have professional potential, is not yet a profession, and much is unknown about the relative effectiveness of what police do. Consequently, in this area, public opinion about crime and related problems may be as useful as police expertise.

Community expectations of police are both reasonable and unreasonable. A police organization's response to community expectations is based on one of the following reasons: (1) they want to keep the public happy, or avoid making them unhappy, because it is politically wise to do so; (2) the activity is or is not within the scope of the police role and/or police professionalism, as defined by the police organization or officer; (3) it is not considered important enough to warrant the investment of police resources in the manner that the community desires. Community expectations of police, either reasonable or unreasonable, are products of what citizens see police do in "real life" and in the media (e.g., television shows and movies) and of the image "sold" to the public by the police themselves.

Historically, the media has distorted police activities, making police work appear to be more dramatic and dangerous than it is and making the police appear to be more capable in responding to problems (e.g., solving crimes, subduing suspects, and using force) than they are in reality. Police have contributed to this by promising to wage, and win, the "war on crime." The methods they use—patrol, investigations, adoption of the latest scientific advances and technology, and crime prevention—do not seem to have more than a minor impact on the crime rate. However, to be fair, the police may actually prevent a large number of crimes, because it is not possible to accurately determine the number of crimes that do not occur because of the existence of police, regardless of the strategies or tactics employed.

Police managers and organizations have had to live with the legacy of twentieth-century reformers. Police continue to try to convince the public that they are making progress toward a questionable goal (i.e., having a substantial impact on crime). When the public criticizes the police for failing to achieve this goal, the police are likely to blame the public for lack of support and demand more resources. This, of course, perpetuates the legacy and the cycle continues. To the degree that the public expects the police to substantially reduce the crime rate, the expectation is unreasonable. To the degree that police managers continue to suggest that this is an achievable goal, they are deceiving the public. Making unreasonable demands and promising unachievable results exacerbates the integration of community and organizational expectations. The police organization must listen to what the community wants, but it must also be honest about telling the public what it is possible to achieve. In other words, the police should take a more active role in *educating the community* regarding realistic and achievable expectations.

Another major problem in integrating expectations involves communities that have a substantial poor or minority population. These areas are often characterized by extensive criminal activity. For the police, these communities represent a serious and potentially dangerous problem. Given that, historically, police have been heavy-handed and discriminatory in such areas, many residents do not trust the police to assist them or treat them fairly. While they may actually want more police assistance, they do not always want the type of assistance that has been provided.

The lack of trust between the police and these communities makes expectation-integration very difficult. The police expect trouble and the public expects unacceptable behavior by the police. This mutual animosity breeds misunderstanding and creates communication problems. Such a situation may be helped by hiring more minority officers, but this is far from clear, given the behavioral adjustment many minority officers appear to make (i.e., they are more likely to adopt a police mind-set rather than a minority community frame of reference).

To begin to integrate community and organization expectations, each party must agree on what it is possible to achieve. Unless expectations are made clear and achievable, integration is not possible; and before this can be accomplished, a *climate of trust* must be restored, particularly in minority communities. The police are responsible for convincing citizens that their concerns will be taken into consideration and, if reasonable, result in changes in police behavior and activities. The police should not promise what they cannot deliver, and the public should not expect what the police cannot achieve.

## Models of Democratic Policing

As discussed in chapter 2, the models of community policing represent different organizational adjustments that are made in response to conflicting expectations about the police role. The adjustments made result from the dominant influence of one of the major sources of expectations in the E-I model, namely, community, organization, and employee. Since employees, until the advent of labor unions and associations, have rarely been an important voice, they created their own "police style," which was a product of the rules and values of the police worker's culture.

The *political-watchman model* was the product of influential political groups in the community. The *legalistic-professional model*, first proposed by civic-minded reformers, was taken over by police leaders who advocated the professionalization of police. Thus, organizational expectations became more important than either those of employees or of the community. This model paid "lip service" to the community in the form of public relations programs designed to create an acceptable image (e.g., the police distributed brochures describing important police activities, visited schools, and provided tours of the police building).

The *community-service model* emerged in the 1960s in response to the perceived nonresponsiveness of the legalistic-professional model, which is based on a mechanistic organizational system and narrowly conceived professional expertise. This development was paralleled by more research into police activities, which created a "scientific" perspective among some police agencies. That is, they became more problem oriented in the sense that they "studied" problems before developing solutions. This is what we call the *rational-contingency approach*.

Certain aspects of our community-service and rational-contingency models of policing have been described in recent years as community-oriented and problem-oriented policing. Both of these were discussed in previous chapters and will be addressed here as essentially one model, called *community policing*. In effect, community policing is both a philosophy and a method of policing; it is based on building a relationship of mutual trust with all segments of the community, listening carefully to community concerns, and responding to problems based on systematic analysis. The latter requires at least some police officers to develop the skills required to conduct reliable and valid research. Community policing can exist without the research component, and a problem-oriented approach can exist without the basic community orientation. However, we consider them both to be integral to the community policing approach.

Kelling (1988) describes the changes that are occurring in police work as a "quiet revolution." This revolution or movement toward community-oriented policing in some cities requires that police make fundamental changes in their orientation. For example, police do not consider themselves the "first line of defense" against crime, rather they believe that community institutions have this responsibility. Kelling provides the following example to illustrate this point:

> Should police have the responsibility for controlling a neighborhood youth who, say, is bullying other children? Of course not. The first line of defense in a neighborhood against a troublesome youth is the youth's family (or extended family). . . . On occasion police will be called: Suppose that the youth is severely bullying other children to the point of injuring them. Is the bully's family relieved of responsibility? Are neighbors? The school? . . . The answer to these questions is no. . . . We expect families, neighbors, teachers, and others to be responsible and prudent (p. 2).

If the assumption is made that community institutions are the most important defense against crime, then the police role is to "stimulate and buttress" the community's ability to respond effectively to the crime problem. One of the most important changes police must make is to focus on problems more than incidents. Rather than viewing each problem individually, the problems are considered within a broader context. For example, it is not uncommon in many cities to find that a large number of calls to police are from the same locations and neighborhoods. Instead of responding to each one as a separate incident, the police can attempt to determine what problems exist in these locations and work to alter or reduce the need for a police response (Kelling 1988; Moore, Trojanowicz, and Kelling 1988).

Eck and Spelman (1987) provide an example of how problem-oriented, rather than incident-oriented, policing works. In Newport News, Virginia, the problem-oriented approach was adopted in 1986. One of the initial targets was a series of burglaries in the New Briarfield Apartments. This 450-unit apartment complex built in 1942 was regarded as the worst housing in the city and it had the highest crime rate.

The police surveyed one-third of the residents to determine their concerns and found that they were primarily concerned about burglaries and the physical deterioration of the complex. The police determined that there was an apparent relationship between the condition of the complex and the crime rate. Consequently, they began to work with the residents and other city agencies to clean up the area: abandoned appliances and cars were removed, streets were swept, trash was removed, and potholes were filled. In addition, the police began to work with other city agencies to help the tenants tear down the apartment complex and find new housing.

While the long-term consequences of this effort are unknown, the initial results were positive (i.e., the crime rate declined). Using a community, problem-oriented approach, the police determined, in a rational manner, the concerns of the community. Instead of focusing on separate incidents, such as a specific crime (although responses to crimes continued), the police worked to determine why so many crimes occurred in the apartment complex. Once this was determined, at least in part, officers worked to change the conditions that contributed to the crime problem. Part of this effort required the police to mobilize the occupants of the apartments to help themselves.

As can be seen from this example, the community-oriented approach significantly changes the role of the police. Riechers and Roberg (in press) have provided an interesting analysis of community policing as it relates to organization and management problems. They suggest that community policing began in the 1950s and 1960s with the development of community relations programs that were designed to increase interaction with the community. However, many of these programs were superficial in nature. For many police agencies, community relations meant nothing more than projecting a positive image in the community. For others, such programs were based on the assumption that if the public understood the police, they could not think ill of them. Consequently, community relations work was directed toward educating the public about police problems and the police point of view. Only rarely did such programs deal meaningfully with community problems, the lack of trust, and inappropriate officer behavior.

Further attempts were made in the 1970s with the emergence of team policing, which as we have noted, had mixed results. All team policing programs involved some form of decentralization of organizational activities in an effort to develop closer ties with the community. Team policing failed because it did not take into consideration the changes that would be required in the organization and management of police departments and in police behavior. Although both community relations programs and team policing can be considered precursors of a community-oriented approach, they are not as comprehensive as what is currently known as community policing.

## Assumptions of Community Policing

While community policing programs vary, they do tend to share common assumptions (Riechers and Roberg, in press). However, a debate now rages over whether community policing is a revival of programs, some of which failed (e.g., some team policing projects), or an attempt to revive, in effect, the positive aspects of the "neighborhood" cop of the political-watchman model. Proponents of community policing argue that it is different from past programs and previous models in several important ways; most significantly, because it is both a philosophy and a method of policing.

Previous attempts to reform the legalistic-professional model tried to graft new programs onto old philosophies, organizational designs, and management practices. The "new" community policing purports to change all of this or at least to recognize that past practices in these areas are potential problems that must be overcome if community policing is to be successful. This is an important consideration because if many agencies adopt this approach to policing, it means a significant departure from past police practices. From a futuristic perspective, we are on the verge of a trend that either will radically change policing in the United States or will eventually be seen as another "failed" attempt at reform, much like team policing. Riechers and Roberg analyze the critical assumptions that provide the foundation for community policing; five of these assumptions are discussed in this section.

**Assumption 1:** Community policing, through increased activities and visibility, will reduce the public's fear of crime.

**Assumption 2:** Communities, or the public, are of "one mind"; a homogeneous populace whose satisfaction or dissatisfaction with the police can be readily measured.

In addressing these assumptions, Manning (1984) suggests that many groups in society do not want increased levels of police activity. He cites Mastrofski (1983), who found that wealthier households use police services at a significantly greater rate than low-income households for less serious crime, less serious order-maintenance problems, and to obtain information. Lower-income households (about 75 percent black in this study) use police services more for violent crimes and more serious order-maintenance problems. Manning concludes that the demand for police service "depends on the social class composition, race, and age of the neighborhood" (p. 224).

Given these findings, can the police define who the community is and determine community needs? Obviously, there is no single community, and thus no single way to conduct "community policing." For example, Alpert and Dunham (1986), in a study of community preferences and responses to different styles of policing conducted in Dade County, Florida, found that the degree of importance placed on certain tasks commonly used to evaluate police officers (by police agencies) differed among neighborhoods according to demographic characteristics (e.g., race, income, and newness of neighborhood). In addition, Brown and Wycoff (1987), in a study of fear reduction in Houston, found that fear of crime was reduced as a result of increasing police–citizen nonadversarial contact, but only for certain groups. Blacks and renters did not share in the benefits of the program to the same extent as other racial groups and homeowners.

On the other hand, evaluations of foot patrol programs, which are closely associated with community policing, tend to contradict some of these findings. Research findings indicate that foot patrol is successful in reducing citizen fear and increasing citizen satisfaction (Esbensen 1987; Police Foundation 1982). However, research on the Citizen Oriented Police Enforcement (COPE) project in Baltimore County, which included foot patrol, showed that only when the initial awareness of the police presence was low did citizens notice an increased police presence (Cordner 1986). If increased police activity in a nonadversarial role is needed to reduce fear of crime and increased activity is noticed only when previously limited in scope, then there is an obvious limit on the degree to which fear can be reduced. To obtain substantial reductions in high crime areas may require a massive investment of police resources, perhaps resulting in inadequate resources in other areas.

Another important finding of Mastrofski (1983) addresses the measurement of citizen satisfaction or dissatisfaction. He found that citizens are more likely to be pleased with police responses to noncrime-related incidents (e.g., order maintenance) and more likely to be displeased with police responses to serious crime incidents. Since low-income minority communities are often characterized by serious crime problems, there may be a limit to which the police can satisfy low-income communities. In addition, any finding of increased satisfaction may not be meaningful, since, in general, most people are already satisfied with their police (Esbensen 1987; Manning 1984).

ASSUMPTION 3: The police should be responsible for actively helping to define and shape community norms.

This assumption is closely related to the goal, espoused by Wilson and Kelling (1982), Kelling (1985, 1987), and Sykes (1986), of using police as agents of informal social control. This assumption may result in a violation of the political neutrality of the police (to be discussed as assumption 4). In addition, as Walker (1984) has pointed out, in the past, injustices and corruption occurred as a result of police enforcement of nonlegal norms. As just discussed, there are many different communities with varying expectations and, practically speaking, it would be difficult, if not impossible, to identify and keep track of them all. Consequently, the police would be able to select the expectations to which they would respond (i.e., most likely the ones they would agree with).

Manning (1984, p. 217) states that "there is a certain contentiousness in claiming that the police know the informal control mechanisms found in a community, can accommodate them, and can in some fashion act to enhance them." He further notes that the informal control mechanisms of a community may be overtly illegal and in conflict with the duty of the police to enforce the laws. Also, informal control mechanisms can be discriminatory. Many people still do not want certain groups in their community. Taken to an extreme, it is certainly possible that this could result in the removal of "undesirables" from the community. The "good old days" of the political-watchman model involved such police behavior. Some people were taken to the outskirts of town or placed on some form of public transportation and told not to come back.

ASSUMPTION 4: Community policing can be done without violating the political neutrality of the police.

Short (1983) argues that there is a basic incompatibility between the political neutrality of police and community policing. In her experiences with community policing in England, she found that using police as an agency of informal social control was incompatible with their political neutrality. Short discovered that community policing projects frequently focused on what they considered to be the causes of crime. Consequently, police organizations became involved in various social service agencies (e.g., welfare and housing), including making decisions about how funds for community projects should be distributed. Short suggests that there is ". . . a danger that community policing will lead more and more policemen to behave—for perfectly good reasons—. . . like politicians" (p. 72). This becomes necessary because to win the trust of the community, the police must help the members of that community. Police may become advocates for selected community interests, functioning much like an elected official except that they are not elected. Under such conditions, the police are not directly accountable, as are politicians, for their behavior.

This assumption further raises the question of the degree to which the police are politically neutral regardless of the model of policing utilized. Although police make political choices all the time, particularly individual police officers who function as ministers of the law, political corruption has been recognized as a potentially serious problem since the latter part of the nineteenth century. While the legalistic-professional model, developed to reduce if not eliminate corrupt and irresponsible behavior, may be somewhat political in nature, it is probably less political than either the community-service or rational-contingency model.

ASSUMPTION 5: Police organizations, given their current mechanistic characteristics and quality of personnel, can be sensitive and responsive enough to accomplish the goals of community policing.

Goldstein (1987) argues that, historically, police organizations have tended to focus on secondary goals related to management and personnel practices rather than on the quality of police service (e.g., responding to public needs or equal or just treatment). While this is accurate to some degree, the quality of police service is essentially a result of the management and personnel practices of an organization. Such goals may be classified as "secondary," but they are of primary concern if successful results are to be accomplished. Police innovations are probably more likely to succeed or fail due to management or personnel reasons than due to other factors.

For instance, are police personnel ready to fulfill the demands of community policing? In undertaking community policing, which includes a problem orientation, police officers are expected to alleviate specific problems that they have helped to identify by working with the community. They are supposed to develop creative and innovative solutions in a fair, just, and legal manner. This requires skills such as problem conceptualization, synthesis and analysis of information, development of action plans, program evaluation, and communication of results and policy implications. These skills may require higher education (beyond the high school level) and, in some instances, advanced education beyond the baccalaureate degree. Of course, the police organization, in keeping with a mechanistic approach, may decide to centralize problem analysis and the development of innovative solutions. The officer would work only on the problems identified by the organization, using the solutions developed by "specialists." In an organic system, the officer is an active participant in all phases of the process. In the mechanistic system, the officer responds to the organization's direction concerning both problems and solutions. If many police officers are perceived by the organization not to have the necessary individual skills to implement community policing, a mechanistic orientation will probably continue to prevail.

Another important consideration is whether police departments have the organizational structure and management orientation that can facilitate the development of a community policing program. Community policing involves a significant change in the philosophy of policing toward a more organic, rather than a mechanistic, approach. How such changes will be accepted by police managers, especially middle-level managers, is crucial. In order to successfully implement community policing, middle-level managers must be able to act as change agents, supportive of change and innovation. Furthermore, the reward structure utilized in a majority of police departments may pose an additional problem. The current emphasis on law enforcement-related activities will need to be altered to reflect an equal emphasis on activities that are community service oriented. In the past (e.g., the team policing experiment), police managers have demonstrated a reluctance, if not an inability, to significantly alter traditional police organization and management practices.

## Critical Assumptions Assessed

Will community policing be an important future trend in policing? While the analysis of the above assumptions suggests serious potential problems, it may be possible to overcome some or all of them. It is also possible that proponents of the approach will simply deny that any problems exist, much as police leaders in the 1960s insisted that police did not discriminate against minority groups. Some police organizations appear to be gradually moving toward a community policing concept without any significant problems, at least so far.

Recently, for example, one of the largest police departments in the United States, Houston, Texas, announced its intention to restructure its entire department in this manner (*Law Enforcement News* 1988). Other agencies, however, continue to cling to a more legalistic and mechanistic approach. Although there may be some progress in this area in the near future, it is important not to expect too much to change in most police departments. Many small and moderate-sized agencies probably will argue that they have always had a community orientation (Skolnick and Bayley 1986), although as community policing is described in this chapter, the argument would not be valid. Communities with serious crime problems (e.g., drug problems and/or gang violence) may think it impossible, or at least impractical, to radically restructure their approach to police work. They may argue that they must continue to stress visibility and apprehension to fight crime, and the community may expect them to do precisely that.

It is also important for police not to create false hopes with community policing. In fact, probably not much will change in the long run in terms of crime rates or fear levels. While there may be some slight gains, and the public may feel better about the police and their safety, there may be no actual change in the probability that residents will or will not be victimized. Crime is largely the result of the age composition of the population, economic conditions, family structure, and moral training; it has little to do with the police response, whatever that might be. If police try to sell community policing as a panacea for the crime, fear, and police–community relationship problems, it will be, as in the past, another example of creating unreasonable expectations and false hopes.

Community policing has the potential of putting citizens more in control of the police, possibly helping them to feel safer, and improving officer satisfaction (through job enrichment activities); it may even have a limited, long-term impact on certain types of crime. But community policing may also create serious problems related to police involvement in the political process of allocating resources, who gets helped and who does not, and the manner in which they are helped. For example, a group of community elites—those individuals most closely aligned with the police—may emerge and use their influence and power to profit from professional courtesy. In other words, certain individuals and groups could rise "above" the law and not be held accountable for violating many minor and moderately serious laws.

Additionally, such a change in the philosophy of policing will not be well received by the "old guard" in many police organizations. As a result, such departments may remain in turmoil for a substantial period, at least until these employees are replaced (through attrition, termination, or retirement) or converted to the "new approach." As suggested previously, the role of executives and middle managers is crucial if such changes are to take place and endure. Managers must listen to, and be concerned about, the expectations of those who agree with and who oppose organizational changes. They must be able to separate selfish employee concerns from those that identify realistic problems. To do otherwise only results in imposing change rather than creating innovation. The former reflects a mechanistic orientation, while the latter is more organic.

## Managerial Perspectives and Problems

Will police managers move toward the development of a different perspective concerning managerial practices in the next decade? Certainly this is possible in organizations that adopt a community orientation. However, even without adopting this approach, perspectives concerning management in general may change. In Madison, Wisconsin, for example, the police organization implemented what is called *bottoms-up management* (*Law Enforcement News* 1987). This is really little more than the participatory decision making (or management) described in the last chapter, where employees are allowed extensive participation in the organization in terms of identifying and solving police problems. Nevertheless, bottoms-up management is an interesting approach that may gain some support and improve the quality of work life in the organization.

In Madison, interested officers were given one-sixth of the organization's resources to police one-sixth of the city in any way they wanted. About forty officers, civilians, and a ten-person planning group worked together to identify problems and develop responses. Part of the discussion centered on organization design and management practices. What resulted was essentially an organic policing model; jobs were enriched because officers had more involvement in making decisions about what work they did and how they did it.

When officers interacted as a group, it was not possible to determine the ranks of participants during discussions. Officers tended to interact based on what they knew and could contribute. Even the persons who were to function as leaders were determined not by rank, but based on the criteria required to meet the responsibilities of the position, given the current activities. As noted, this process is closely linked to organic policing; it also has some parallels to the "democratic model" of policing proposed by Angell (1971) and discussed in chapter 3. Early reports indicate that this bottoms-up approach to management has been well received by both participants and the community (*Law Enforcement News* 1987).

However, the officers participating in this program were volunteers, which means they were already interested in this approach. It is possible that many officers (e.g., those with lower-level needs) would not want to work in such an organizational environment, particularly middle managers, who might have to sacrifice the influence they exert by virtue of the status and authority granted to them by the organization. It is important again to point out that one of the major reasons team policing experiments failed was the reluctance of middle managers to change their role and relationship with subordinates. Bottoms-up management could fail or have limited applicability for the same reasons. In addition, there are the possible problems of community policing already noted earlier. We hope that the lessons to be learned regarding reducing the resistance to change, as well as the processes of organizational development, will be practiced in attempts to implement such innovative approaches.

Other potential developments in police management have been discussed by Moore (1988). Moore foresees some possible changes in how police organizations are evaluated and in the role of mid- and lower-level managers. We will first discuss some of the implications if more emphasis is placed on *fear levels* as a measure of police organization effectiveness rather than on the *crime rate*. And, second, we will address the possible changing role of mid- and lower-level managers.

Citizens' concern about crime may be more easily influenced than the crime rate by police activities. This is particularly true if a community-oriented approach is adopted (Moore and Trojanowicz 1988); that is, greater interaction and influence with the public. Using fear levels as a measure of police success has several potential problems, however. While crime rates in a community can be manipulated by police reporting practices (e.g., a policy is established that unless the officer believes that a victim is telling the truth about a crime, he or she does not take a report), fear levels may be even easier to manipulate. For example, police agencies may find that assigning more officers to an area for a short time before they survey fear levels may cause a sharp decline in the levels. In addition, there is also the problem of research design and data collection. In these surveys, unless rigorous methodological techniques and data analysis are employed, changes of 5 or 10 percent may mean very little and may even give false impressions. When an organization can easily manipulate the criteria used to determine its effectiveness, the temptation to do so may negate any productive consequences or police–community understanding that might be derived from using fear levels as a measure of police effectiveness.

The role of mid- and lower-level managers may change from essentially a *bureaucrat* who enforces organization rules to a *coach*. This is the leader and change agent, discussed in chapter 12, who teaches officers how to do police work, reinforces the purpose and values of the organization, and allows them flexibility in doing their job. Of course, some middle managers already have such styles, but more may adopt this orientation in the future.

However, it is probably more important for managers to develop a *contingency approach* than one style, whether that of a bureaucrat or a coach.

Moore is also an advocate of what he calls the *corporate* perspective on policing. In general, this perspective is that the police "represent a bundle of assets" and the role of managers is to find the "highest value" use for those assets. Corporations do not tend to retain a fixed idea about their product but instead examine their organization in terms of resources (what the organization is capable of doing) and then identify products or services that would be of value to organization members and clients or shareholders, in this case, the public. This perspective, according to Moore, will undoubtedly broaden the role of police in the community. However, he believes that an expanded role will strengthen the relationship with the community and facilitate more effective responses to the crime problem.

Adoption of a business analogy, like that of a corporate model, has been quite common in police work. Whenever organization and management reforms have been suggested in the past, students of policing often suggest that police organizations should be "run" like a business or, in this instance, a corporation. Remember that the bureaucratic or mechanistic model currently being criticized by Moore and others was essentially adopted from the private sector. And while the corporate model may be more flexible than the bureaucratic, it has limitations, namely that public and private management are substantially different undertakings, as already discussed in chapter 1.

Finally, Di Grazia (1984) suggests that the primary emphasis in the future should be placed on the *quality of personnel* in police work. He believes that police work should become an elite calling. Only the very best applicants should be considered. An important part of such a trend would be a tendency to stress higher education, along with attempts to attract interested and dedicated individuals. For Di Grazia, unlike community policing advocates in general, the future of policing is to be found in upgrading the quality of personnel and not necessarily in organization redesign and management practices, although he believes that these are also important. Interestingly, if community policing as we are describing it (i.e., with a significantly expanded role concept and increased sophistication of job requirements) is to be effectively implemented, increased emphasis on the quality of personnel is undoubtedly necessary.

Historically, Di Grazia's theme is a common one in law enforcement. Almost every generation of police leaders (except some who believe that increasing educational requirements will make the employment of minorities more difficult) has recommended employing better-educated candidates. In the final analysis, the future of policing in general, and police management in particular, may be more strongly influenced by the quality of personnel recruited into the field than by any other factor. If police organization and management are to change to any significant degree in the near future, the change will most likely be led by organization members who are motivated by higher-order needs, who perceive the need for change, and who are capable of acting as change agents.

We hope the information contained throughout this text will help students and managers alike to more fully understand police organizational behavior, in assessing managerial practices, and, when necessary, in promoting organizational change to improve the quality of work environments and employee satisfaction and performance. If police managerial practices are to be improved, we must look toward the future and not be afraid to implement timely and constructive changes that will benefit not only the police but society as well.

## Summary

The E-I model introduced in the first chapter has two major expectation-integration problems: one involving the employee and the organization, and one involving the organization and the community. The integration of employee and organization expectations is made more difficult because a humanistic orientation does not prevail in the management of most police organizations. To control officer behavior, among other reasons, a mechanistic system has dominated police organization and management; such a system tends to place more emphasis on organizational expectations than on employee concerns. The use of this mechanistic approach for a prolonged period has created considerable divisiveness between management and workers. These two groups—managers and workers—participate in the same organization, but they may have substantially different ideas about the police role and appropriate police behavior.

The second integration problem of the E-I model involves organizational and community expectations. Communities are diverse with potentially different expectations about police activities and behavior. Community expectations of the police may be both reasonable and unreasonable. These expectations are products of what the public sees the police do in "real life" and in the media, as well as the image sold to the public by the police. Another problem in this area is minority groups and their unique concerns about the police. Historically, police have tended to see minority group areas, particularly in urban communities, as a serious police problem. In return, minorities have wanted more police protection but usually have not trusted the police to treat them fairly. This lack of trust makes the integration of organization–community expectations more difficult.

The models of policing that have evolved historically have resulted in movement toward both a community-service and rational-contingency approach. This is discussed as community policing in this chapter, which includes a problem orientation. While initial evaluations of community policing appear promising in terms of reducing fear of crime and improving police–citizen relationships and job satisfaction, it is potentially a threat to the political neutrality of police. Additionally, implementation problems due to mechanistic structures and quality of personnel may prove troublesome.

Emerging managerial perspectives in the police field include the bottoms-up style utilized in Madison, Wisconsin and the corporate analogy to manage organizations. The first approach substantially increases employee participation and appears to be a promising innovation in making police departments more organic. The corporate analogy continues a long-established trend of basing police innovation on concepts from the private sector and it may or may not prove useful. Another recommendation calls for a greater emphasis on the quality of police personnel, especially with respect to higher education for police officers. It is questionable whether significant changes can be made in police organization and management without an increased emphasis on the quality of police personnel.

## Discussion Questions

1. What are the most difficult problems in integrating employee and organization expectations?
2. What are the most difficult problems in integrating organizational and community expectations?
3. Define community policing. How is it related to problem-oriented policing? How is it related to community relations programs and team policing?
4. Identify and explain the five assumptions on which community policing is based. Do you think these assumptions tend to indicate that community policing will be more or less effective than other forms of policing? Why?
5. How would you go about implementing community policing in a police department?
6. What is bottoms-up management and how does it work? Do you think it has potential for improving effectiveness of police organizations? Why?
7. What is the corporate perspective as it relates to police management? Do you think this is a useful way of thinking about the police? Why?
8. Explain how you think the police will change in the next decade or two. How will such changes influence you either as an employee or a member of the community, or both?

# References

Alpert, A. P. and Dunham, R. G., *Policing Urban America* (Prospect Heights, Ill.: Waveland Press, 1986).

Angell, J. E., "Toward an Alternative to the Classic Police Organizational Arrangements: A Democratic Model," *Criminology* 9(1971): 185–206.

Brown, L. P. and Wycoff, M. A., "Policing Houston: Reducing Fear and Improving Service," *Crime and Delinquency* 33, no. 1(1987): 71–89.

Commission on Accreditation for Law Enforcement Agencies, *Standards for Law Enforcement Agencies* (Fairfax, Va.: CALEA, 1984).

Cordner, G. W., "Fear of Crime and the Police: An Evaluation of a Fear-Reduction Strategy," *Journal of Police Science and Administration* 14, no. 3(1986): 223–233.

Di Grazia, R., "What Century Are We In, Anyway?" *Law Enforcement News*, March 12, 1984, p. 8.

Eck, J. E. and Spelman, W., *Problem-Solving: Problem-Oriented Policing in Newport News*. Police Executive Research Forum. (Washington, D.C.: National Institute of Justice, 1987).

Esbensen, F. A., "Foot Patrols: Of What Value?" *American Journal of Police* 6, no. 1(1987): 45–65.

Goldstein, H., "Toward Community-Oriented Policing: Potential, Basic Requirements, and Threshold Questions," *Crime and Delinquency* 33, no. 1(1987): 6–30.

Kelling, G. L., "Order Maintenance, the Quality of Urban Life, and the Police: A Line of Argument," in *Police Leadership in America*, ed. W. A. Geller (New York: Praeger, 1985), pp. 296–308.

———, "Acquiring a Taste for Order: The Community and the Police," *Crime and Delinquency* 33, no. 1(1987): 90–102.

———, *Police and Communities: The Quiet Revolution. Perspective on Policing* (Washington, D.C.: National Institute of Justice, 1988).

Klockars, C. B., "Order Maintenance, the Quality of Life and the Police," in *Police Leadership in America*, ed. W. A. Geller (New York: Praeger, 1985), pp. 309–321.

Law Enforcement News, "Madison PD Eyes 'Bottoms-Up' Management," June 9, 1987, p. 1.

———, "Houston To Assess Police Model," March 15, 1988, p. 1.

Manning, P. K., "Community Policing," *American Journal of Police* 3, no. 2(1984): 205–227.

Mastrofski, S., "The Police and Non-Crime Services," in *Evaluating Performance of Criminal Justice Agencies*, G. P. Whitaker and C. C. Phillips (Beverly Hills, Calif.: Sage, 1983), pp. 33–61.

Moore, M. H., Interview, *Law Enforcement News*, April 15, 1988, pp. 6–7.

Moore, M. H. and Trojanowicz, R. C. *Policing and the Fear of Crime. Perspectives on Policing* (Washington, D.C.: National Institute of Justice, 1988).

Moore, M. H., Trojanowicz, R. C., and Kelling, G. L., *Crime and Policing. Perspectives on Policing* (Washington, D.C.: National Institute of Justice, 1988).

Police Foundation, *The Newark Foot Patrol Experiment* (Washington, D.C.: Police Foundation, 1982).

Riechers, L. M. and Roberg, R. R., "Community Policing: A Critical Review of Underlying Assumptions." In press.

Short, C., "Community Policing—Beyond Slogans," in *The Future of Policing*, ed. T. Bennet (Cambridge, England: Institute of Criminology, 1983), pp. 67–81.

Skolnick, J. H. and Bayley, D. H., *The New Blue Line: Police Innovation in Six American Cities* (New York: Free Press, 1986).

Sykes, G. W., "Street Justice: A Moral Defense of Order Maintenance Policing," *Justice Quarterly* 3, no. 4(1986): 497–512.

Walker, S., "Broken Windows and Fractured History: The Use and Misuse of History in Recent Police Patrol Analysis," *Justice Quarterly* 1, no. 1(1984): 75–90.

Wilson, J. Q. and Kelling, G. L., "Broken Windows," *Atlantic Monthly* 249(1982): 29–38.

# Index

# Photo Credits